A Galaxy Next Door

Gido Amagakure

3

CONTENTS

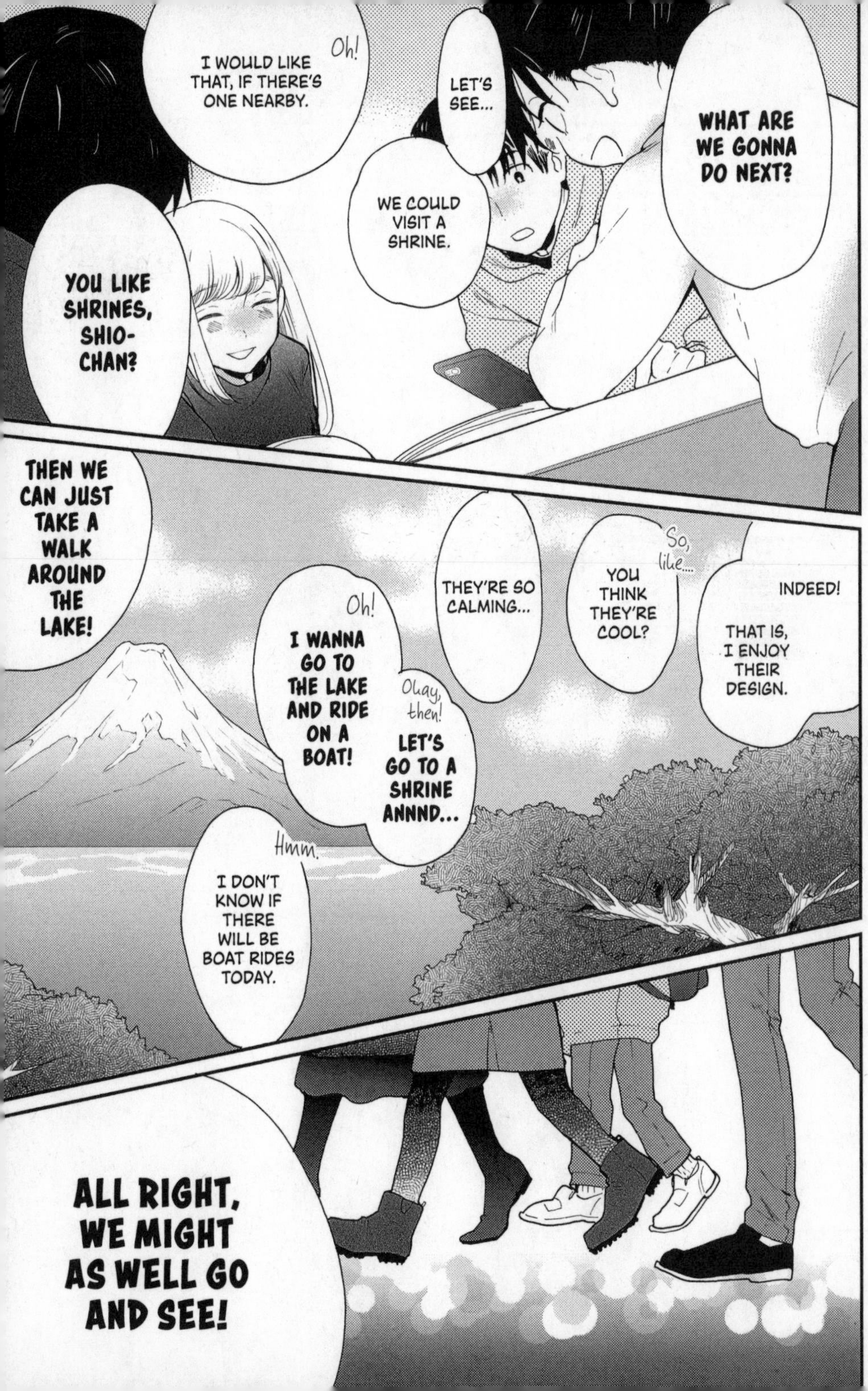
WHAT ARE WE GONNA DO NEXT?
LET'S SEE...
WE COULD VISIT A SHRINE.
Oh!
I WOULD LIKE THAT, IF THERE'S ONE NEARBY.
YOU LIKE SHRINES, SHIO-CHAN?
INDEED!
THAT IS, I ENJOY THEIR DESIGN.
So, like...
YOU THINK THEY'RE COOL?
THEY'RE SO CALMING...
Okay, then!
LET'S GO TO A SHRINE ANNND...
Oh!
I WANNA GO TO THE LAKE AND RIDE ON A BOAT!
Hmm.
I DON'T KNOW IF THERE WILL BE BOAT RIDES TODAY.
THEN WE CAN JUST TAKE A WALK AROUND THE LAKE!
ALL RIGHT, WE MIGHT AS WELL GO AND SEE!

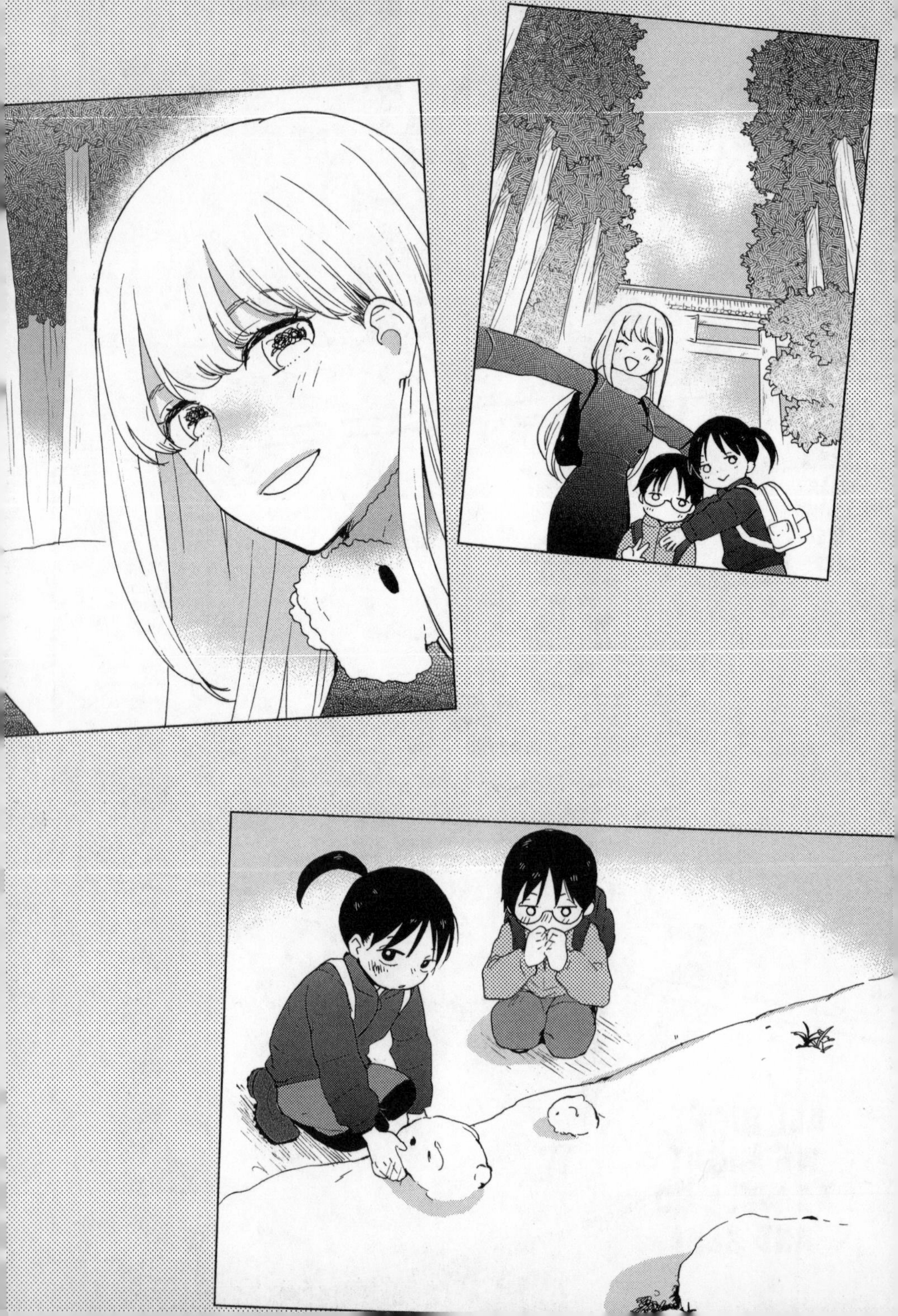

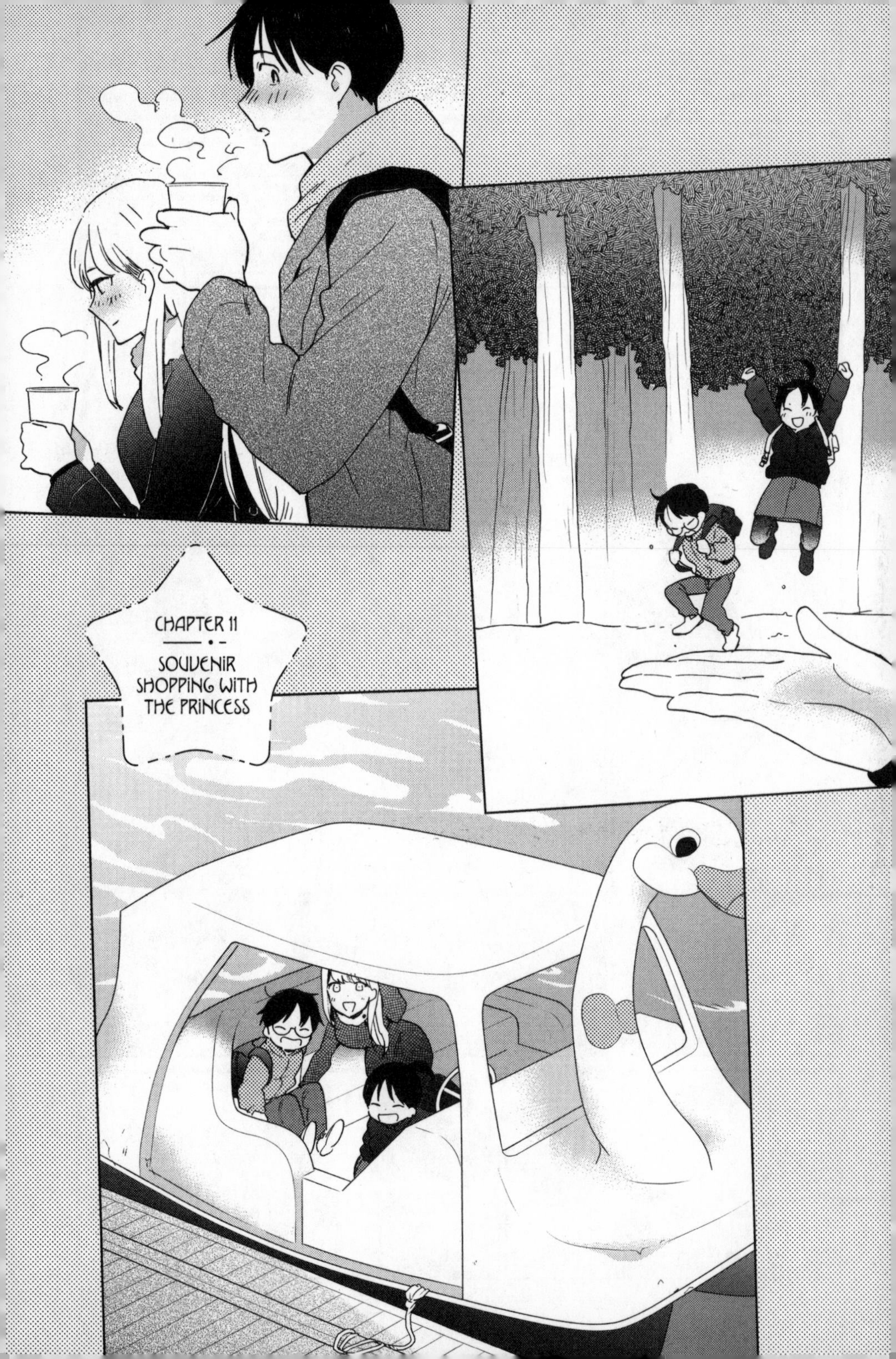
CHAPTER 11
SOUVENIR SHOPPING WITH THE PRINCESS

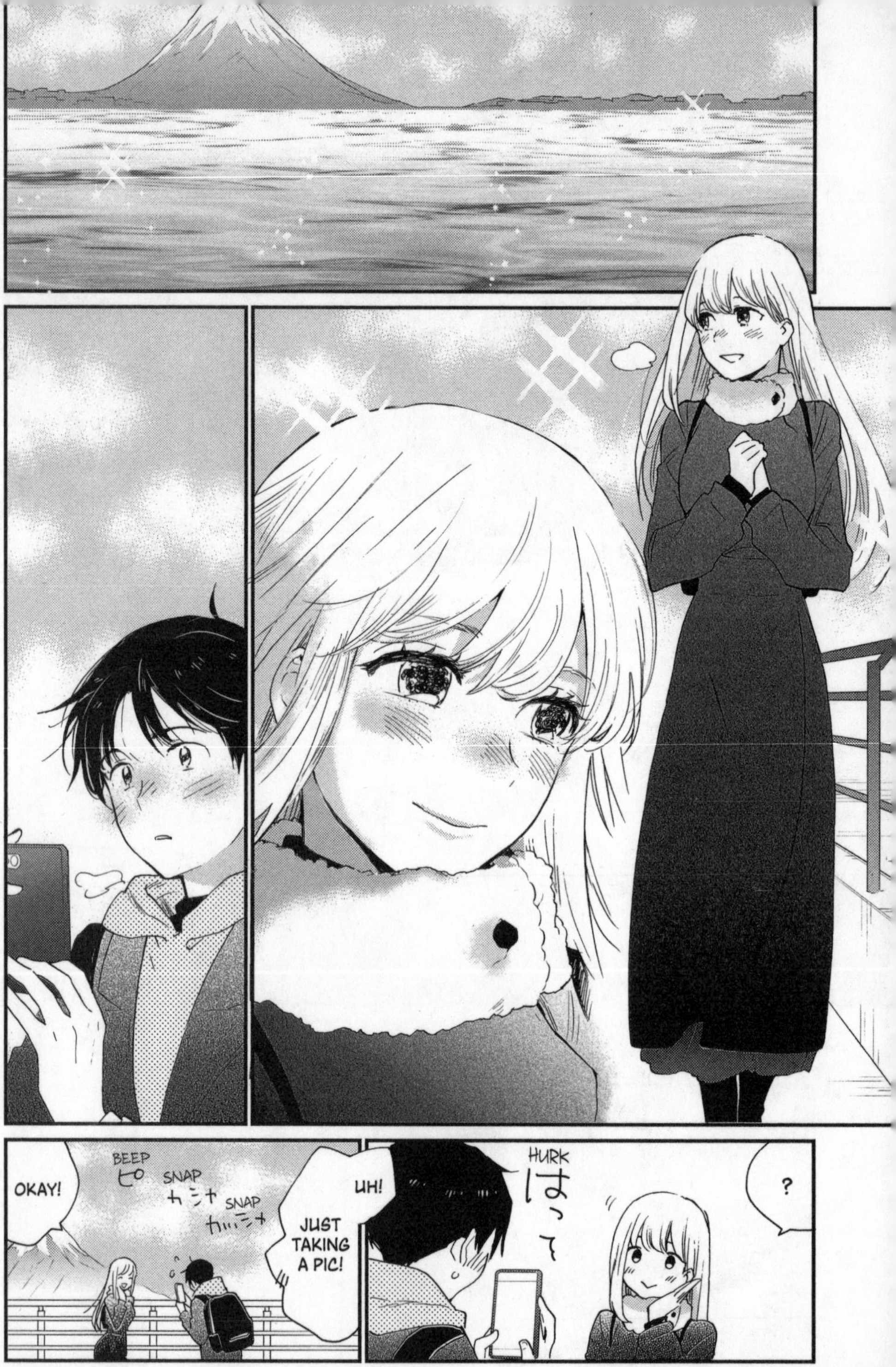
?
HURK
はって
UH!
JUST TAKING A PIC!
BEEP
ピ
SNAP
カシャ
SNAP
カシャ
OKAY!

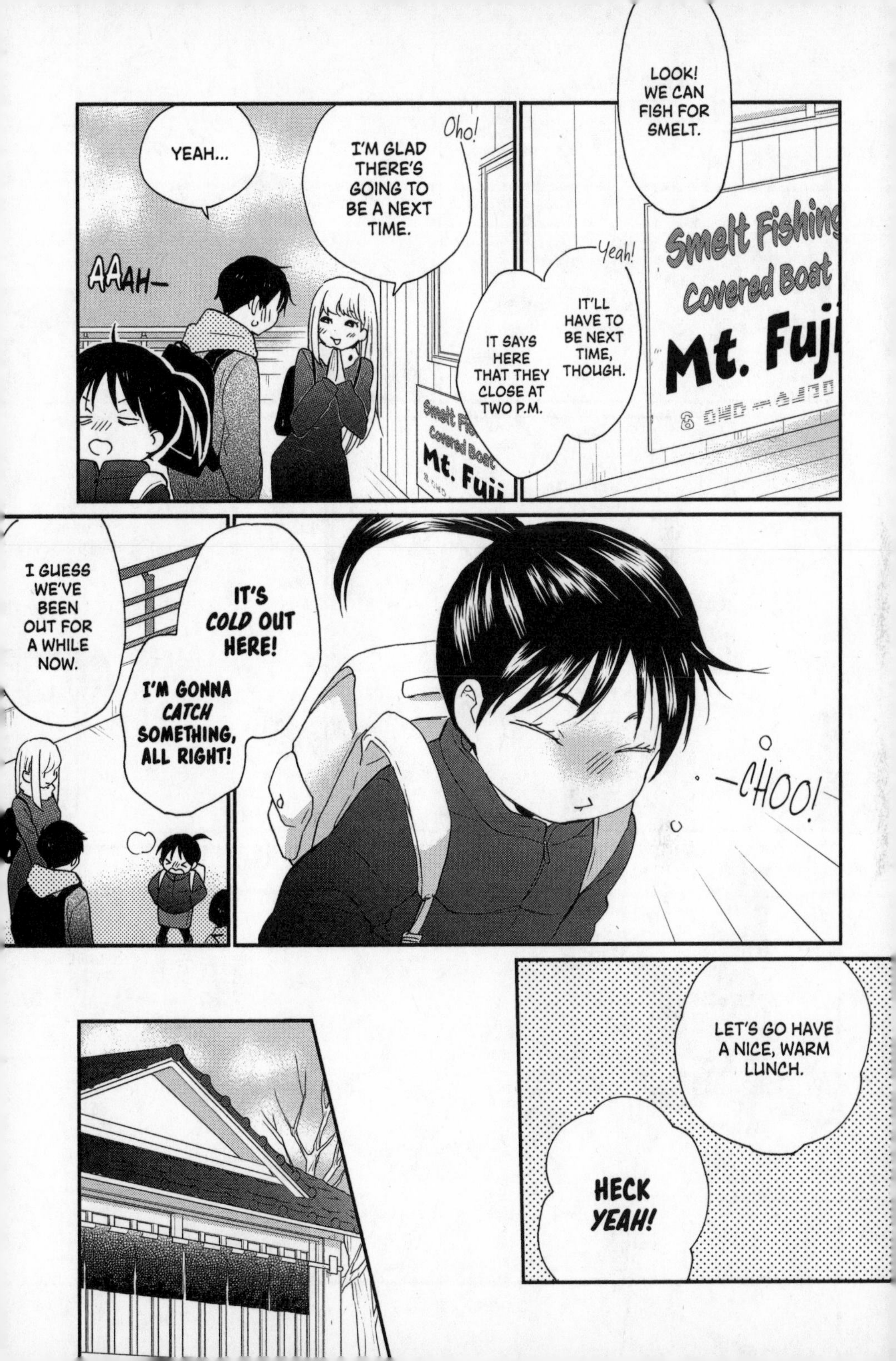
LOOK! WE CAN FISH FOR SMELT.
Smelt Fishing Covered Boat Mt. Fuji
Yeah!
IT'LL HAVE TO BE NEXT TIME, THOUGH.
IT SAYS HERE THAT THEY CLOSE AT TWO P.M.
Oho!
I'M GLAD THERE'S GOING TO BE A NEXT TIME.
YEAH...
AAAH—
—CHOO!
IT'S COLD OUT HERE!
I'M GONNA CATCH SOMETHING, ALL RIGHT!
I GUESS WE'VE BEEN OUT FOR A WHILE NOW.
LET'S GO HAVE A NICE, WARM LUNCH.
HECK YEAH!

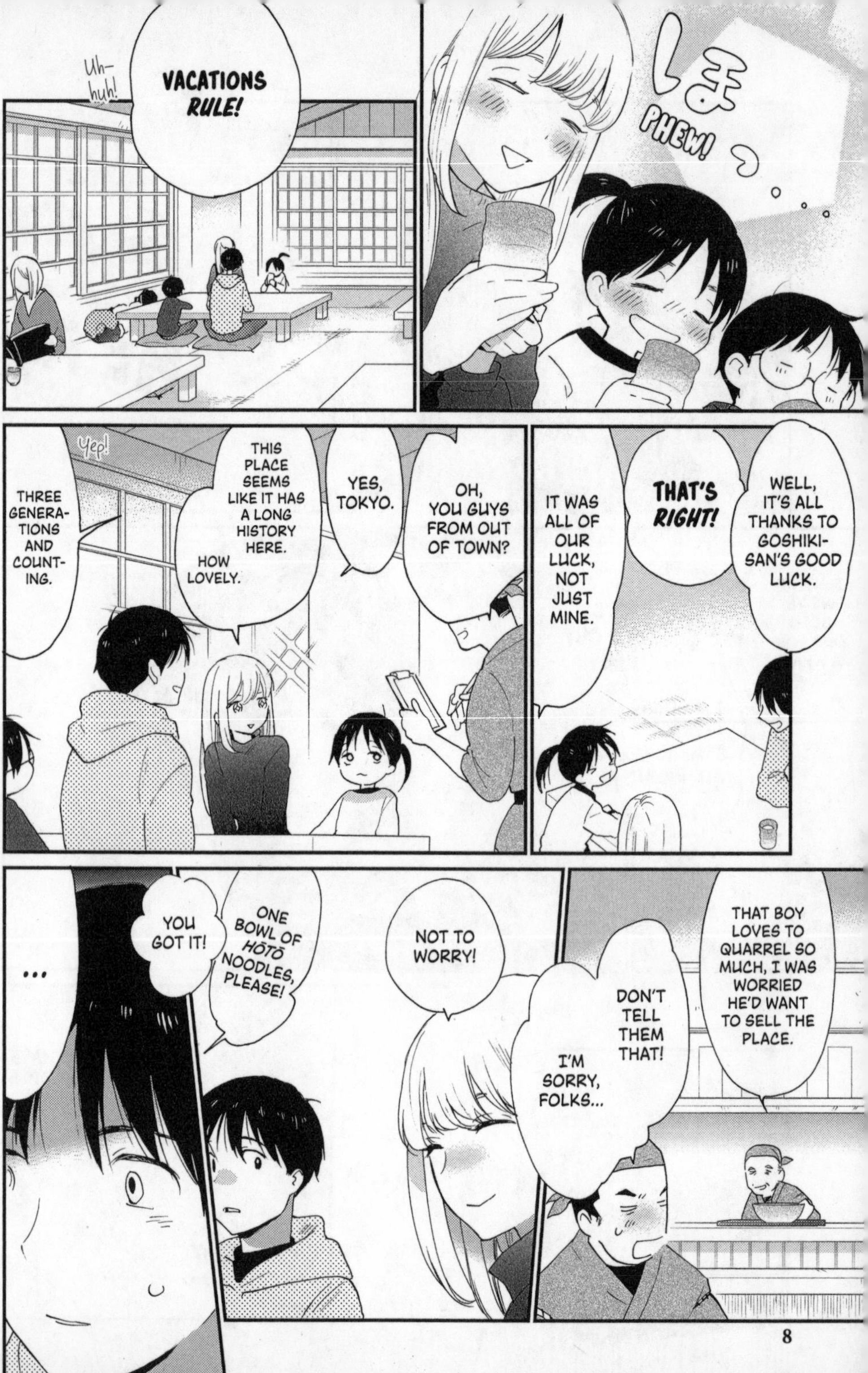
PHEW!
VACATIONS RULE!
Uh-huh!
WELL, IT'S ALL THANKS TO GOSHIKI-SAN'S GOOD LUCK.
THAT'S RIGHT!
IT WAS ALL OF OUR LUCK, NOT JUST MINE.
OH, YOU GUYS FROM OUT OF TOWN?
YES, TOKYO.
THIS PLACE SEEMS LIKE IT HAS A LONG HISTORY HERE.
HOW LOVELY.
Yep!
THREE GENERATIONS AND COUNTING.
THAT BOY LOVES TO QUARREL SO MUCH, I WAS WORRIED HE'D WANT TO SELL THE PLACE.
DON'T TELL THEM THAT!
I'M SORRY, FOLKS...
NOT TO WORRY!
ONE BOWL OF HŌTŌ NOODLES, PLEASE!
YOU GOT IT!
...

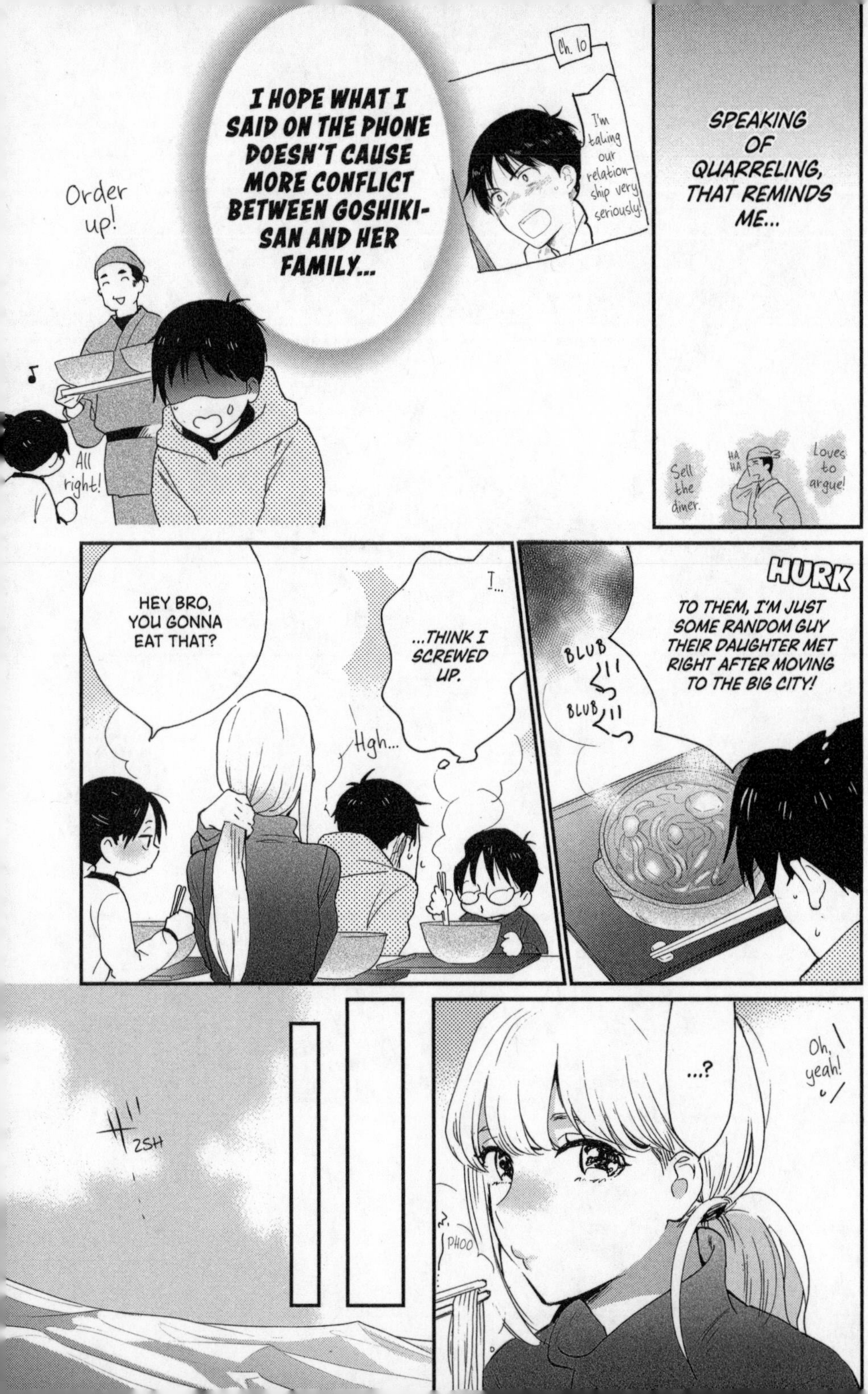
SPEAKING OF QUARRELING, THAT REMINDS ME...
Ch. 10
I'm taking our relationship very seriously!
Loves to argue!
HA HA
Sell the diner.
I HOPE WHAT I SAID ON THE PHONE DOESN'T CAUSE MORE CONFLICT BETWEEN GOSHIKI-SAN AND HER FAMILY...
Order up!
All right!
HURK
TO THEM, I'M JUST SOME RANDOM GUY THEIR DAUGHTER MET RIGHT AFTER MOVING TO THE BIG CITY!
BLUB
BLUB
I...
...THINK I SCREWED UP.
Hgh...
HEY BRO, YOU GONNA EAT THAT?
Oh, yeah!
...?
PHOO
ZSH

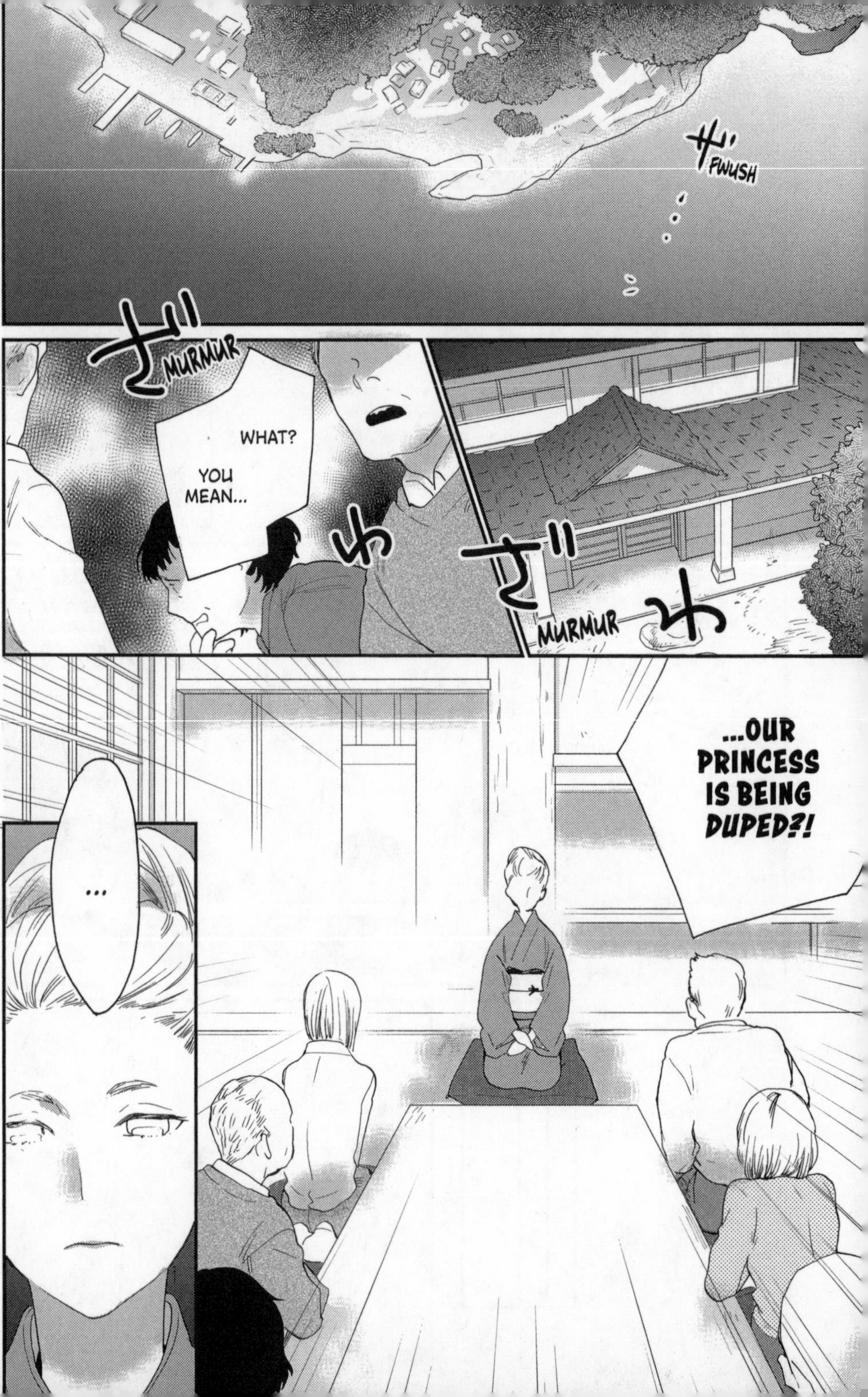

ザッ
FWUSH
ざわ
MURMUR
ざわ
MURMUR
WHAT?
YOU MEAN...
...OUR PRINCESS IS BEING DUPED?!
...

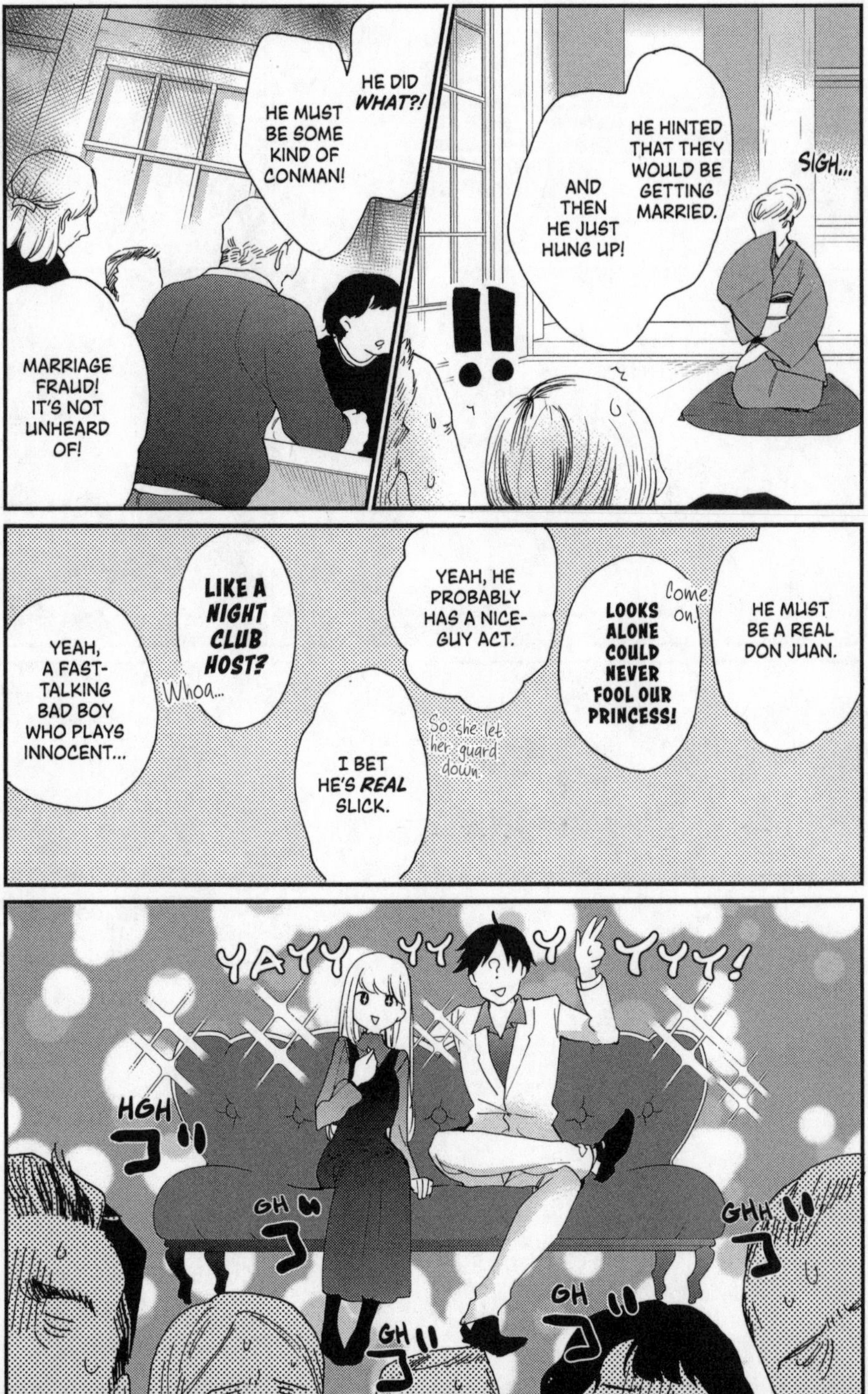
HE HINTED THAT THEY WOULD BE GETTING MARRIED.
AND THEN HE JUST HUNG UP!
SIGH...
!!
HE DID WHAT?!
HE MUST BE SOME KIND OF CONMAN!
MARRIAGE FRAUD! IT'S NOT UNHEARD OF!
HE MUST BE A REAL DON JUAN.
Come on.
LOOKS ALONE COULD NEVER FOOL OUR PRINCESS!
So she let her guard down.
YEAH, HE PROBABLY HAS A NICE-GUY ACT.
I BET HE'S REAL SLICK.
LIKE A NIGHT CLUB HOST?
Whoa...
YEAH, A FAST-TALKING BAD BOY WHO PLAYS INNOCENT...
YAYYYYYYYY!
GHH
GH
HGH
GH
GH

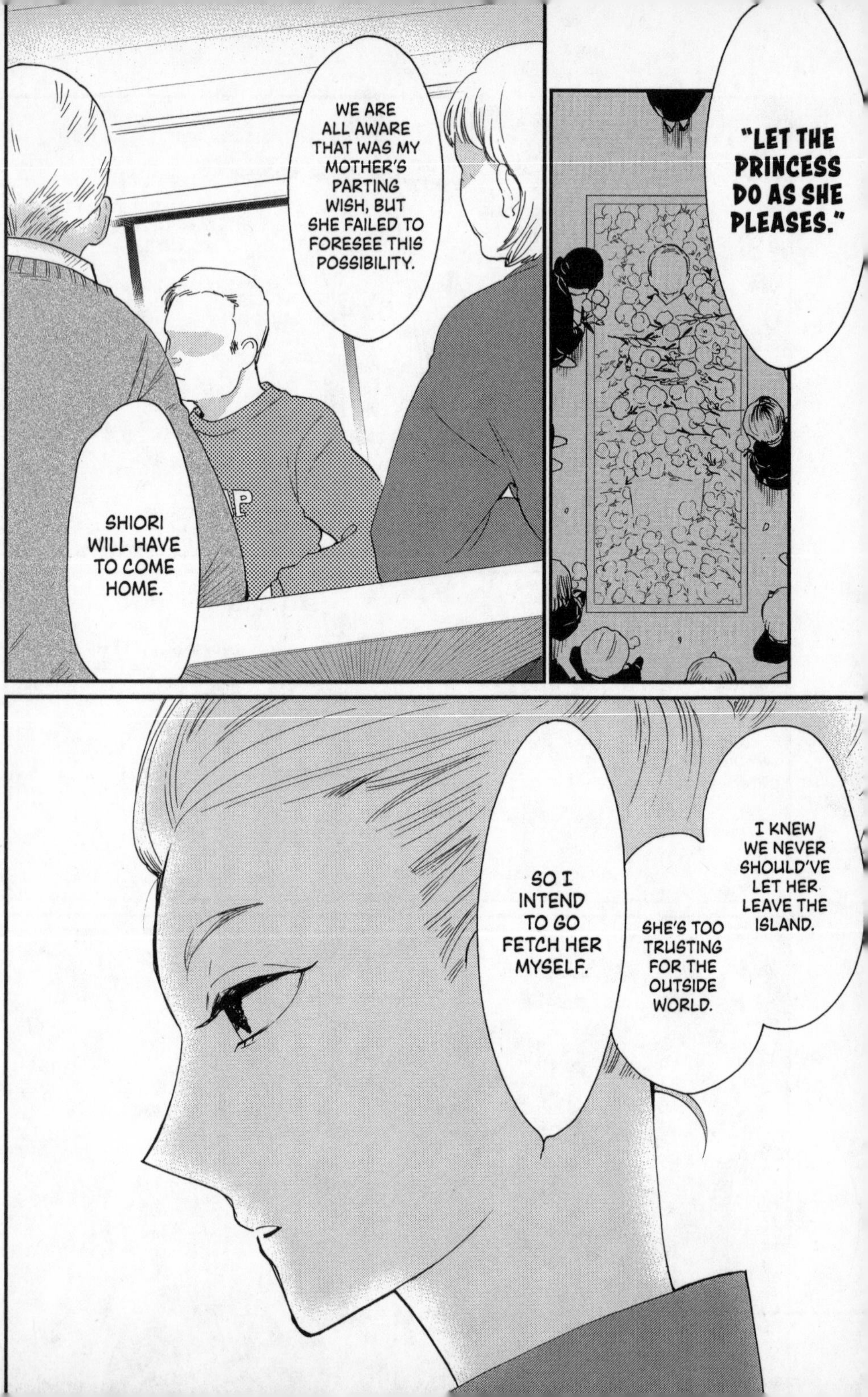
"LET THE PRINCESS DO AS SHE PLEASES."
WE ARE ALL AWARE THAT WAS MY MOTHER'S PARTING WISH, BUT SHE FAILED TO FORESEE THIS POSSIBILITY.
SHIORI WILL HAVE TO COME HOME.
I KNEW WE NEVER SHOULD'VE LET HER LEAVE THE ISLAND.
SHE'S TOO TRUSTING FOR THE OUTSIDE WORLD.
SO I INTEND TO GO FETCH HER MYSELF.

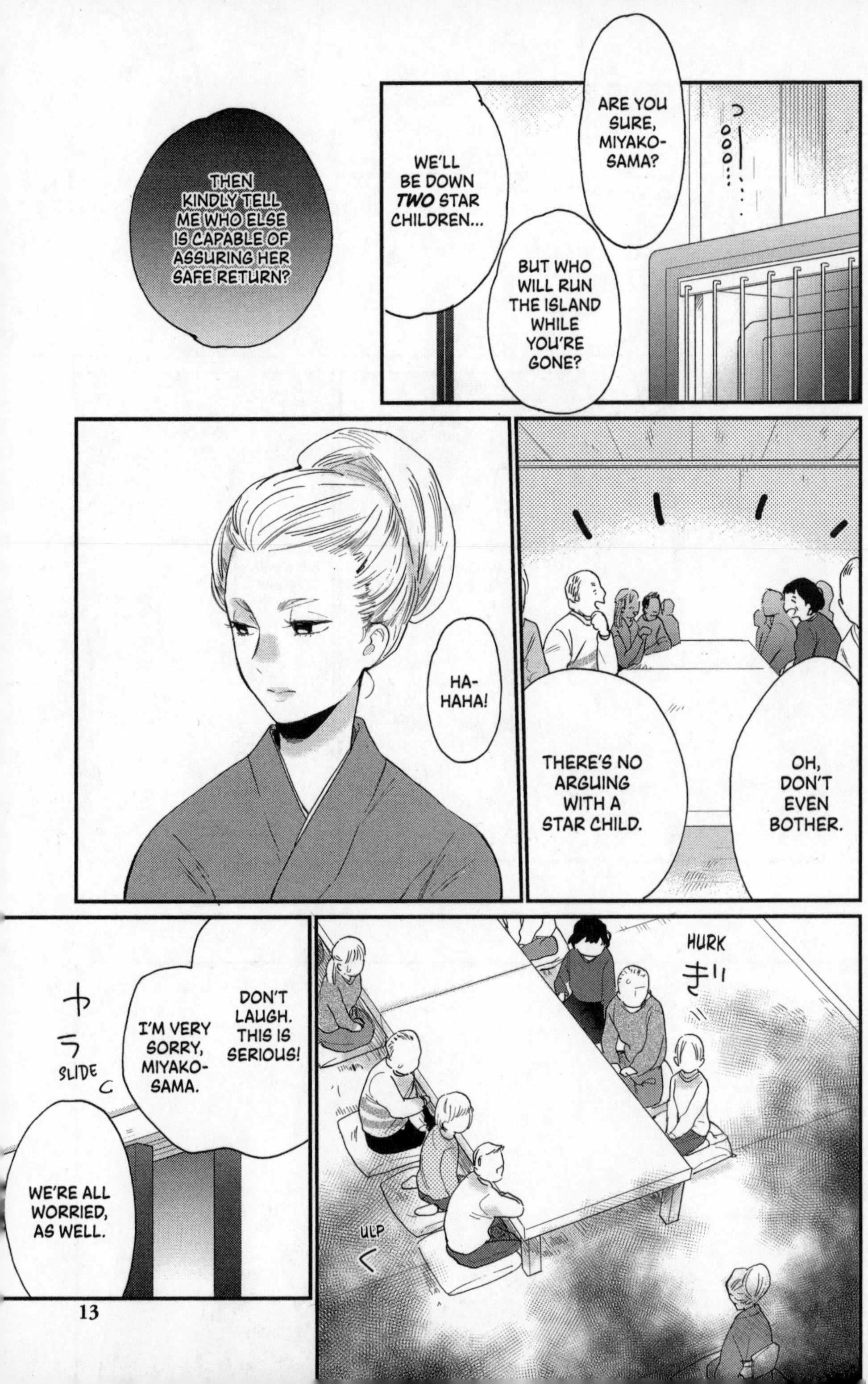
ARE YOU SURE, MIYAKO-SAMA?
つ... OOO...
WE'LL BE DOWN TWO STAR CHILDREN...
BUT WHO WILL RUN THE ISLAND WHILE YOU'RE GONE?
THEN KINDLY TELL ME WHO ELSE IS CAPABLE OF ASSURING HER SAFE RETURN?
OH, DON'T EVEN BOTHER.
THERE'S NO ARGUING WITH A STAR CHILD.
HA-HAHA!
HURK
きぃ
ULP
く
DON'T LAUGH. THIS IS SERIOUS!
I'M VERY SORRY, MIYAKO-SAMA.
ヤラ
SLIDE
WE'RE ALL WORRIED, AS WELL.

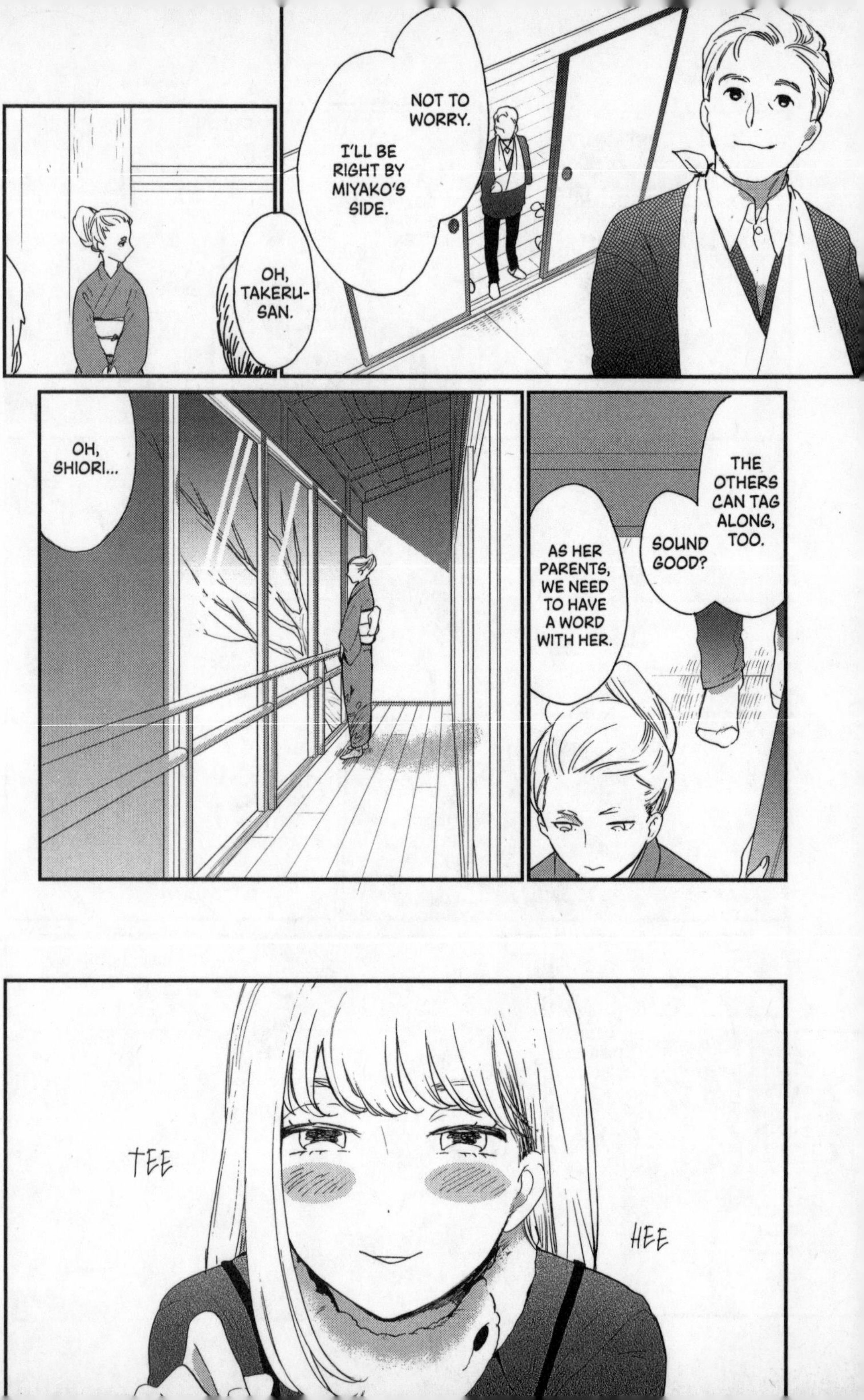
NOT TO WORRY.
I'LL BE RIGHT BY MIYAKO'S SIDE.
OH, TAKERU-SAN.
THE OTHERS CAN TAG ALONG, TOO.
SOUND GOOD?
AS HER PARENTS, WE NEED TO HAVE A WORD WITH HER.
OH, SHIORI...
TEE
HEE

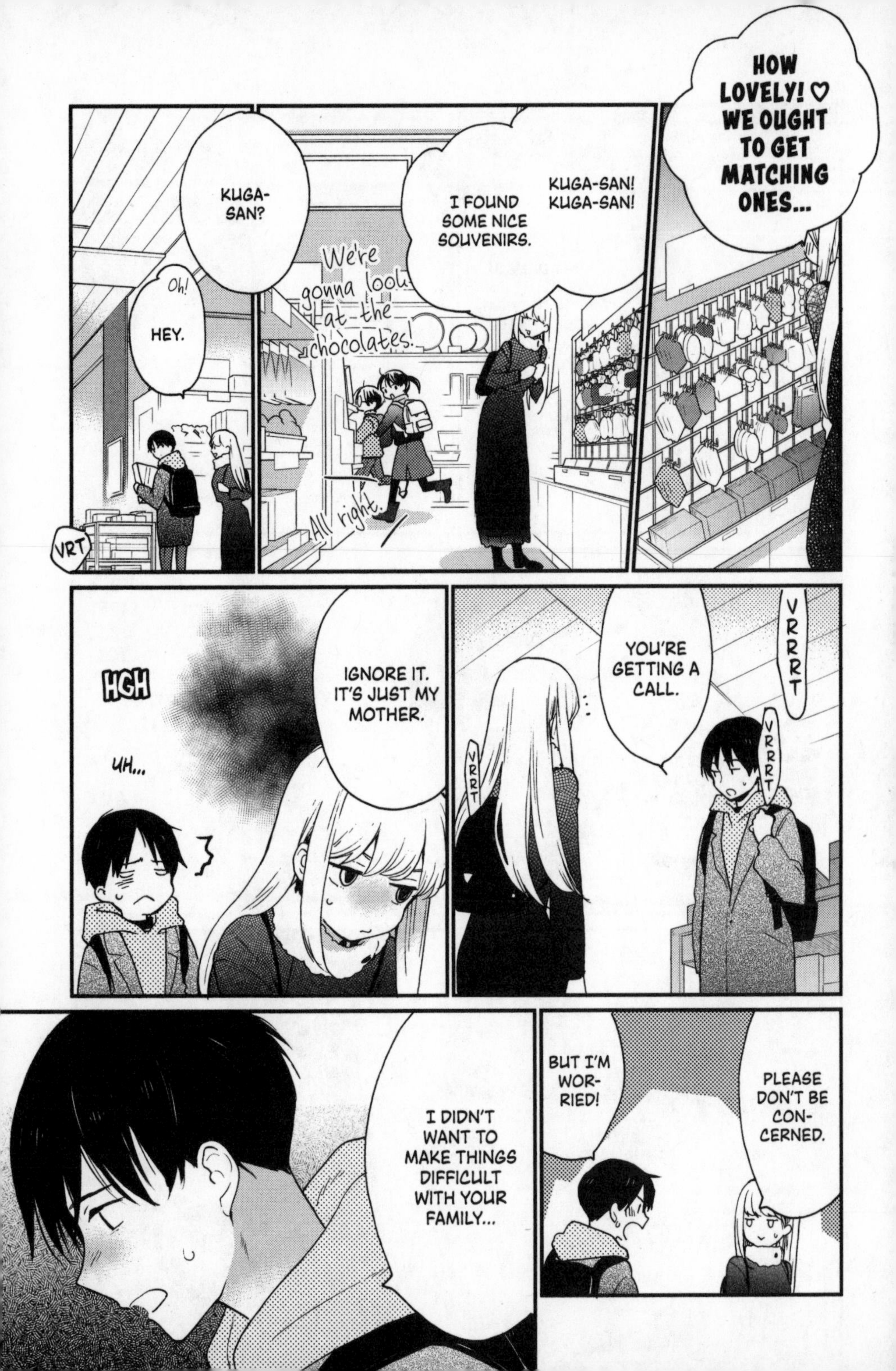
HOW LOVELY! ♡ WE OUGHT TO GET MATCHING ONES...
KUGA-SAN! KUGA-SAN!
I FOUND SOME NICE SOUVENIRS.
We're gonna look at the chocolates!
All right.
KUGA-SAN?
Oh!
HEY.
VRT
VRRRT
YOU'RE GETTING A CALL.
VRRRT
VRRT
IGNORE IT. IT'S JUST MY MOTHER.
HGH
UH...
PLEASE DON'T BE CON-CERNED.
BUT I'M WOR-RIED!
I DIDN'T WANT TO MAKE THINGS DIFFICULT WITH YOUR FAMILY...

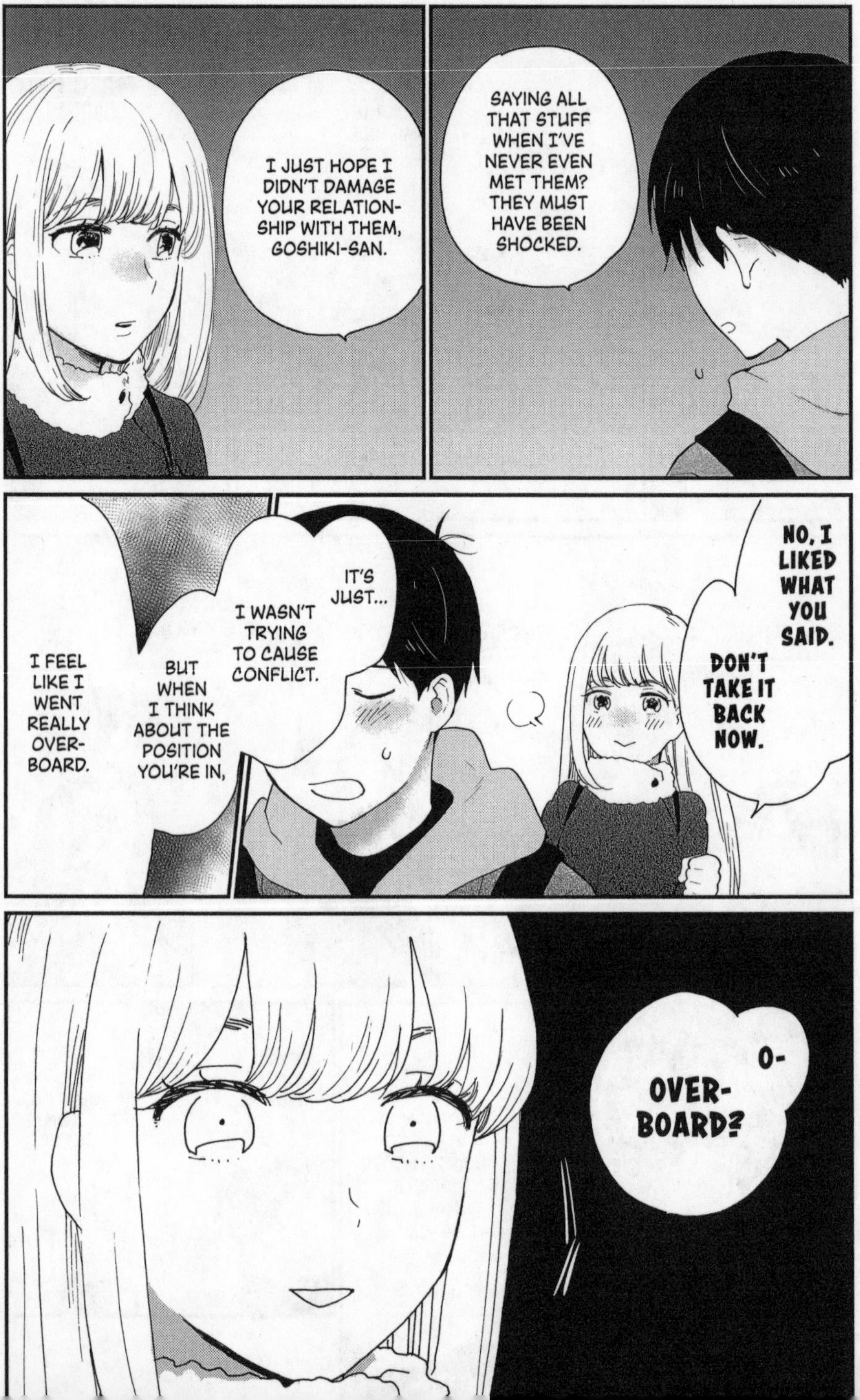
SAYING ALL THAT STUFF WHEN I'VE NEVER EVEN MET THEM? THEY MUST HAVE BEEN SHOCKED.
I JUST HOPE I DIDN'T DAMAGE YOUR RELATION-SHIP WITH THEM, GOSHIKI-SAN.
NO, I LIKED WHAT YOU SAID.
DON'T TAKE IT BACK NOW.
IT'S JUST...
I WASN'T TRYING TO CAUSE CONFLICT.
BUT WHEN I THINK ABOUT THE POSITION YOU'RE IN,
I FEEL LIKE I WENT REALLY OVER-BOARD.
O-
OVER-BOARD?

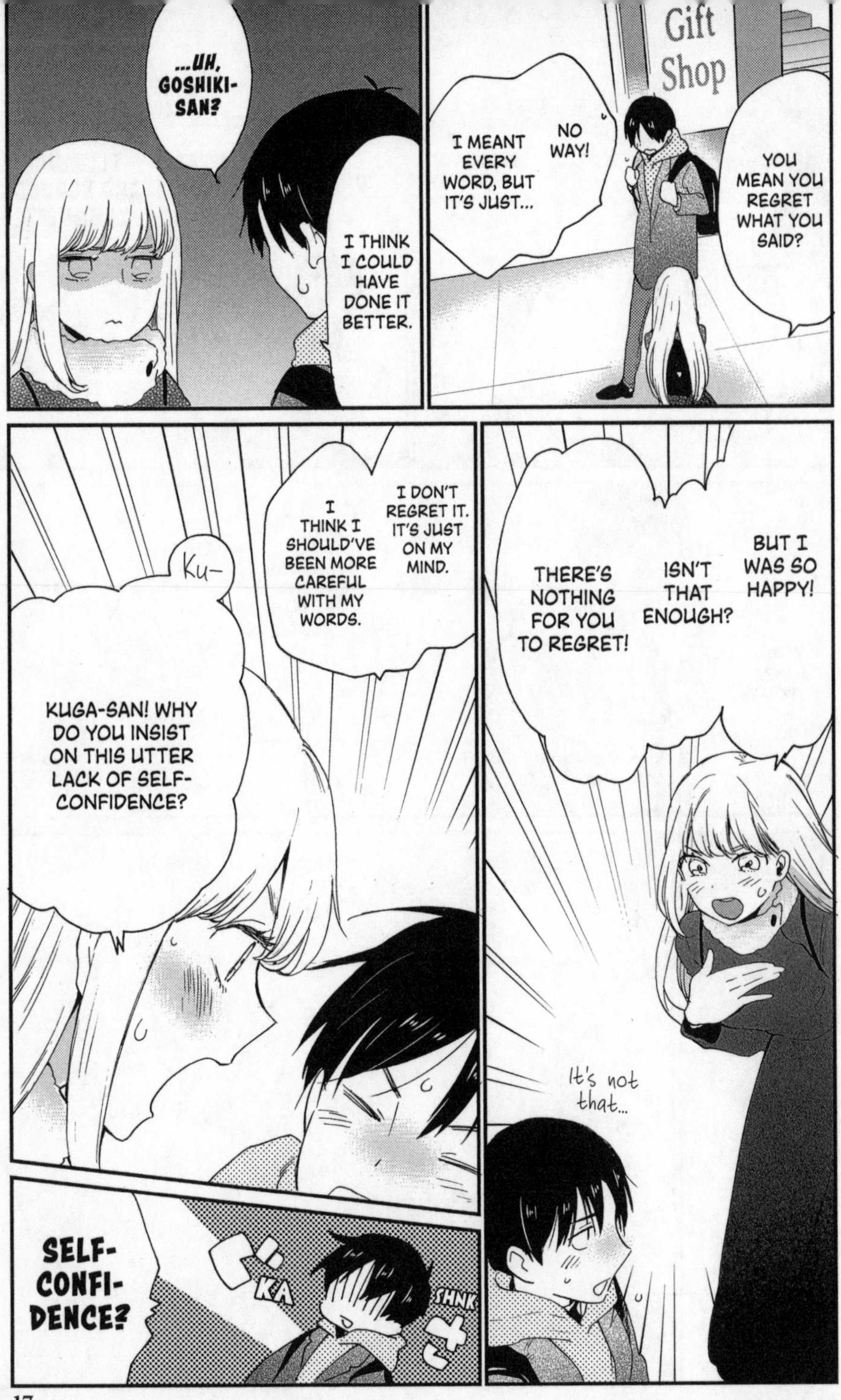
Gift Shop
YOU MEAN YOU REGRET WHAT YOU SAID?
NO WAY!
I MEANT EVERY WORD, BUT IT'S JUST...
I THINK I COULD HAVE DONE IT BETTER.
...UH, GOSHIKI-SAN?
BUT I WAS SO HAPPY!
ISN'T THAT ENOUGH?
THERE'S NOTHING FOR YOU TO REGRET!
It's not that...
I DON'T REGRET IT. IT'S JUST ON MY MIND.
I THINK I SHOULD'VE BEEN MORE CAREFUL WITH MY WORDS.
Ku-
KUGA-SAN! WHY DO YOU INSIST ON THIS UTTER LACK OF SELF-CONFIDENCE?
SHNK
KA
SELF-CONFI-DENCE?

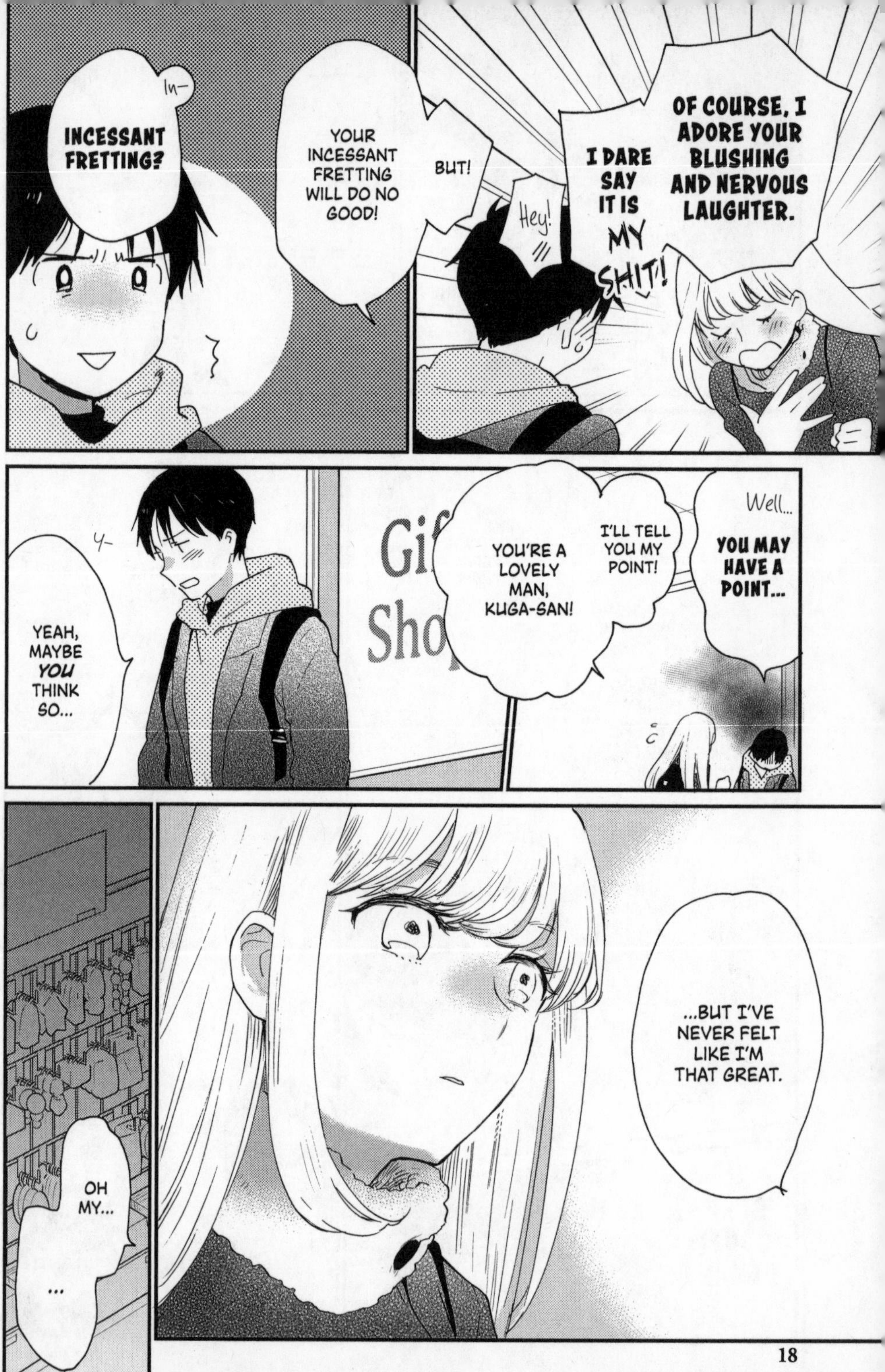
OF COURSE, I ADORE YOUR BLUSHING AND NERVOUS LAUGHTER.
I DARE SAY IT IS MY SHIT!
Hey!
BUT!
YOUR INCESSANT FRETTING WILL DO NO GOOD!
In-
INCESSANT FRETTING?
Well...
YOU MAY HAVE A POINT...
I'LL TELL YOU MY POINT!
YOU'RE A LOVELY MAN, KUGA-SAN!
Y-
YEAH, MAYBE YOU THINK SO...
...BUT I'VE NEVER FELT LIKE I'M THAT GREAT.
OH MY...
...

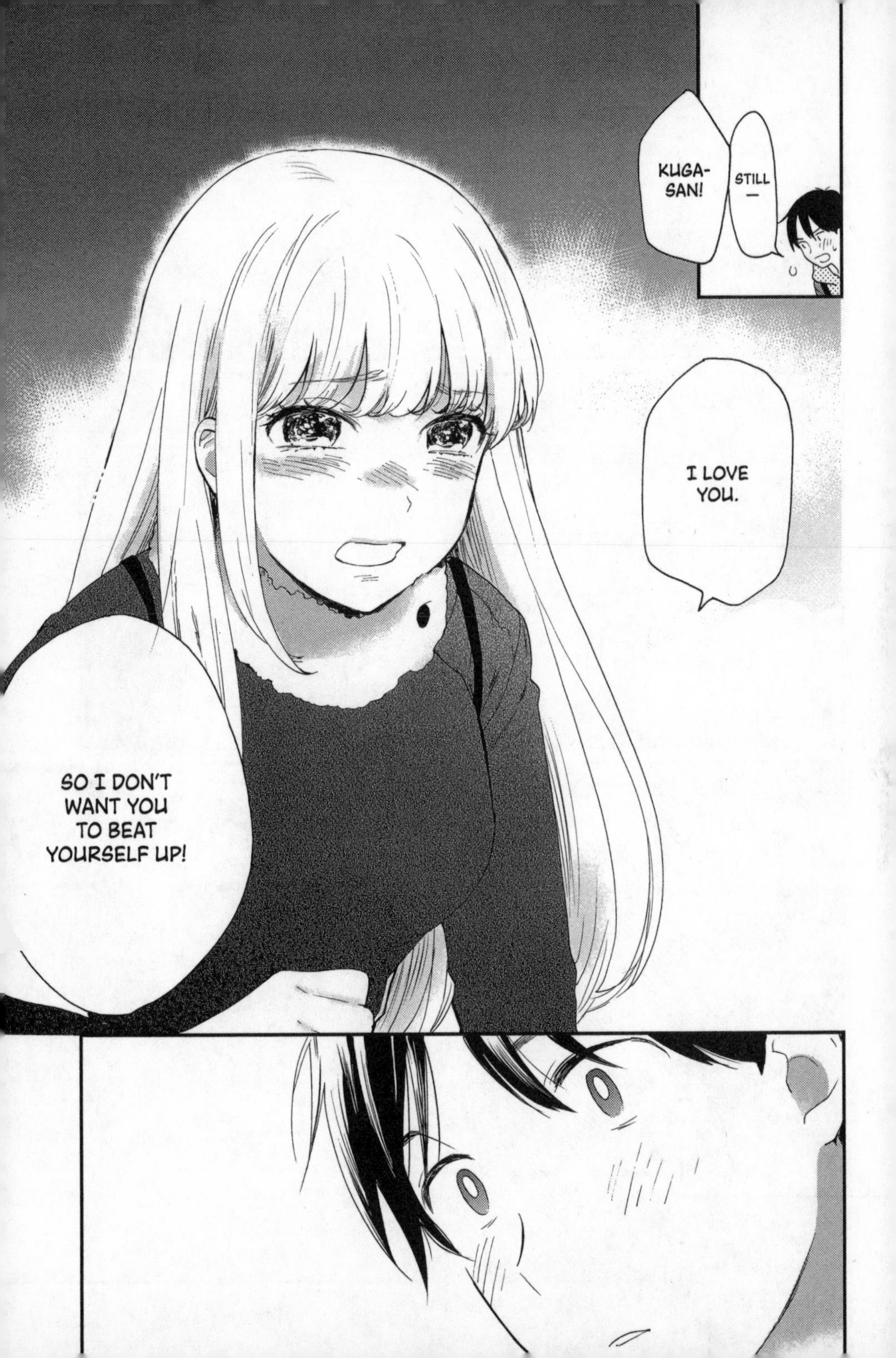
STILL —
KUGA-SAN!
I LOVE YOU.
SO I DON'T WANT YOU TO BEAT YOURSELF UP!

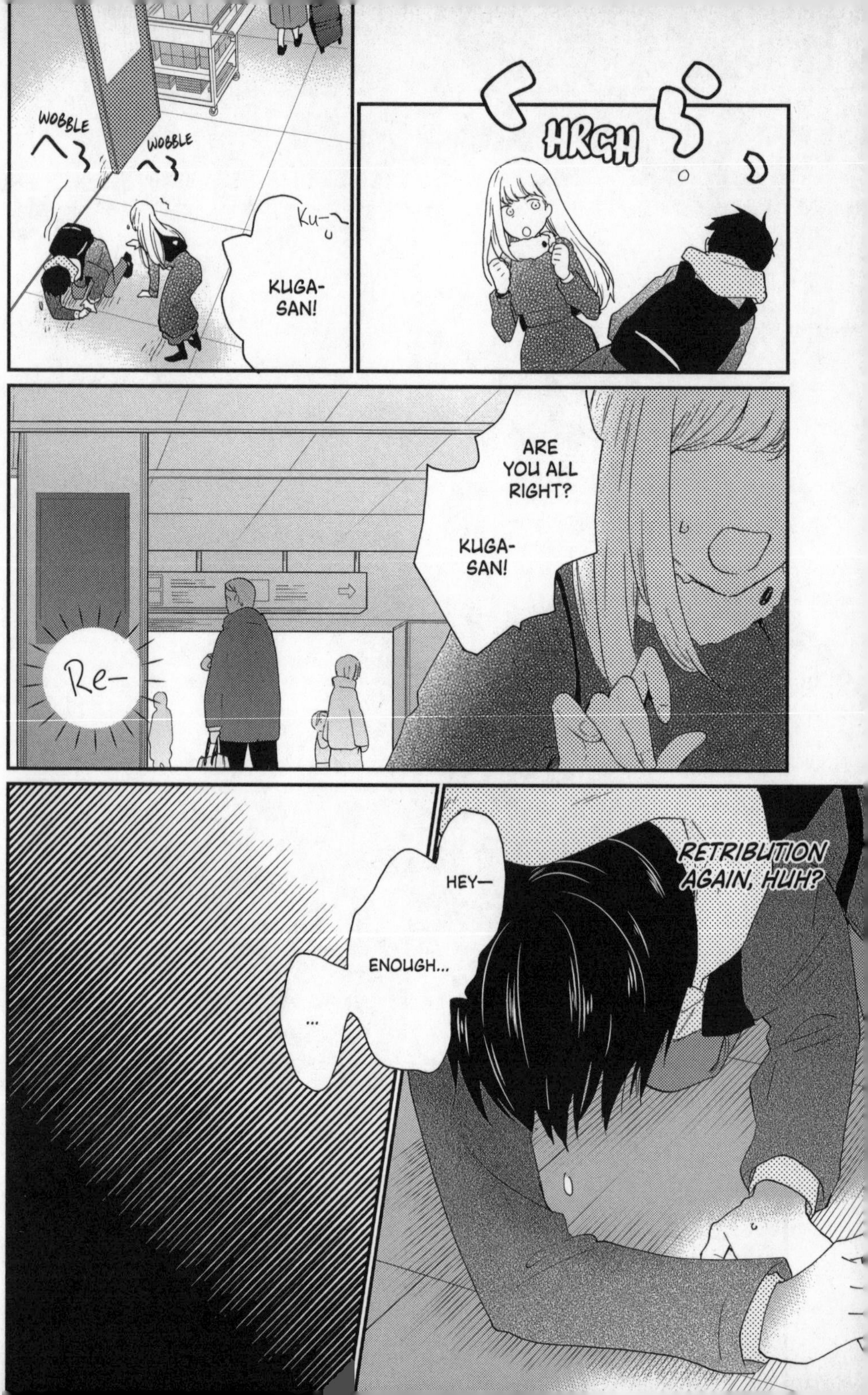
HRGH
WOBBLE
WOBBLE
Ku–
KUGA-SAN!
ARE YOU ALL RIGHT?
KUGA-SAN!
Re–
RETRIBUTION AGAIN, HUH?
HEY—
ENOUGH...
...

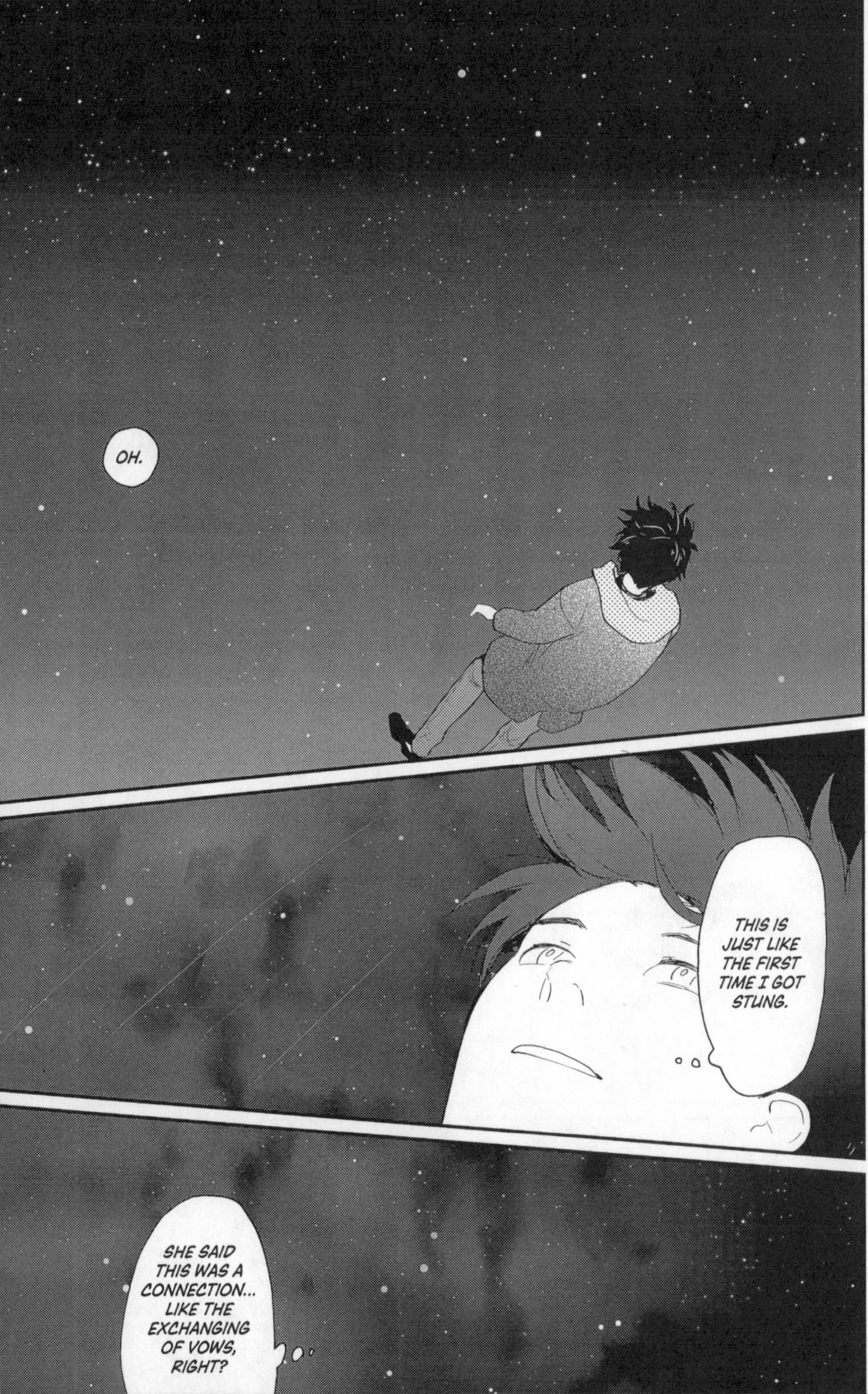
OH.
THIS IS JUST LIKE THE FIRST TIME I GOT STUNG.
SHE SAID THIS WAS A CONNECTION... LIKE THE EXCHANGING OF VOWS, RIGHT?

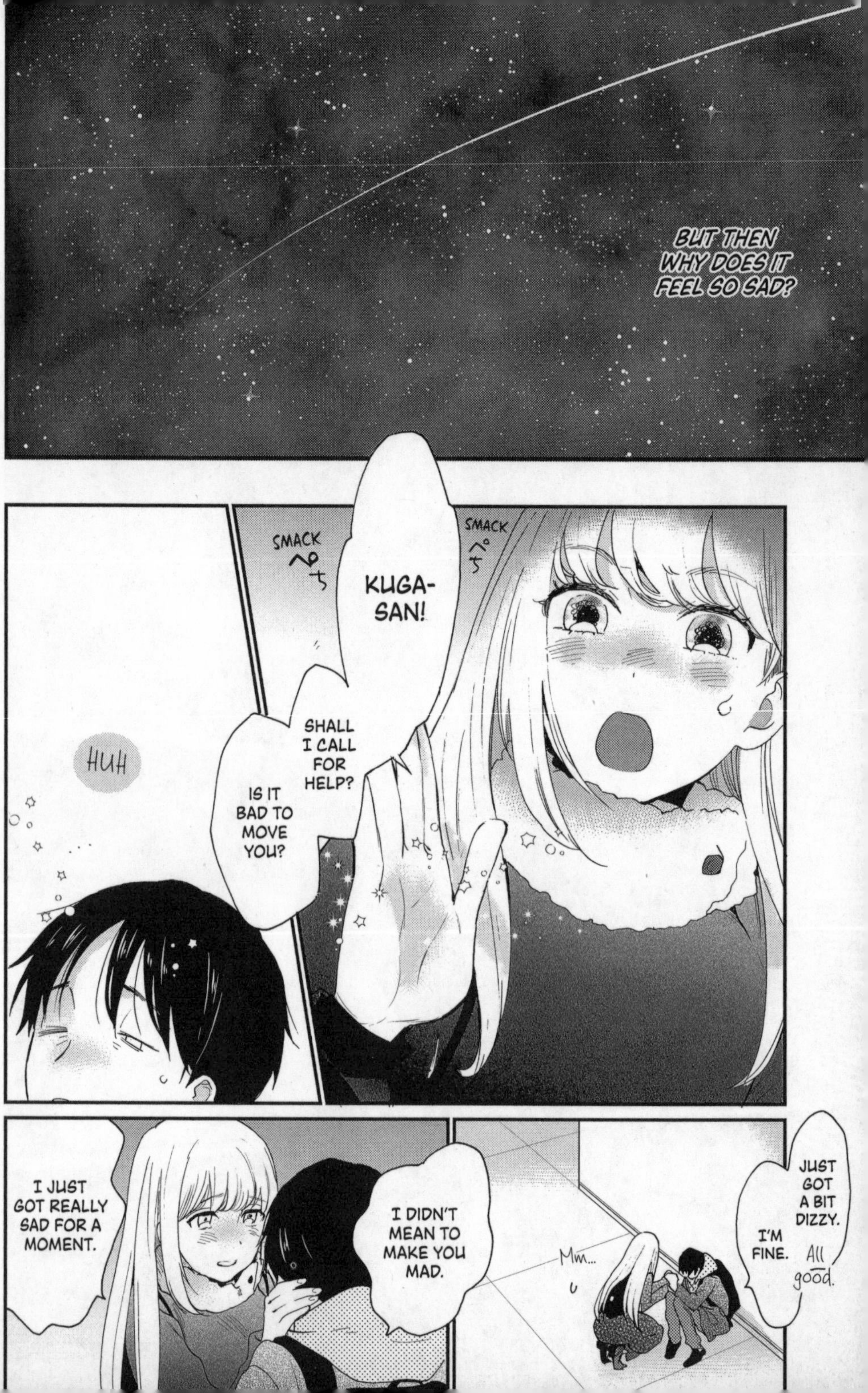
BUT THEN WHY DOES IT FEEL SO SAD?
SMACK
SMACK
KUGA-SAN!
SHALL I CALL FOR HELP?
IS IT BAD TO MOVE YOU?
HUH
JUST GOT A BIT DIZZY.
I'M FINE.
All good.
Mm...
I DIDN'T MEAN TO MAKE YOU MAD.
I JUST GOT REALLY SAD FOR A MOMENT.

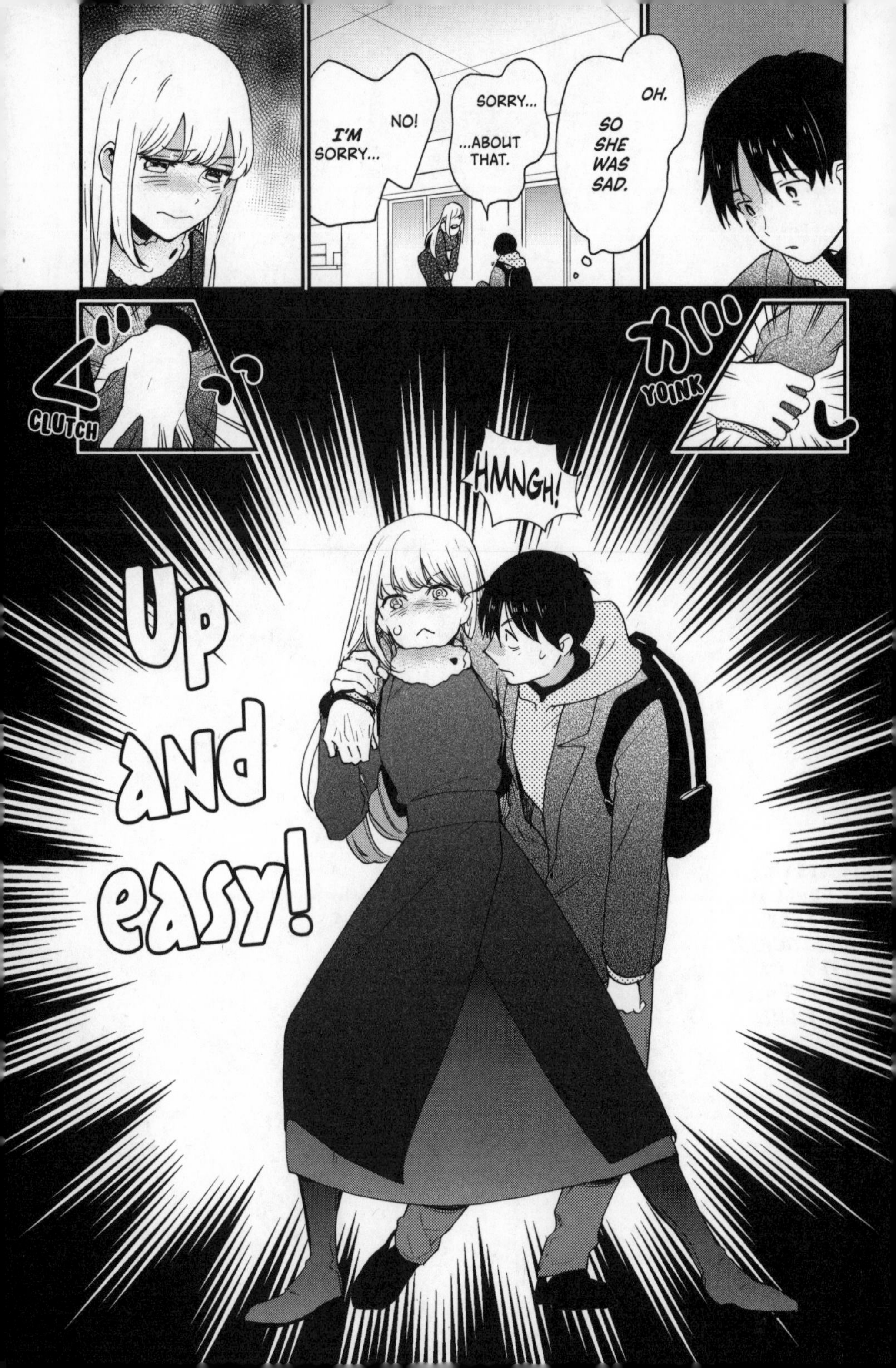
OH.
SO SHE WAS SAD.
SORRY... ...ABOUT THAT.
NO! I'M SORRY...
YOINK
CLUTCH
HMNGH!
Up and easy!

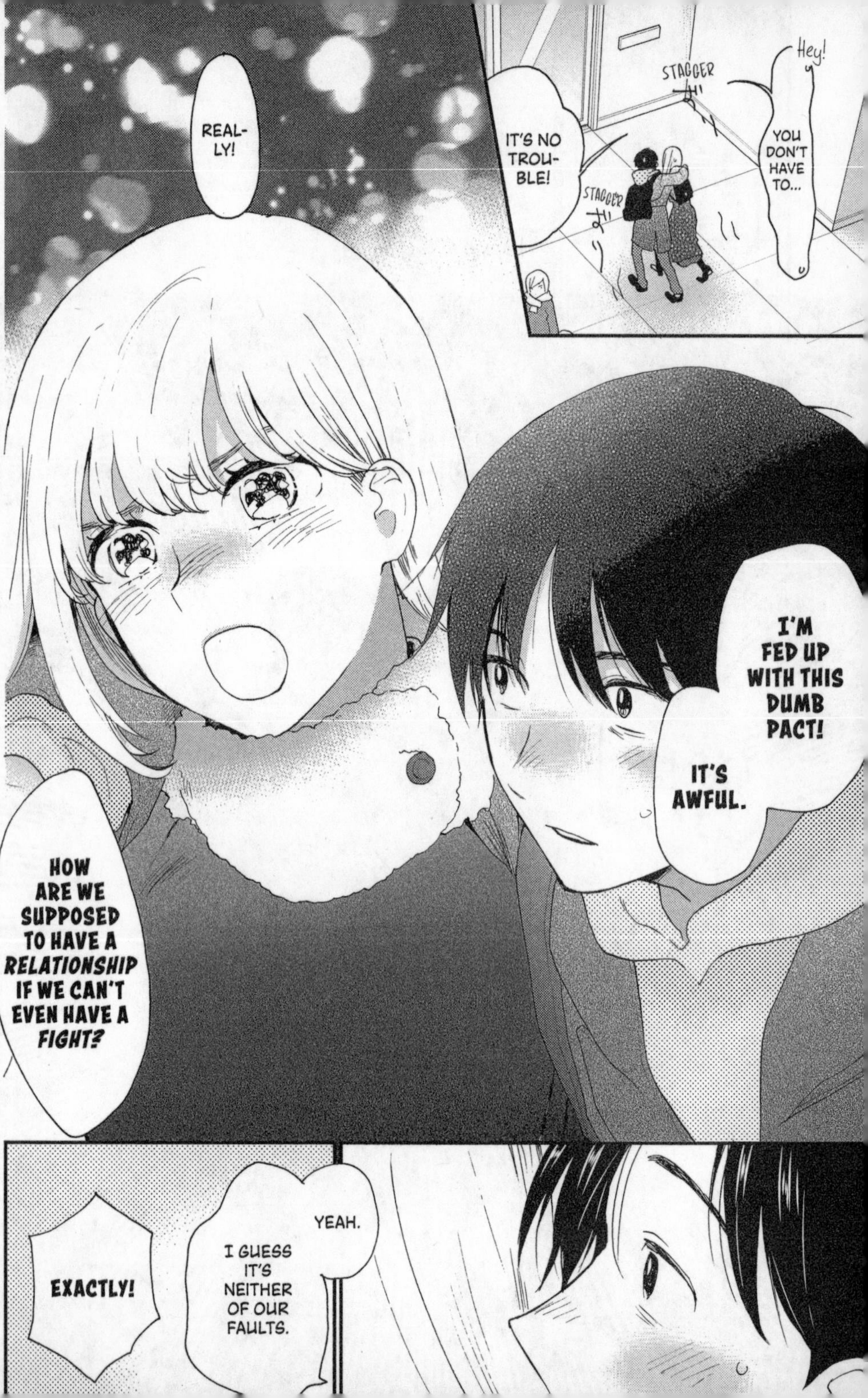
Hey!
YOU DON'T HAVE TO...
STAGGER
IT'S NO TROUBLE!
STAGGER
I'M FED UP WITH THIS DUMB PACT!
IT'S AWFUL.
REAL-LY!
HOW ARE WE SUPPOSED TO HAVE A *RELATIONSHIP* IF WE CAN'T EVEN HAVE A *FIGHT?*
YEAH.
I GUESS IT'S NEITHER OF OUR FAULTS.
EXACTLY!

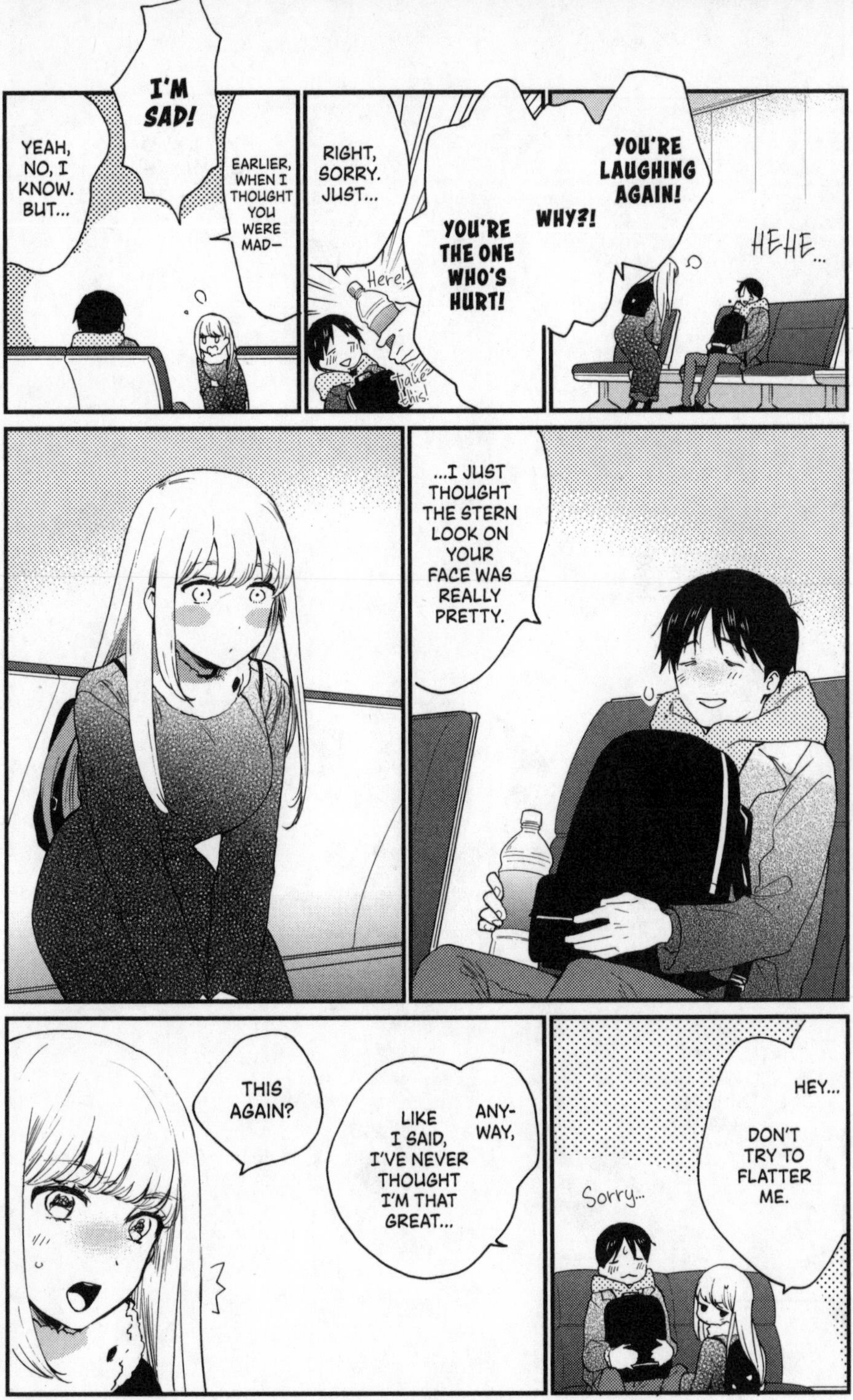
YOU'RE LAUGHING AGAIN!
HEHE...
WHY?!
YOU'RE THE ONE WHO'S HURT!
Here!
Take this!
RIGHT, SORRY. JUST...
EARLIER, WHEN I THOUGHT YOU WERE MAD—
I'M SAD!
YEAH, NO, I KNOW. BUT...
...I JUST THOUGHT THE STERN LOOK ON YOUR FACE WAS REALLY PRETTY.
HEY...
DON'T TRY TO FLATTER ME.
Sorry...
ANYWAY,
LIKE I SAID, I'VE NEVER THOUGHT I'M THAT GREAT...
THIS AGAIN?

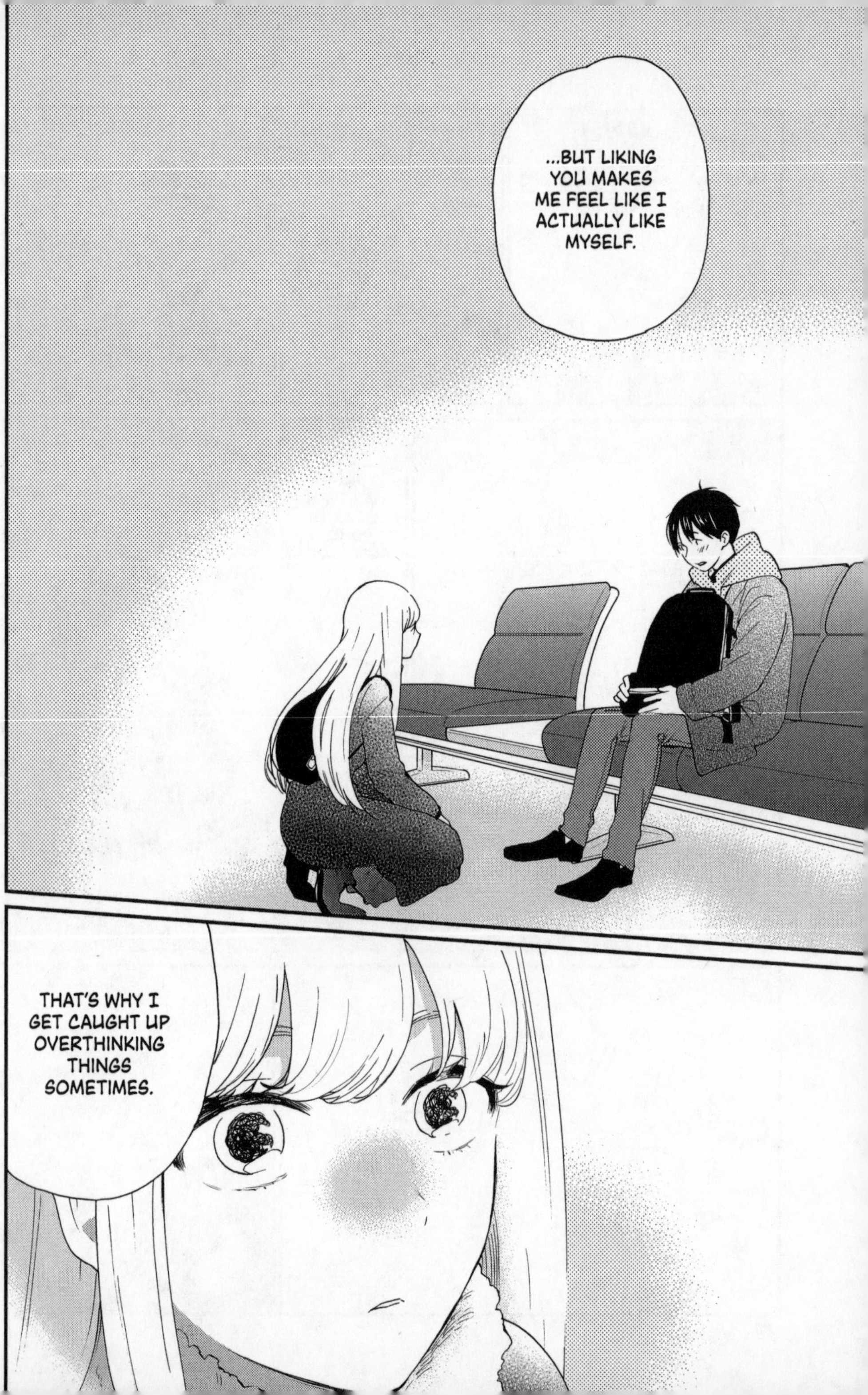
...BUT LIKING YOU MAKES ME FEEL LIKE I ACTUALLY LIKE MYSELF.
THAT'S WHY I GET CAUGHT UP OVERTHINKING THINGS SOMETIMES.

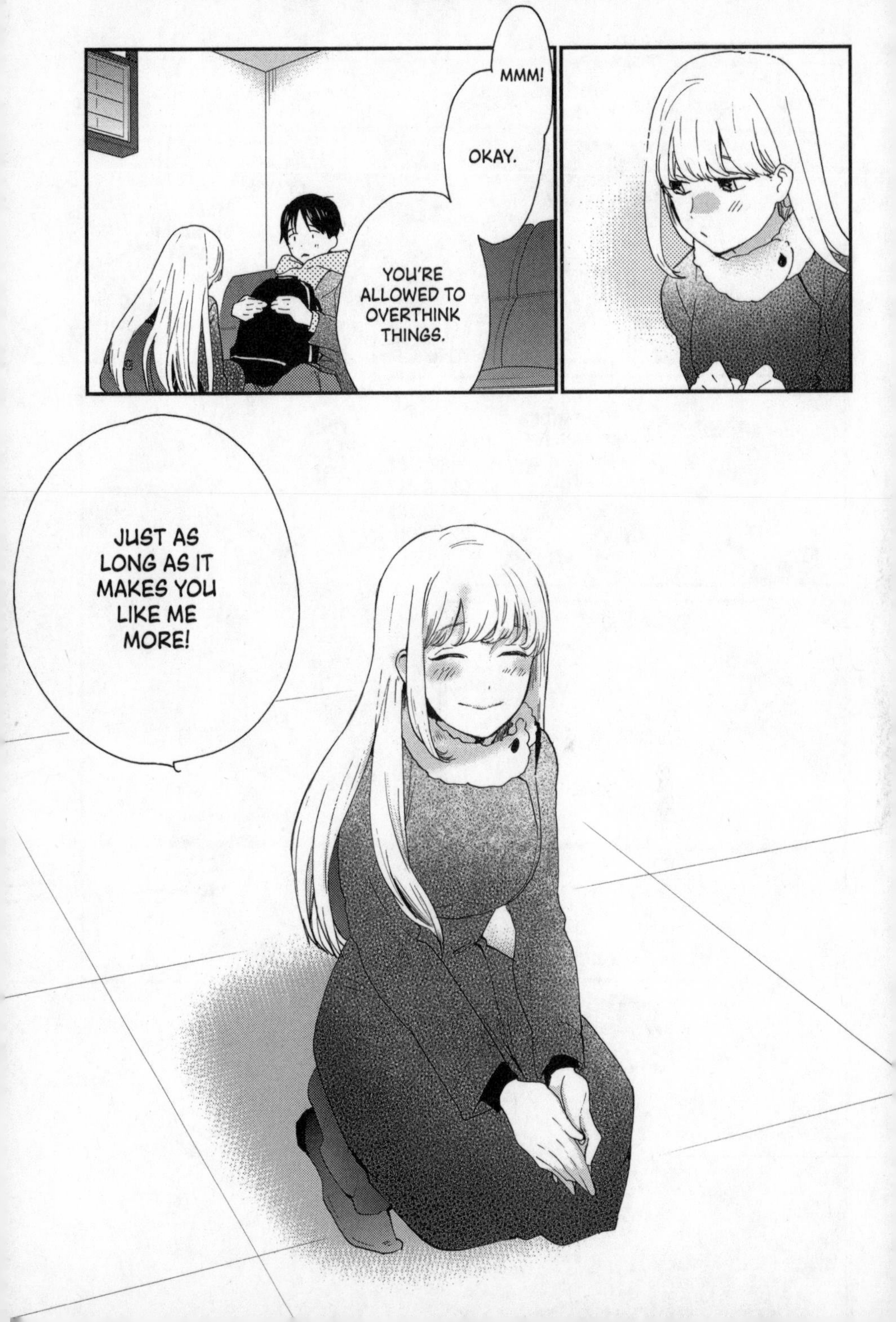
MMM!
OKAY.
YOU'RE ALLOWED TO OVERTHINK THINGS.
JUST AS LONG AS IT MAKES YOU LIKE ME MORE!

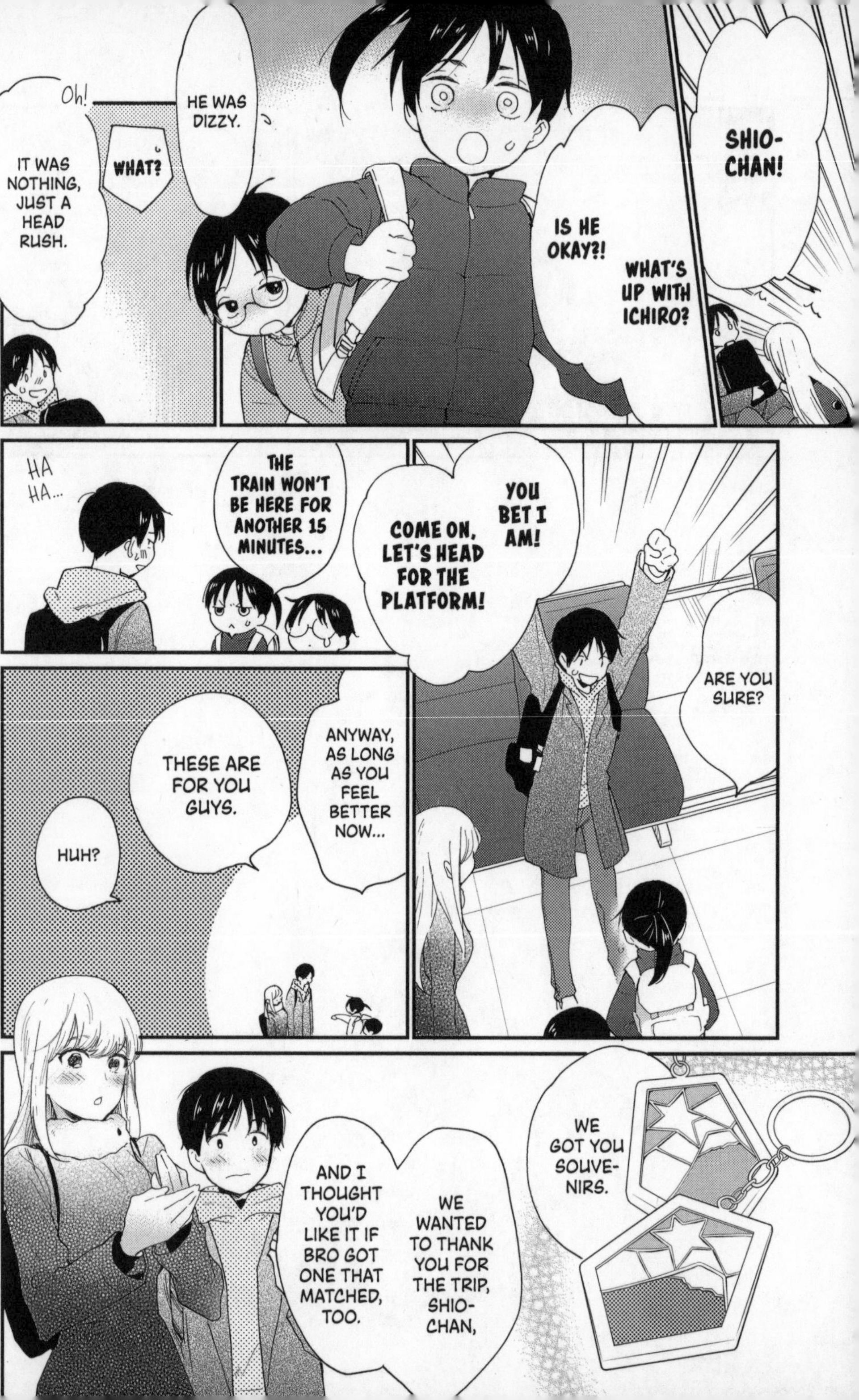

SHIO-CHAN!
WHAT'S UP WITH ICHIRO?
IS HE OKAY?!
HE WAS DIZZY.
WHAT?
Oh!
IT WAS NOTHING, JUST A HEAD RUSH.
YOU BET I AM!
COME ON, LET'S HEAD FOR THE PLATFORM!
ARE YOU SURE?
THE TRAIN WON'T BE HERE FOR ANOTHER 15 MINUTES...
HA HA...
ANYWAY, AS LONG AS YOU FEEL BETTER NOW...
THESE ARE FOR YOU GUYS.
HUH?
WE GOT YOU SOUVE-NIRS.
WE WANTED TO THANK YOU FOR THE TRIP, SHIO-CHAN,
AND I THOUGHT YOU'D LIKE IT IF BRO GOT ONE THAT MATCHED, TOO.

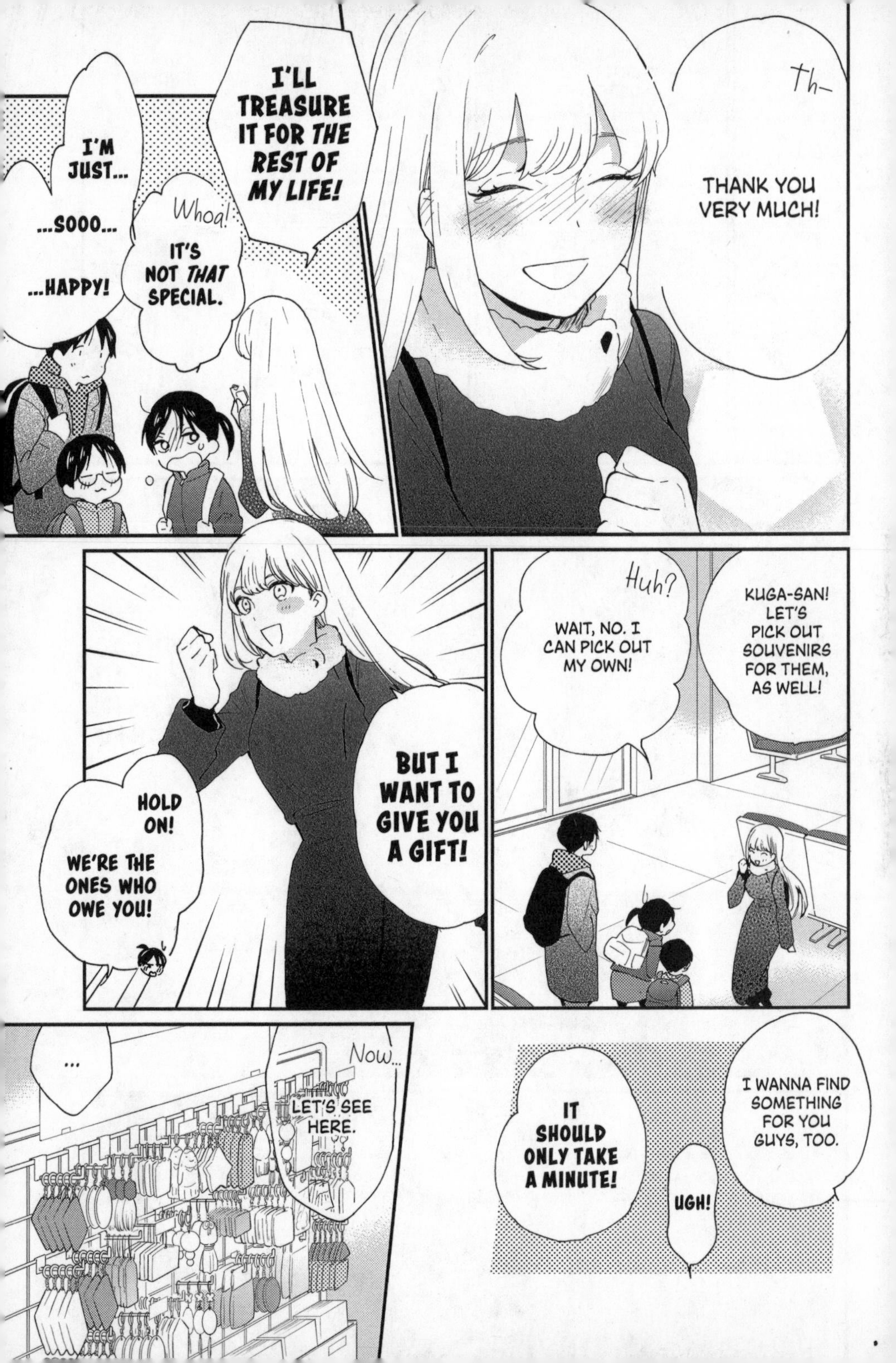
Th–
THANK YOU VERY MUCH!
I'LL TREASURE IT FOR *THE* *REST OF* *MY LIFE!*
Whoa!
IT'S NOT *THAT* SPECIAL.
I'M JUST...
...SOOO...
...HAPPY!
KUGA-SAN! LET'S PICK OUT SOUVENIRS FOR THEM, AS WELL!
Huh?
WAIT, NO. I CAN PICK OUT MY OWN!
BUT I WANT TO GIVE YOU A GIFT!
HOLD ON!
WE'RE THE ONES WHO OWE YOU!
I WANNA FIND SOMETHING FOR YOU GUYS, TOO.
IT SHOULD ONLY TAKE A MINUTE!
UGH!
Now...
LET'S SEE HERE.
...

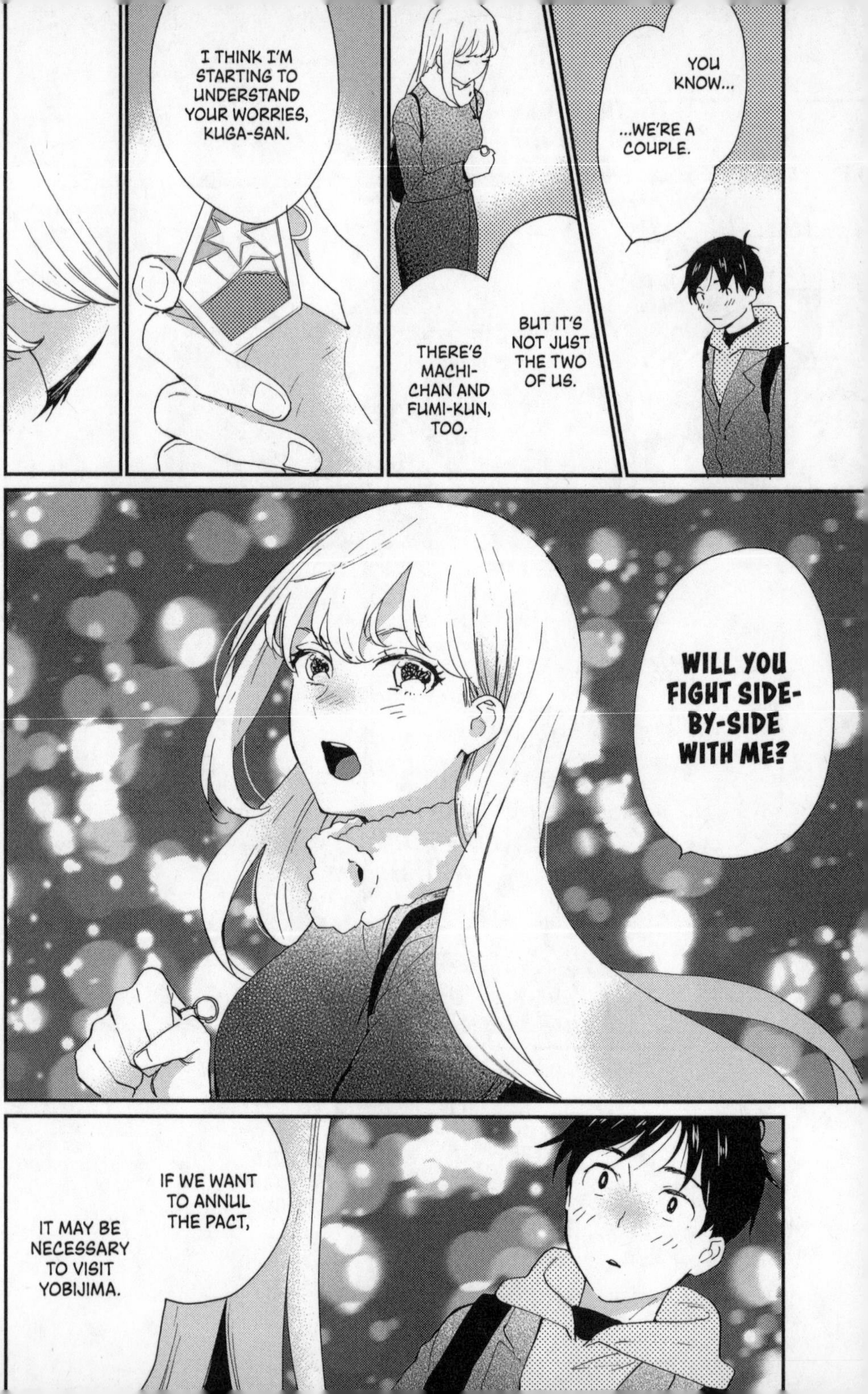
YOU KNOW...
...WE'RE A COUPLE.
BUT IT'S NOT JUST THE TWO OF US.
THERE'S MACHI-CHAN AND FUMI-KUN, TOO.
I THINK I'M STARTING TO UNDERSTAND YOUR WORRIES, KUGA-SAN.
WILL YOU FIGHT SIDE-BY-SIDE WITH ME?
IF WE WANT TO ANNUL THE PACT,
IT MAY BE NECESSARY TO VISIT YOBIJIMA.

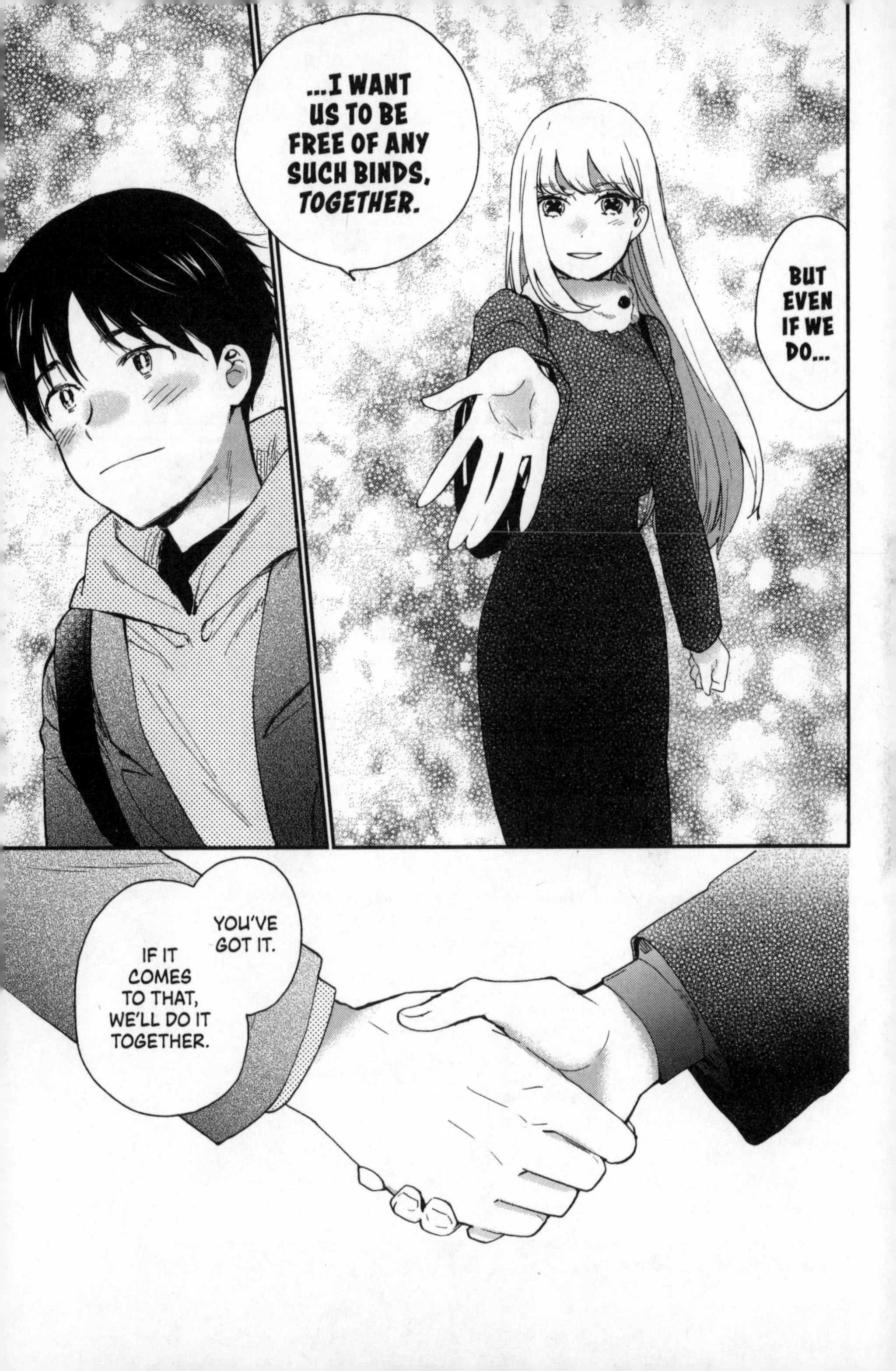

BUT EVEN IF WE DO...
...I WANT US TO BE FREE OF ANY SUCH BINDS. *TOGETHER.*
YOU'VE GOT IT.
IF IT COMES TO THAT, WE'LL DO IT TOGETHER.

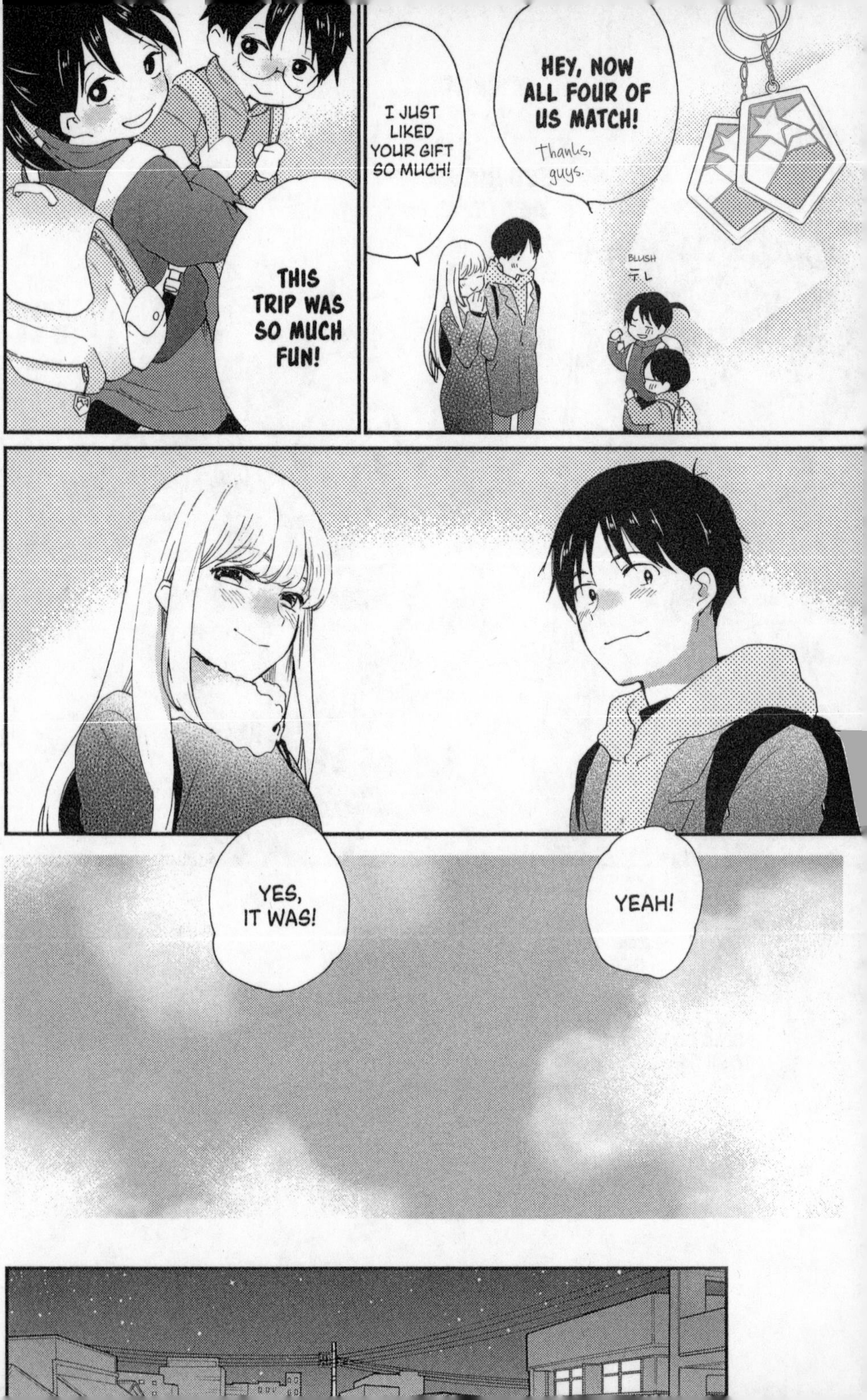
HEY, NOW ALL FOUR OF US MATCH!
Thanks, guys.
I JUST LIKED YOUR GIFT SO MUCH!
BLUSH
THIS TRIP WAS SO MUCH FUN!
YEAH!
YES, IT WAS!

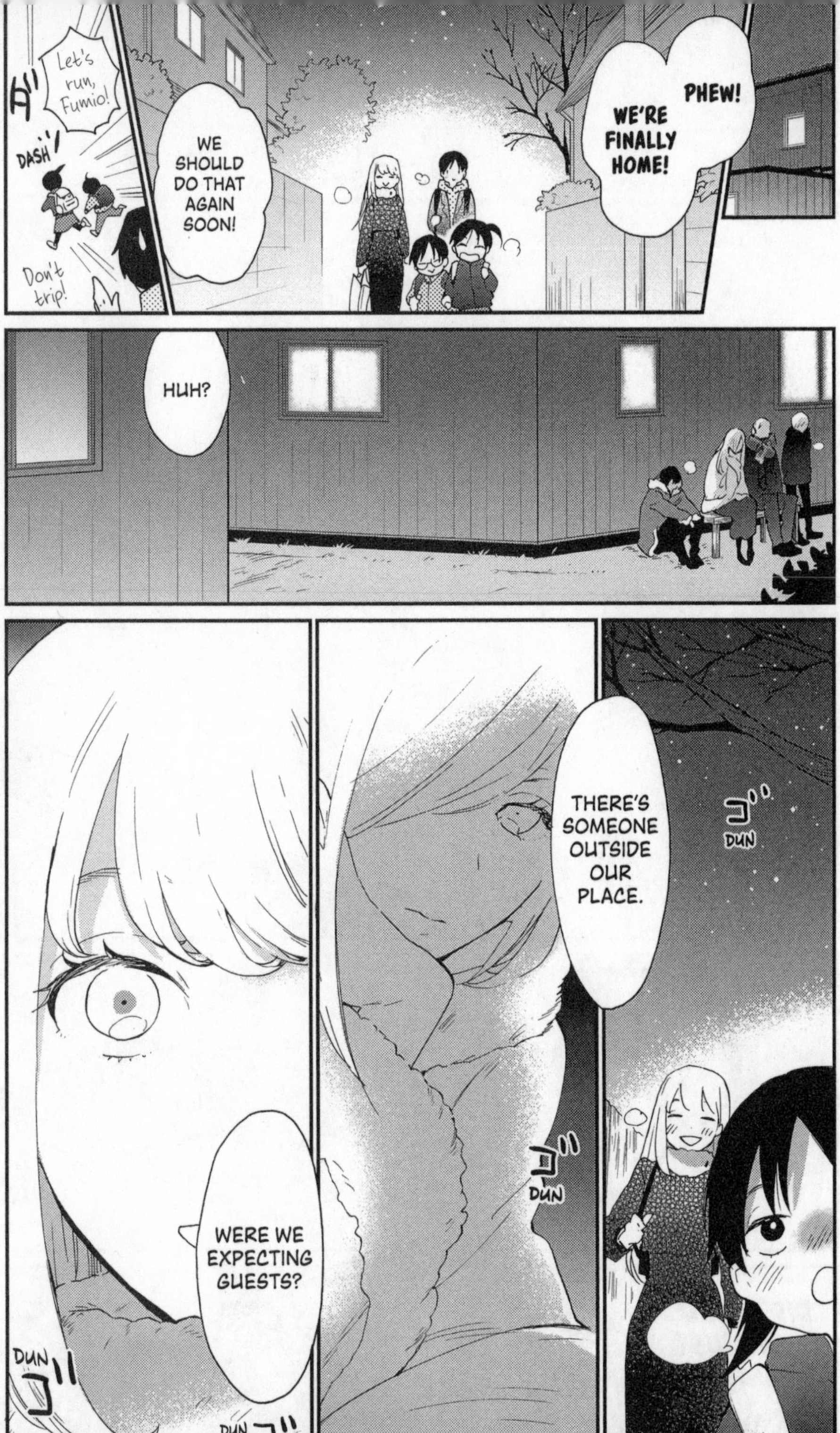
PHEW!
WE'RE FINALLY HOME!
WE SHOULD DO THAT AGAIN SOON!
Let's run, Fumio!
DASH
Don't trip!
HUH?
THERE'S SOMEONE OUTSIDE OUR PLACE.
DUN
WERE WE EXPECTING GUESTS?
DUN
DUN
DUN

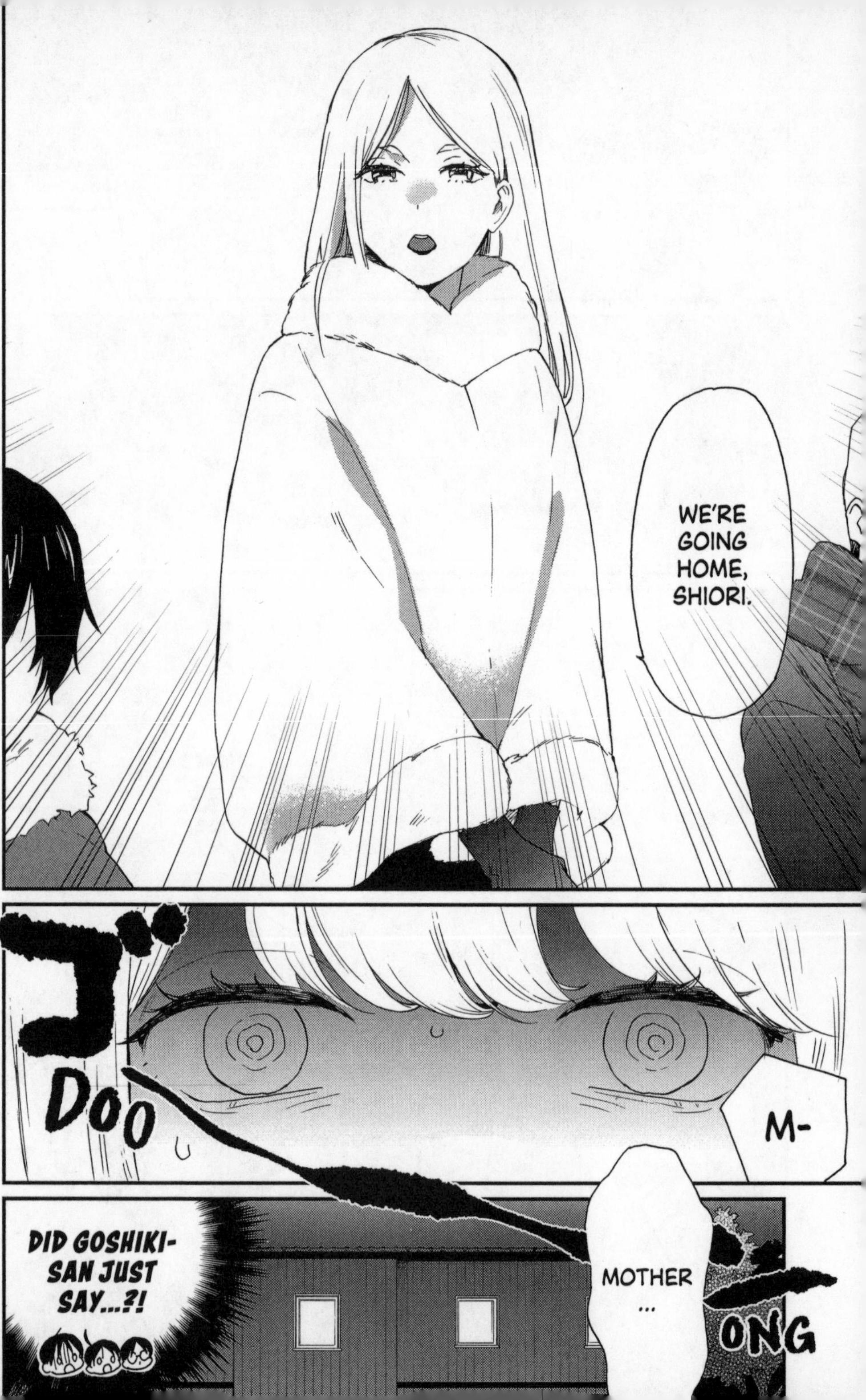
WE'RE GOING HOME, SHIORI.
M-
ゴ
DOO
MOTHER ...
ONG
DID GOSHIKI-SAN JUST SAY...?!

CHAPTER 11 ♦ END

A Galaxy Next Door

Gido
Amagakure

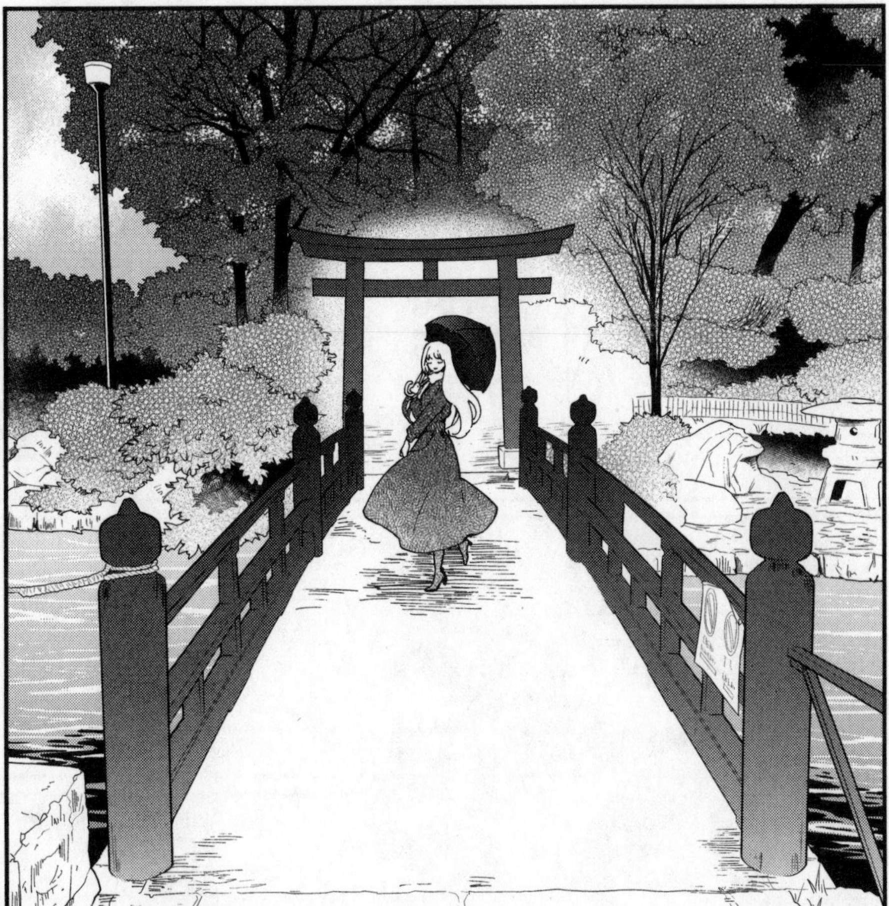

CHAPTER 12

A FAMILY MEETING WITH THE PRINCESS

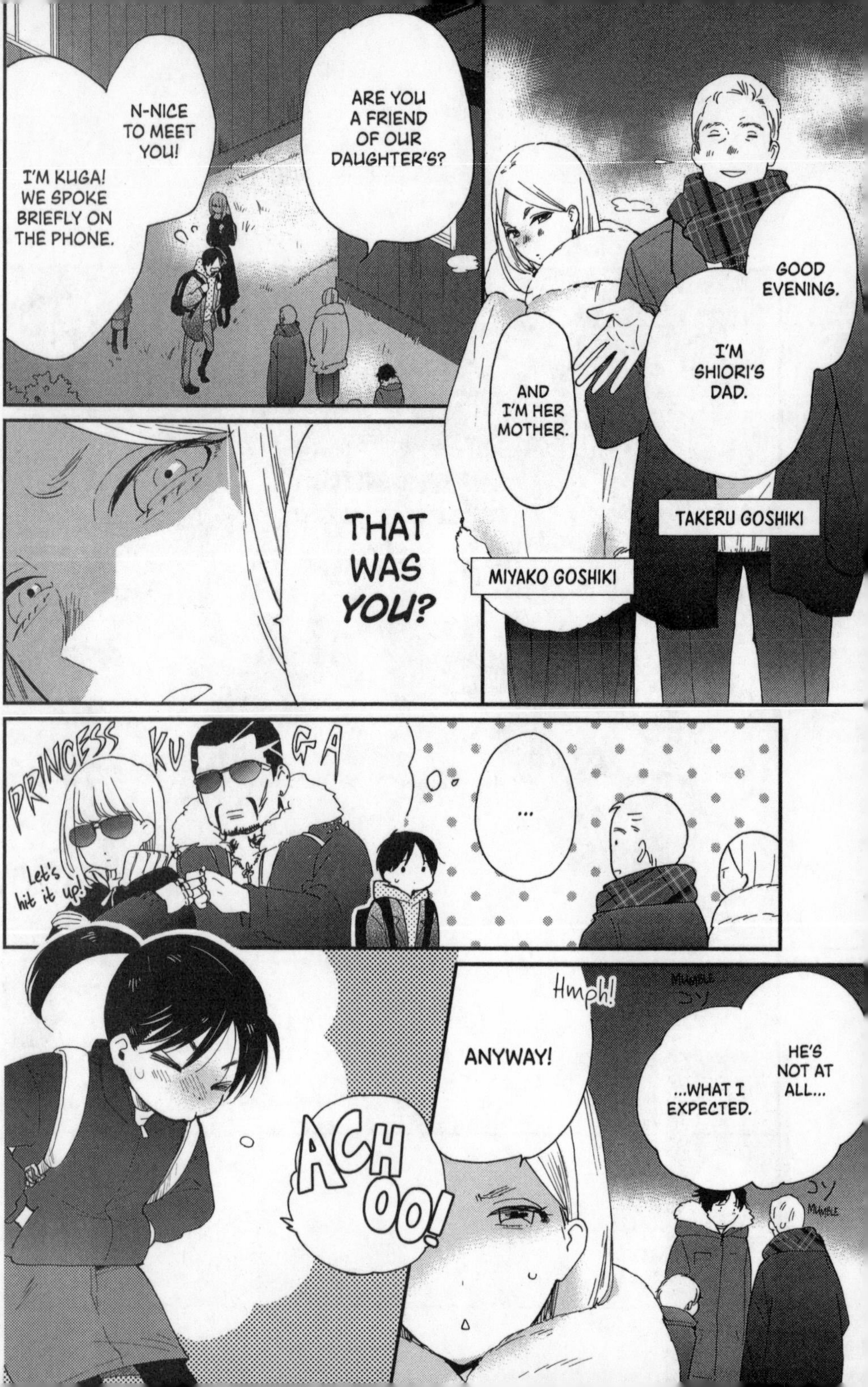
GOOD EVENING.
I'M SHIORI'S DAD.
TAKERU GOSHIKI
AND I'M HER MOTHER.
MIYAKO GOSHIKI
ARE YOU A FRIEND OF OUR DAUGHTER'S?
N-NICE TO MEET YOU!
I'M KUGA! WE SPOKE BRIEFLY ON THE PHONE.
THAT WAS YOU?
...
PRINCESS KUGA
Let's hit it up!
MUMBLE
HE'S NOT AT ALL...
...WHAT I EXPECTED.
MUMBLE
Hmph!
ANYWAY!
ACHOO!

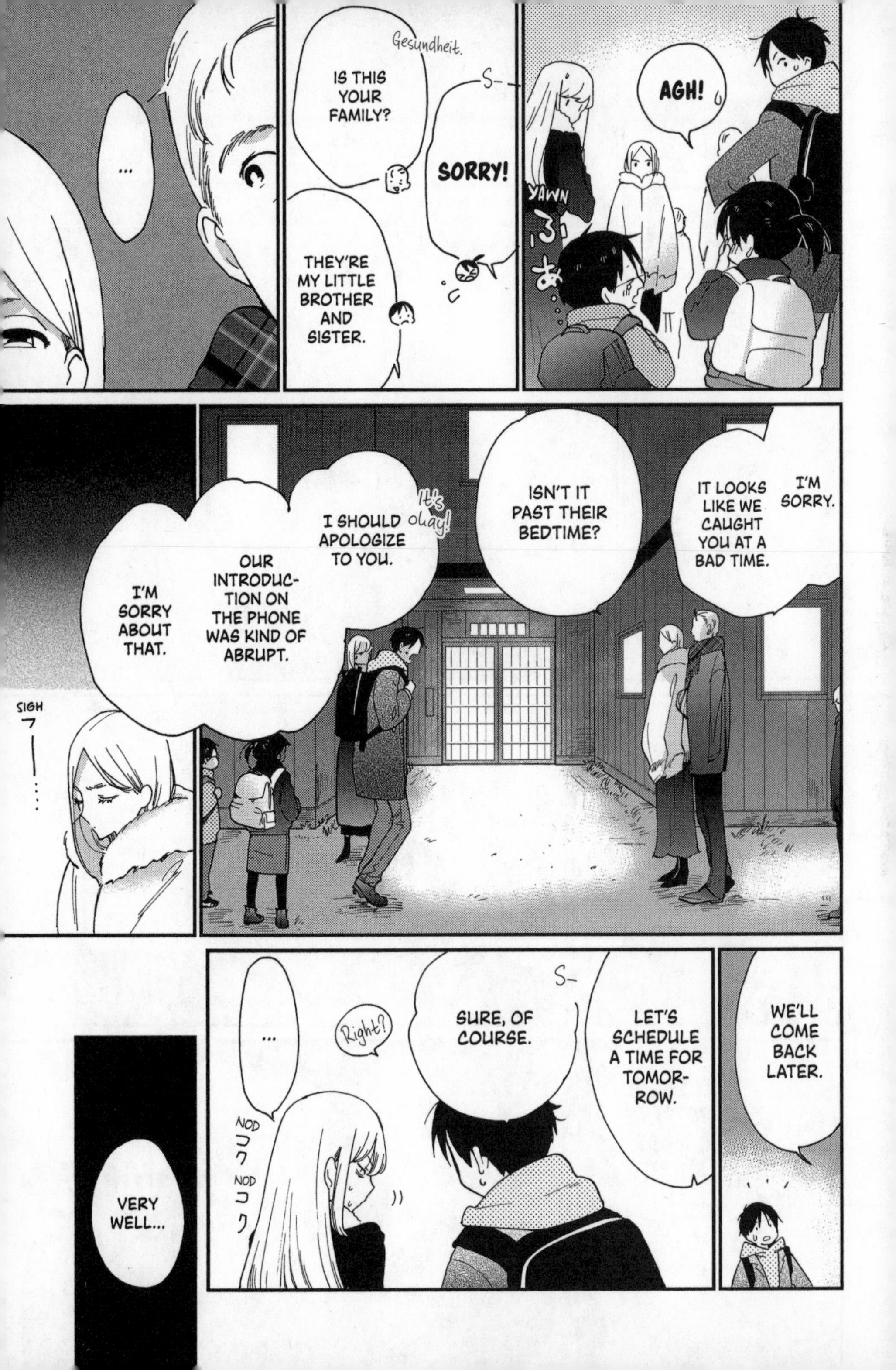
AGH!
YAWN
ふぁ
Gesundheit.
IS THIS YOUR FAMILY?
S–
SORRY!
THEY'RE MY LITTLE BROTHER AND SISTER.
...
I'M SORRY.
IT LOOKS LIKE WE CAUGHT YOU AT A BAD TIME.
ISN'T IT PAST THEIR BEDTIME?
It's okay!
I SHOULD APOLOGIZE TO YOU.
OUR INTRODUCTION ON THE PHONE WAS KIND OF ABRUPT.
I'M SORRY ABOUT THAT.
SIGH
...
WE'LL COME BACK LATER.
LET'S SCHEDULE A TIME FOR TOMORROW.
S–
SURE, OF COURSE.
Right?
...
NOD
コク
NOD
コク
VERY WELL...

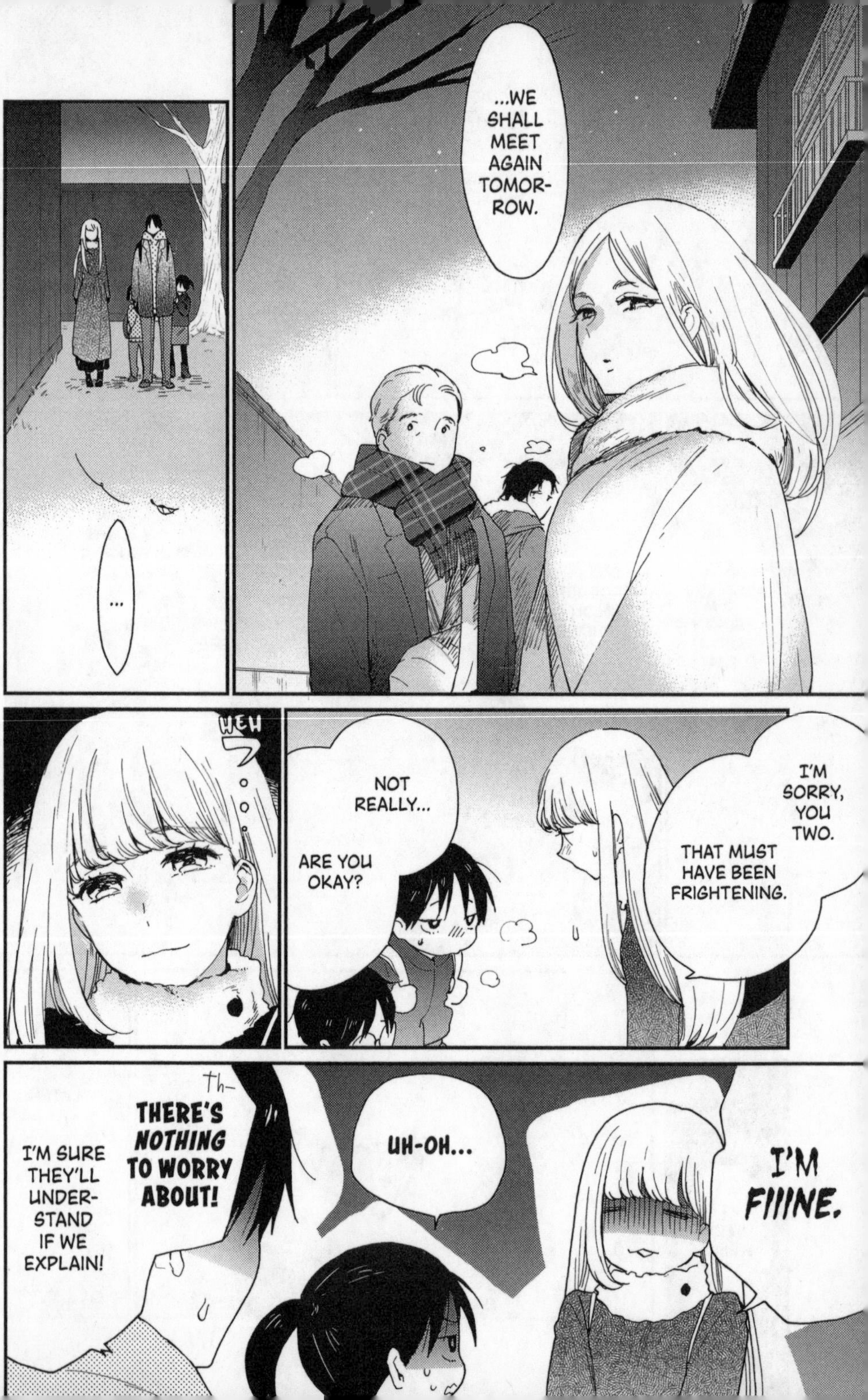
...WE SHALL MEET AGAIN TOMOR-ROW.
...
I'M SORRY, YOU TWO.
THAT MUST HAVE BEEN FRIGHTENING.
NOT REALLY...
ARE YOU OKAY?
WEH
I'M FIIINE.
UH-OH...
Th-
THERE'S NOTHING TO WORRY ABOUT!
I'M SURE THEY'LL UNDER-STAND IF WE EXPLAIN!

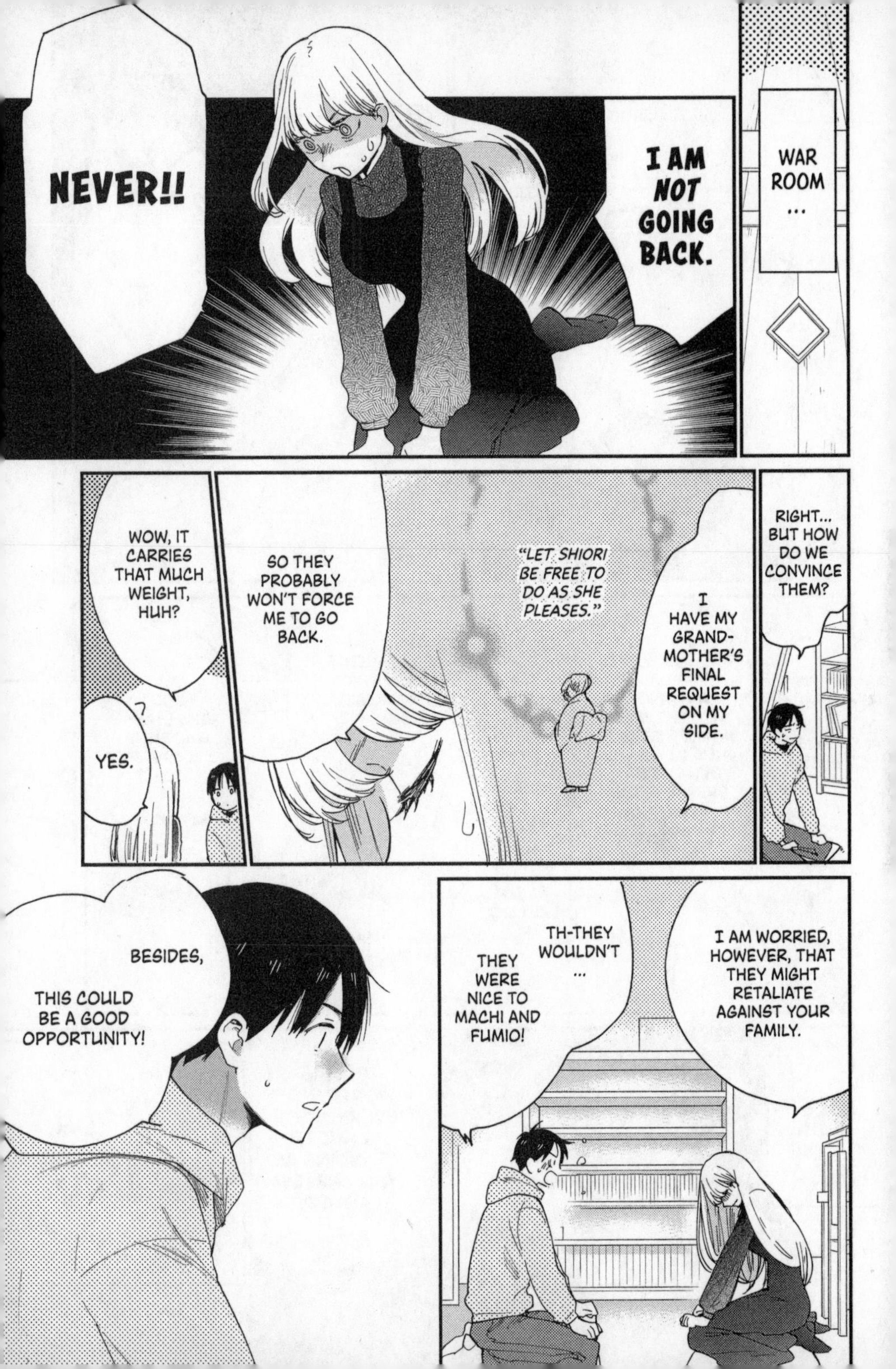
WAR ROOM ...
I AM *NOT* GOING BACK.
NEVER!!
RIGHT... BUT HOW DO WE CONVINCE THEM?
I HAVE MY GRAND-MOTHER'S FINAL REQUEST ON MY SIDE.
"LET SHIORI BE FREE TO DO AS SHE PLEASES."
SO THEY PROBABLY WON'T FORCE ME TO GO BACK.
WOW, IT CARRIES THAT MUCH WEIGHT, HUH?
YES.
I AM WORRIED, HOWEVER, THAT THEY MIGHT RETALIATE AGAINST YOUR FAMILY.
TH-THEY WOULDN'T ...
THEY WERE NICE TO MACHI AND FUMIO!
BESIDES,
THIS COULD BE A GOOD OPPORTUNITY!

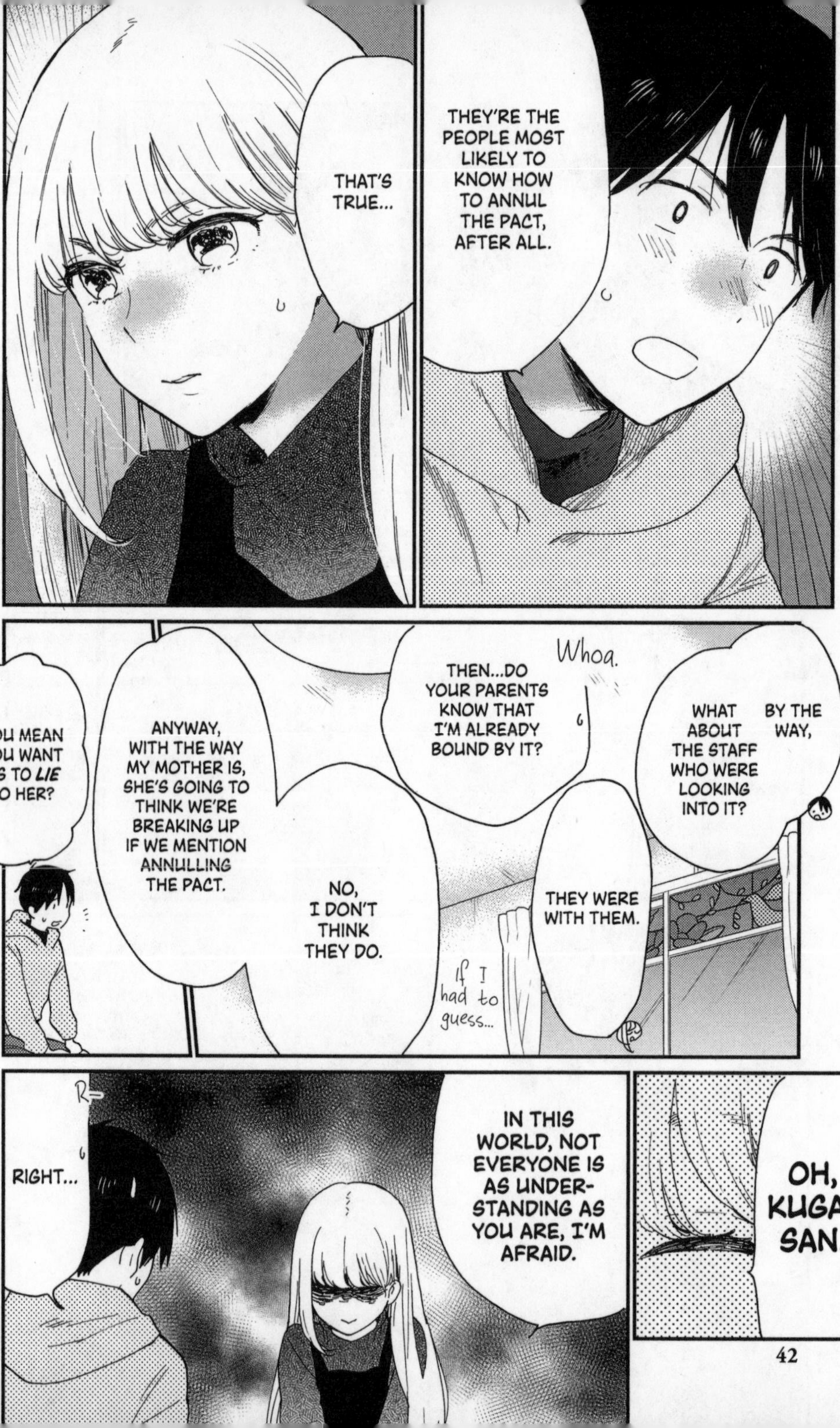
THEY'RE THE PEOPLE MOST LIKELY TO KNOW HOW TO ANNUL THE PACT, AFTER ALL.
THAT'S TRUE...
BY THE WAY, WHAT ABOUT THE STAFF WHO WERE LOOKING INTO IT?
THEY WERE WITH THEM.
Whoa.
THEN...DO YOUR PARENTS KNOW THAT I'M ALREADY BOUND BY IT?
If I had to guess...
NO, I DON'T THINK THEY DO.
ANYWAY, WITH THE WAY MY MOTHER IS, SHE'S GOING TO THINK WE'RE BREAKING UP IF WE MENTION ANNULLING THE PACT.
YOU MEAN YOU WANT US TO *LIE* TO HER?
OH, KUGA-SAN.
IN THIS WORLD, NOT EVERYONE IS AS UNDER-STANDING AS YOU ARE, I'M AFRAID.
R—
RIGHT...

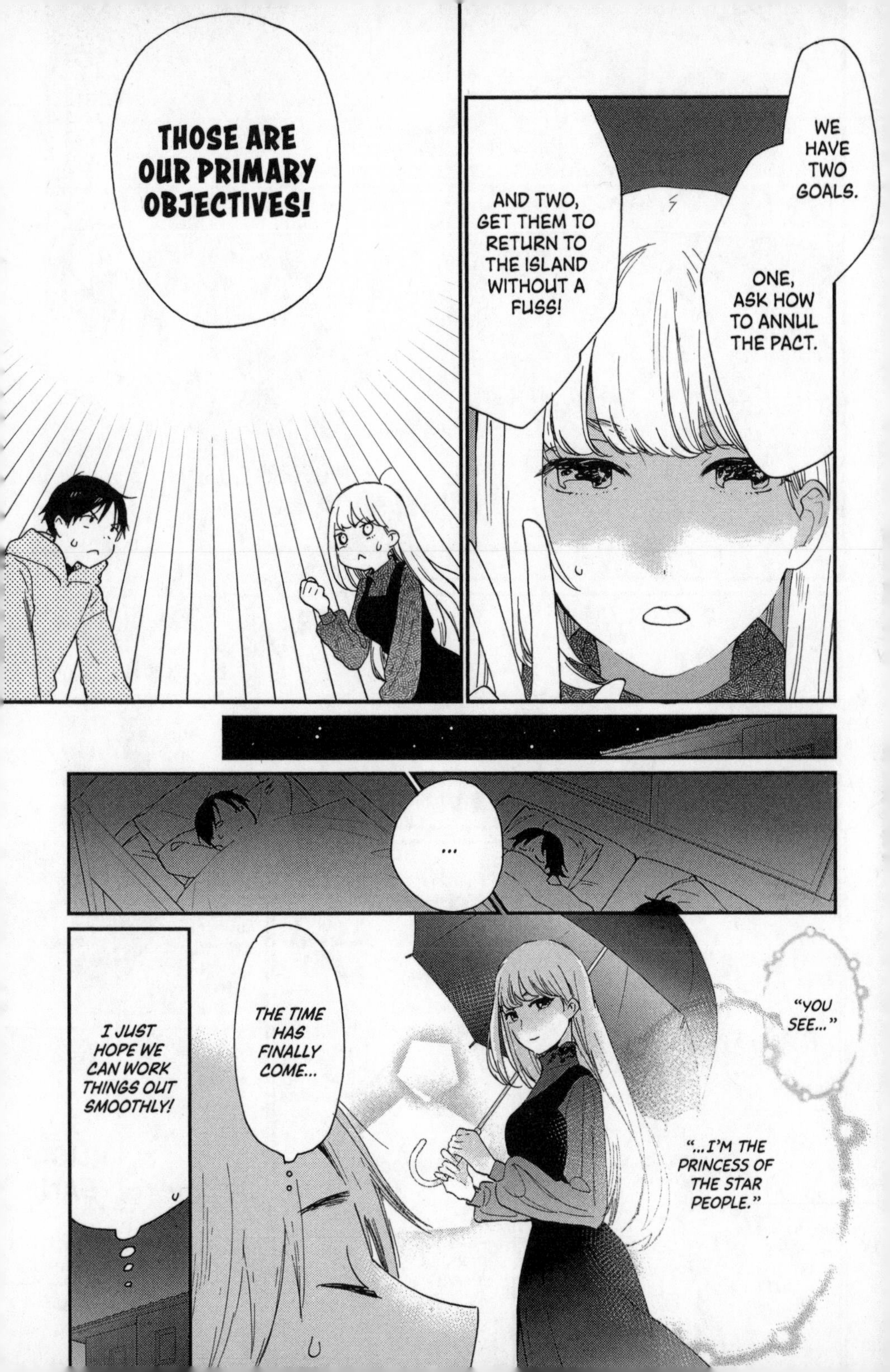
WE HAVE TWO GOALS.
ONE, ASK HOW TO ANNUL THE PACT.
AND TWO, GET THEM TO RETURN TO THE ISLAND WITHOUT A FUSS!
THOSE ARE OUR PRIMARY OBJECTIVES!
...
"YOU SEE..."
"...I'M THE PRINCESS OF THE STAR PEOPLE."
THE TIME HAS FINALLY COME...
I JUST HOPE WE CAN WORK THINGS OUT SMOOTHLY!

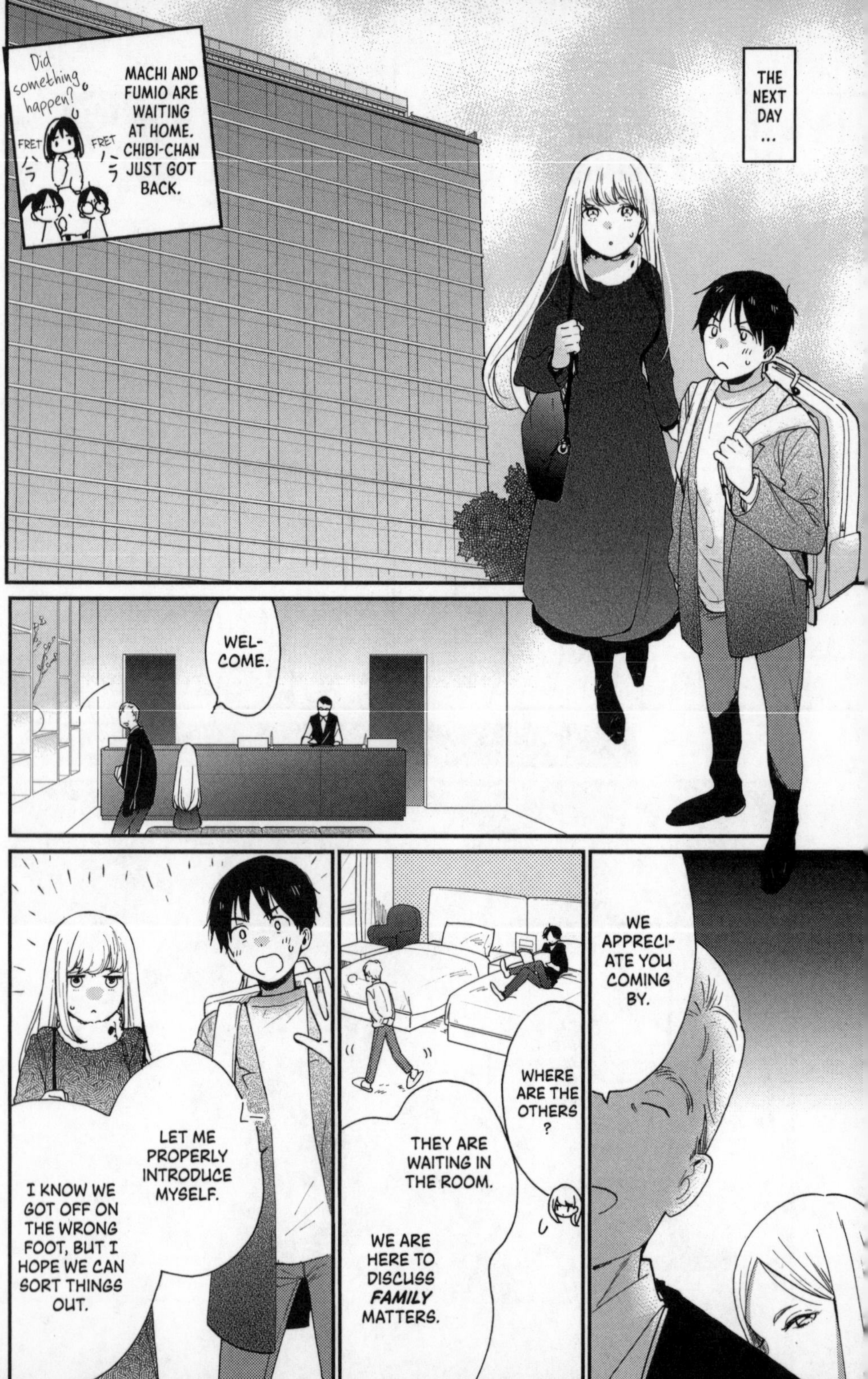
THE NEXT DAY ...
MACHI AND FUMIO ARE WAITING AT HOME. CHIBI-CHAN JUST GOT BACK.
Did something happen?
FRET
ハラ
FRET
ハラ
WEL-COME.
WE APPRECI-ATE YOU COMING BY.
WHERE ARE THE OTHERS?
THEY ARE WAITING IN THE ROOM.
WE ARE HERE TO DISCUSS ***FAMILY*** MATTERS.
LET ME PROPERLY INTRODUCE MYSELF.
I KNOW WE GOT OFF ON THE WRONG FOOT, BUT I HOPE WE CAN SORT THINGS OUT.

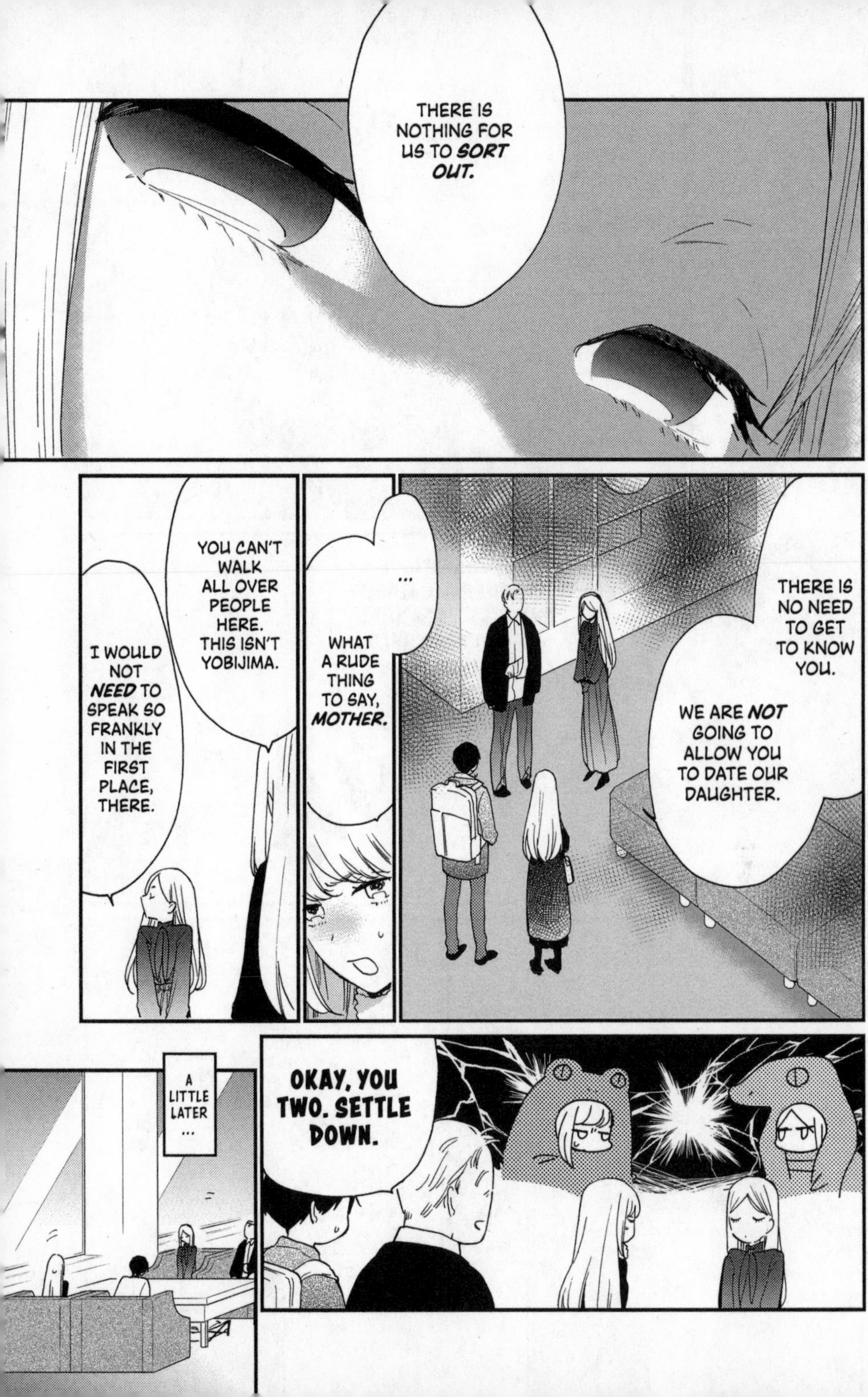
THERE IS NOTHING FOR US TO *SORT OUT.*
THERE IS NO NEED TO GET TO KNOW YOU.
WE ARE *NOT* GOING TO ALLOW YOU TO DATE OUR DAUGHTER.
...
WHAT A RUDE THING TO SAY, *MOTHER.*
YOU CAN'T WALK ALL OVER PEOPLE HERE. THIS ISN'T YOBIJIMA.
I WOULD NOT *NEED* TO SPEAK SO FRANKLY IN THE FIRST PLACE, THERE.
OKAY, YOU TWO. SETTLE DOWN.
A LITTLE LATER ...

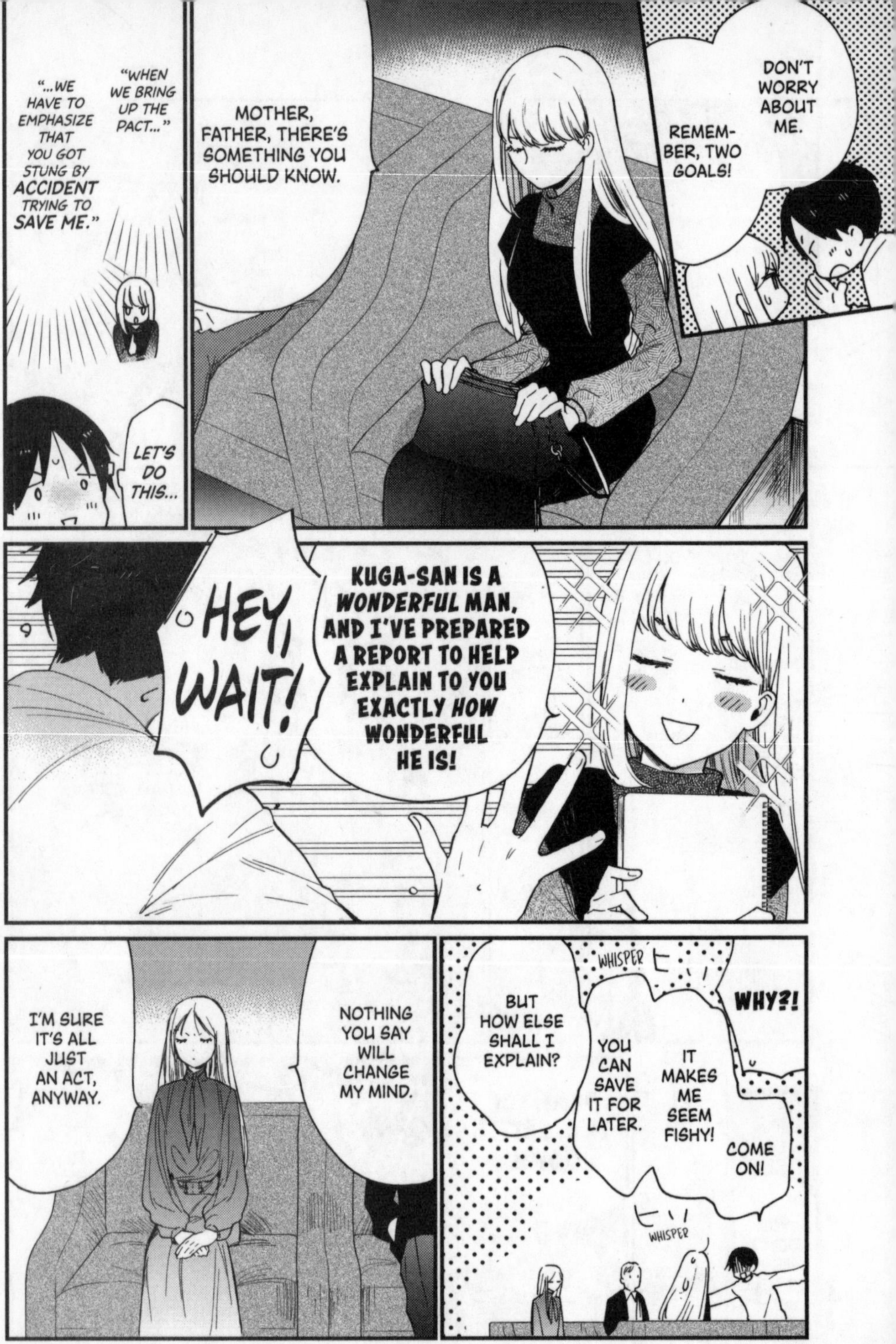
DON'T WORRY ABOUT ME.
REMEMBER, TWO GOALS!
MOTHER, FATHER, THERE'S SOMETHING YOU SHOULD KNOW.
"WHEN WE BRING UP THE PACT..."
"...WE HAVE TO EMPHASIZE THAT YOU GOT STUNG BY ACCIDENT TRYING TO SAVE ME."
LET'S DO THIS...
KUGA-SAN IS A WONDERFUL MAN, AND I'VE PREPARED A REPORT TO HELP EXPLAIN TO YOU EXACTLY HOW WONDERFUL HE IS!
HEY, WAIT!
WHY?!
WHISPER
BUT HOW ELSE SHALL I EXPLAIN?
IT MAKES ME SEEM FISHY!
COME ON!
YOU CAN SAVE IT FOR LATER.
WHISPER
NOTHING YOU SAY WILL CHANGE MY MIND.
I'M SURE IT'S ALL JUST AN ACT, ANYWAY.

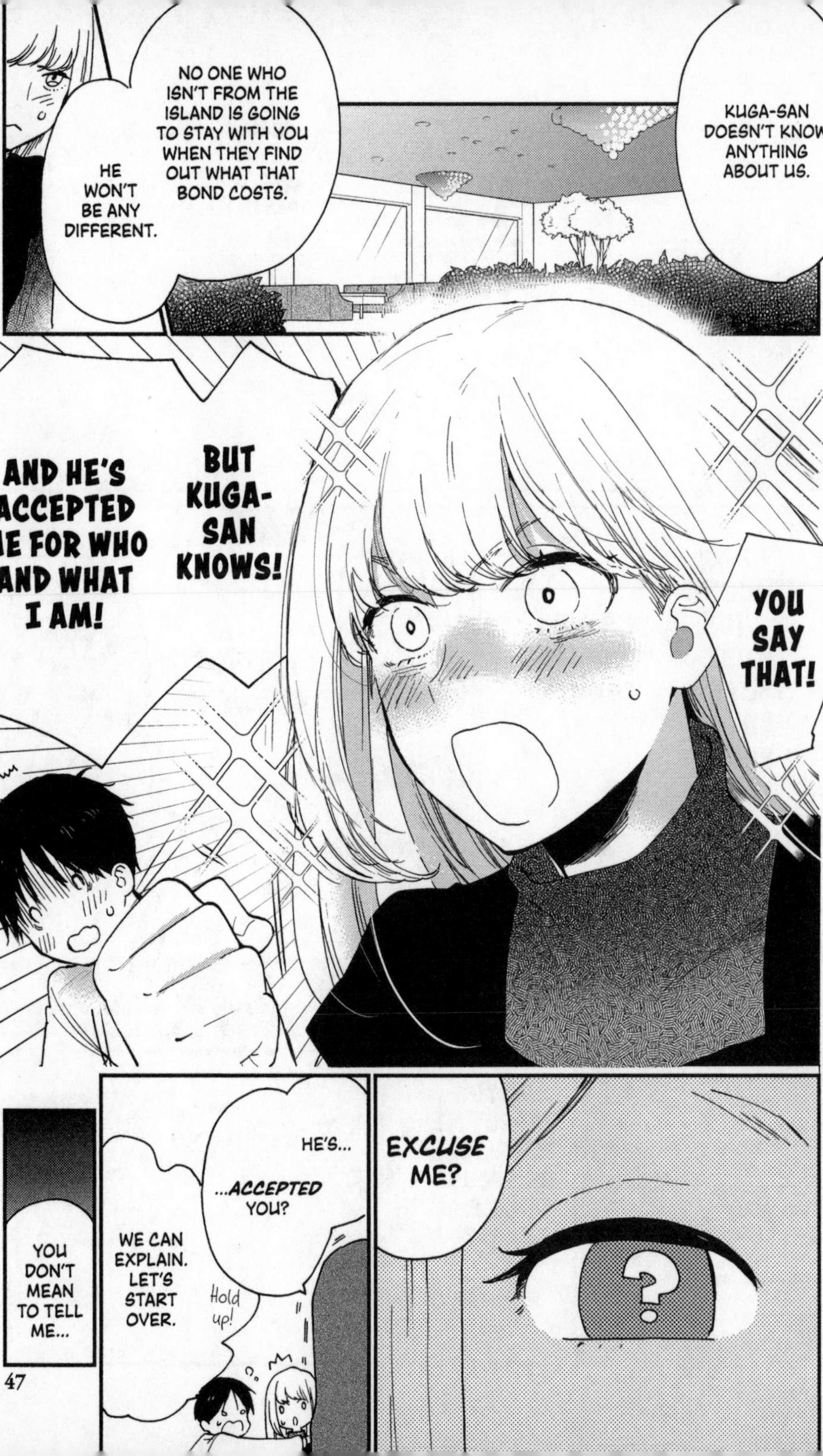
KUGA-SAN DOESN'T KNOW ANYTHING ABOUT US.
NO ONE WHO ISN'T FROM THE ISLAND IS GOING TO STAY WITH YOU WHEN THEY FIND OUT WHAT THAT BOND COSTS.
HE WON'T BE ANY DIFFERENT.
YOU SAY THAT!
BUT KUGA-SAN KNOWS!
AND HE'S ACCEPTED ME FOR WHO AND WHAT I AM!
EXCUSE ME?
HE'S...
...ACCEPTED YOU?
WE CAN EXPLAIN. LET'S START OVER.
Hold up!
YOU DON'T MEAN TO TELL ME...

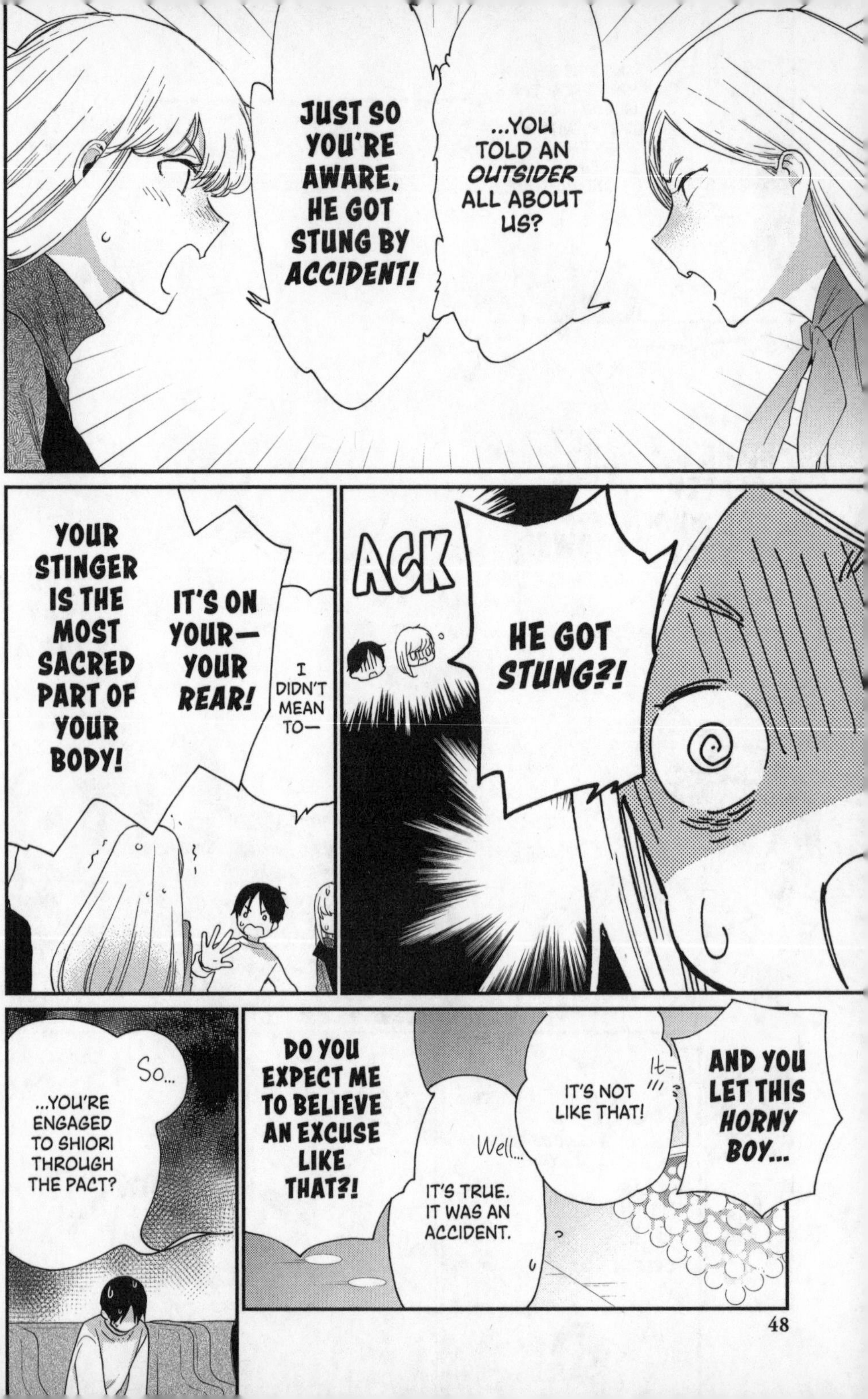
...YOU TOLD AN OUTSIDER ALL ABOUT US?
JUST SO YOU'RE AWARE, HE GOT STUNG BY ACCIDENT!
ACK
HE GOT STUNG?!
YOUR STINGER IS THE MOST SACRED PART OF YOUR BODY!
IT'S ON YOUR— YOUR REAR!
I DIDN'T MEAN TO—
AND YOU LET THIS HORNY BOY...
It—
IT'S NOT LIKE THAT!
DO YOU EXPECT ME TO BELIEVE AN EXCUSE LIKE THAT?!
Well...
IT'S TRUE. IT WAS AN ACCIDENT.
So...
...YOU'RE ENGAGED TO SHIORI THROUGH THE PACT?

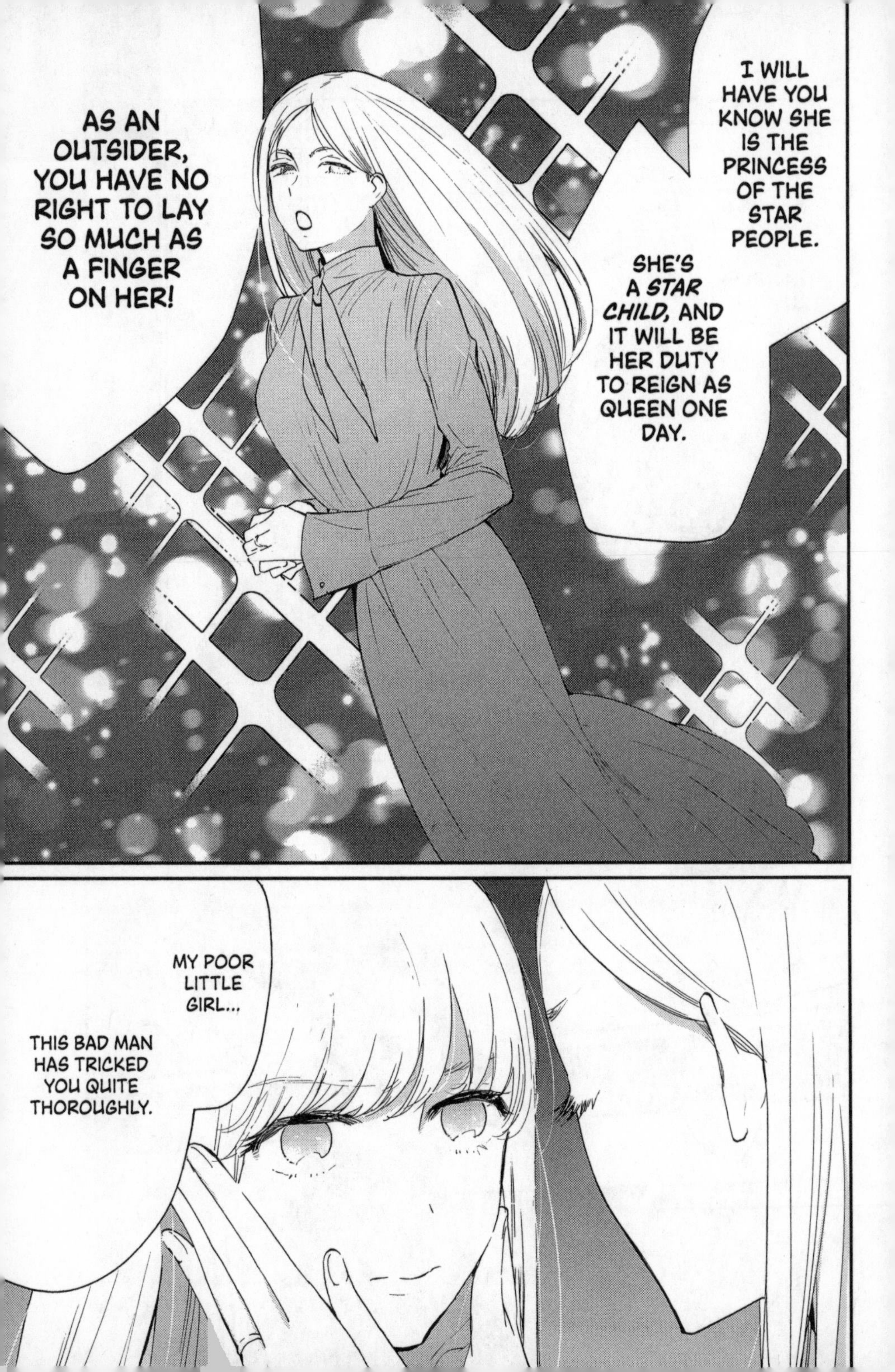
I WILL HAVE YOU KNOW SHE IS THE PRINCESS OF THE STAR PEOPLE.
SHE'S A *STAR CHILD,* AND IT WILL BE HER DUTY TO REIGN AS QUEEN ONE DAY.
AS AN OUTSIDER, YOU HAVE NO RIGHT TO LAY SO MUCH AS A FINGER ON HER!
MY POOR LITTLE GIRL...
THIS BAD MAN HAS TRICKED YOU QUITE THOROUGHLY.

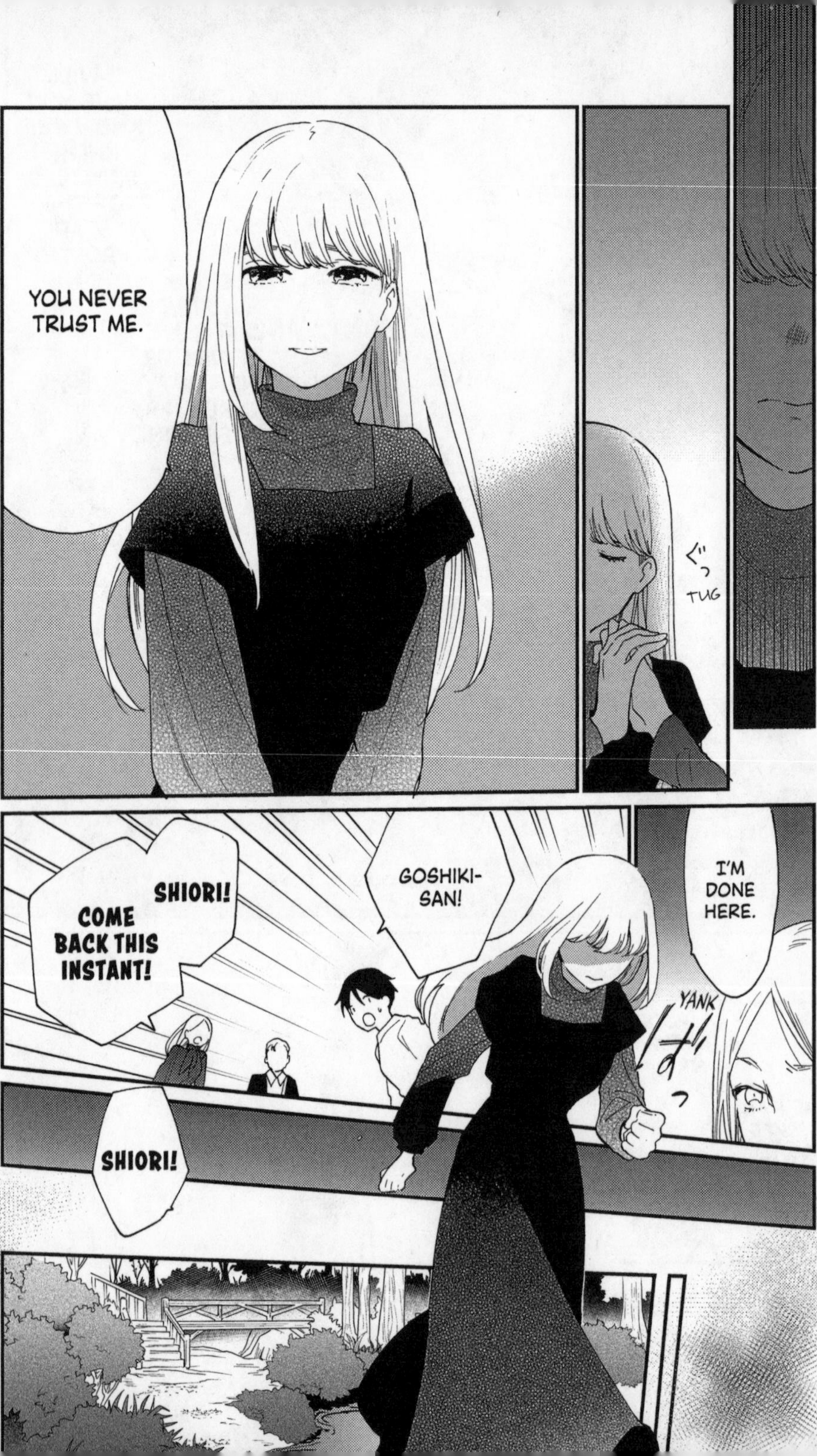
ぐっ
TUG
YOU NEVER TRUST ME.
I'M DONE HERE.
YANK
GOSHIKI-SAN!
SHIORI! COME BACK THIS INSTANT!
SHIORI!

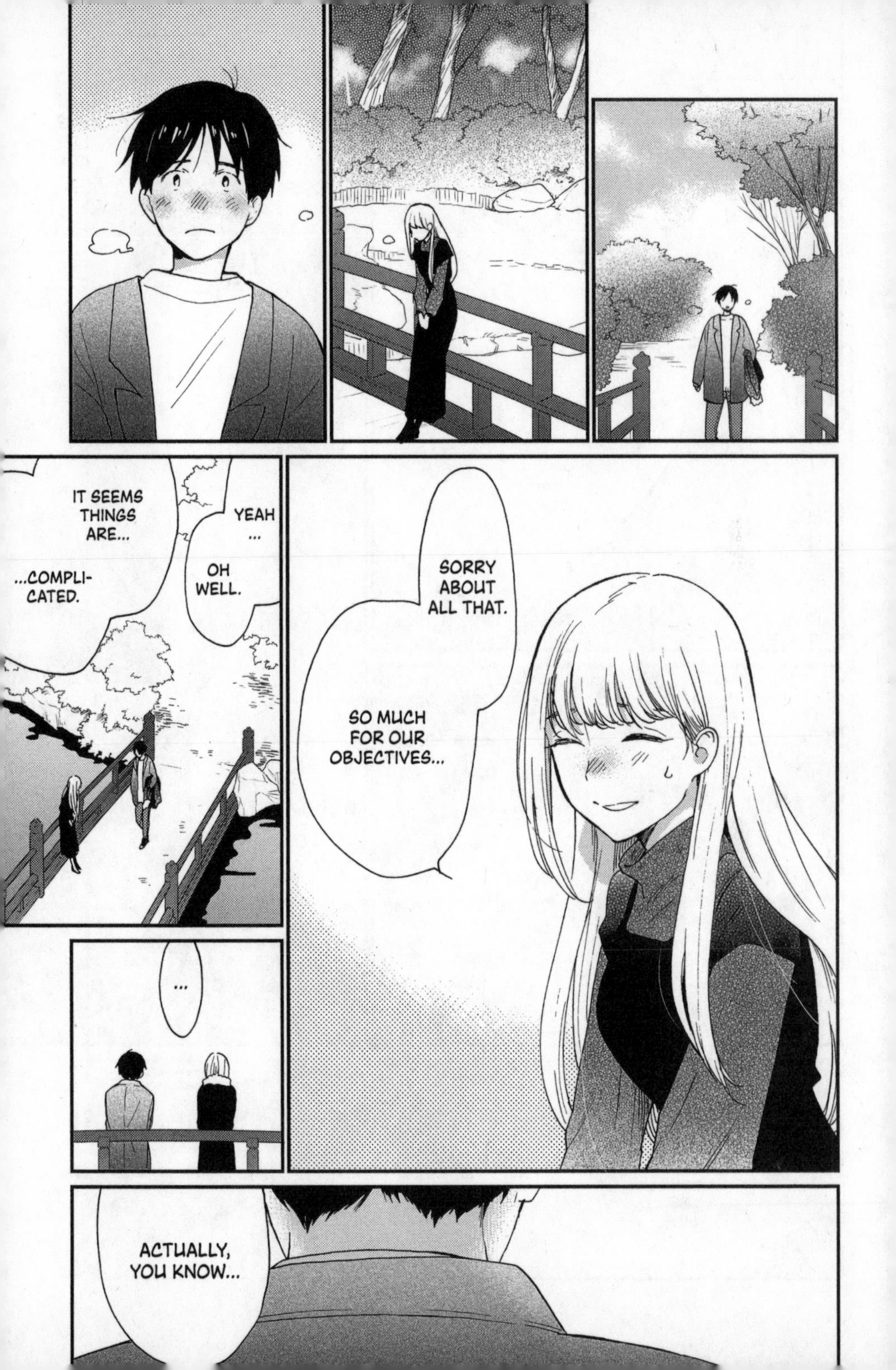
SORRY ABOUT ALL THAT.
SO MUCH FOR OUR OBJECTIVES...
IT SEEMS THINGS ARE...
...COMPLICATED.
YEAH...
OH WELL.
...
ACTUALLY, YOU KNOW...

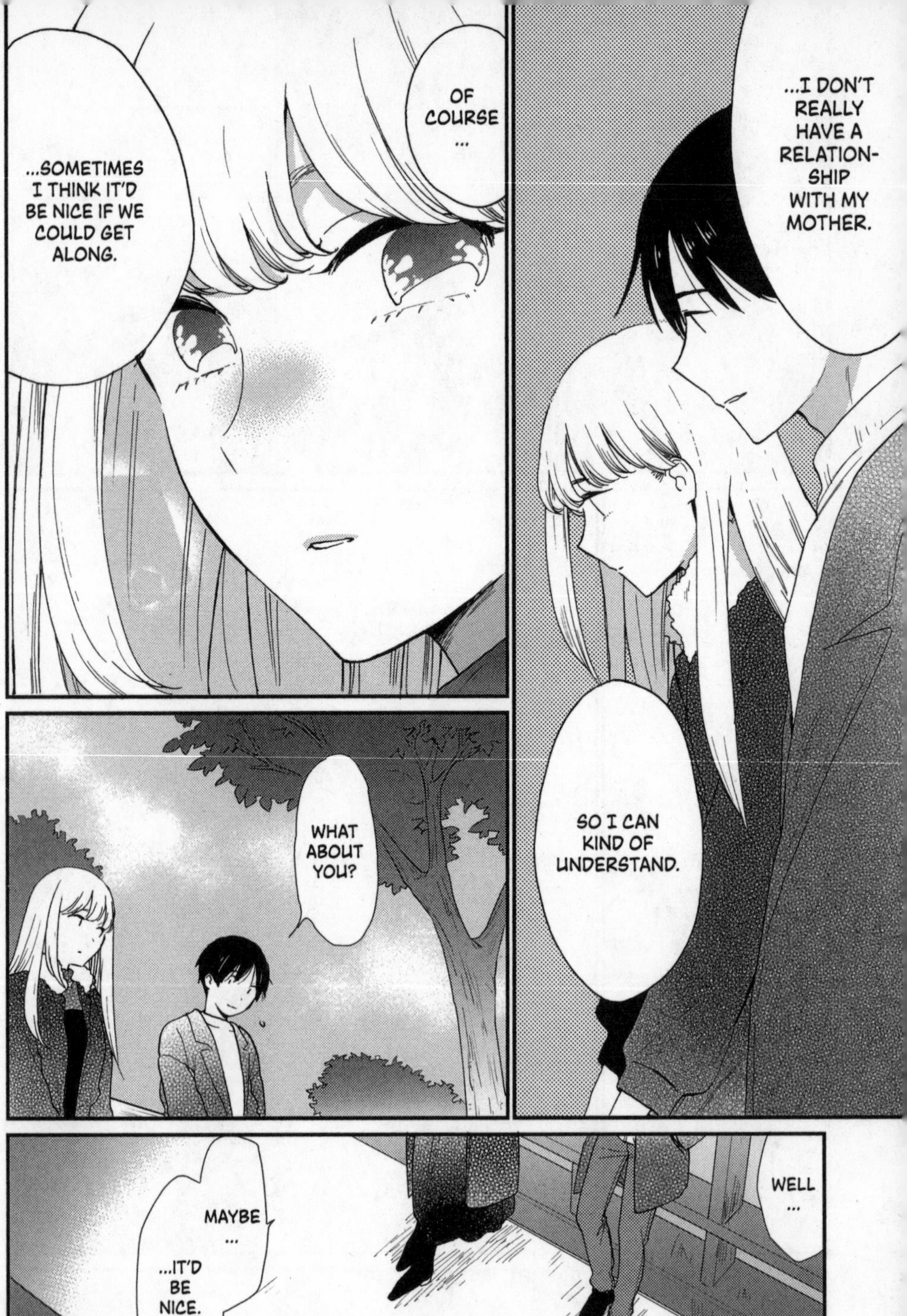
...I DON'T REALLY HAVE A RELATIONSHIP WITH MY MOTHER.
SO I CAN KIND OF UNDERSTAND.
OF COURSE ...
...SOMETIMES I THINK IT'D BE NICE IF WE COULD GET ALONG.
WHAT ABOUT YOU?
WELL ...
MAYBE ...
...IT'D BE NICE.

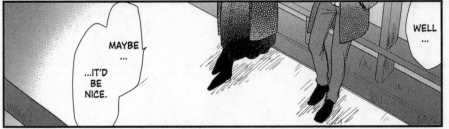

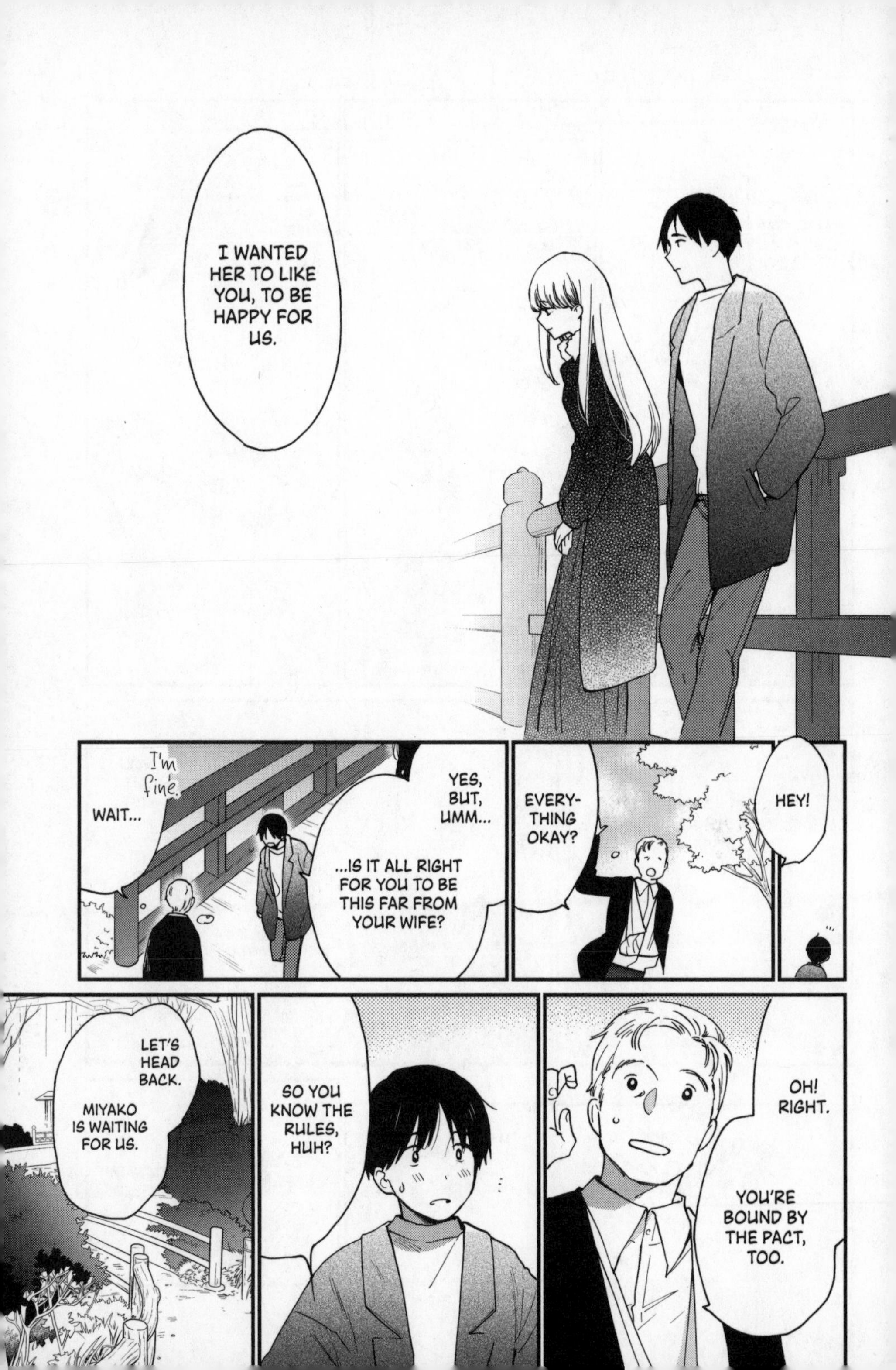

I WANTED HER TO LIKE YOU, TO BE HAPPY FOR US.
HEY!
EVERY-THING OKAY?
YES, BUT, UMM...
...IS IT ALL RIGHT FOR YOU TO BE THIS FAR FROM YOUR WIFE?
I'm fine.
WAIT...
OH! RIGHT.
YOU'RE BOUND BY THE PACT, TOO.
SO YOU KNOW THE RULES, HUH?
LET'S HEAD BACK.
MIYAKO IS WAITING FOR US.

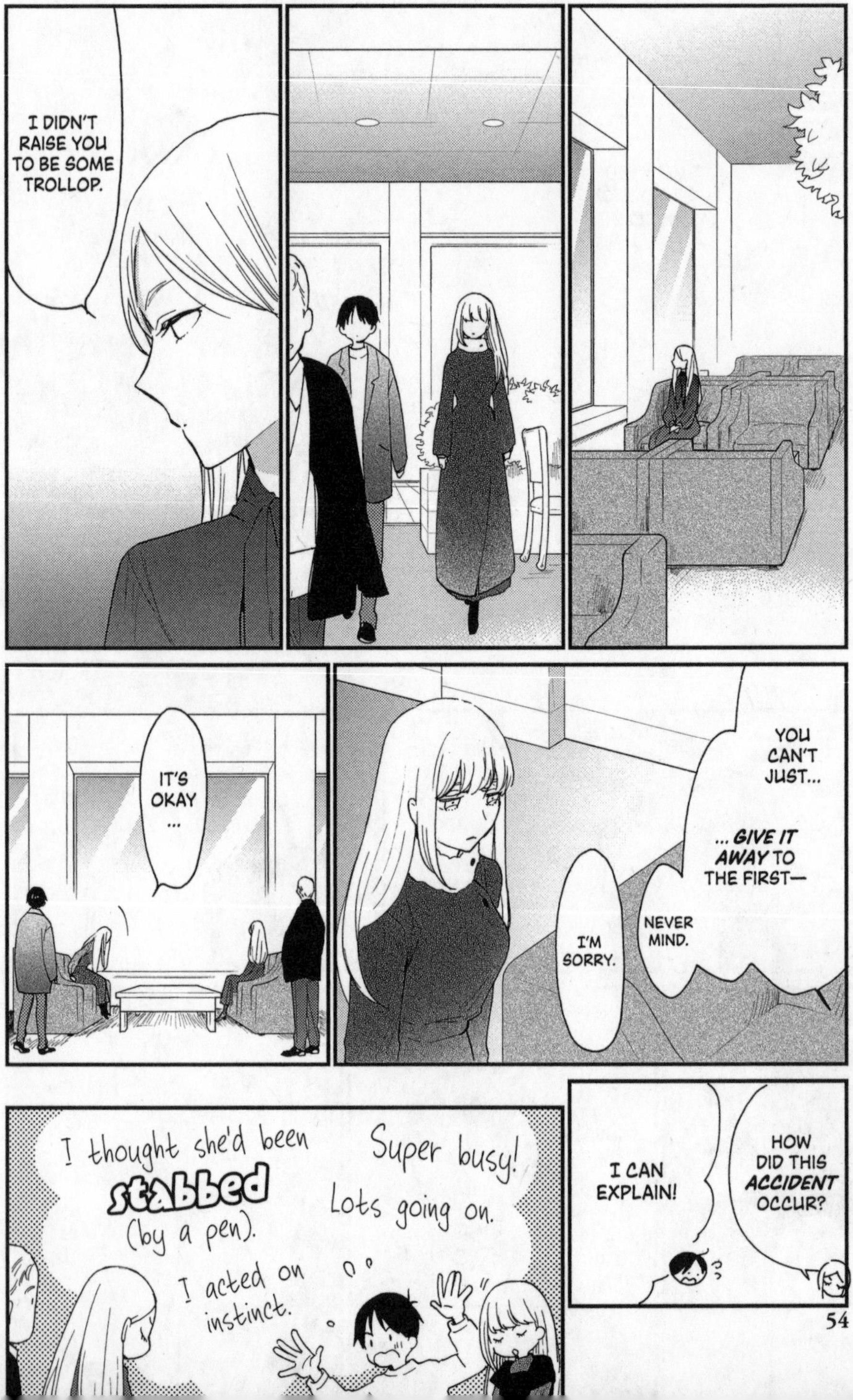
I DIDN'T RAISE YOU TO BE SOME TROLLOP.
YOU CAN'T JUST...
... GIVE IT AWAY TO THE FIRST—
NEVER MIND.
I'M SORRY.
IT'S OKAY ...
HOW DID THIS ACCIDENT OCCUR?
I CAN EXPLAIN!
Super busy! Lots going on.
I thought she'd been stabbed (by a pen).
I acted on instinct.

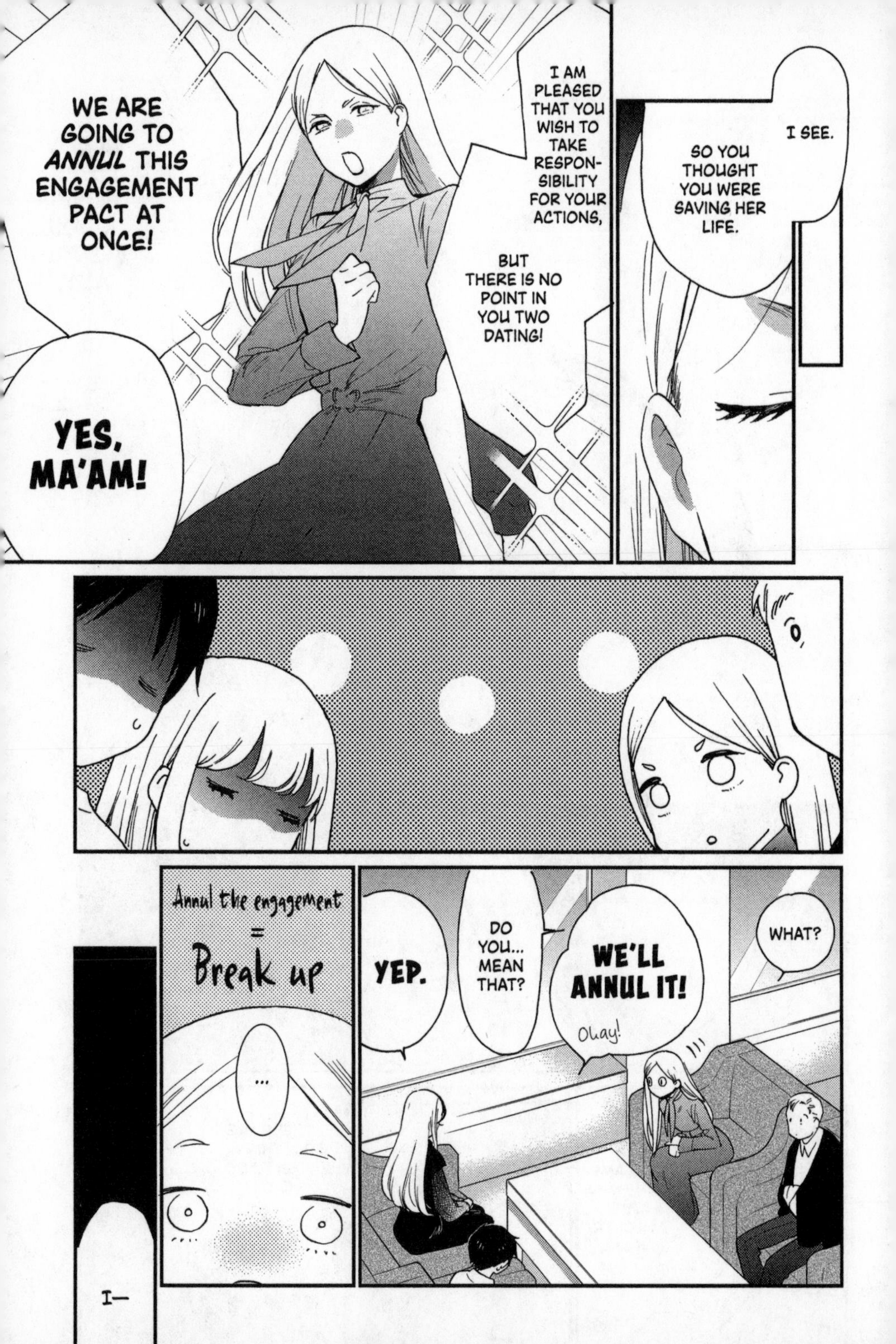
I SEE.
SO YOU THOUGHT YOU WERE SAVING HER LIFE.
I AM PLEASED THAT YOU WISH TO TAKE RESPONSIBILITY FOR YOUR ACTIONS,
BUT THERE IS NO POINT IN YOU TWO DATING!
WE ARE GOING TO *ANNUL* THIS ENGAGEMENT PACT AT ONCE!
YES, MA'AM!
WHAT?
WE'LL ANNUL IT!
Okay!
DO YOU... MEAN THAT?
YEP.
Annul the engagement = Break up
...
I—

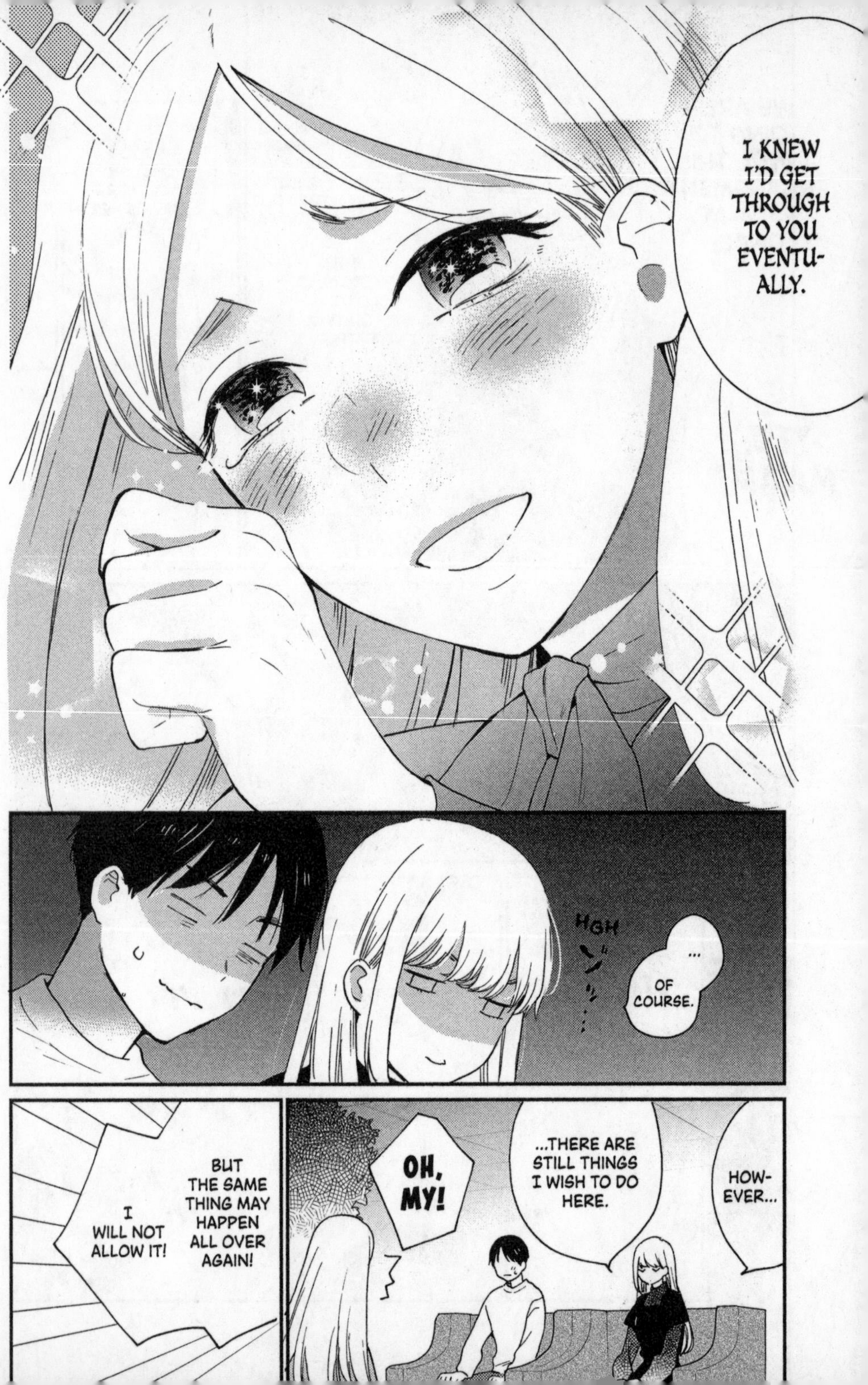
I KNEW I'D GET THROUGH TO YOU EVENTU-ALLY.
HGH
... OF COURSE.
HOW-EVER...
...THERE ARE STILL THINGS I WISH TO DO HERE.
OH, MY!
BUT THE SAME THING MAY HAPPEN ALL OVER AGAIN!
I WILL NOT ALLOW IT!

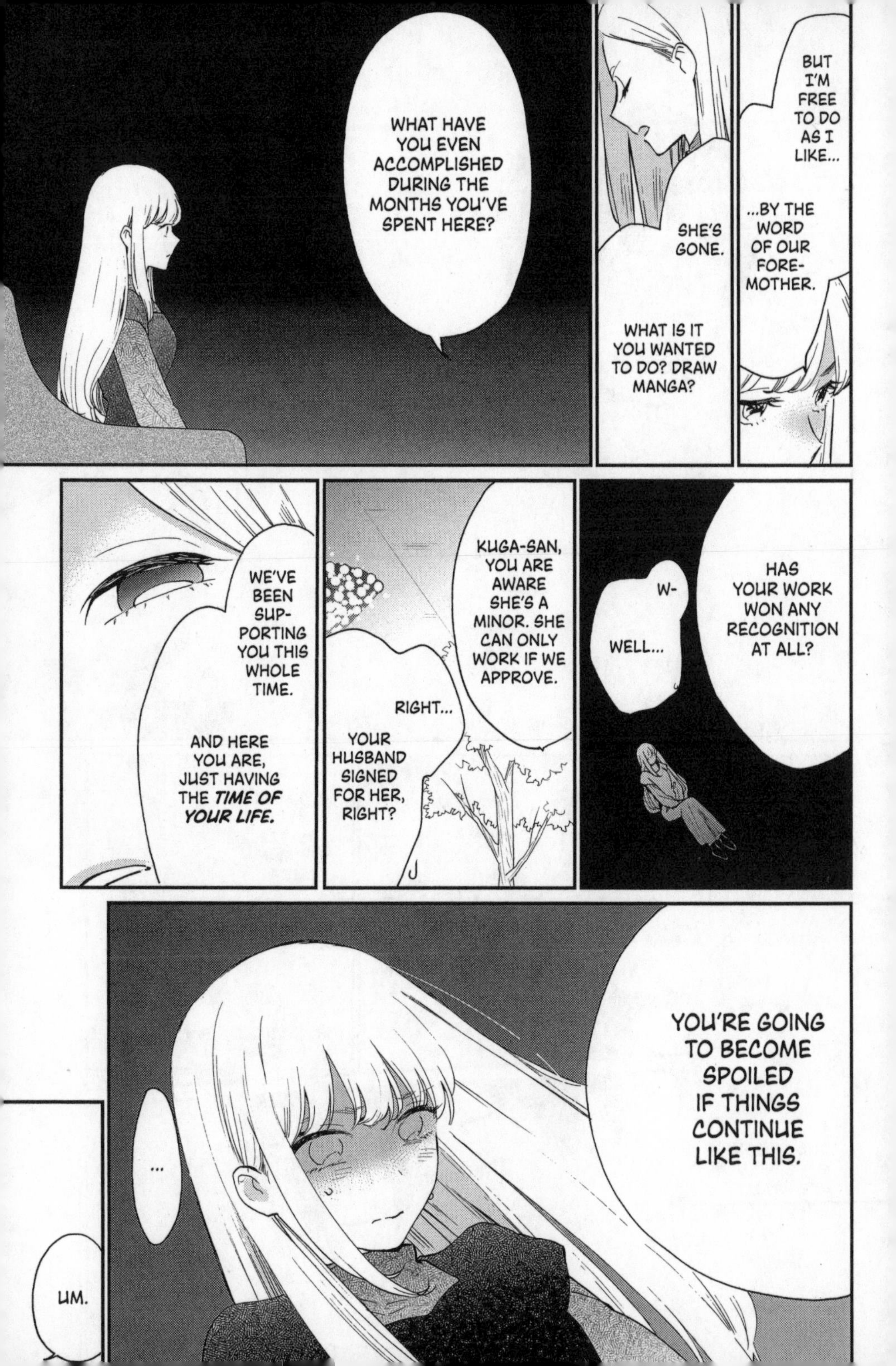
BUT I'M FREE TO DO AS I LIKE...
...BY THE WORD OF OUR FORE-MOTHER.
SHE'S GONE.
WHAT IS IT YOU WANTED TO DO? DRAW MANGA?
WHAT HAVE YOU EVEN ACCOMPLISHED DURING THE MONTHS YOU'VE SPENT HERE?
HAS YOUR WORK WON ANY RECOGNITION AT ALL?
W- WELL...
KUGA-SAN, YOU ARE AWARE SHE'S A MINOR. SHE CAN ONLY WORK IF WE APPROVE.
RIGHT...
YOUR HUSBAND SIGNED FOR HER, RIGHT?
WE'VE BEEN SUP-PORTING YOU THIS WHOLE TIME.
AND HERE YOU ARE, JUST HAVING THE *TIME OF YOUR LIFE.*
YOU'RE GOING TO BECOME SPOILED IF THINGS CONTINUE LIKE THIS.
...
UM.

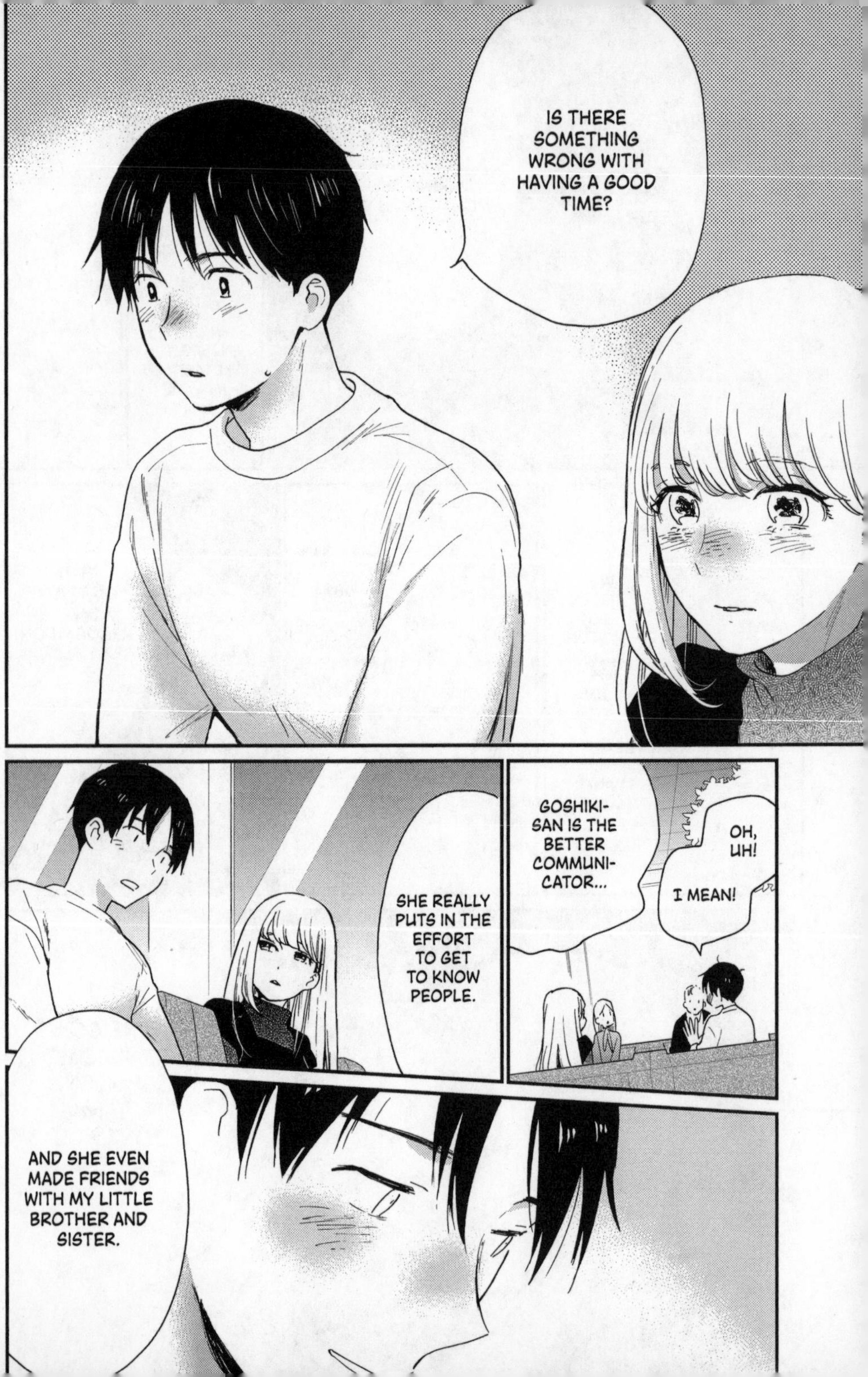
IS THERE SOMETHING WRONG WITH HAVING A GOOD TIME?
OH, UH!
I MEAN!
GOSHIKI-SAN IS THE BETTER COMMUNICATOR...
SHE REALLY PUTS IN THE EFFORT TO GET TO KNOW PEOPLE.
AND SHE EVEN MADE FRIENDS WITH MY LITTLE BROTHER AND SISTER.

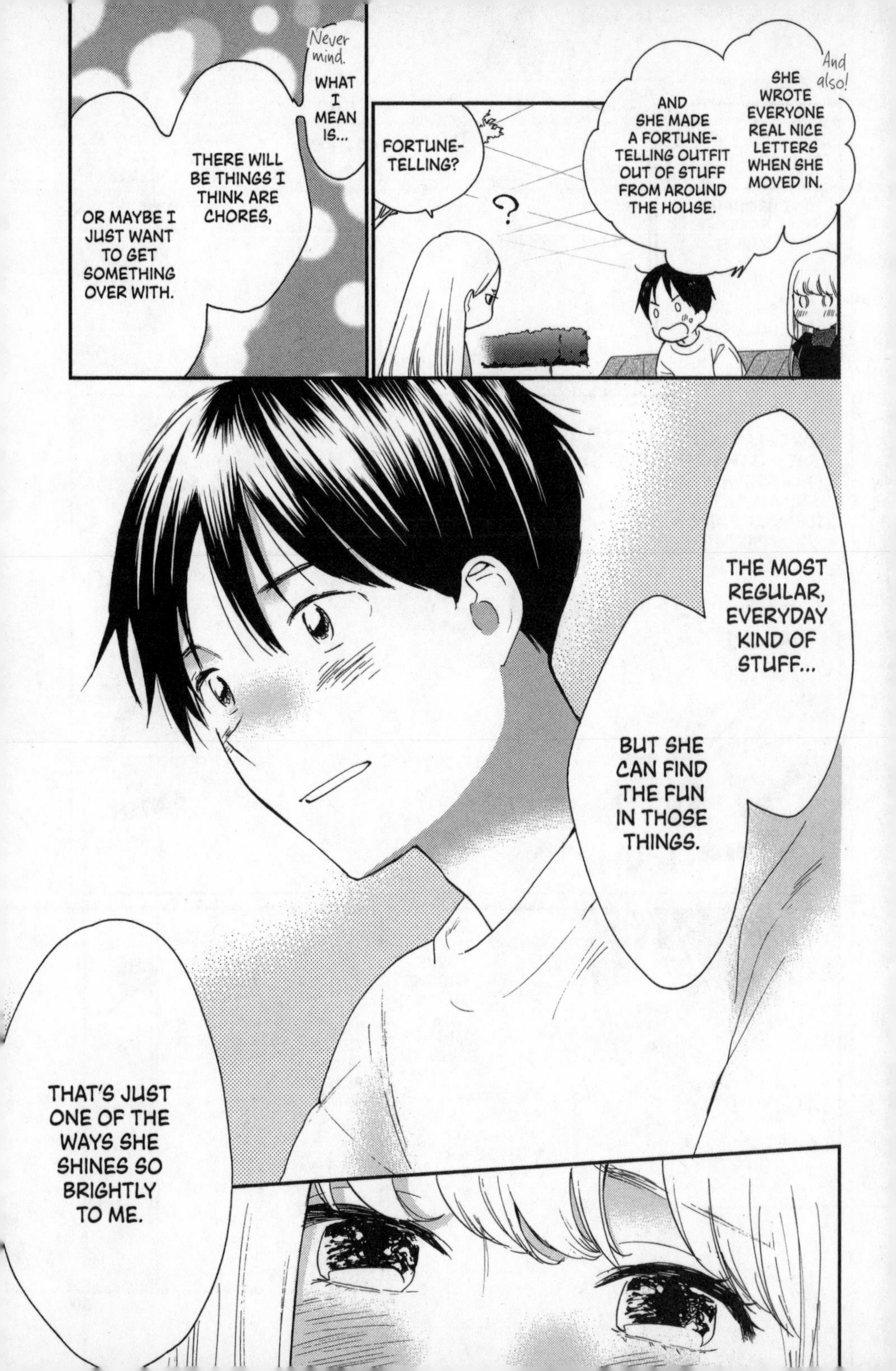
AND SHE MADE A FORTUNE-TELLING OUTFIT OUT OF STUFF FROM AROUND THE HOUSE.
And also!
SHE WROTE EVERYONE REAL NICE LETTERS WHEN SHE MOVED IN.
FORTUNE-TELLING?
Never mind.
WHAT I MEAN IS...
THERE WILL BE THINGS I THINK ARE CHORES,
OR MAYBE I JUST WANT TO GET SOMETHING OVER WITH.
THE MOST REGULAR, EVERYDAY KIND OF STUFF...
BUT SHE CAN FIND THE FUN IN THOSE THINGS.
THAT'S JUST ONE OF THE WAYS SHE SHINES SO BRIGHTLY TO ME.

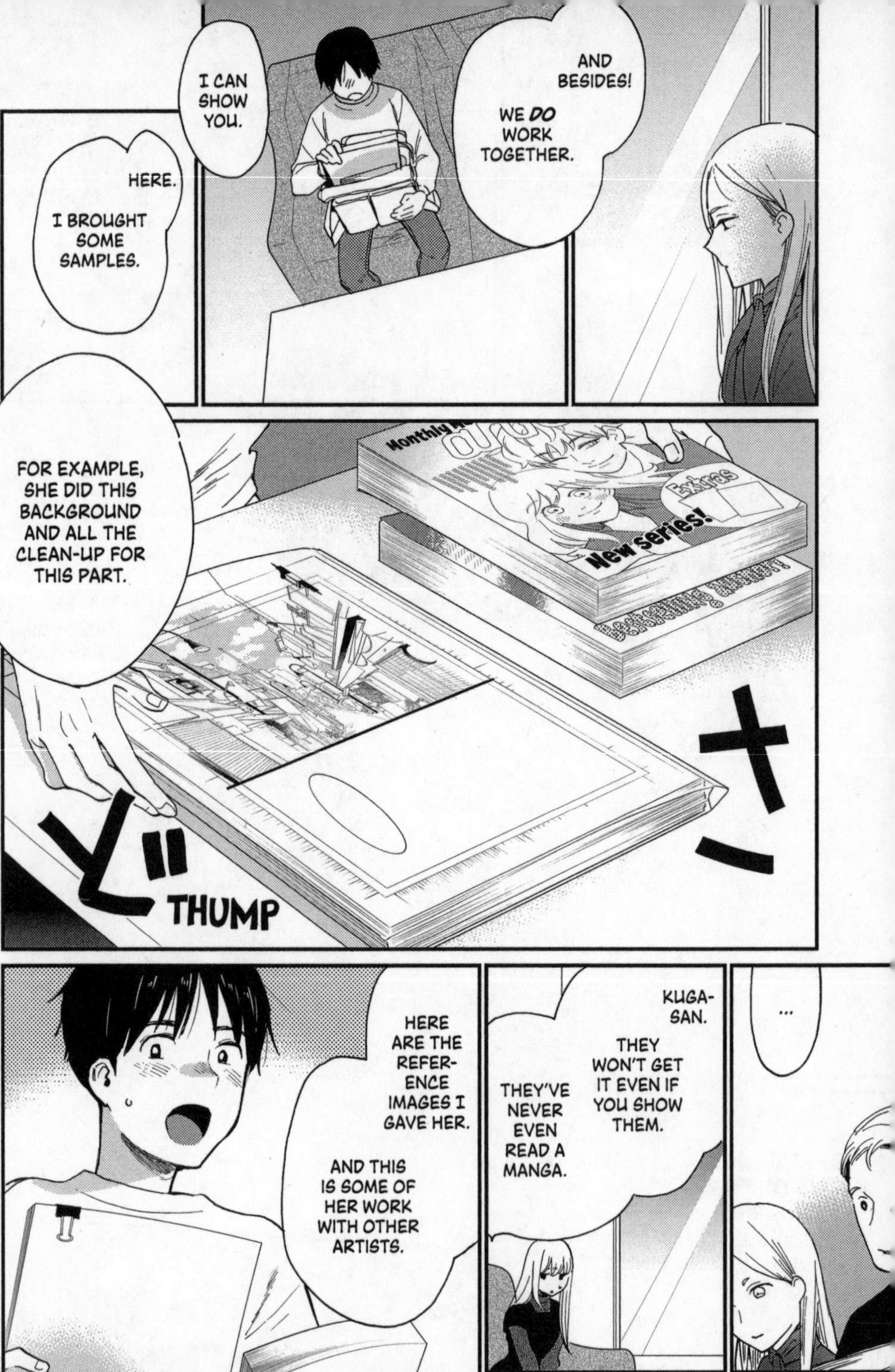
AND BESIDES!
WE DO WORK TOGETHER.
I CAN SHOW YOU.
HERE.
I BROUGHT SOME SAMPLES.
FOR EXAMPLE, SHE DID THIS BACKGROUND AND ALL THE CLEAN-UP FOR THIS PART.
Extras
New series!
THUMP
...
KUGA-SAN.
THEY WON'T GET IT EVEN IF YOU SHOW THEM.
THEY'VE NEVER EVEN READ A MANGA.
HERE ARE THE REFERENCE IMAGES I GAVE HER.
AND THIS IS SOME OF HER WORK WITH OTHER ARTISTS.

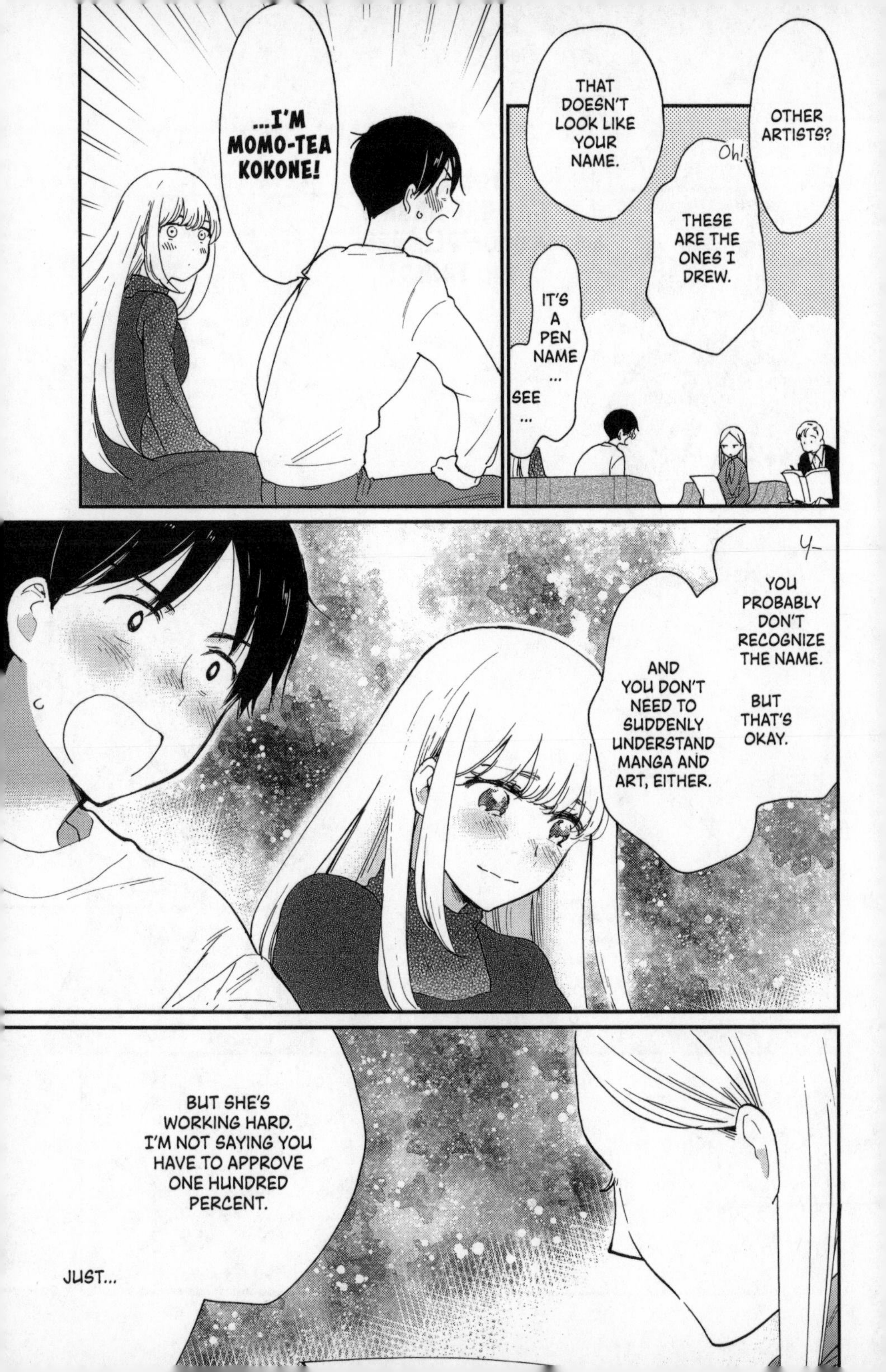
OTHER ARTISTS?
Oh!
THESE ARE THE ONES I DREW.
THAT DOESN'T LOOK LIKE YOUR NAME.
IT'S A PEN NAME... SEE...
...I'M MOMO-TEA KOKONE!
Y-
YOU PROBABLY DON'T RECOGNIZE THE NAME.
BUT THAT'S OKAY.
AND YOU DON'T NEED TO SUDDENLY UNDERSTAND MANGA AND ART, EITHER.
BUT SHE'S WORKING HARD. I'M NOT SAYING YOU HAVE TO APPROVE ONE HUNDRED PERCENT.
JUST...

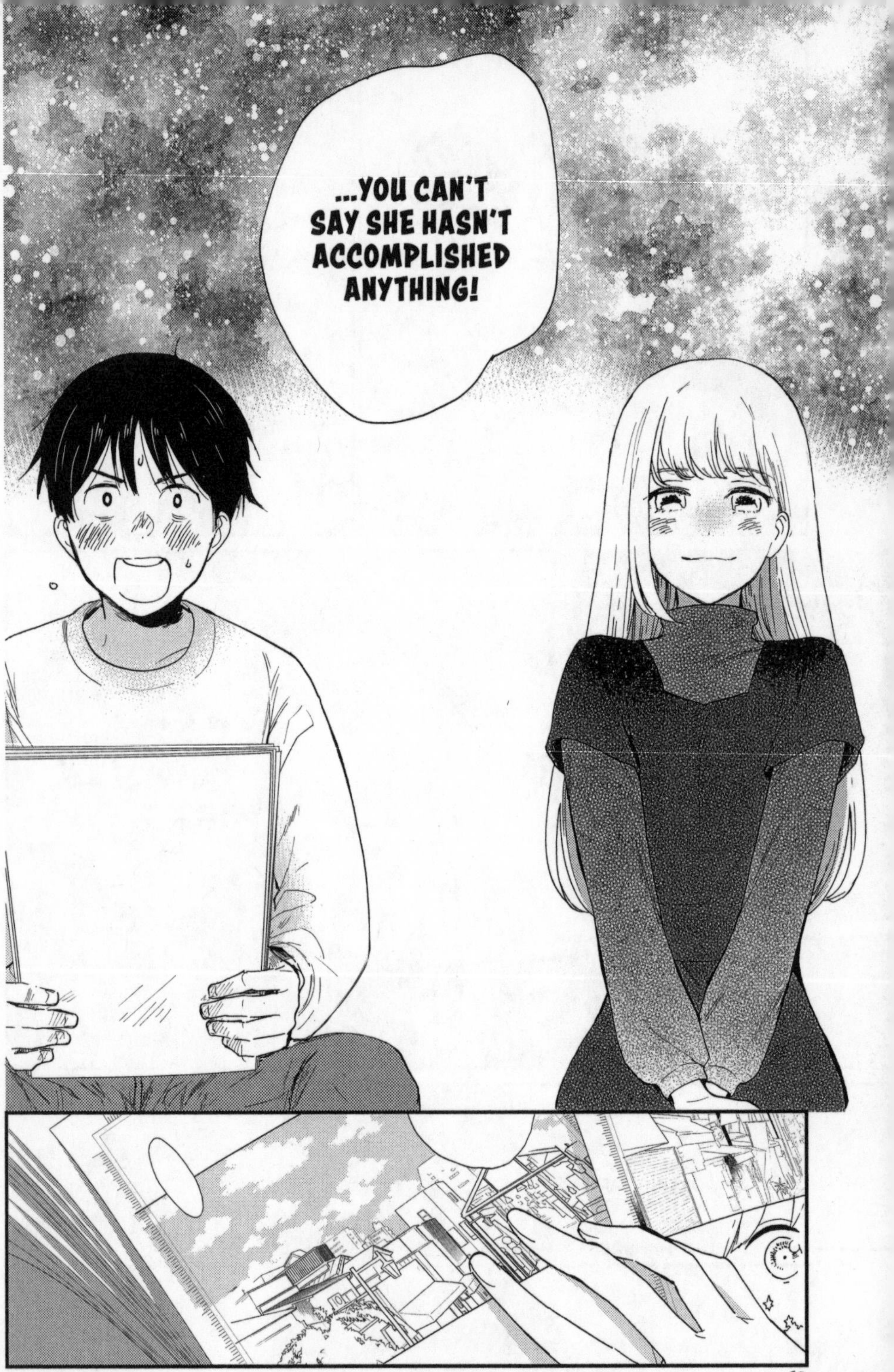
...YOU CAN'T SAY SHE HASN'T ACCOMPLISHED ANYTHING!

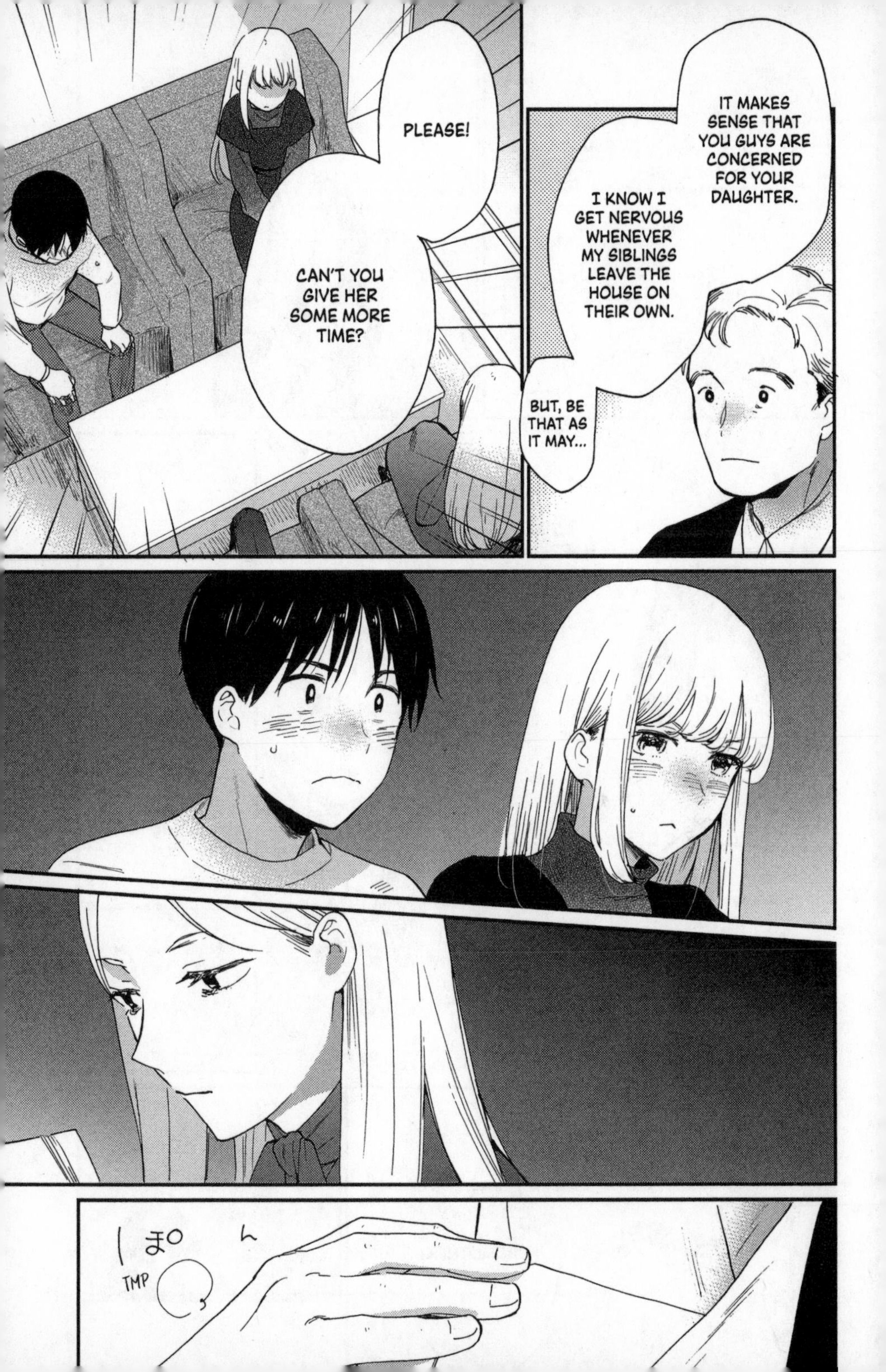
IT MAKES SENSE THAT YOU GUYS ARE CONCERNED FOR YOUR DAUGHTER.
I KNOW I GET NERVOUS WHENEVER MY SIBLINGS LEAVE THE HOUSE ON THEIR OWN.
BUT, BE THAT AS IT MAY...
PLEASE!
CAN'T YOU GIVE HER SOME MORE TIME?
ぽん
TMP

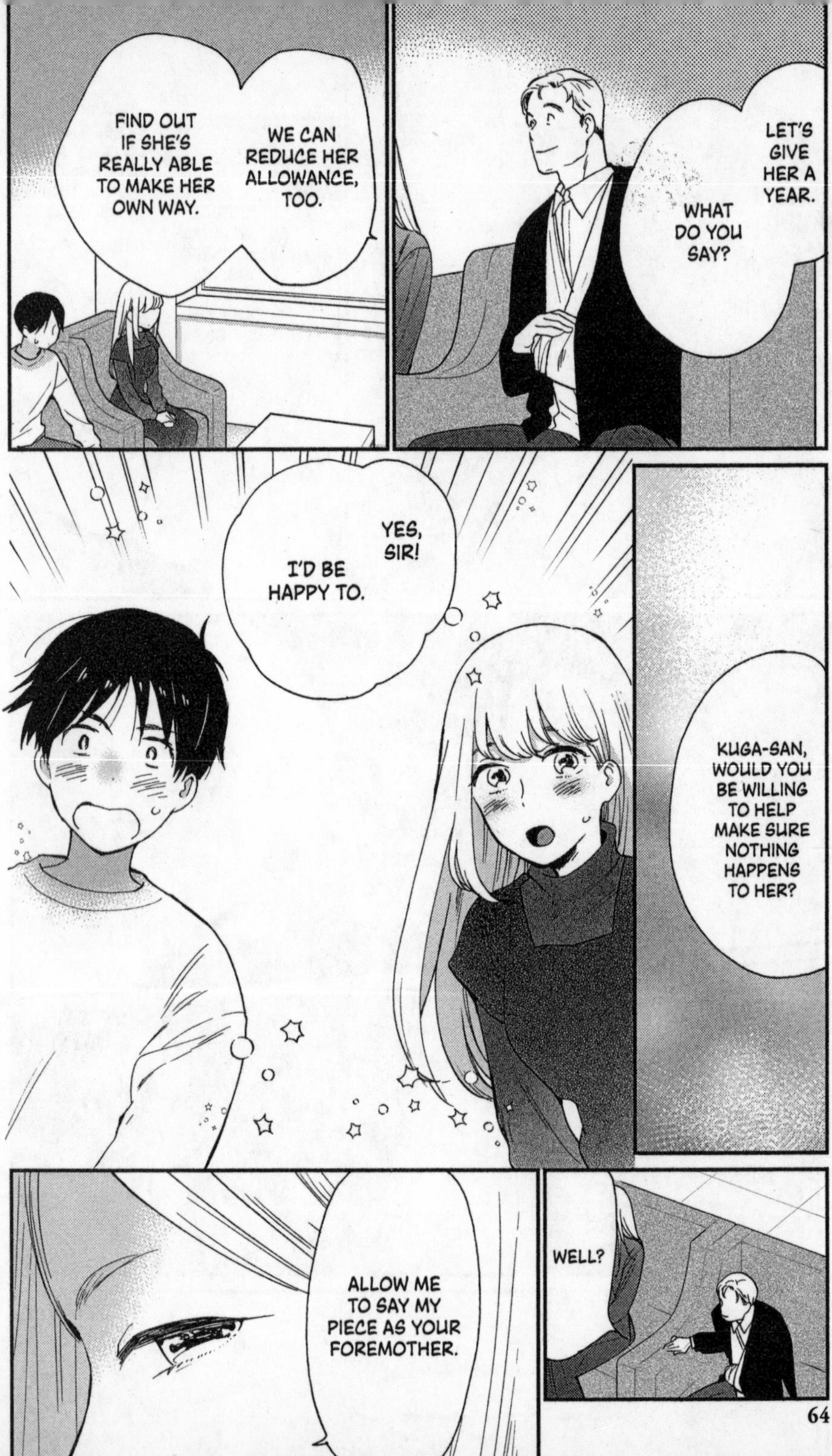
LET'S GIVE HER A YEAR.
WHAT DO YOU SAY?
WE CAN REDUCE HER ALLOWANCE, TOO.
FIND OUT IF SHE'S REALLY ABLE TO MAKE HER OWN WAY.
KUGA-SAN, WOULD YOU BE WILLING TO HELP MAKE SURE NOTHING HAPPENS TO HER?
YES, SIR!
I'D BE HAPPY TO.
WELL?
ALLOW ME TO SAY MY PIECE AS YOUR FOREMOTHER.

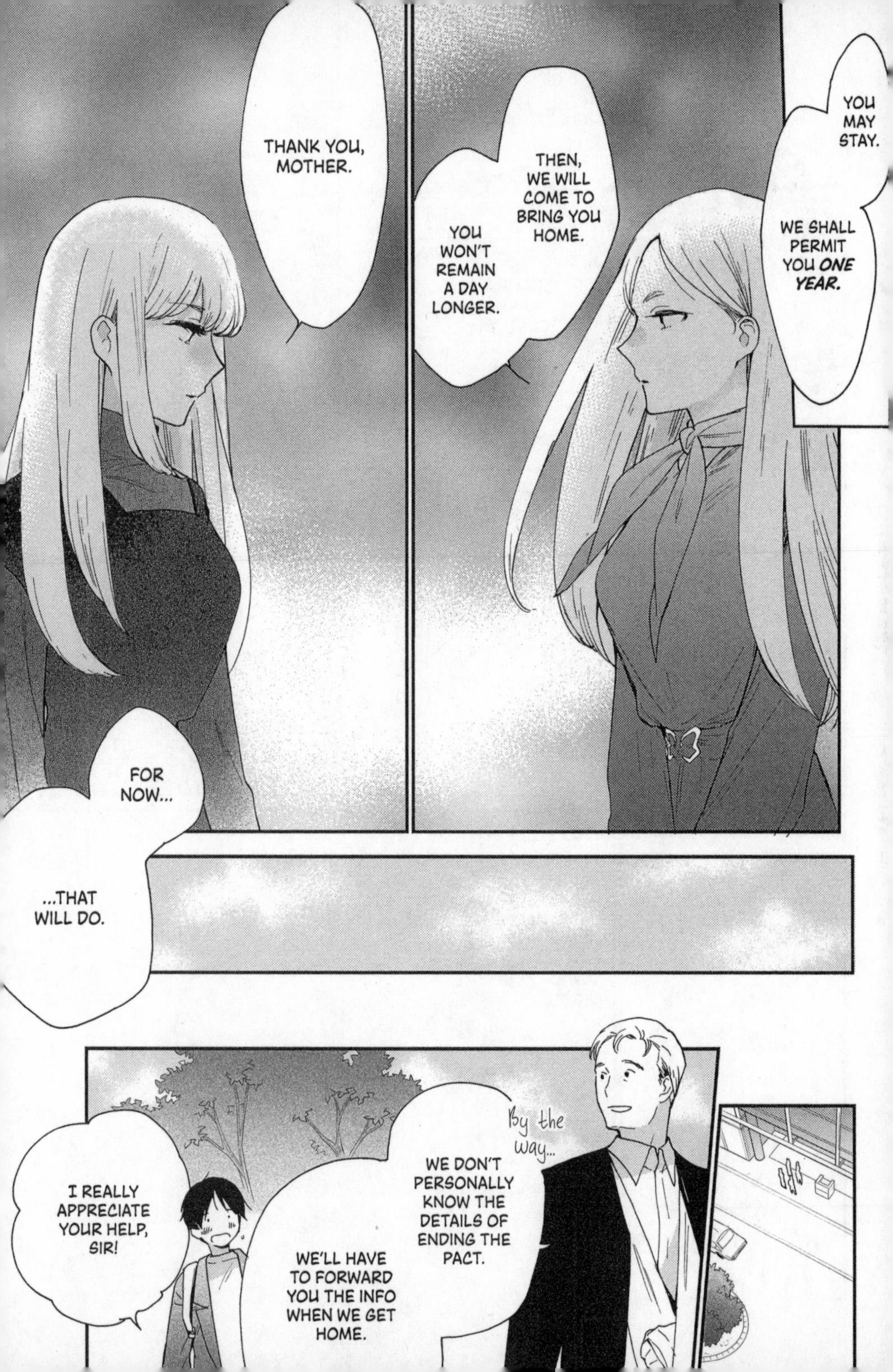
YOU MAY STAY.
WE SHALL PERMIT YOU *ONE YEAR.*
THEN, WE WILL COME TO BRING YOU HOME.
YOU WON'T REMAIN A DAY LONGER.
THANK YOU, MOTHER.
FOR NOW...
...THAT WILL DO.
By the way...
WE DON'T PERSONALLY KNOW THE DETAILS OF ENDING THE PACT.
WE'LL HAVE TO FORWARD YOU THE INFO WHEN WE GET HOME.
I REALLY APPRECIATE YOUR HELP, SIR!

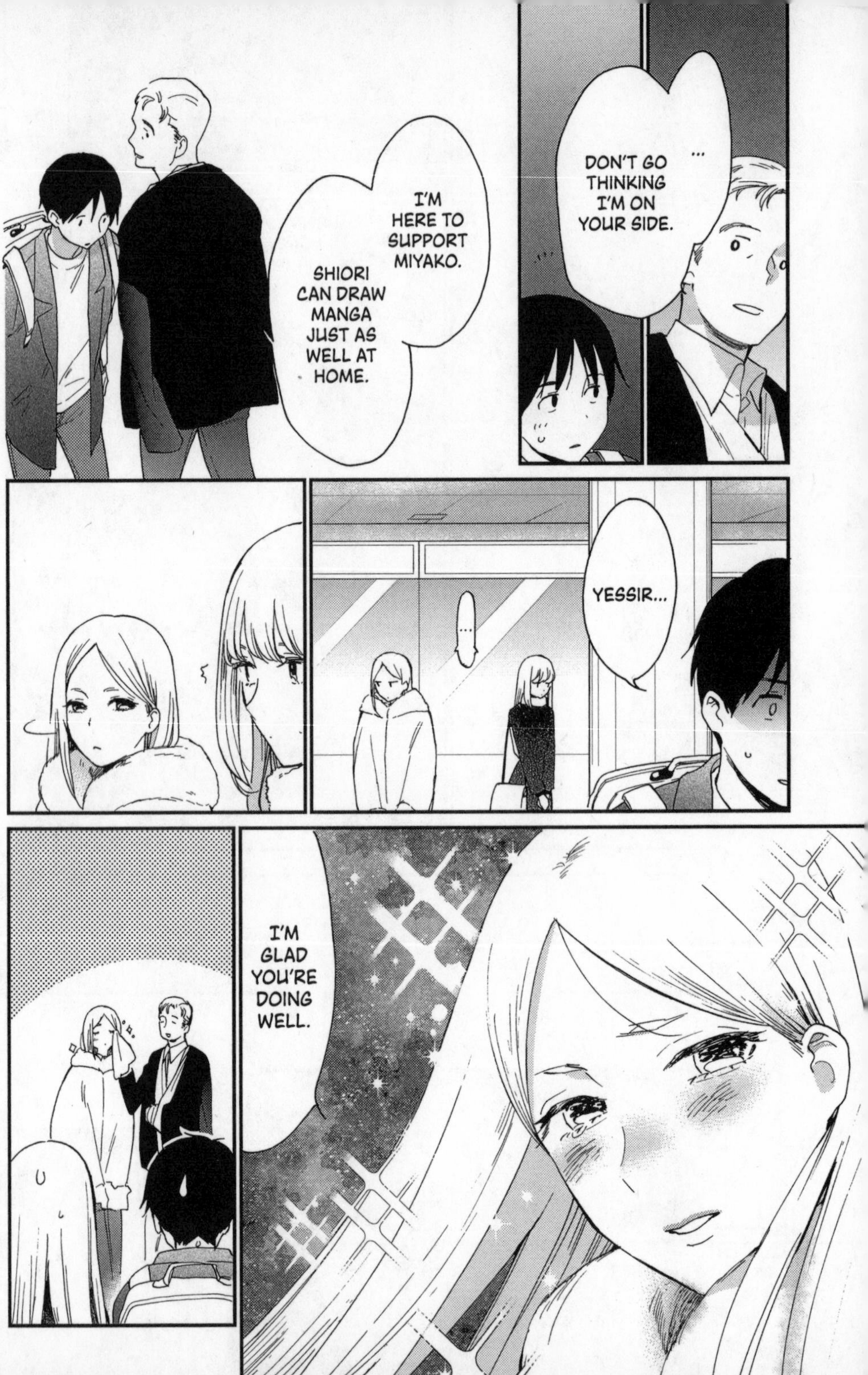
...
DON'T GO THINKING I'M ON YOUR SIDE.
I'M HERE TO SUPPORT MIYAKO.
SHIORI CAN DRAW MANGA JUST AS WELL AT HOME.
YESSIR...
...
I'M GLAD YOU'RE DOING WELL.

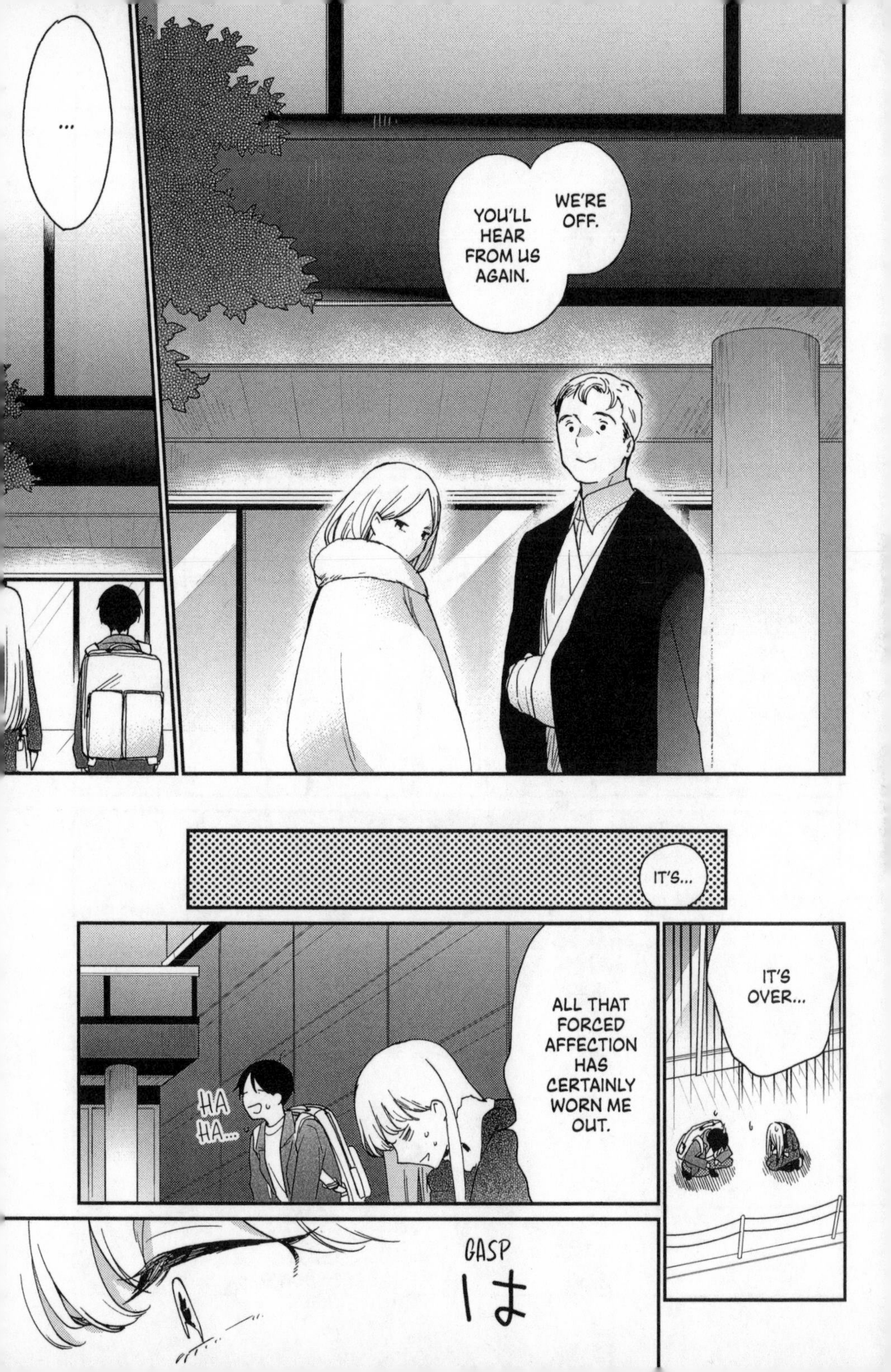
WE'RE OFF.
YOU'LL HEAR FROM US AGAIN.
...
IT'S...
IT'S OVER...
ALL THAT FORCED AFFECTION HAS CERTAINLY WORN ME OUT.
HA HA...
GASP
は

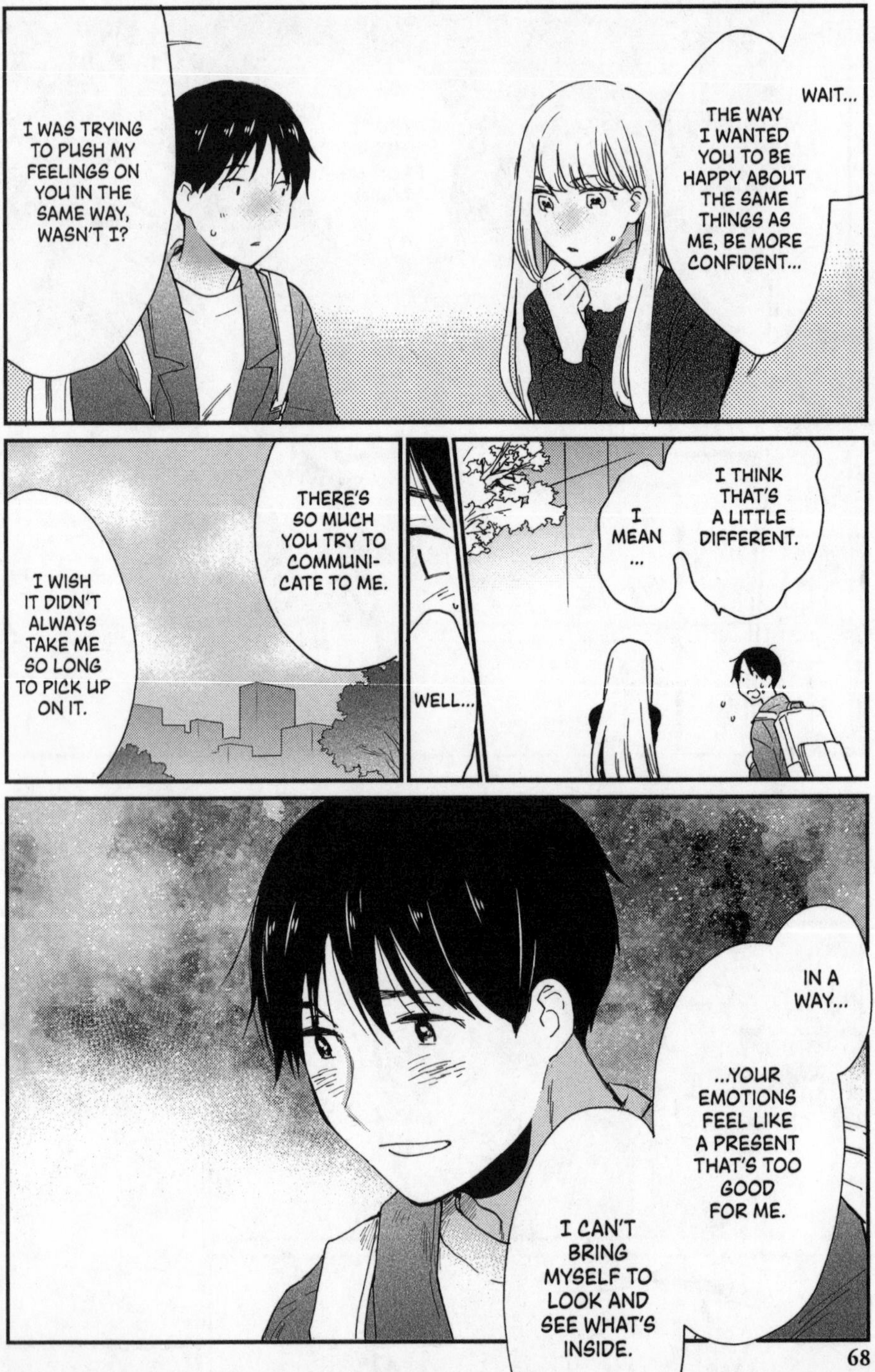
WAIT...
THE WAY I WANTED YOU TO BE HAPPY ABOUT THE SAME THINGS AS ME, BE MORE CONFIDENT...
I WAS TRYING TO PUSH MY FEELINGS ON YOU IN THE SAME WAY, WASN'T I?
I THINK THAT'S A LITTLE DIFFERENT.
I MEAN...
WELL...
THERE'S SO MUCH YOU TRY TO COMMUNICATE TO ME.
I WISH IT DIDN'T ALWAYS TAKE ME SO LONG TO PICK UP ON IT.
IN A WAY...
...YOUR EMOTIONS FEEL LIKE A PRESENT THAT'S TOO GOOD FOR ME.
I CAN'T BRING MYSELF TO LOOK AND SEE WHAT'S INSIDE.

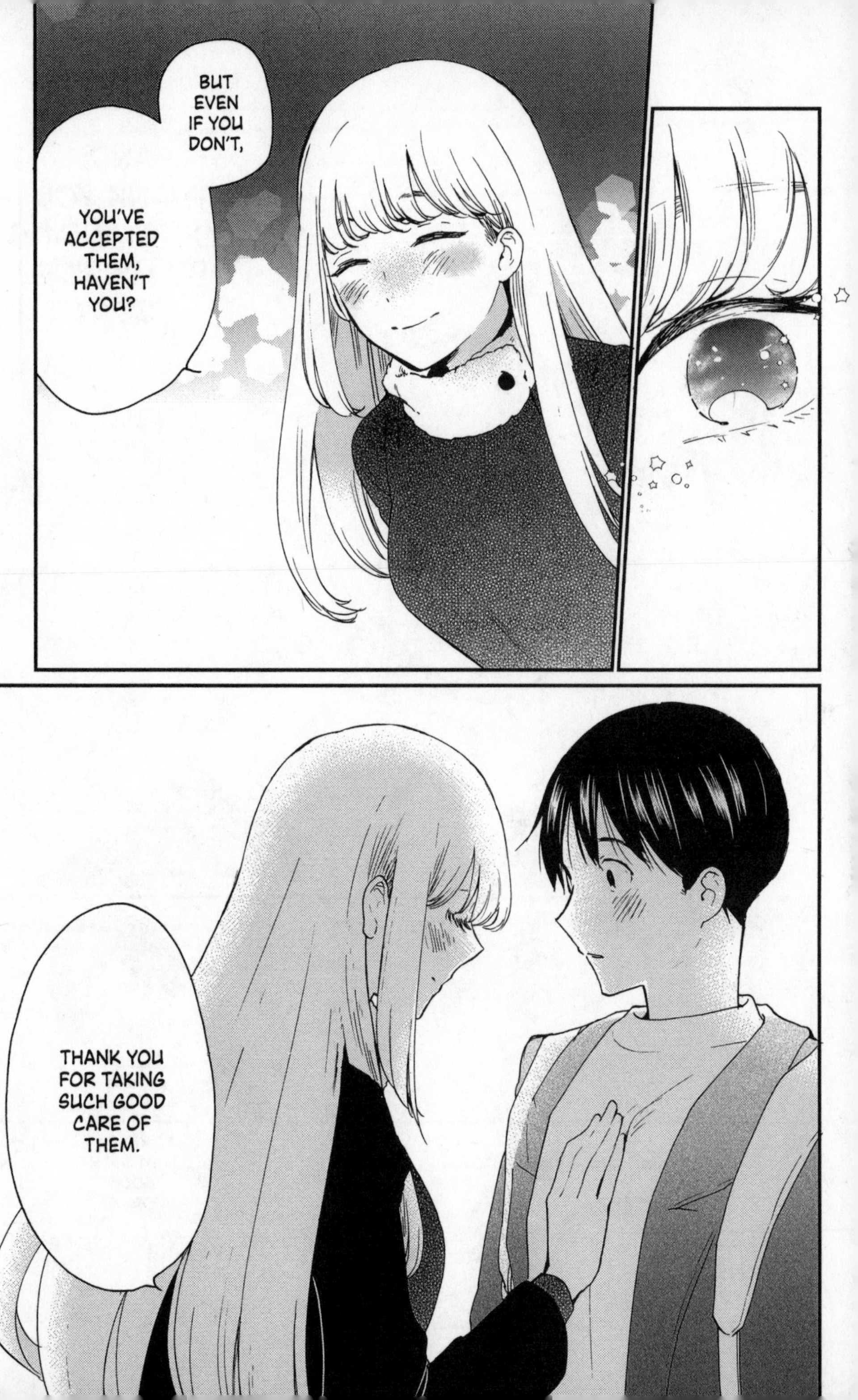
BUT EVEN IF YOU DON'T,
YOU'VE ACCEPTED THEM, HAVEN'T YOU?
THANK YOU FOR TAKING SUCH GOOD CARE OF THEM.

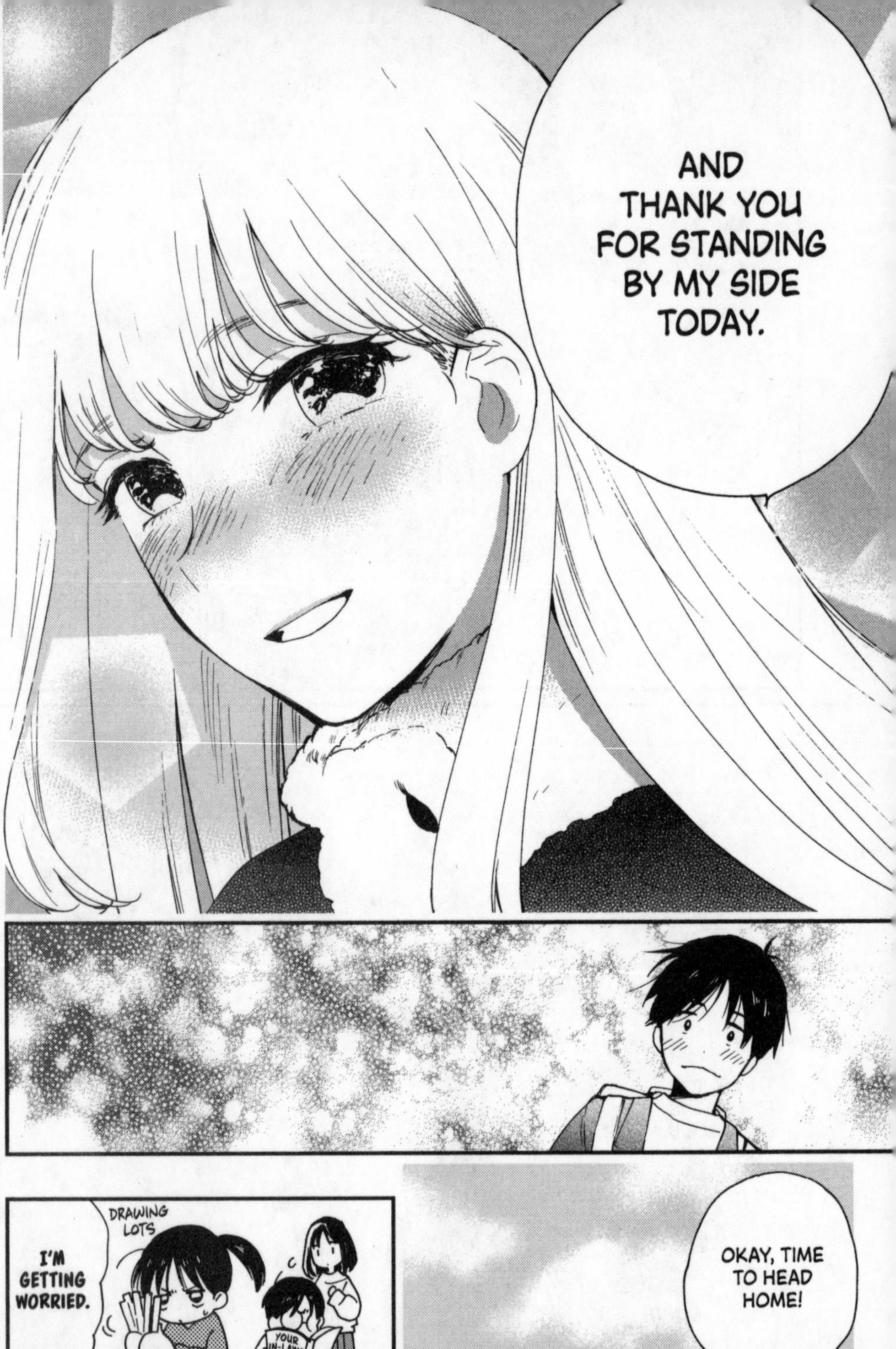
AND THANK YOU FOR STANDING BY MY SIDE TODAY.
OKAY, TIME TO HEAD HOME!
DRAWING LOTS
I'M GETTING WORRIED.
YOUR IN-LAWS AND

CHAPTER 12 ★ END

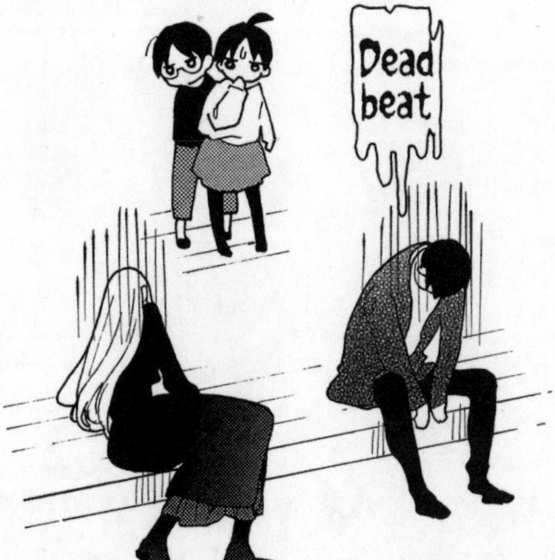
Dead beat

A Galaxy Next Door

Gido Amagakure

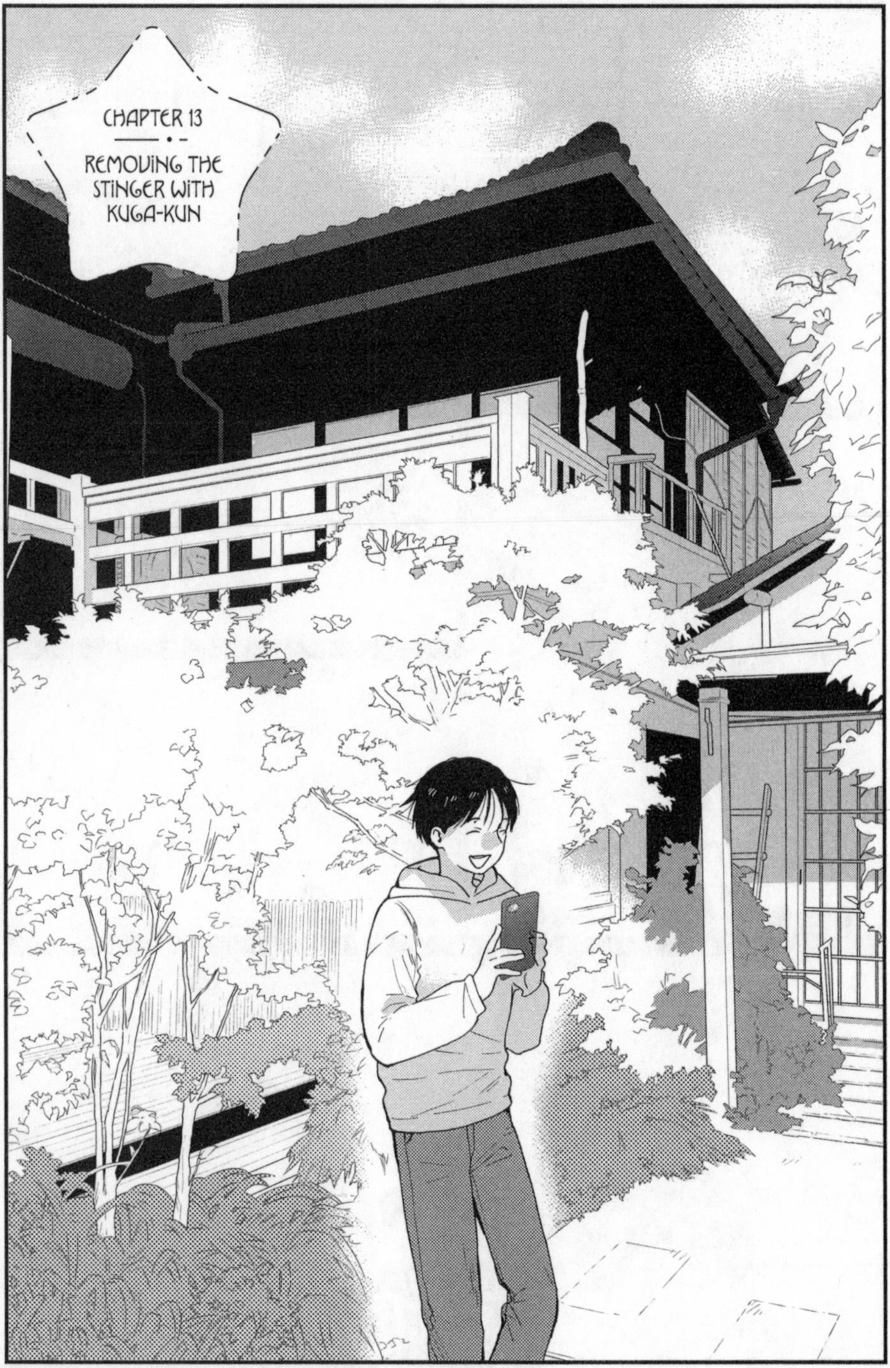
CHAPTER 13
REMOVING THE STINGER WITH KUGA-KUN

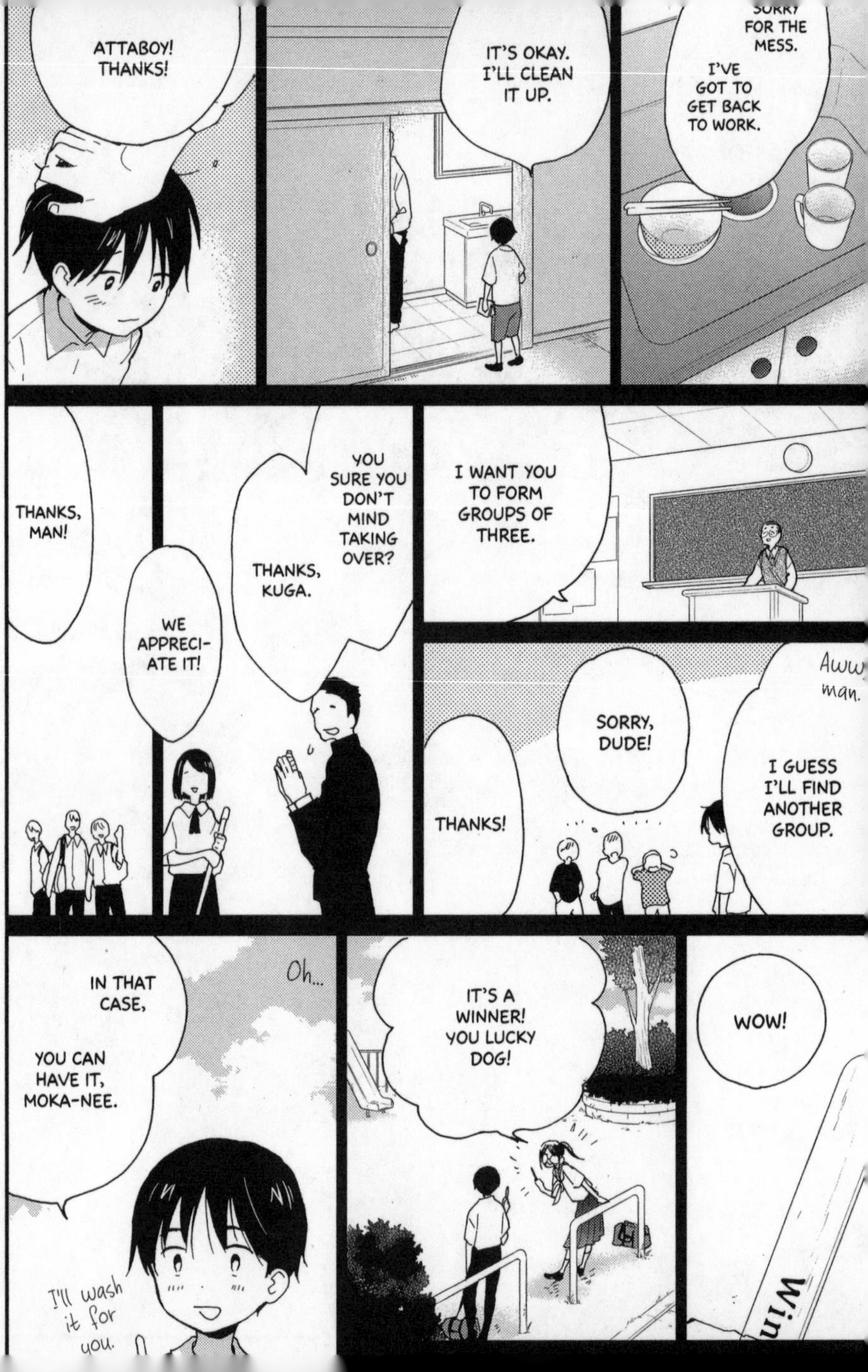
SORRY FOR THE MESS.
I'VE GOT TO GET BACK TO WORK.
IT'S OKAY. I'LL CLEAN IT UP.
ATTABOY! THANKS!
I WANT YOU TO FORM GROUPS OF THREE.
Awww man.
I GUESS I'LL FIND ANOTHER GROUP.
SORRY, DUDE!
THANKS!
YOU SURE YOU DON'T MIND TAKING OVER?
THANKS, KUGA.
WE APPRECIATE IT!
THANKS, MAN!
WOW!
IT'S A WINNER! YOU LUCKY DOG!
Oh...
IN THAT CASE,
YOU CAN HAVE IT, MOKA-NEE.
I'll wash it for you.

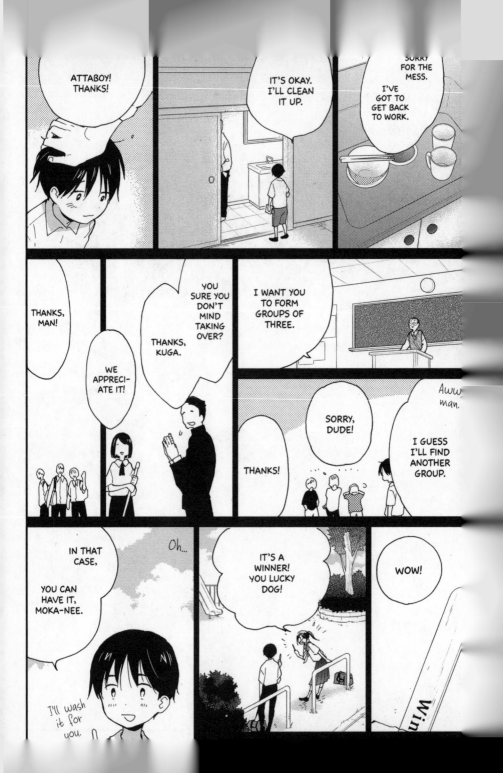

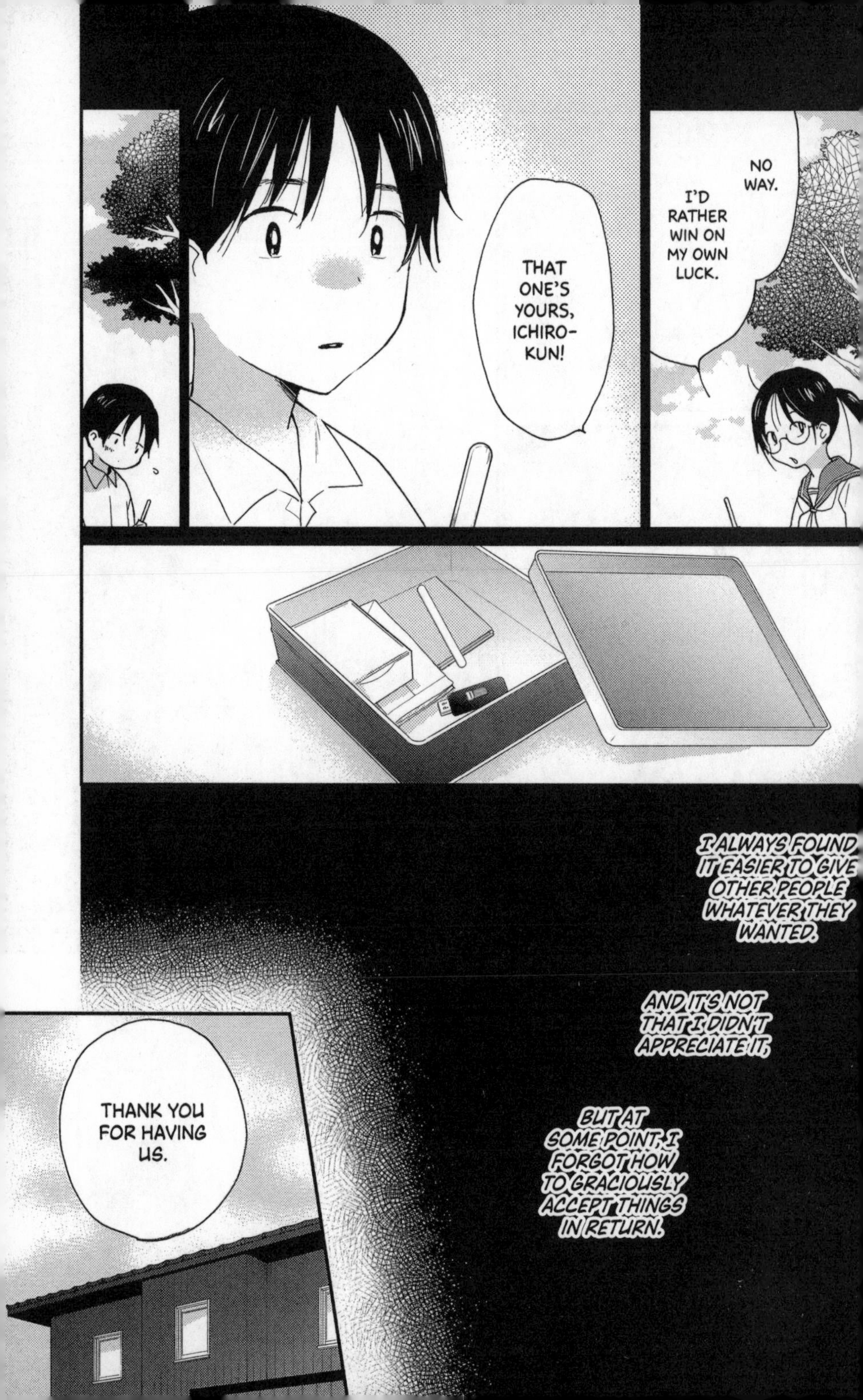
NO WAY.
I'D RATHER WIN ON MY OWN LUCK.
THAT ONE'S YOURS, ICHIRO-KUN!
I ALWAYS FOUND IT EASIER TO GIVE OTHER PEOPLE WHATEVER THEY WANTED.
AND IT'S NOT THAT I DIDN'T APPRECIATE IT,
BUT AT SOME POINT, I FORGOT HOW TO GRACIOUSLY ACCEPT THINGS IN RETURN.
THANK YOU FOR HAVING US.

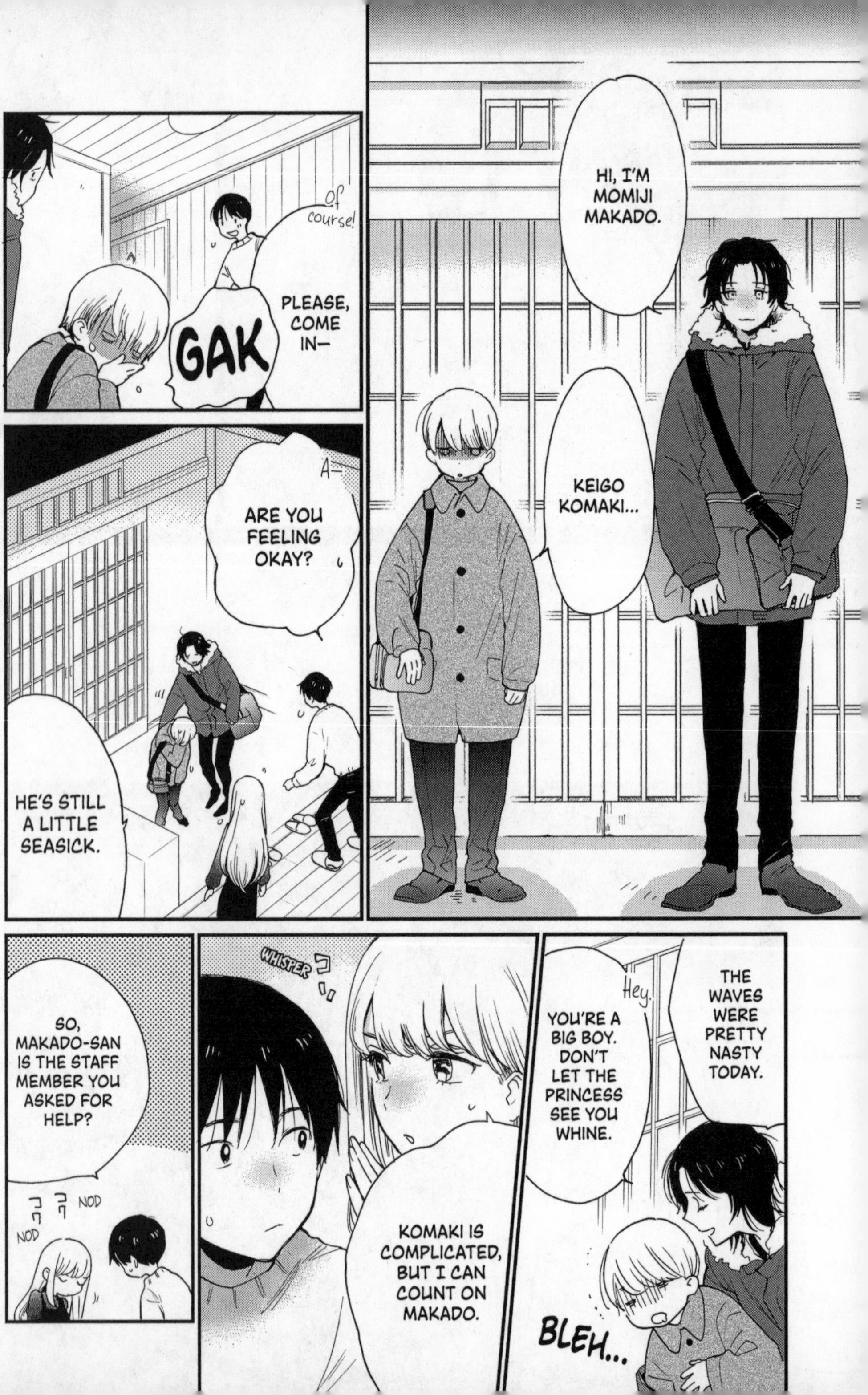

HI, I'M MOMIJI MAKADO.
KEIGO KOMAKI...
Of course!
PLEASE, COME IN—
GAK
A—
ARE YOU FEELING OKAY?
HE'S STILL A LITTLE SEASICK.
THE WAVES WERE PRETTY NASTY TODAY.
Hey.
YOU'RE A BIG BOY. DON'T LET THE PRINCESS SEE YOU WHINE.
BLEH...
WHISPER
KOMAKI IS COMPLICATED, BUT I CAN COUNT ON MAKADO.
SO, MAKADO-SAN IS THE STAFF MEMBER YOU ASKED FOR HELP?
NOD
NOD

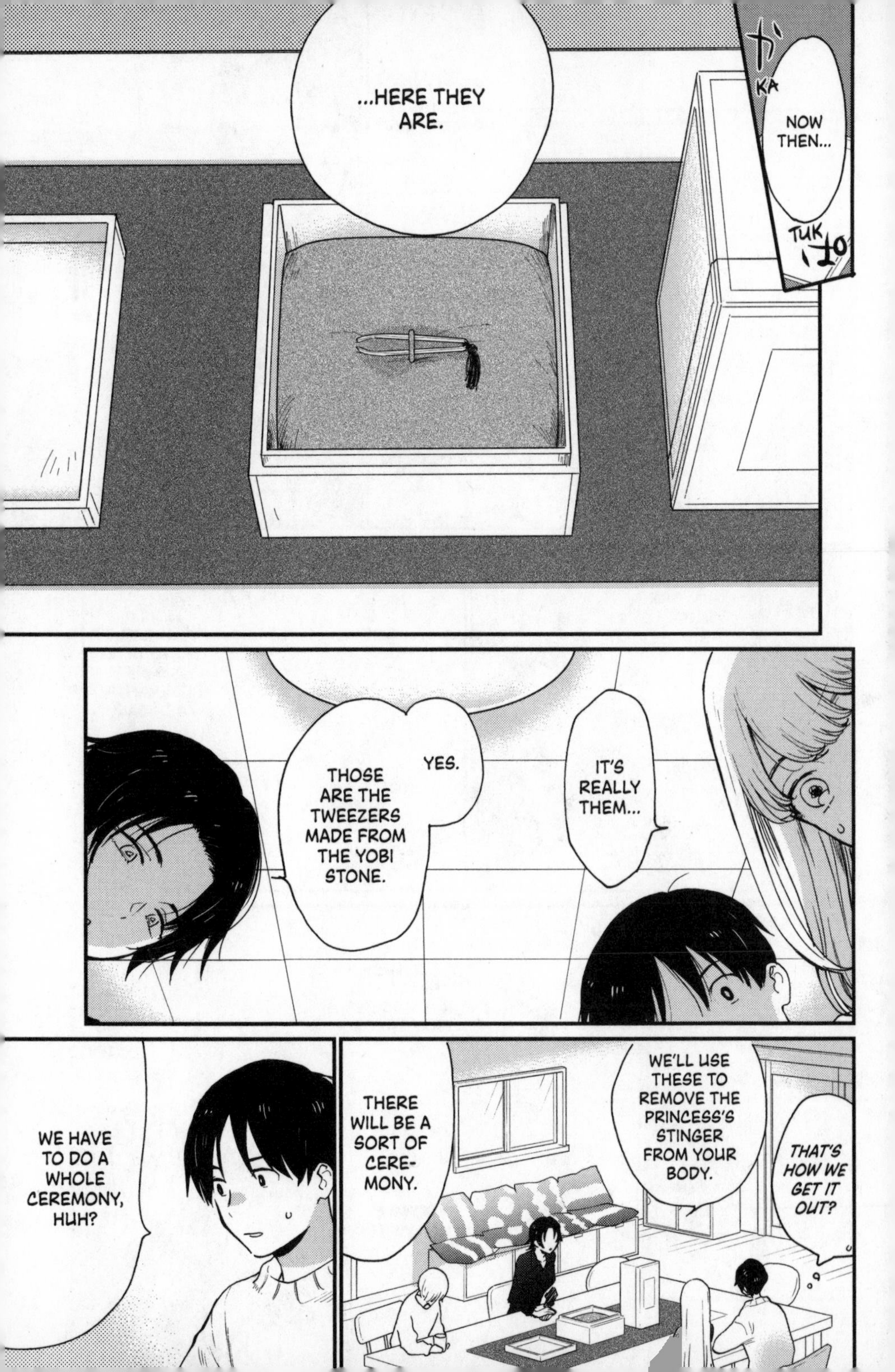
KA
NOW THEN...
TUK
...HERE THEY ARE.
IT'S REALLY THEM...
YES.
THOSE ARE THE TWEEZERS MADE FROM THE YOBI STONE.
THAT'S HOW WE GET IT OUT?
WE'LL USE THESE TO REMOVE THE PRINCESS'S STINGER FROM YOUR BODY.
THERE WILL BE A SORT OF CERE-MONY.
WE HAVE TO DO A WHOLE CEREMONY, HUH?

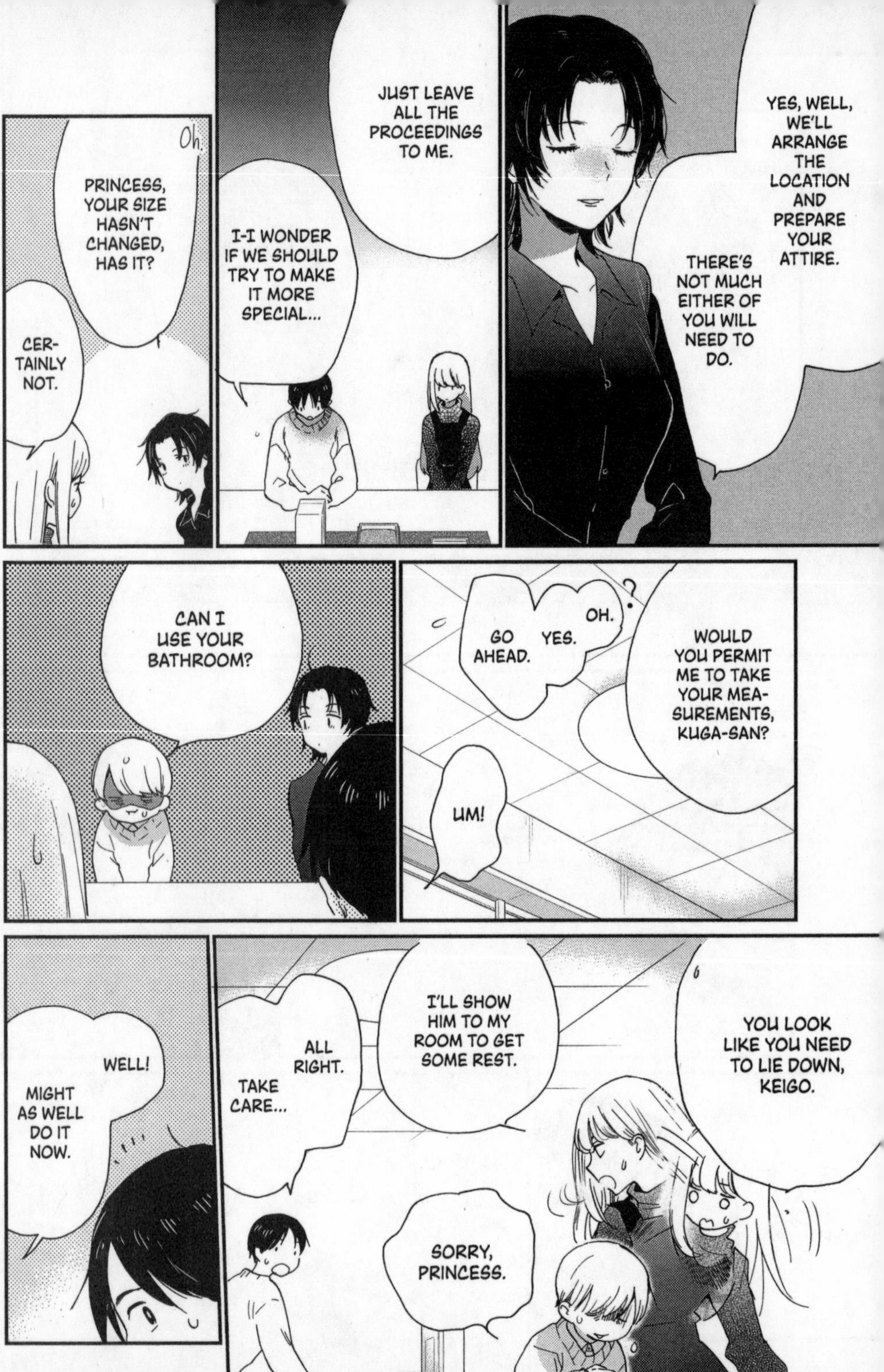
YES, WELL, WE'LL ARRANGE THE LOCATION AND PREPARE YOUR ATTIRE.
THERE'S NOT MUCH EITHER OF YOU WILL NEED TO DO.
JUST LEAVE ALL THE PROCEEDINGS TO ME.
I-I WONDER IF WE SHOULD TRY TO MAKE IT MORE SPECIAL...
Oh.
PRINCESS, YOUR SIZE HASN'T CHANGED, HAS IT?
CER-TAINLY NOT.
WOULD YOU PERMIT ME TO TAKE YOUR MEA-SUREMENTS, KUGA-SAN?
OH.
YES.
GO AHEAD.
UM!
CAN I USE YOUR BATHROOM?
YOU LOOK LIKE YOU NEED TO LIE DOWN, KEIGO.
I'LL SHOW HIM TO MY ROOM TO GET SOME REST.
SORRY, PRINCESS.
ALL RIGHT.
TAKE CARE...
WELL!
MIGHT AS WELL DO IT NOW.

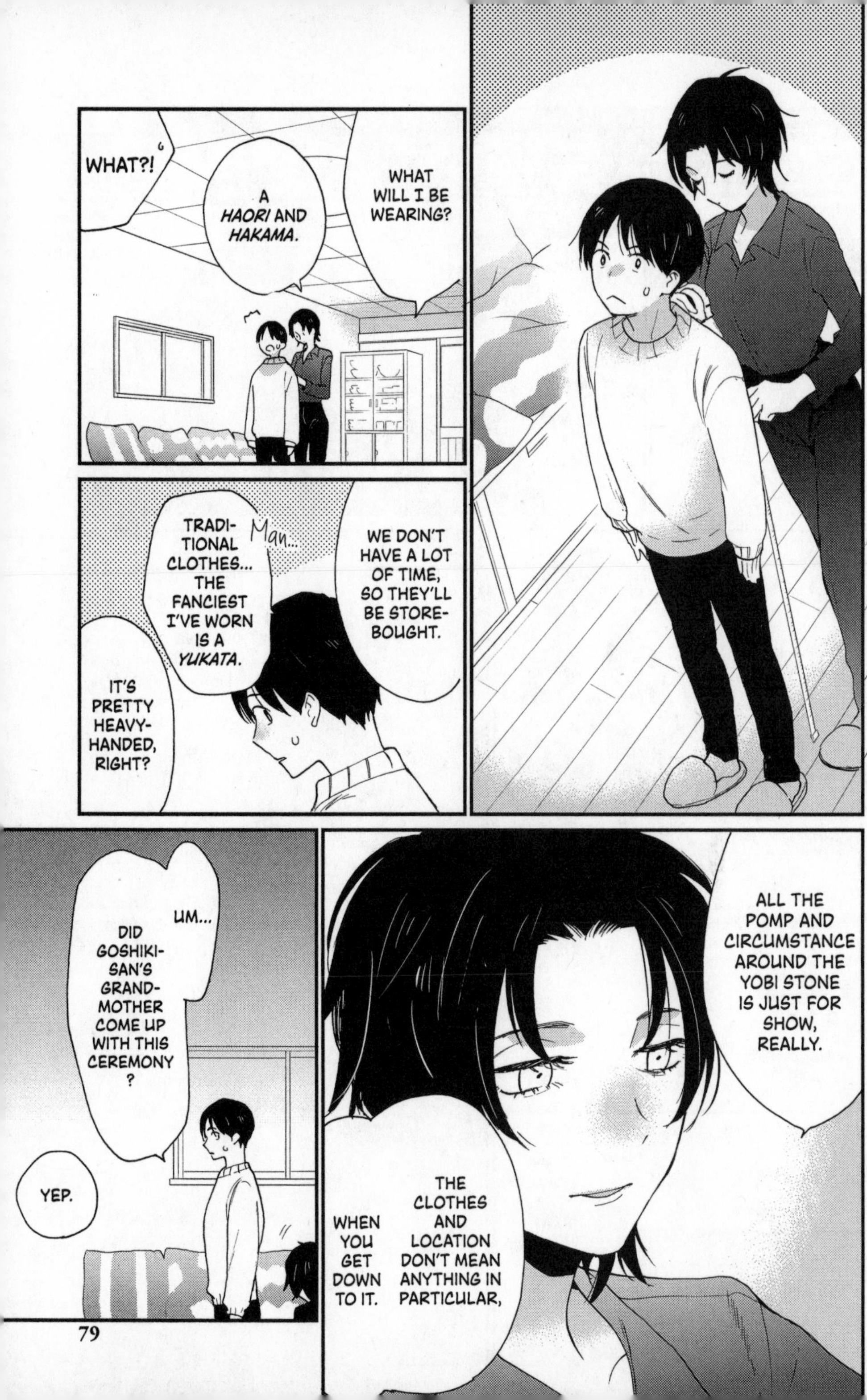

WHAT WILL I BE WEARING?
A *HAORI* AND *HAKAMA*.
WHAT?!
WE DON'T HAVE A LOT OF TIME, SO THEY'LL BE STORE-BOUGHT.
TRADITIONAL CLOTHES... THE FANCIEST I'VE WORN IS A *YUKATA*.
Man...
IT'S PRETTY HEAVY-HANDED, RIGHT?
ALL THE POMP AND CIRCUMSTANCE AROUND THE YOBI STONE IS JUST FOR SHOW, REALLY.
THE CLOTHES AND LOCATION DON'T MEAN ANYTHING IN PARTICULAR,
WHEN YOU GET DOWN TO IT.
UM...
DID GOSHIKI-SAN'S GRANDMOTHER COME UP WITH THIS CEREMONY?
YEP.

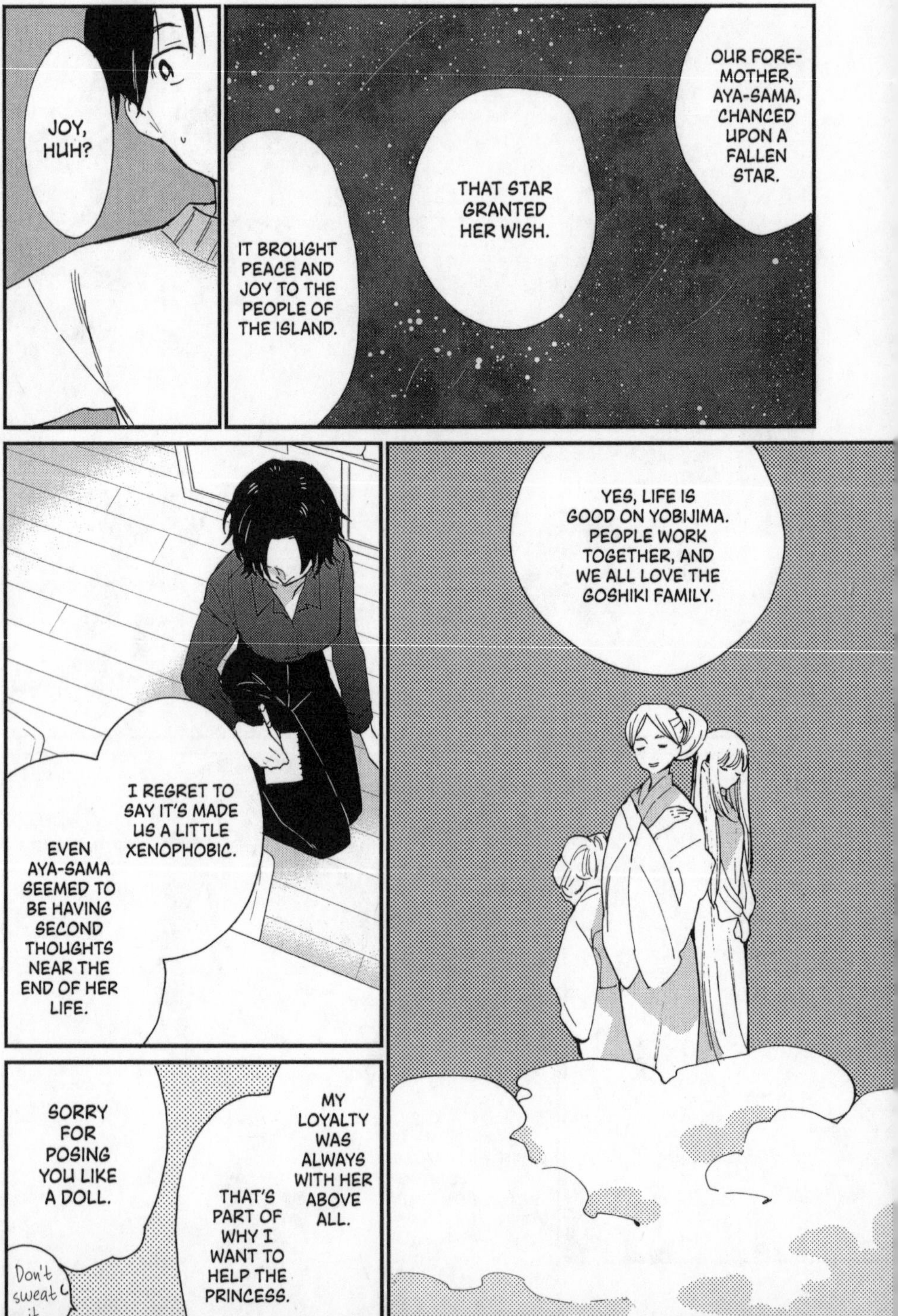
OUR FORE-MOTHER, AYA-SAMA, CHANCED UPON A FALLEN STAR.
THAT STAR GRANTED HER WISH.
IT BROUGHT PEACE AND JOY TO THE PEOPLE OF THE ISLAND.
JOY, HUH?
YES, LIFE IS GOOD ON YOBIJIMA. PEOPLE WORK TOGETHER, AND WE ALL LOVE THE GOSHIKI FAMILY.
I REGRET TO SAY IT'S MADE US A LITTLE XENOPHOBIC.
EVEN AYA-SAMA SEEMED TO BE HAVING SECOND THOUGHTS NEAR THE END OF HER LIFE.
MY LOYALTY WAS ALWAYS WITH HER ABOVE ALL.
THAT'S PART OF WHY I WANT TO HELP THE PRINCESS.
SORRY FOR POSING YOU LIKE A DOLL.
Don't sweat it.

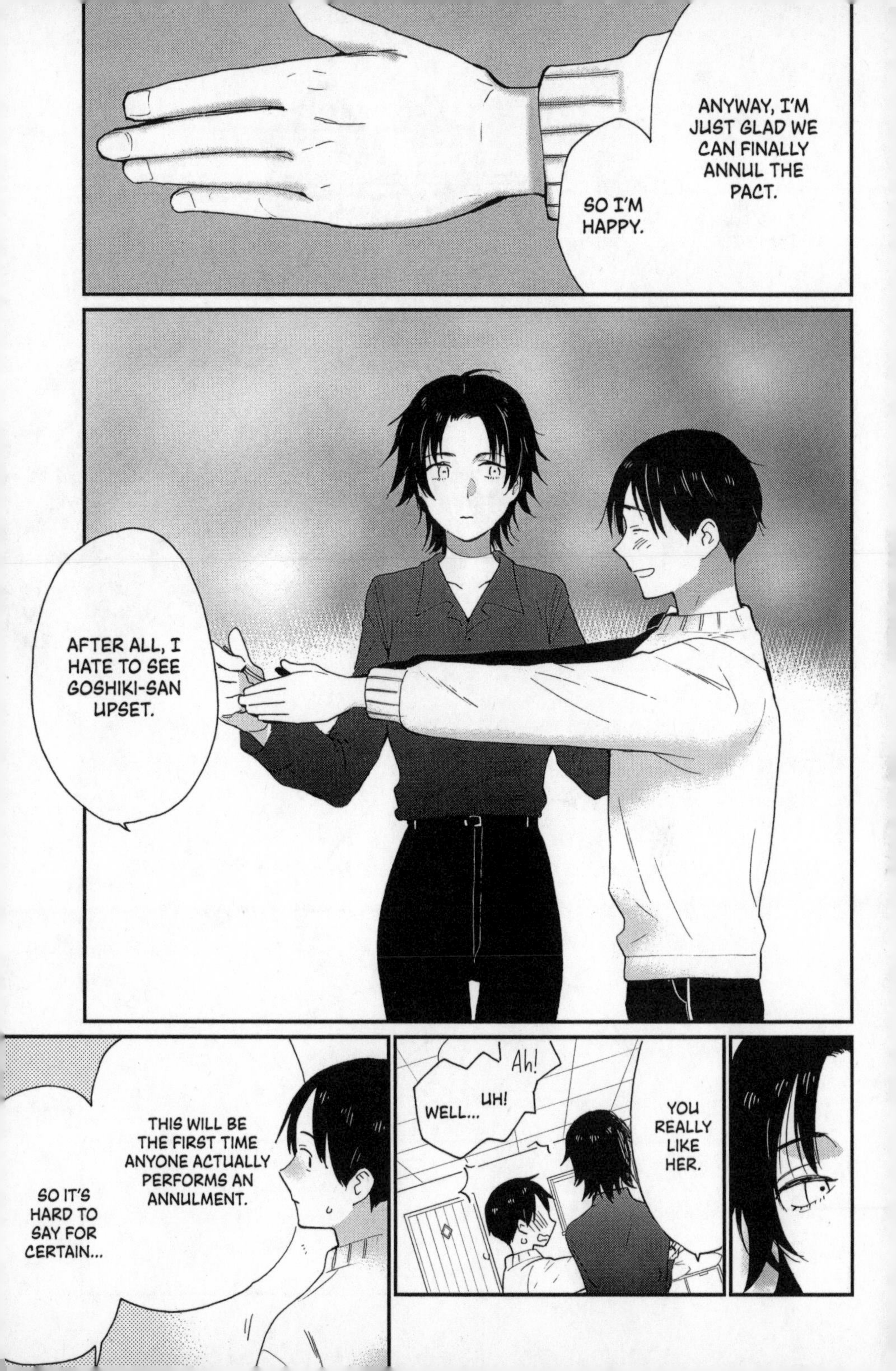
ANYWAY, I'M JUST GLAD WE CAN FINALLY ANNUL THE PACT.
SO I'M HAPPY.
AFTER ALL, I HATE TO SEE GOSHIKI-SAN UPSET.
YOU REALLY LIKE HER.
Ah!
WELL... UH!
THIS WILL BE THE FIRST TIME ANYONE ACTUALLY PERFORMS AN ANNULMENT.
SO IT'S HARD TO SAY FOR CERTAIN...

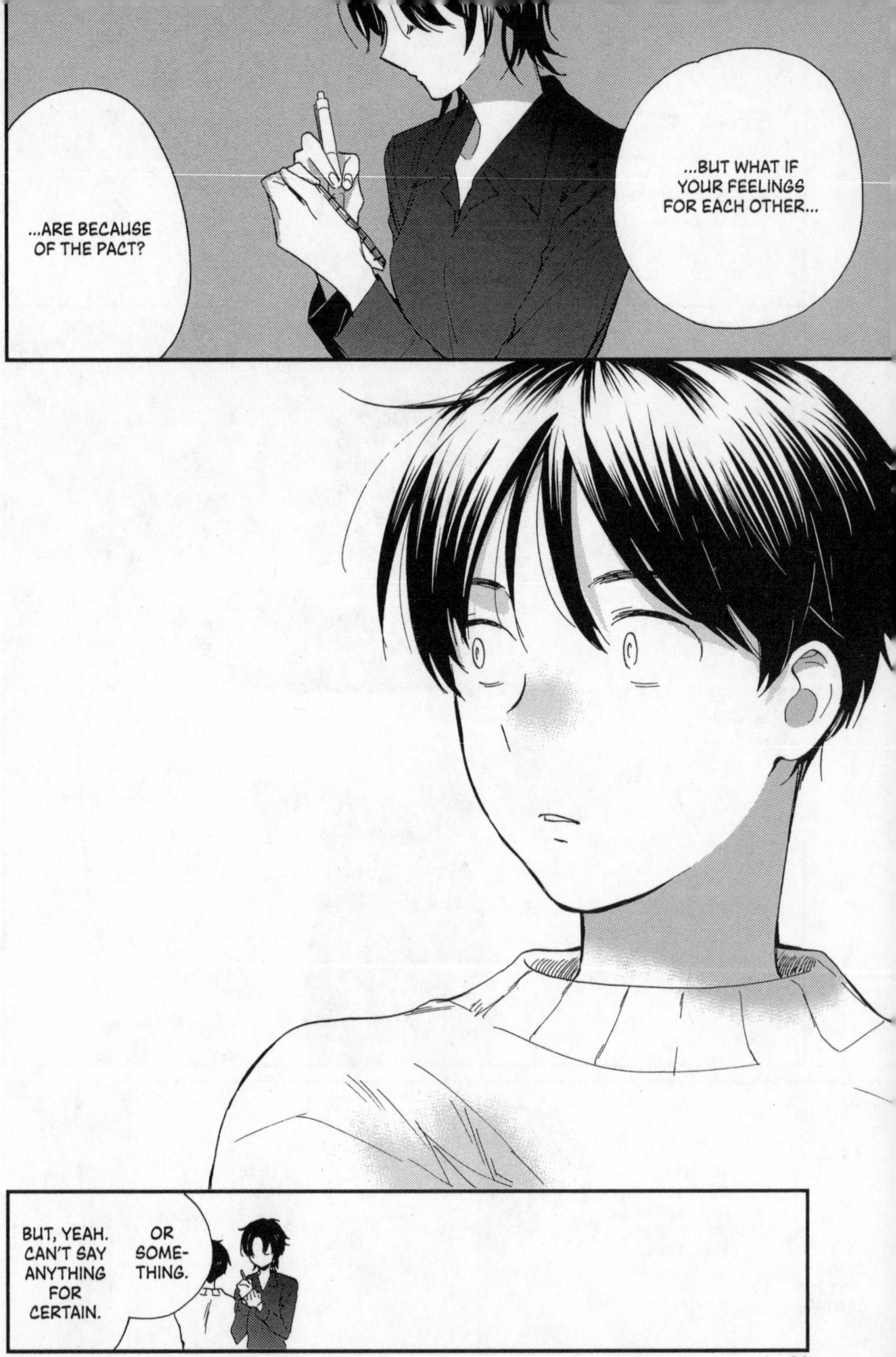
...BUT WHAT IF YOUR FEELINGS FOR EACH OTHER...
...ARE BECAUSE OF THE PACT?
OR SOME-THING.
BUT, YEAH. CAN'T SAY ANYTHING FOR CERTAIN.

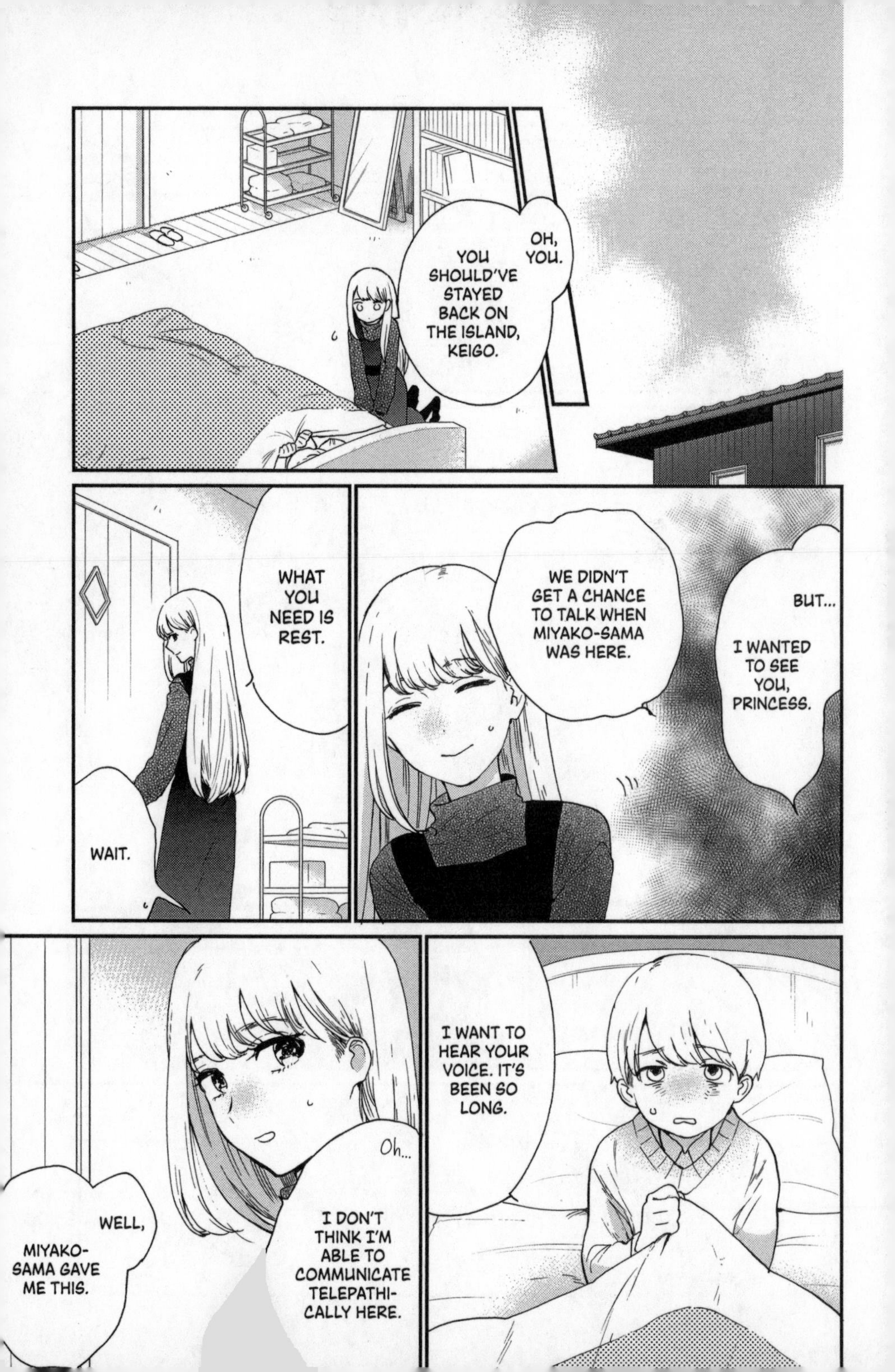
OH, YOU. YOU SHOULD'VE STAYED BACK ON THE ISLAND, KEIGO.
BUT... I WANTED TO SEE YOU, PRINCESS.
WE DIDN'T GET A CHANCE TO TALK WHEN MIYAKO-SAMA WAS HERE.
WHAT YOU NEED IS REST.
WAIT.
I WANT TO HEAR YOUR VOICE. IT'S BEEN SO LONG.
Oh...
I DON'T THINK I'M ABLE TO COMMUNICATE TELEPATHI-CALLY HERE.
WELL, MIYAKO-SAMA GAVE ME THIS.

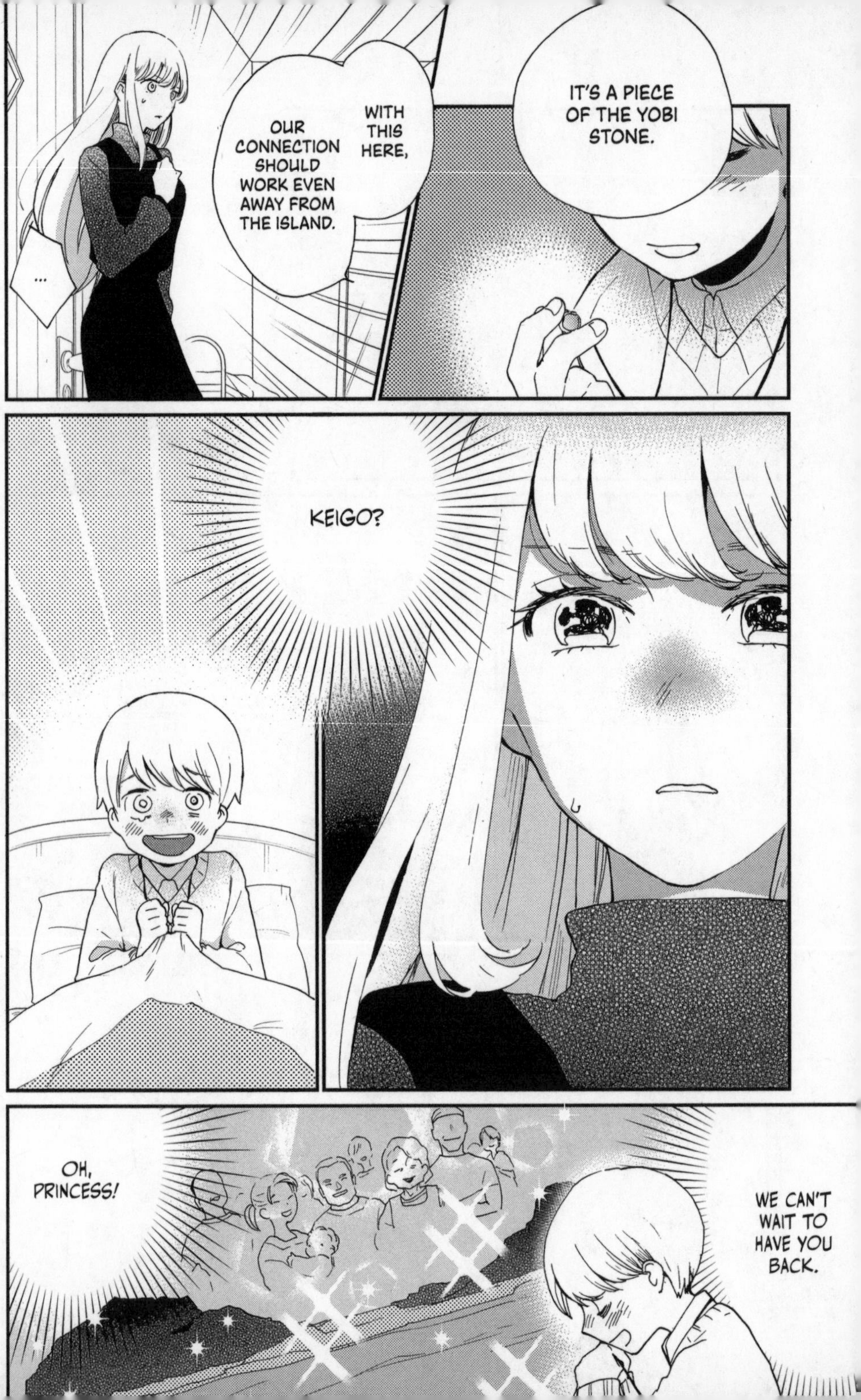
IT'S A PIECE OF THE YOBI STONE.
WITH THIS HERE,
OUR CONNECTION SHOULD WORK EVEN AWAY FROM THE ISLAND.
...
KEIGO?
WE CAN'T WAIT TO HAVE YOU BACK.
OH, PRINCESS!

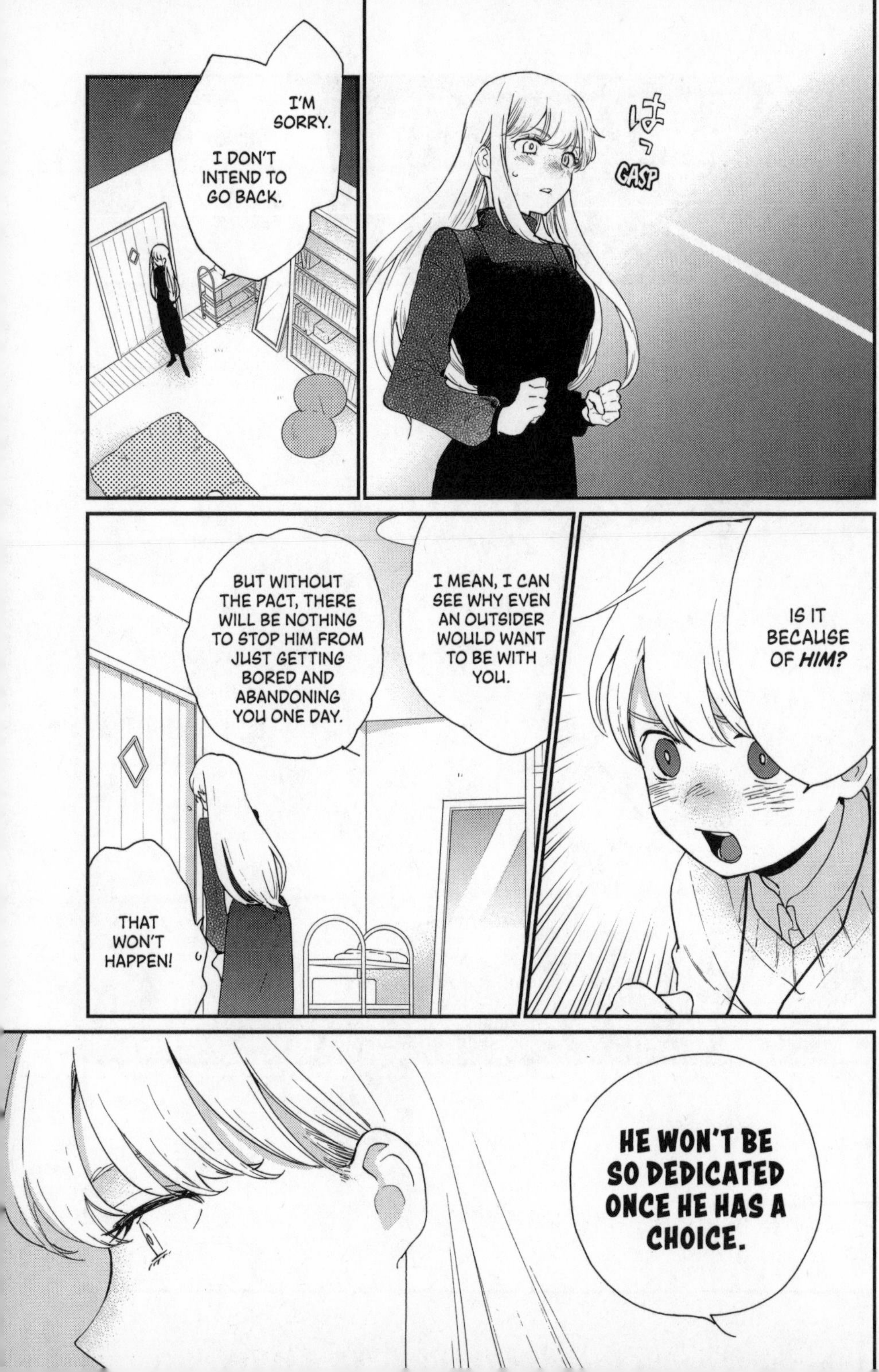
はっ
GASP
I'M SORRY.
I DON'T INTEND TO GO BACK.
IS IT BECAUSE OF HIM?
I MEAN, I CAN SEE WHY EVEN AN OUTSIDER WOULD WANT TO BE WITH YOU.
BUT WITHOUT THE PACT, THERE WILL BE NOTHING TO STOP HIM FROM JUST GETTING BORED AND ABANDONING YOU ONE DAY.
THAT WON'T HAPPEN!
HE WON'T BE SO DEDICATED ONCE HE HAS A CHOICE.

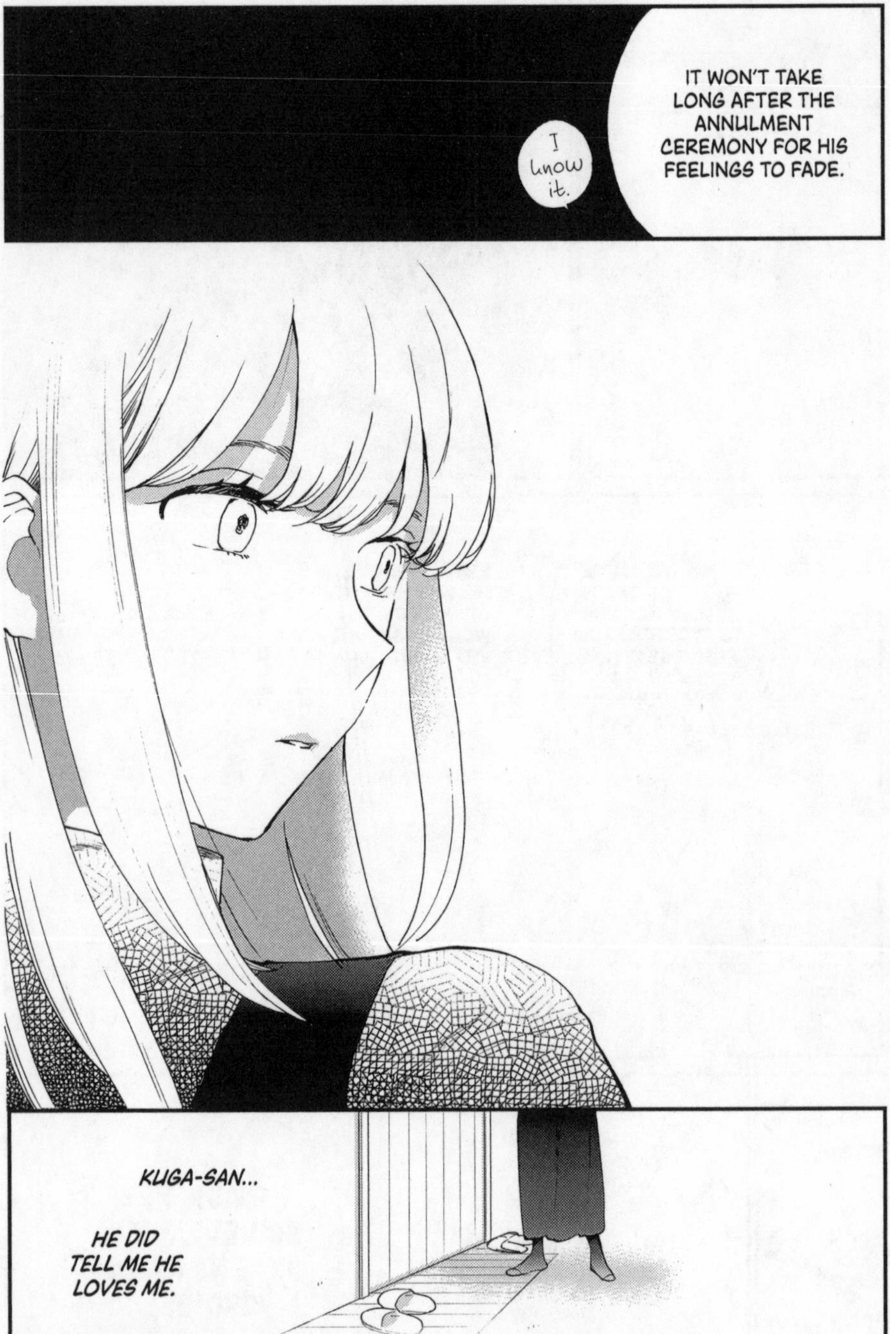
IT WON'T TAKE LONG AFTER THE ANNULMENT CEREMONY FOR HIS FEELINGS TO FADE.
I know it.
KUGA-SAN...
HE DID TELL ME HE LOVES ME.

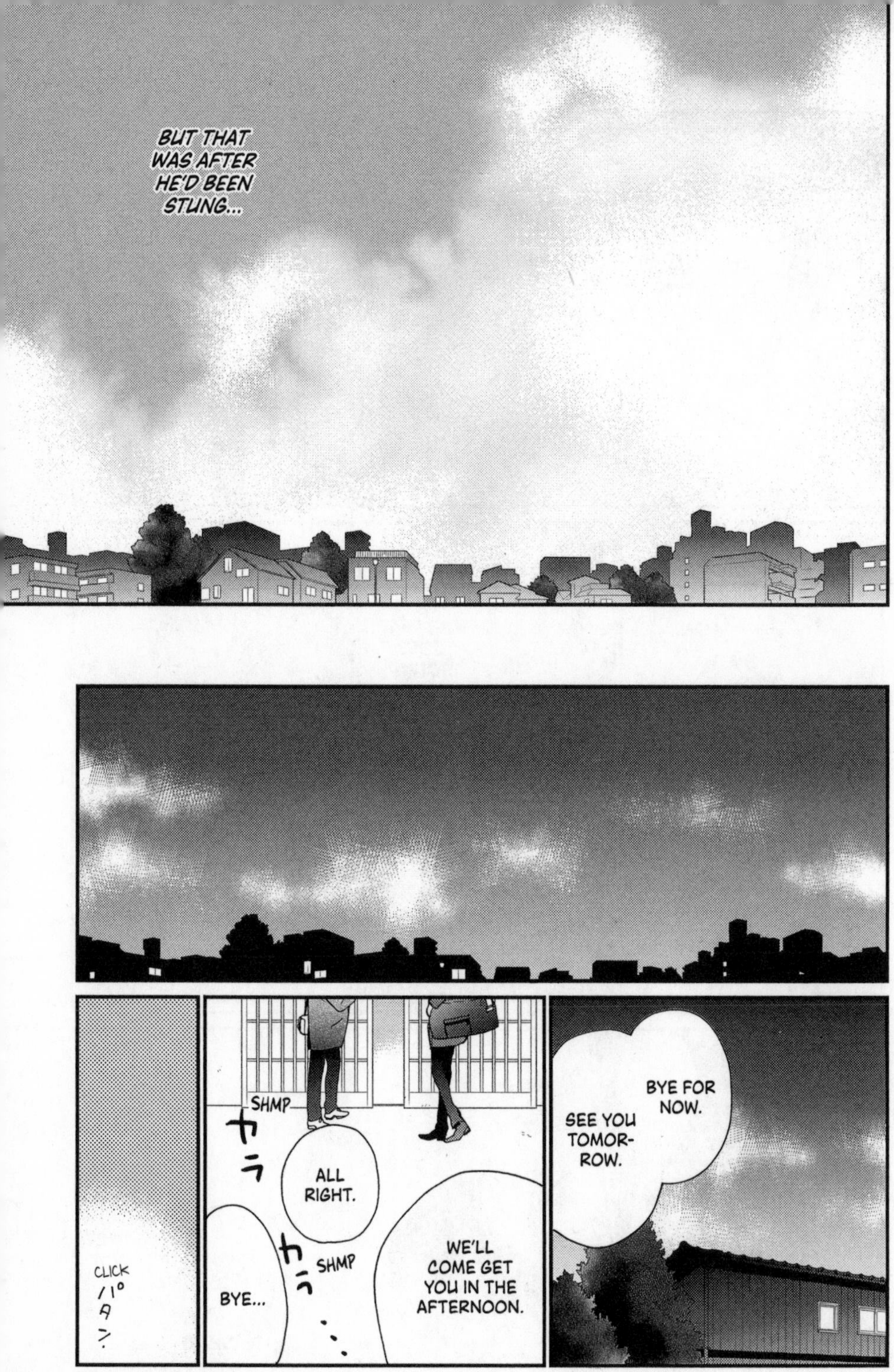
BUT THAT WAS AFTER HE'D BEEN STUNG...
SEE YOU TOMOR-ROW.
BYE FOR NOW.
SHMP
ALL RIGHT.
WE'LL COME GET YOU IN THE AFTERNOON.
SHMP
BYE...
CLICK

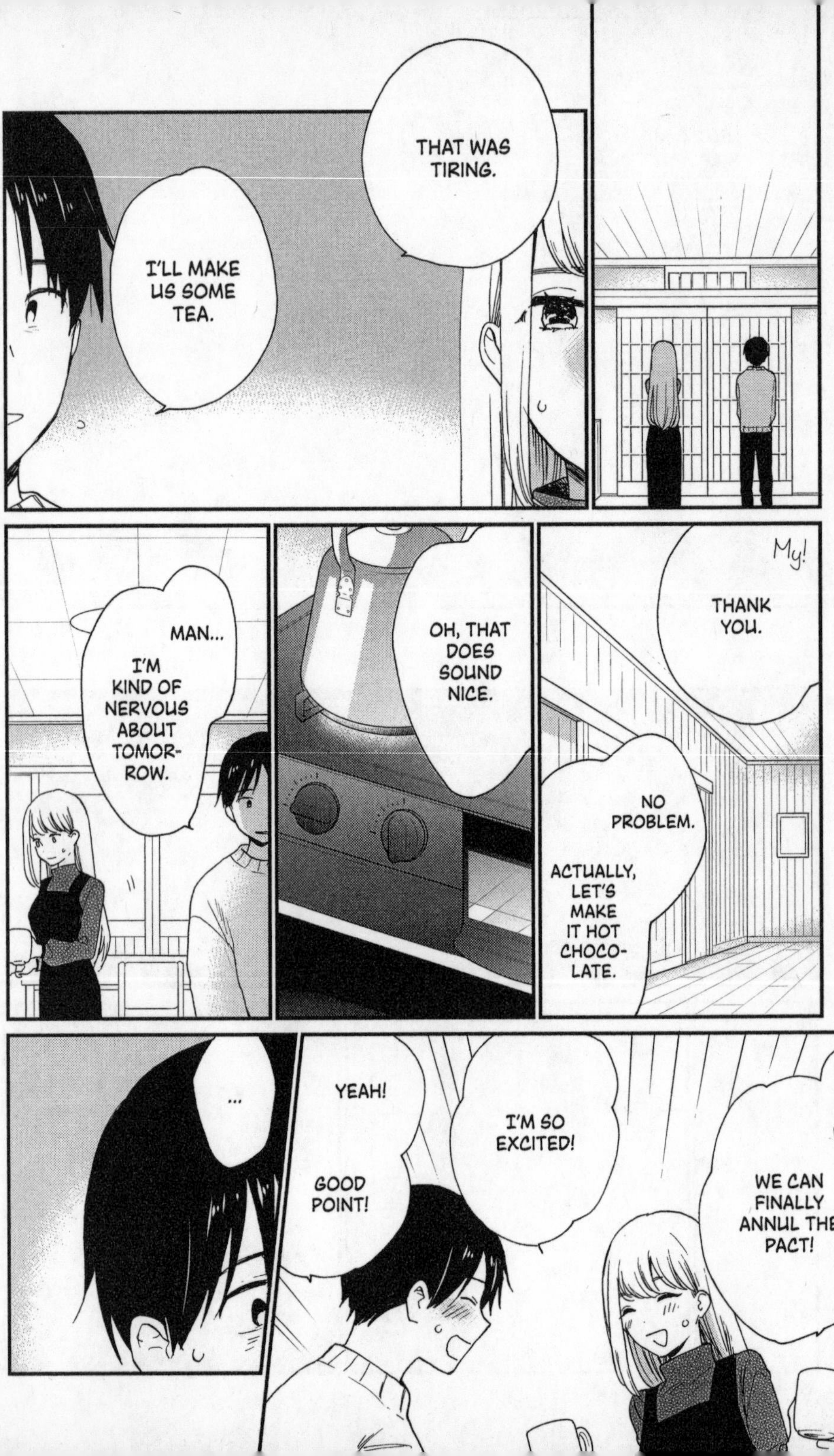
THAT WAS TIRING.
I'LL MAKE US SOME TEA.
My!
THANK YOU.
NO PROBLEM.
ACTUALLY, LET'S MAKE IT HOT CHOCOLATE.
OH, THAT DOES SOUND NICE.
MAN...
I'M KIND OF NERVOUS ABOUT TOMORROW.
BUT WHY?
WE CAN FINALLY ANNUL THE PACT!
I'M SO EXCITED!
YEAH!
GOOD POINT!
...

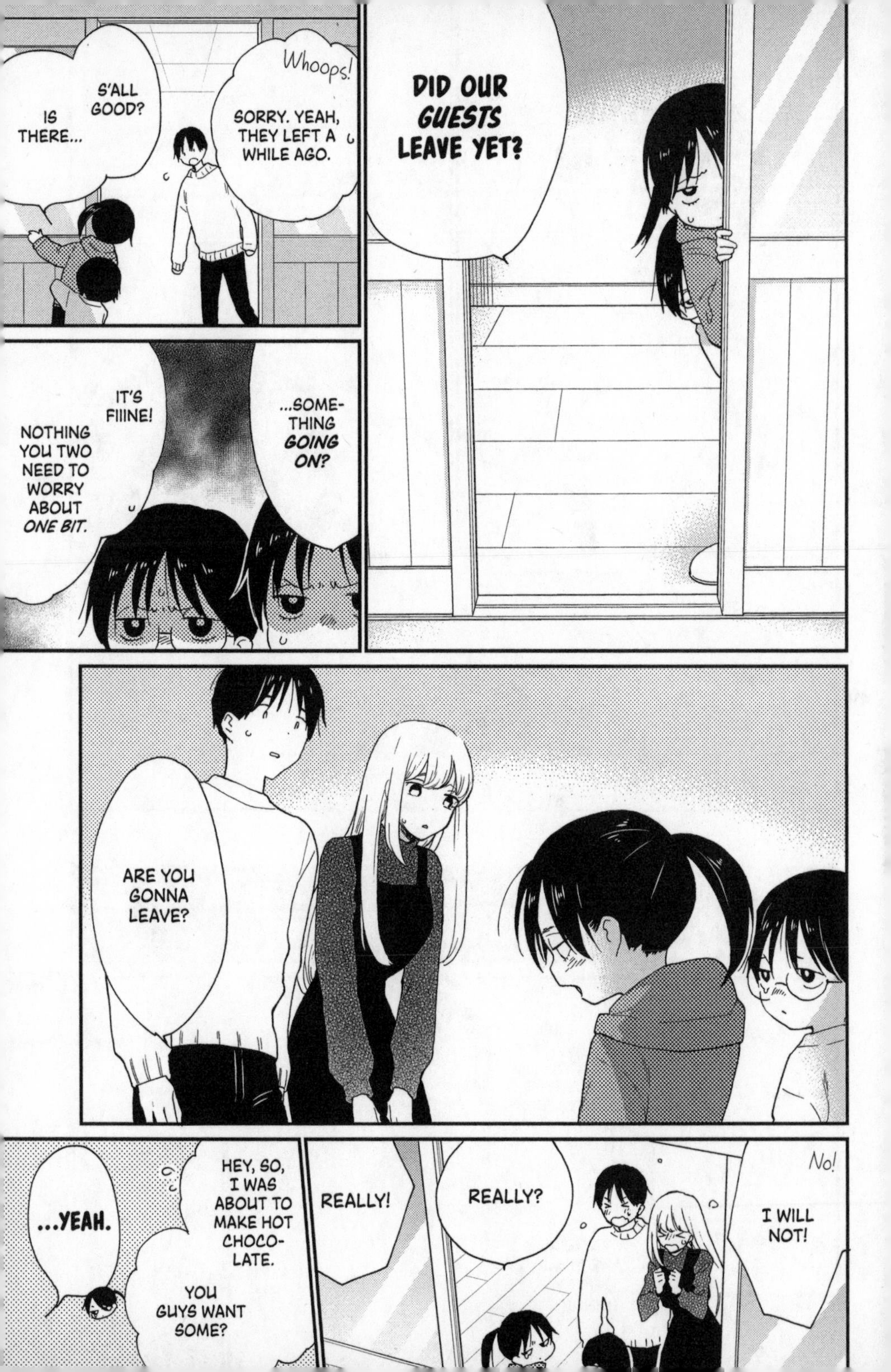
DID OUR *GUESTS* LEAVE YET?
Whoops!
SORRY. YEAH, THEY LEFT A WHILE AGO.
S'ALL GOOD? IS THERE...
...SOME-THING *GOING* ON?
IT'S FIIINE!
NOTHING YOU TWO NEED TO WORRY ABOUT *ONE BIT*.
ARE YOU GONNA LEAVE?
No!
I WILL NOT!
REALLY?
REALLY!
HEY, SO, I WAS ABOUT TO MAKE HOT CHOCO-LATE.
YOU GUYS WANT SOME?
...YEAH.

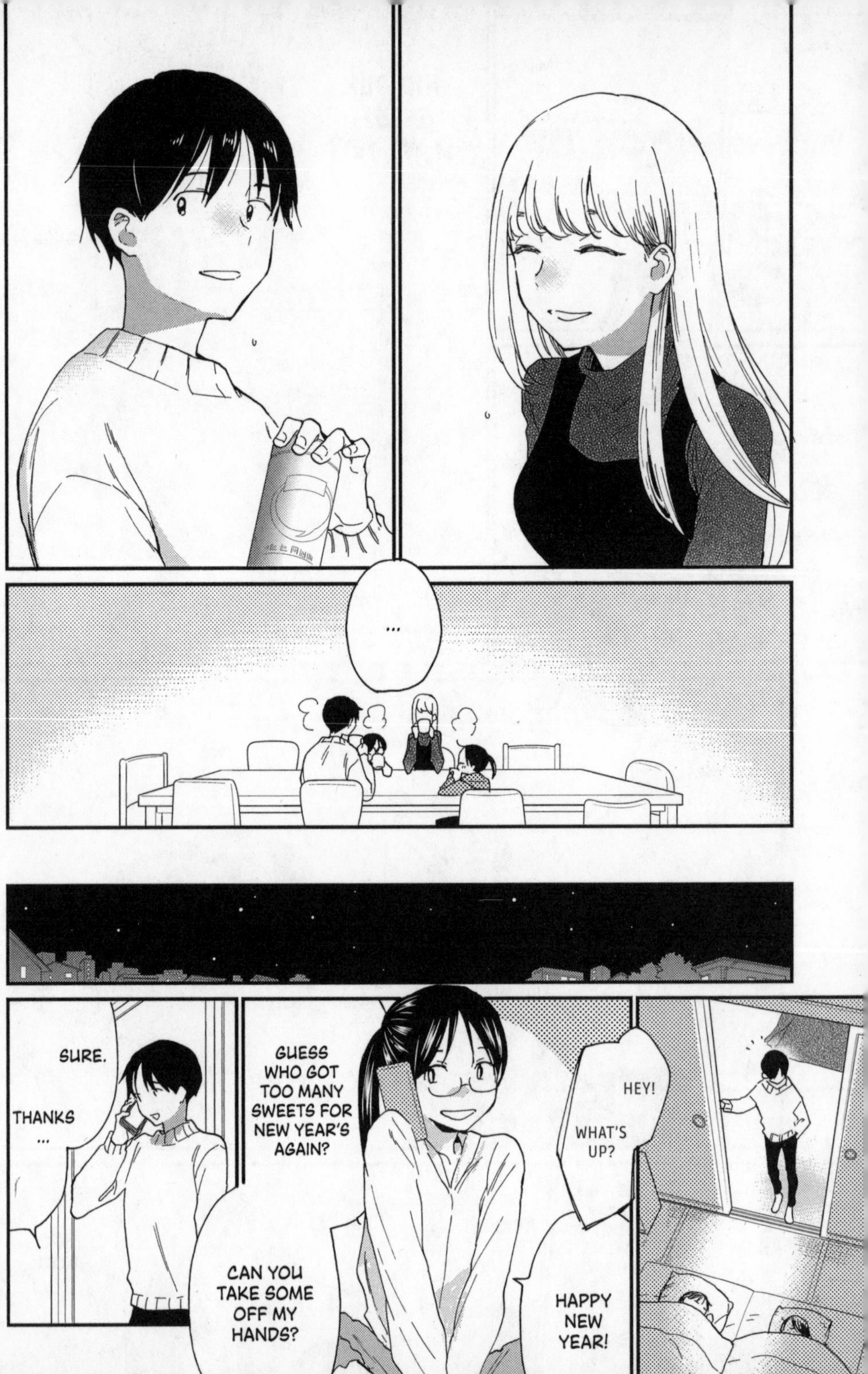
...
HEY!
WHAT'S UP?
HAPPY NEW YEAR!
GUESS WHO GOT TOO MANY SWEETS FOR NEW YEAR'S AGAIN?
CAN YOU TAKE SOME OFF MY HANDS?
SURE.
THANKS ...

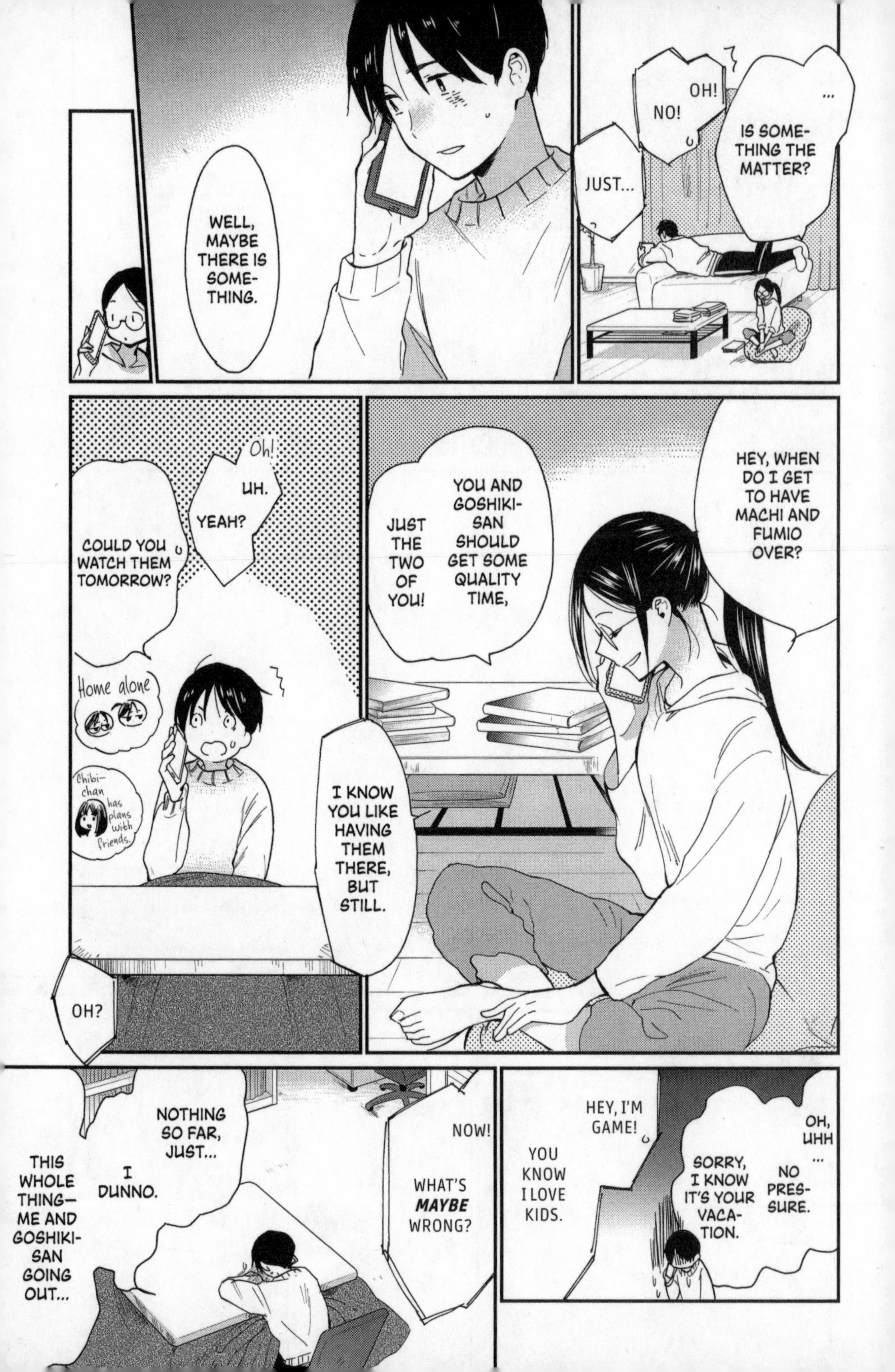
...
IS SOME-THING THE MATTER?
OH! NO!
JUST...
WELL, MAYBE THERE IS SOME-THING.
HEY, WHEN DO I GET TO HAVE MACHI AND FUMIO OVER?
YOU AND GOSHIKI-SAN SHOULD GET SOME QUALITY TIME,
JUST THE TWO OF YOU!
I KNOW YOU LIKE HAVING THEM THERE, BUT STILL.
Oh!
UH.
YEAH?
COULD YOU WATCH THEM TOMORROW?
Home alone
Chibi-chan has plans with friends.
OH?
OH, UHH ...
NO PRES-SURE.
SORRY, I KNOW IT'S YOUR VACA-TION.
HEY, I'M GAME!
YOU KNOW I LOVE KIDS.
NOW!
WHAT'S *MAYBE* WRONG?
NOTHING SO FAR, JUST...
I DUNNO.
THIS WHOLE THING— ME AND GOSHIKI-SAN GOING OUT...

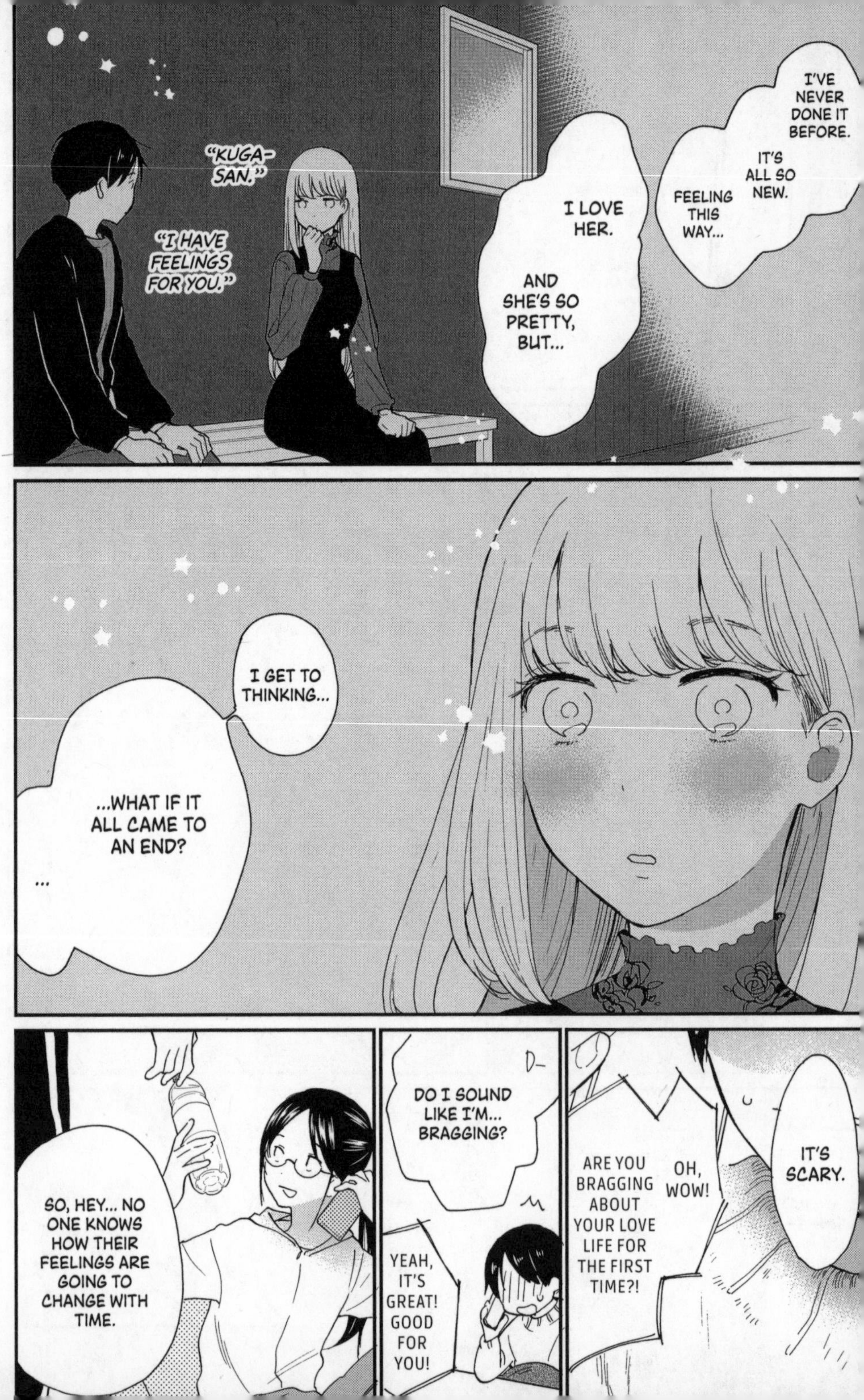
I'VE NEVER DONE IT BEFORE.
IT'S ALL SO NEW.
FEELING THIS WAY...
I LOVE HER.
AND SHE'S SO PRETTY, BUT...
"KUGA-SAN."
"I HAVE FEELINGS FOR YOU."
I GET TO THINKING...
...WHAT IF IT ALL CAME TO AN END?
...
IT'S SCARY.
OH, WOW!
ARE YOU BRAGGING ABOUT YOUR LOVE LIFE FOR THE FIRST TIME?!
D–
DO I SOUND LIKE I'M... BRAGGING?
YEAH, IT'S GREAT! GOOD FOR YOU!
SO, HEY... NO ONE KNOWS HOW THEIR FEELINGS ARE GOING TO CHANGE WITH TIME.

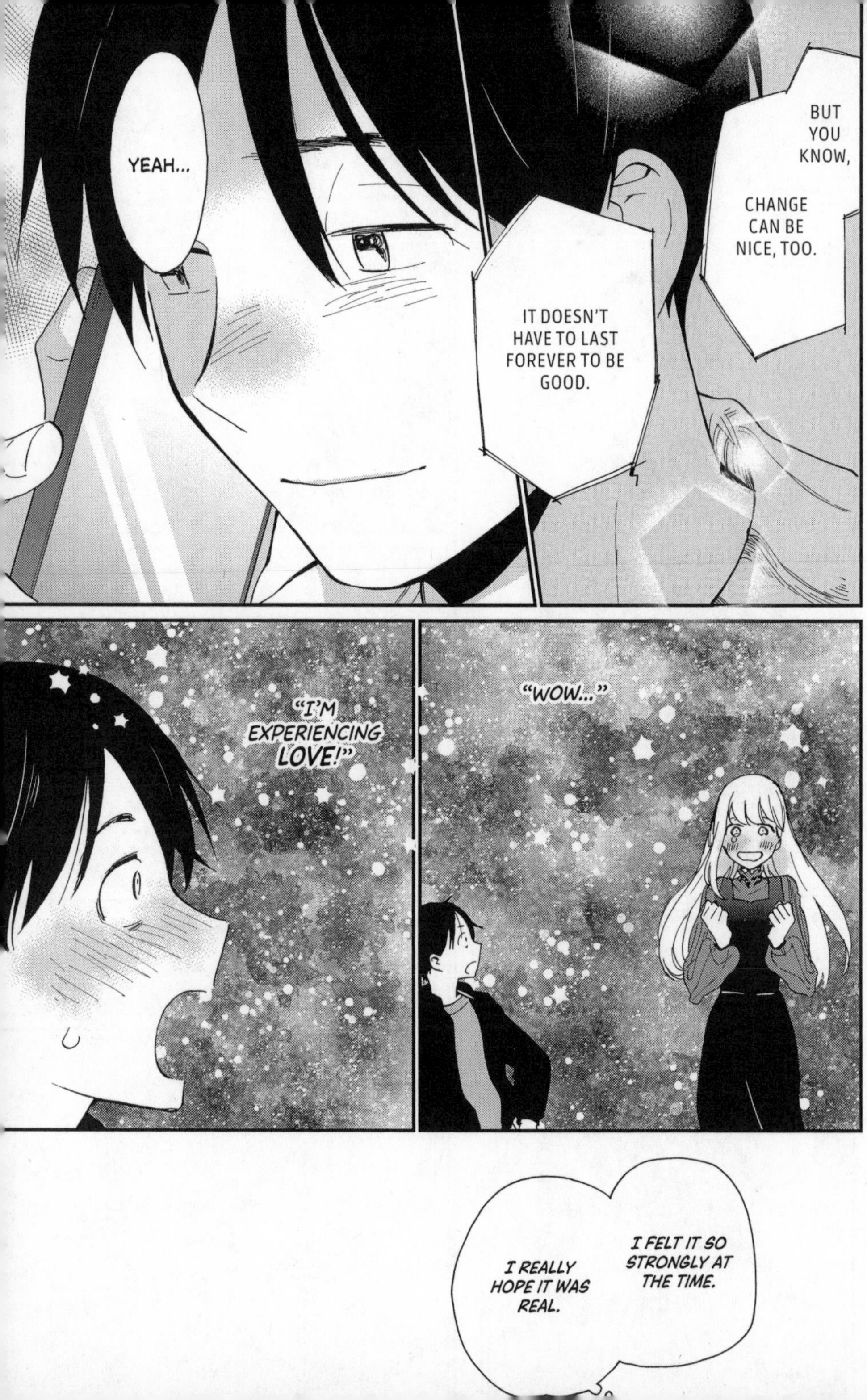
BUT YOU KNOW,
CHANGE CAN BE NICE, TOO.
IT DOESN'T HAVE TO LAST FOREVER TO BE GOOD.
YEAH...
"WOW..."
"I'M EXPERIENCING LOVE!"
I FELT IT SO STRONGLY AT THE TIME.
I REALLY HOPE IT WAS REAL.

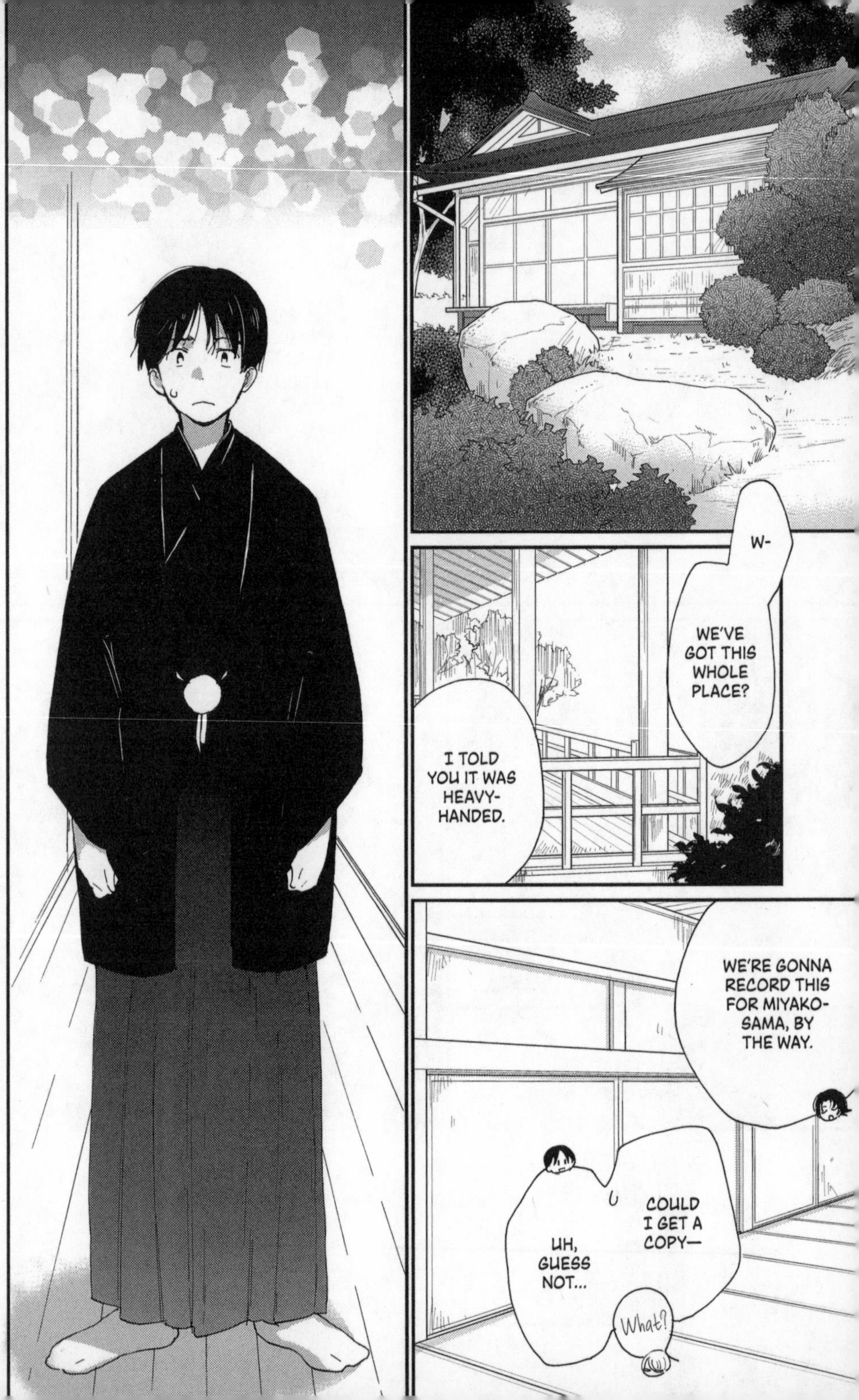
W-
WE'VE GOT THIS WHOLE PLACE?
I TOLD YOU IT WAS HEAVY-HANDED.
WE'RE GONNA RECORD THIS FOR MIYAKO-SAMA, BY THE WAY.
COULD I GET A COPY—
UH, GUESS NOT...
What?

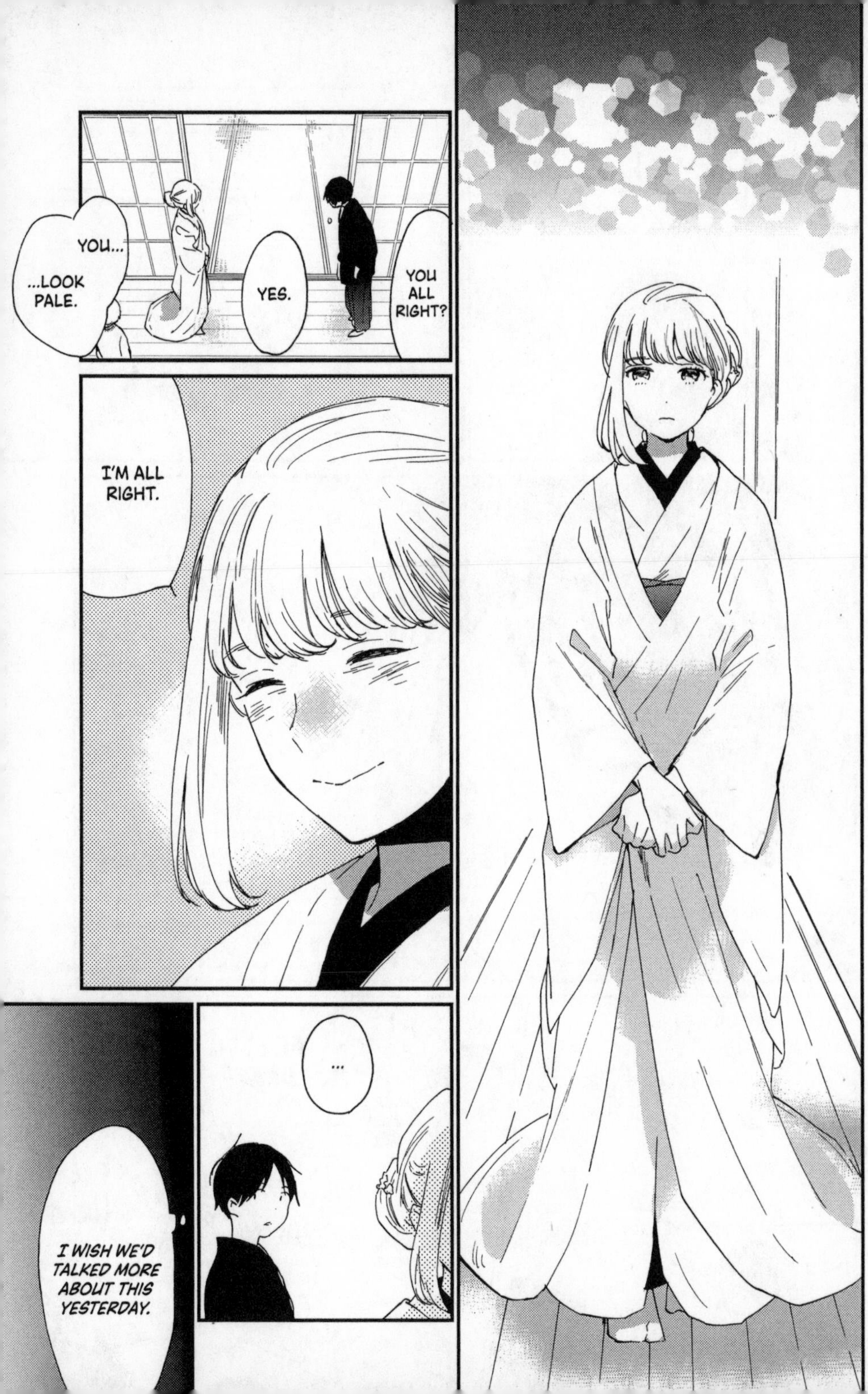
YOU ALL RIGHT?
YES.
YOU...
...LOOK PALE.
I'M ALL RIGHT.
...
I WISH WE'D TALKED MORE ABOUT THIS YESTERDAY.

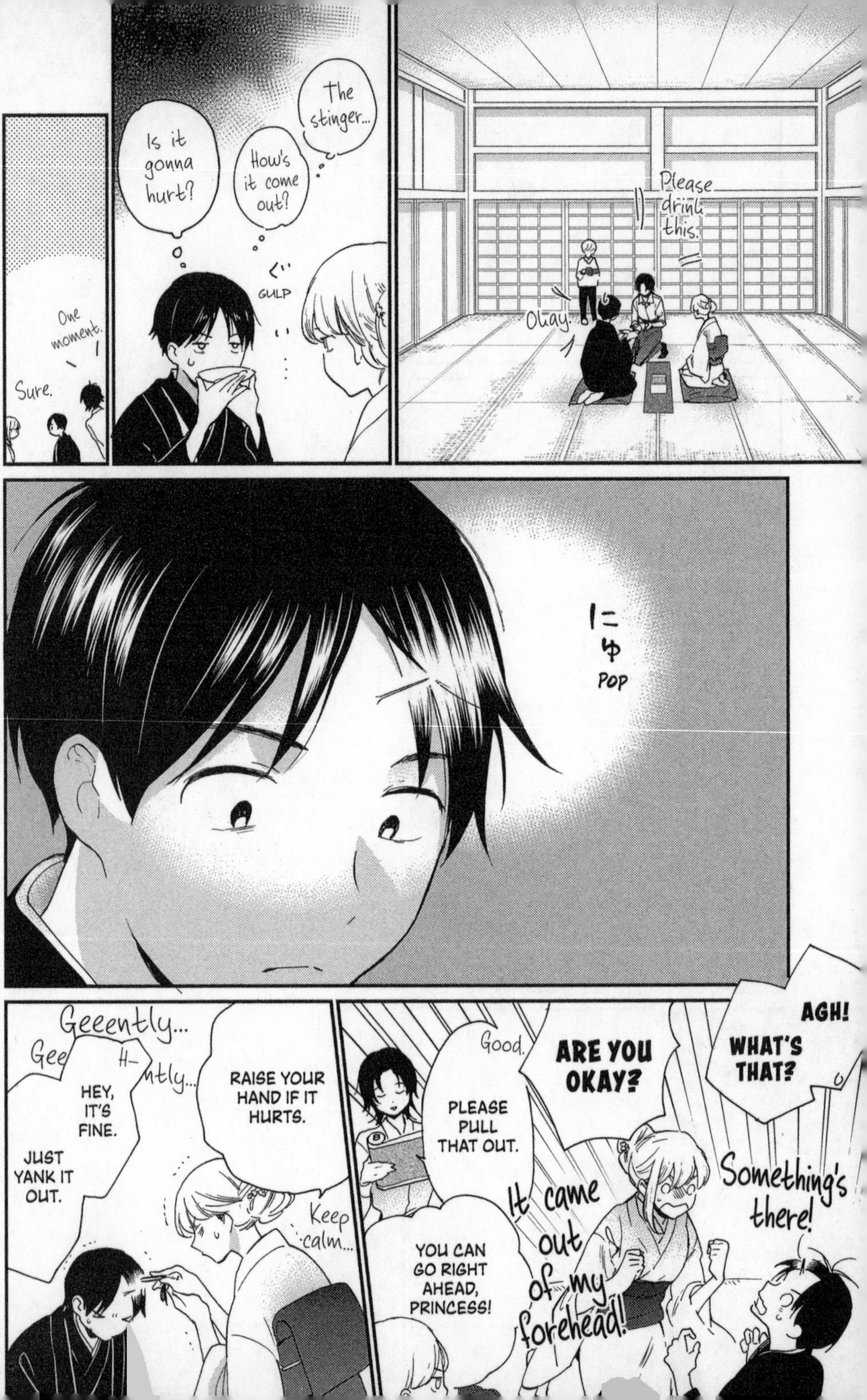
Please drink this.
Okay.
The stinger...
How's it come out?
Is it gonna hurt?
ぐい
GULP
One moment.
Sure.
にゅ
POP
AGH! WHAT'S THAT?
Something's there!
ARE YOU OKAY?
It came out of my forehead!
Good.
PLEASE PULL THAT OUT.
YOU CAN GO RIGHT AHEAD, PRINCESS!
RAISE YOUR HAND IF IT HURTS.
Keep calm...
Geeently...
Gee H– ntly...
HEY, IT'S FINE.
JUST YANK IT OUT.

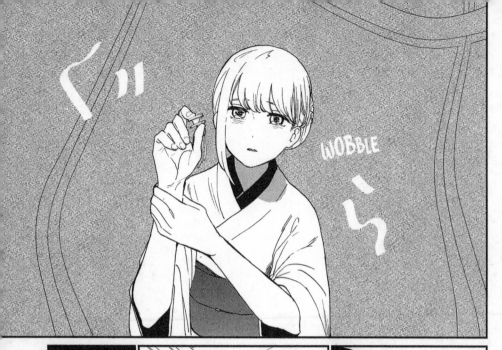

WOBBLE
I'M SCARED.
THIS IS REALLY HAPPENING.
WAI—
I CAN FEEL IT.
THE CONNECTION IS BEING BROKEN.
NO, NO, NO... IF I'D'VE KNOWN IT WOULD BE LIKE THIS, I'D HAVE TRIED TO MAKE HER LAUGH MORE.
INSTEAD OF BEING TOO TIMID TO ACCEPT EVERYTHING SHE OFFERED ME, I SHOULD HAVE BEEN MORE OPEN TO HER FEELINGS—PAID MORE ATTENTION.
I NEED HER TO KNOW HOW MUCH I LOVE HER.

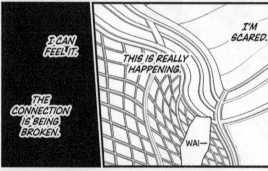

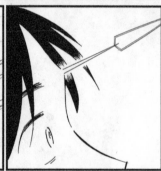

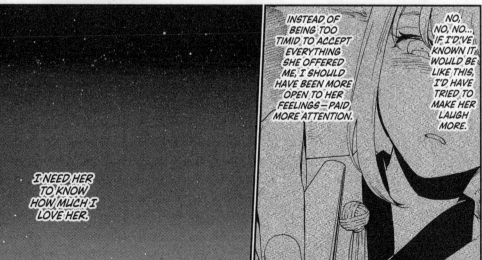

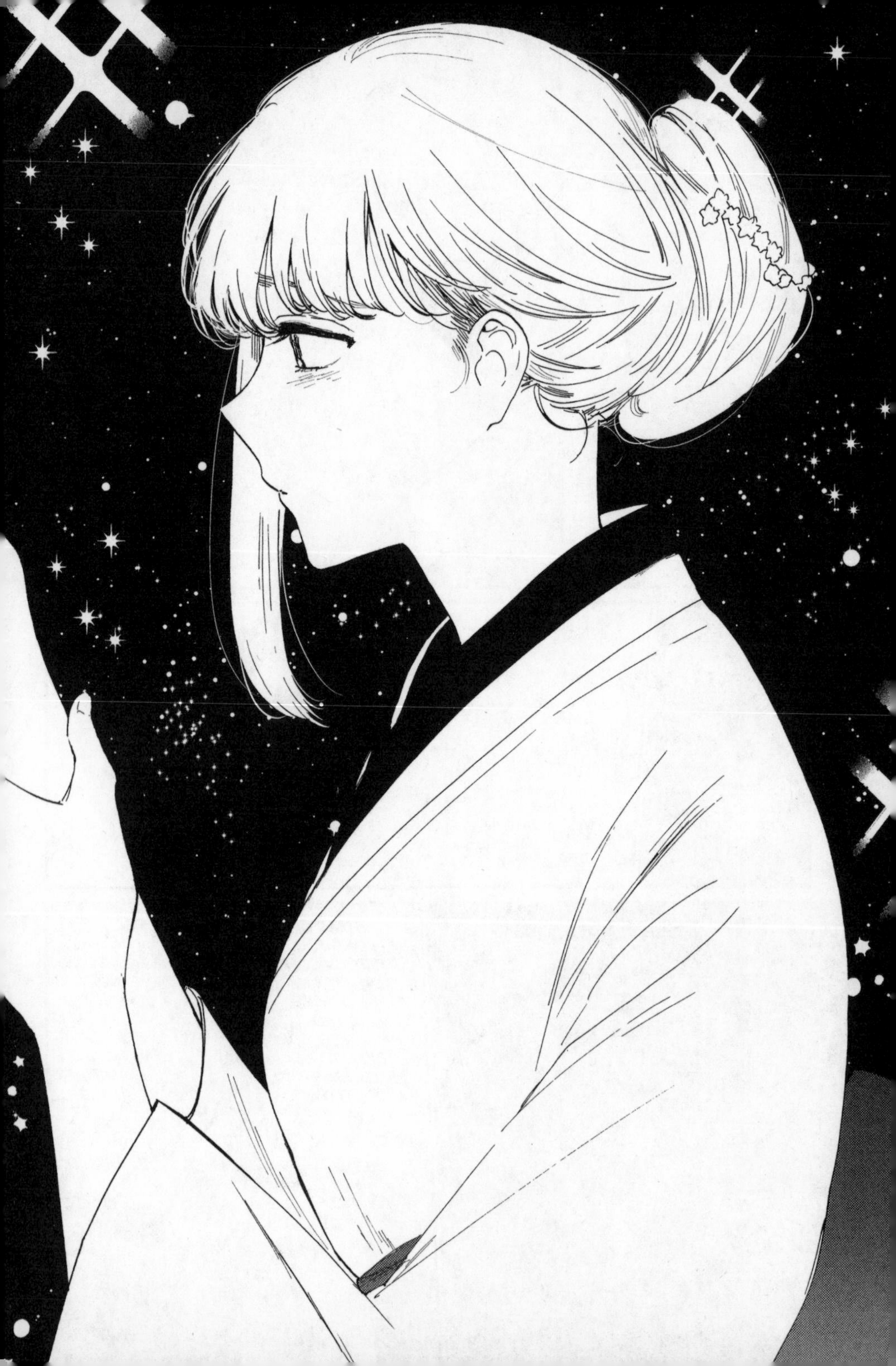

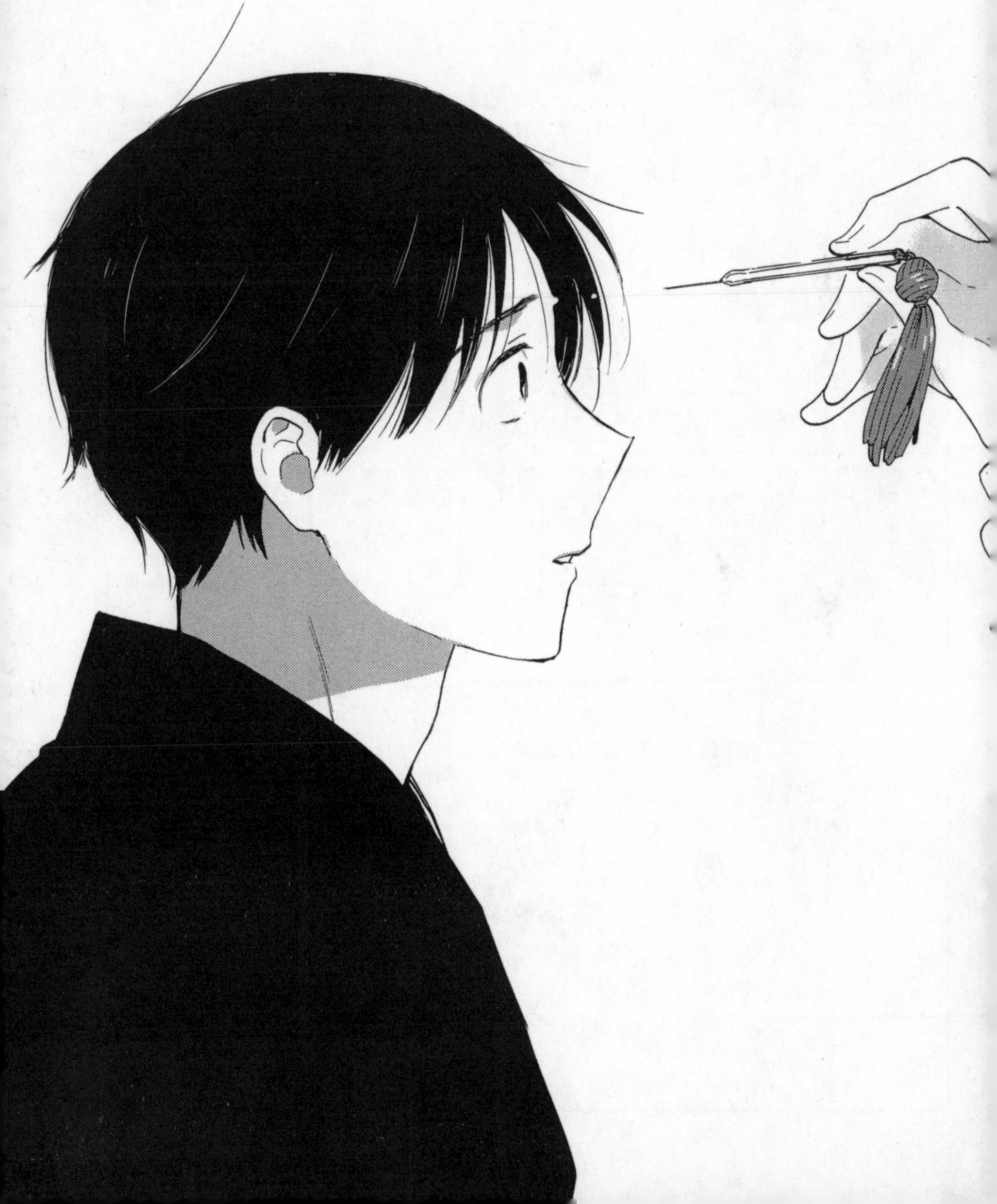

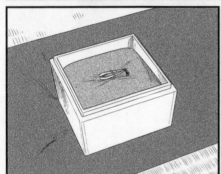

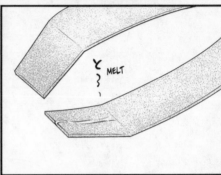

MELT

THAT'S ALL. EVERYTHING WENT ACCORDING TO PLAN.

...

ARE YOU TWO OKAY?

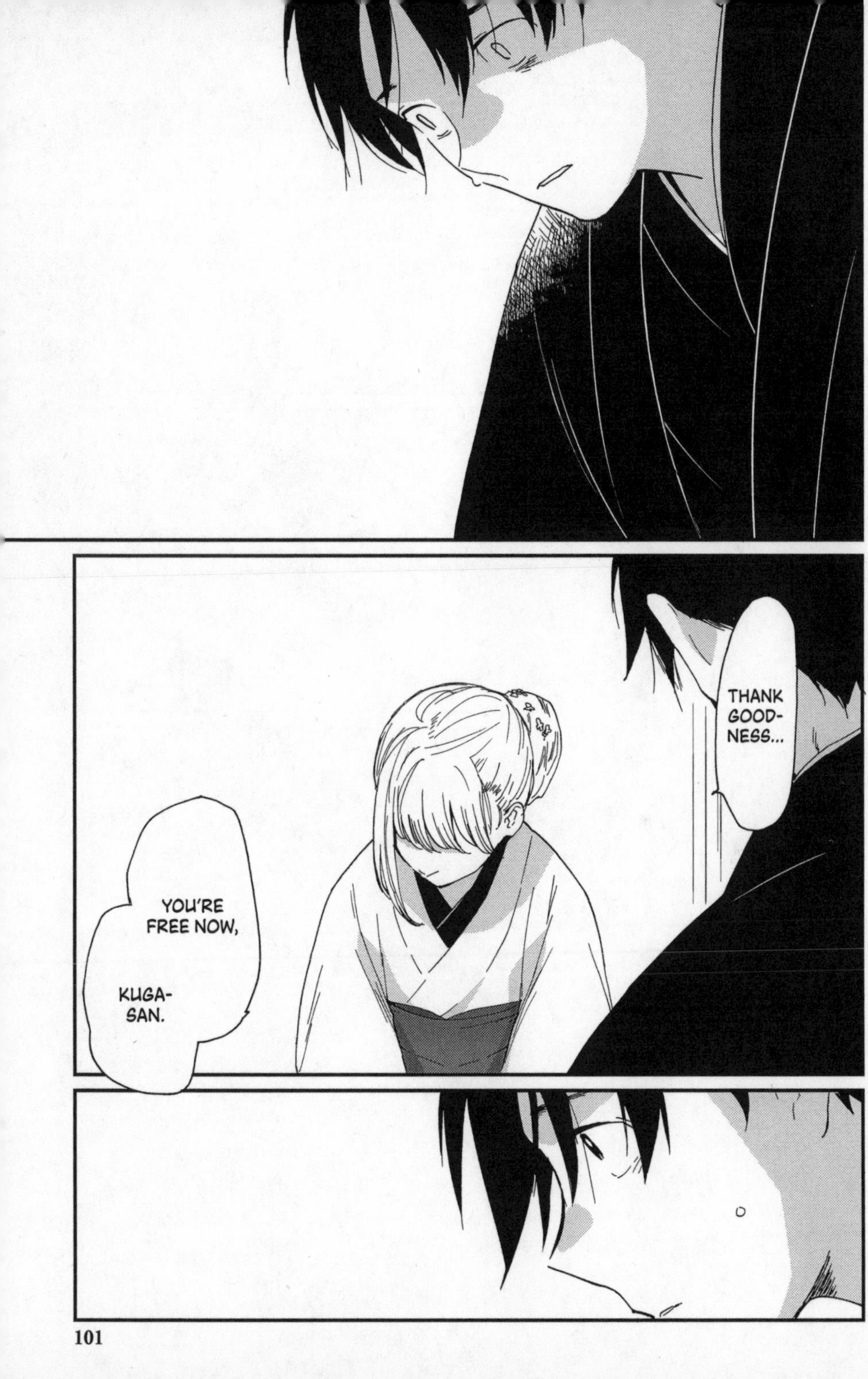
THANK GOOD-NESS...
YOU'RE FREE NOW,
KUGA-SAN.

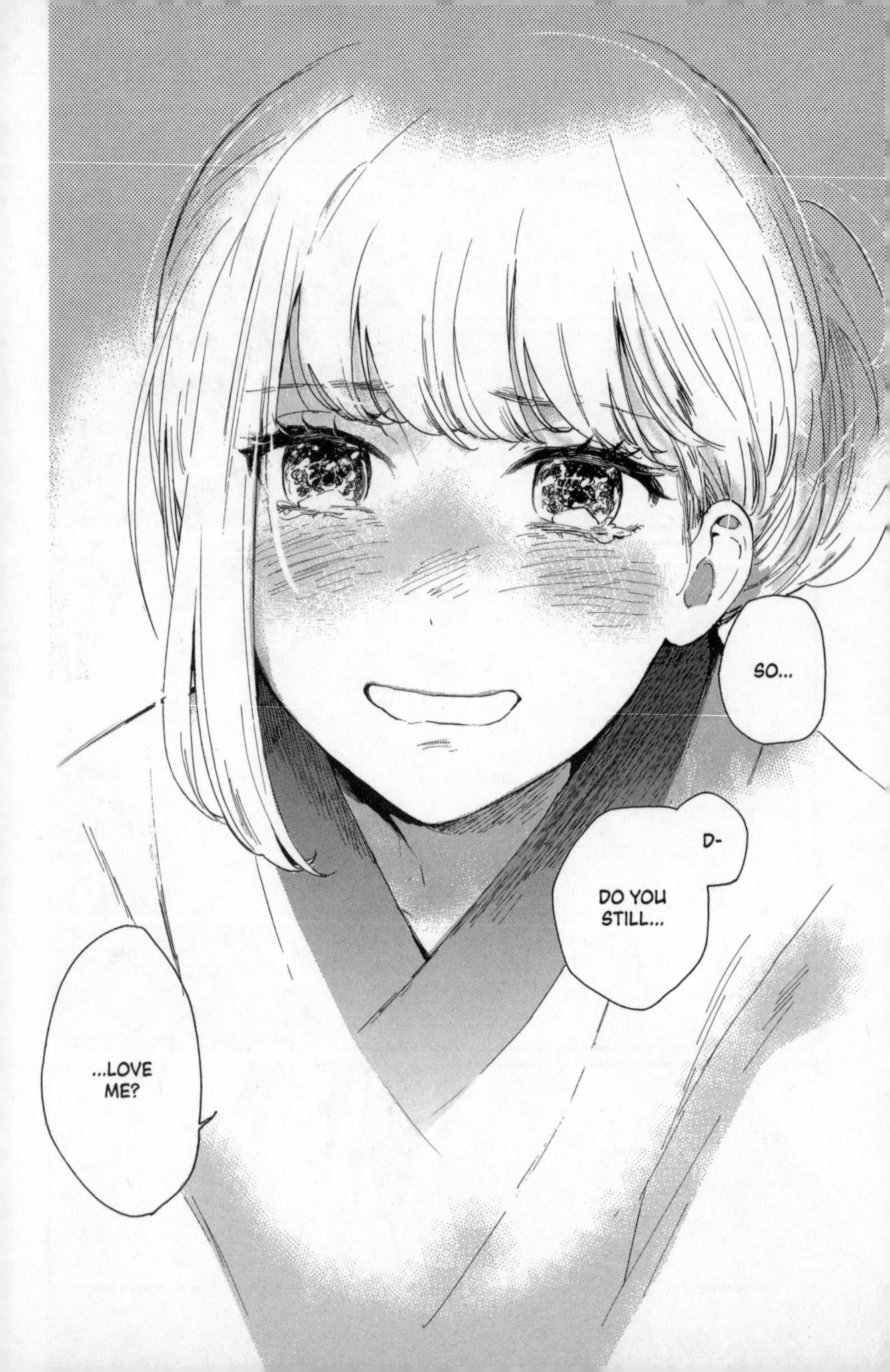
SO...
D-
DO YOU STILL...
...LOVE ME?

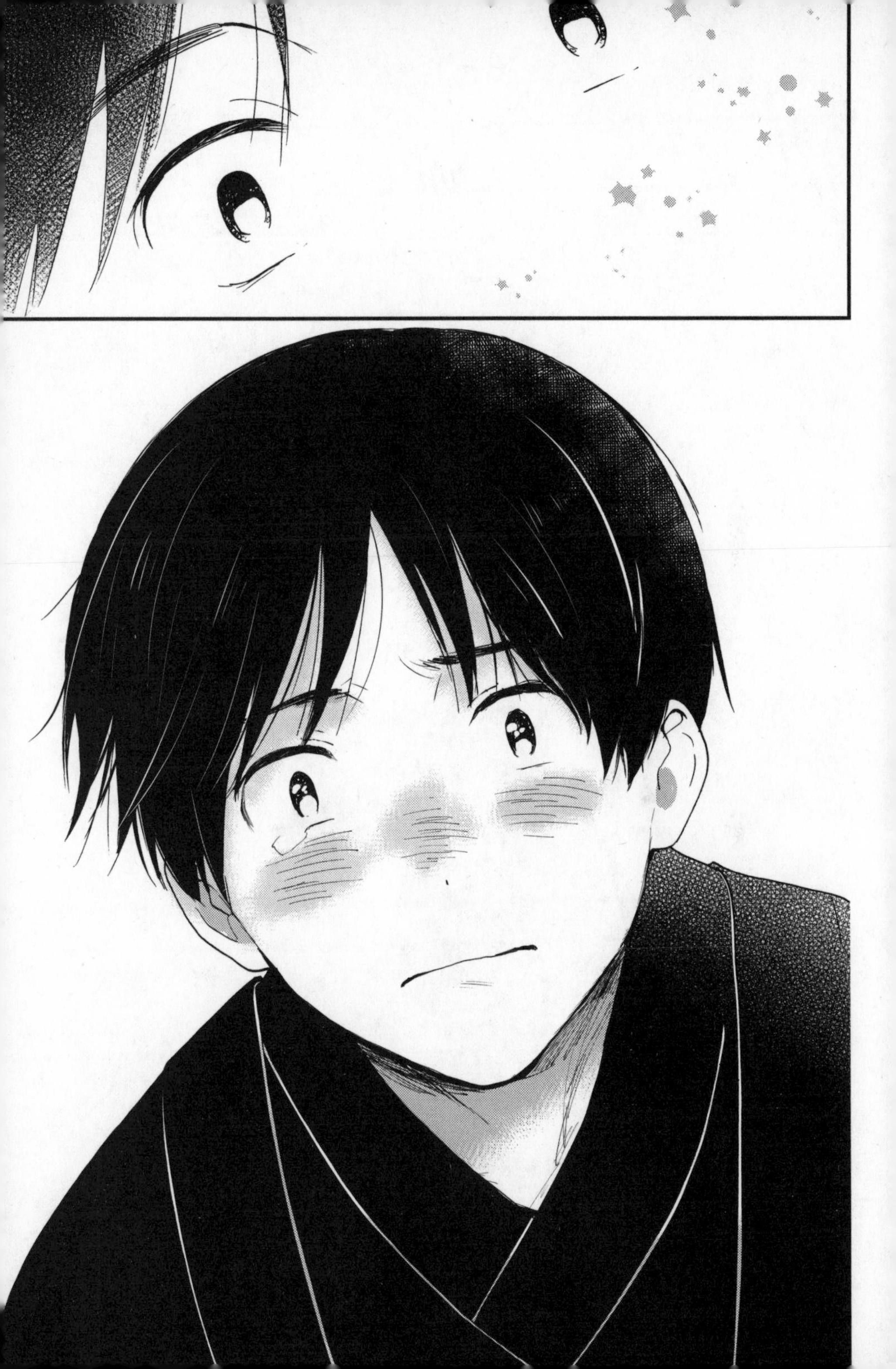

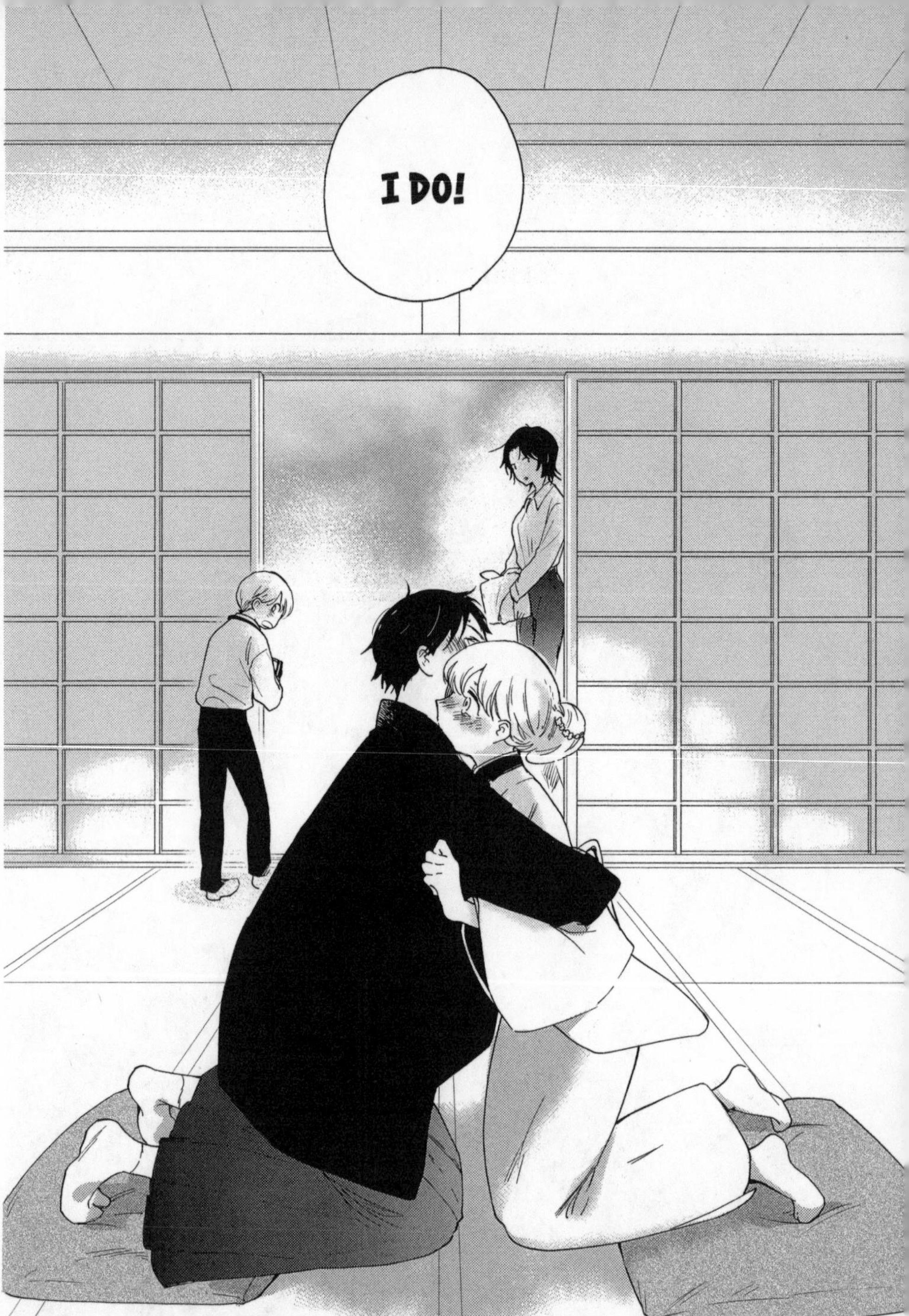
I DO!

CHAPTER 13 ✿ END

A Galaxy Next Door

Gido Amagakure

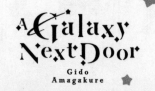

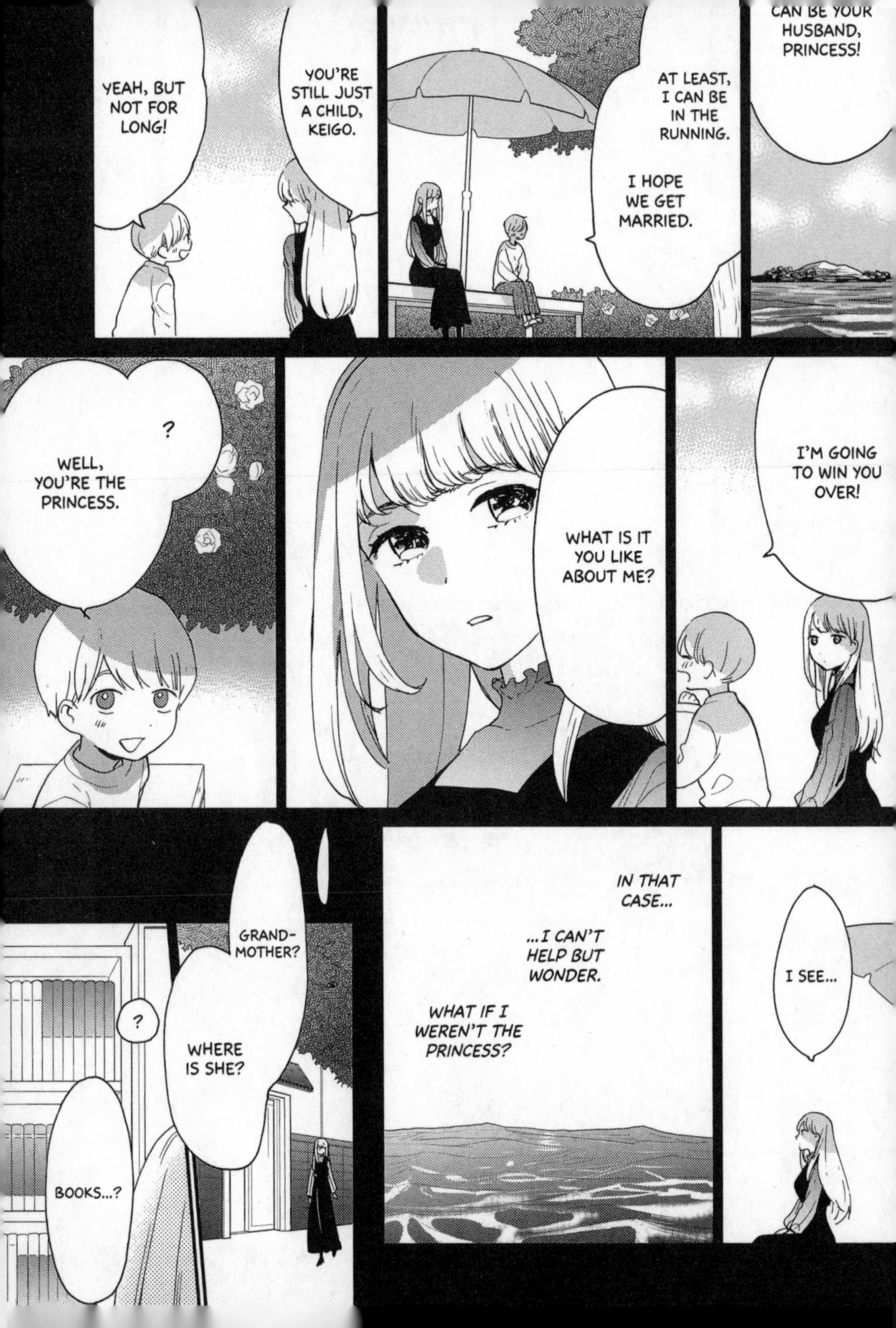
CAN BE YOUR HUSBAND, PRINCESS!
AT LEAST, I CAN BE IN THE RUNNING.
I HOPE WE GET MARRIED.
YOU'RE STILL JUST A CHILD, KEIGO.
YEAH, BUT NOT FOR LONG!
I'M GOING TO WIN YOU OVER!
WHAT IS IT YOU LIKE ABOUT ME?
?
WELL, YOU'RE THE PRINCESS.
I SEE...
IN THAT CASE...
...I CAN'T HELP BUT WONDER.
WHAT IF I WEREN'T THE PRINCESS?
GRAND-MOTHER?
WHERE IS SHE?
?
BOOKS...?

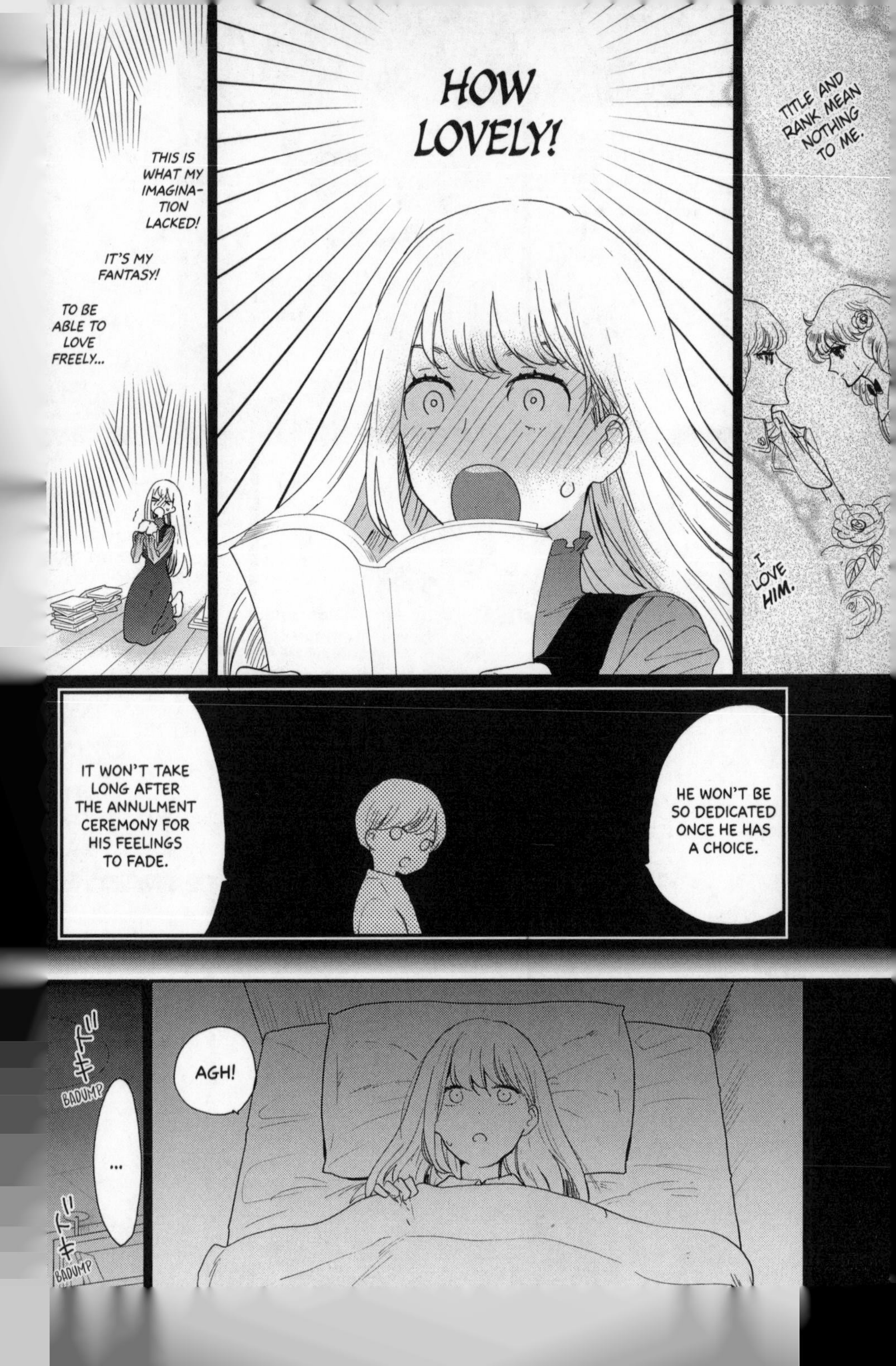
TITLE AND RANK MEAN NOTHING TO ME.
I LOVE HIM.
HOW LOVELY!
THIS IS WHAT MY IMAGINATION LACKED!
IT'S MY FANTASY!
TO BE ABLE TO LOVE FREELY...
HE WON'T BE SO DEDICATED ONCE HE HAS A CHOICE.
IT WON'T TAKE LONG AFTER THE ANNULMENT CEREMONY FOR HIS FEELINGS TO FADE.
AGH!
BADUMP
...
BADUMP

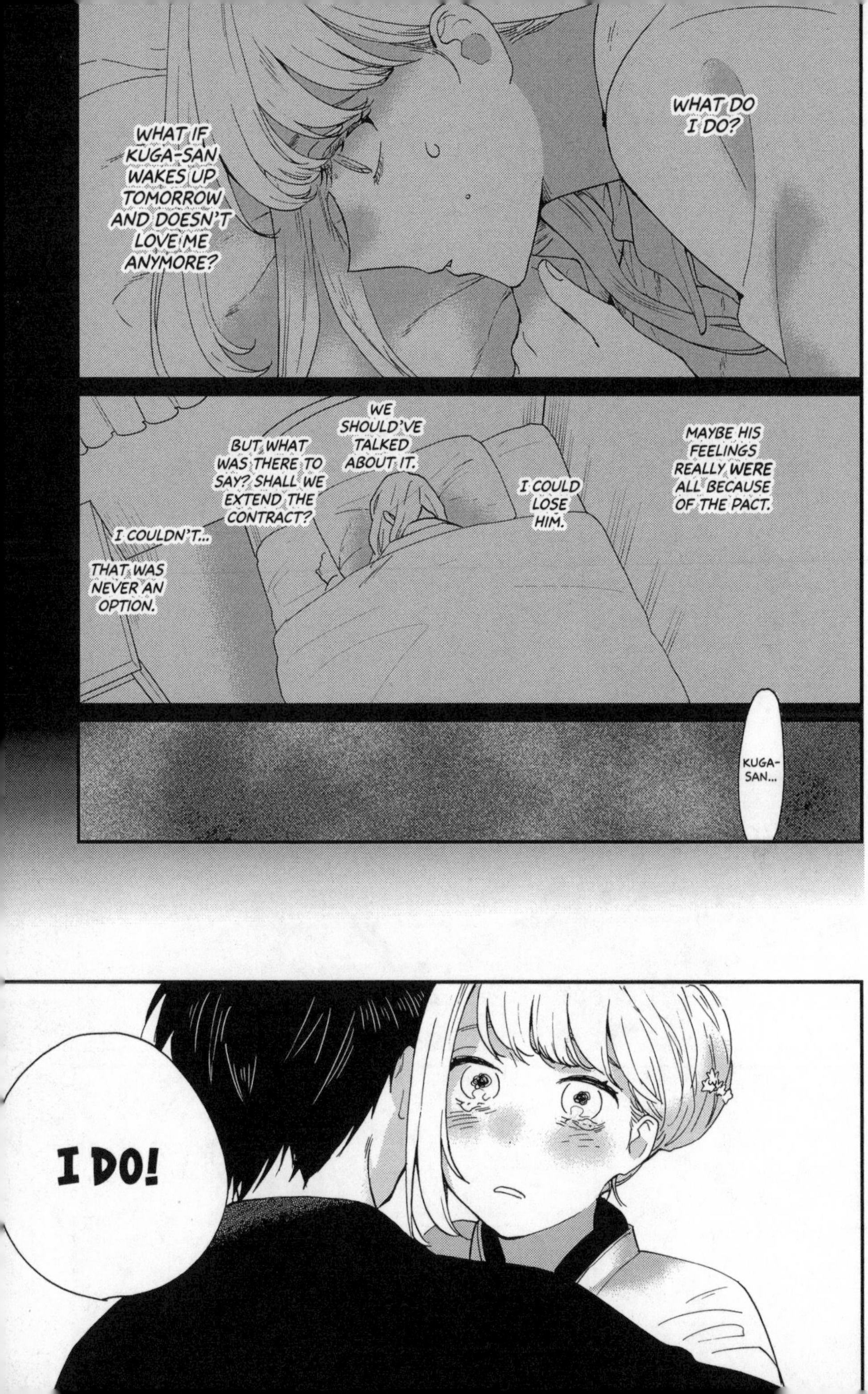
WHAT DO I DO?
WHAT IF KUGA-SAN WAKES UP TOMORROW AND DOESN'T LOVE ME ANYMORE?
MAYBE HIS FEELINGS REALLY WERE ALL BECAUSE OF THE PACT.
I COULD LOSE HIM.
WE SHOULD'VE TALKED ABOUT IT.
BUT WHAT WAS THERE TO SAY? SHALL WE EXTEND THE CONTRACT?
I COULDN'T...
THAT WAS NEVER AN OPTION.
KUGA-SAN...
I DO!

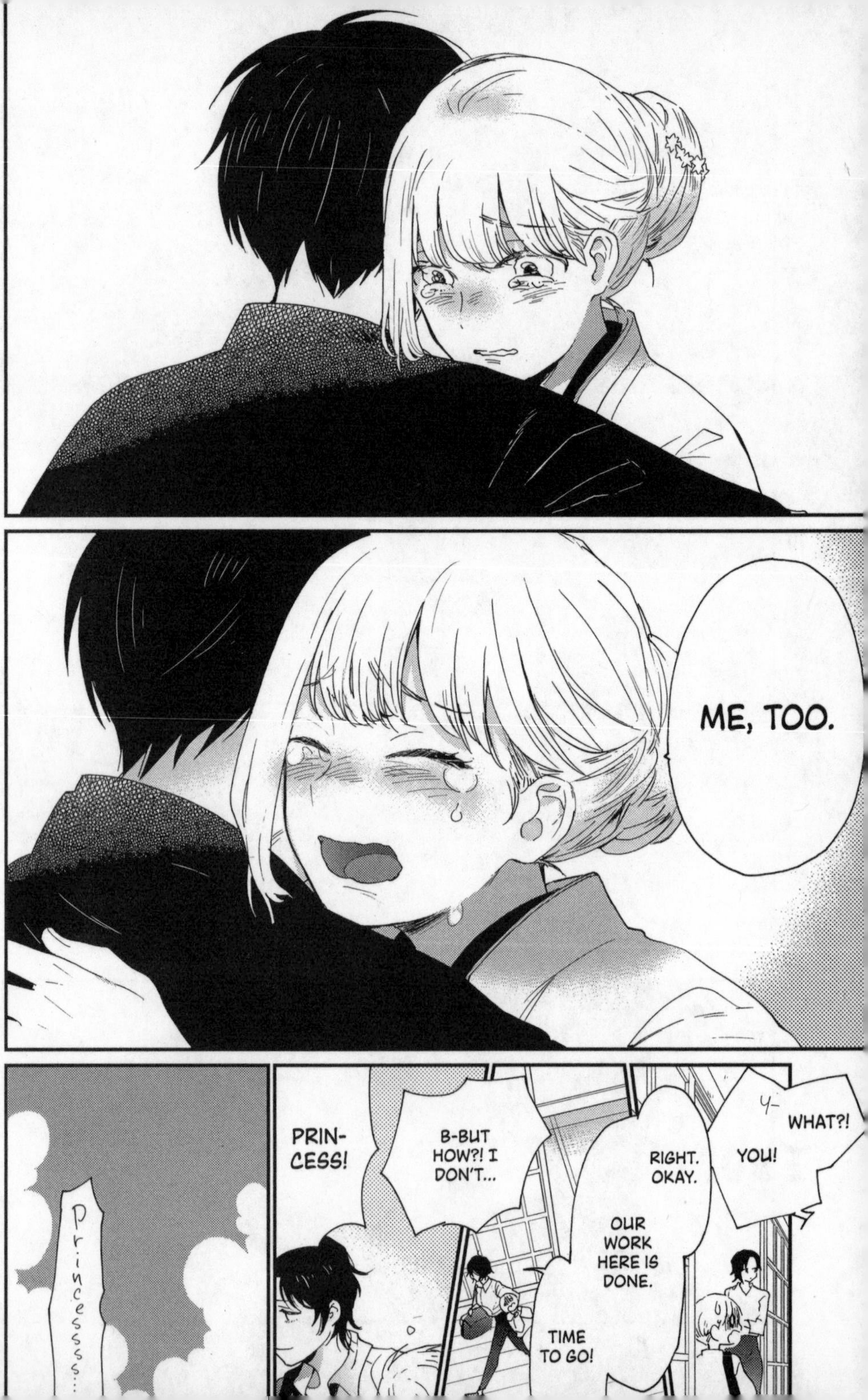
ME, TOO.
Y-
WHAT?!
YOU!
RIGHT. OKAY.
OUR WORK HERE IS DONE.
TIME TO GO!
B-BUT HOW?! I DON'T...
PRIN-CESS!
Princesss...

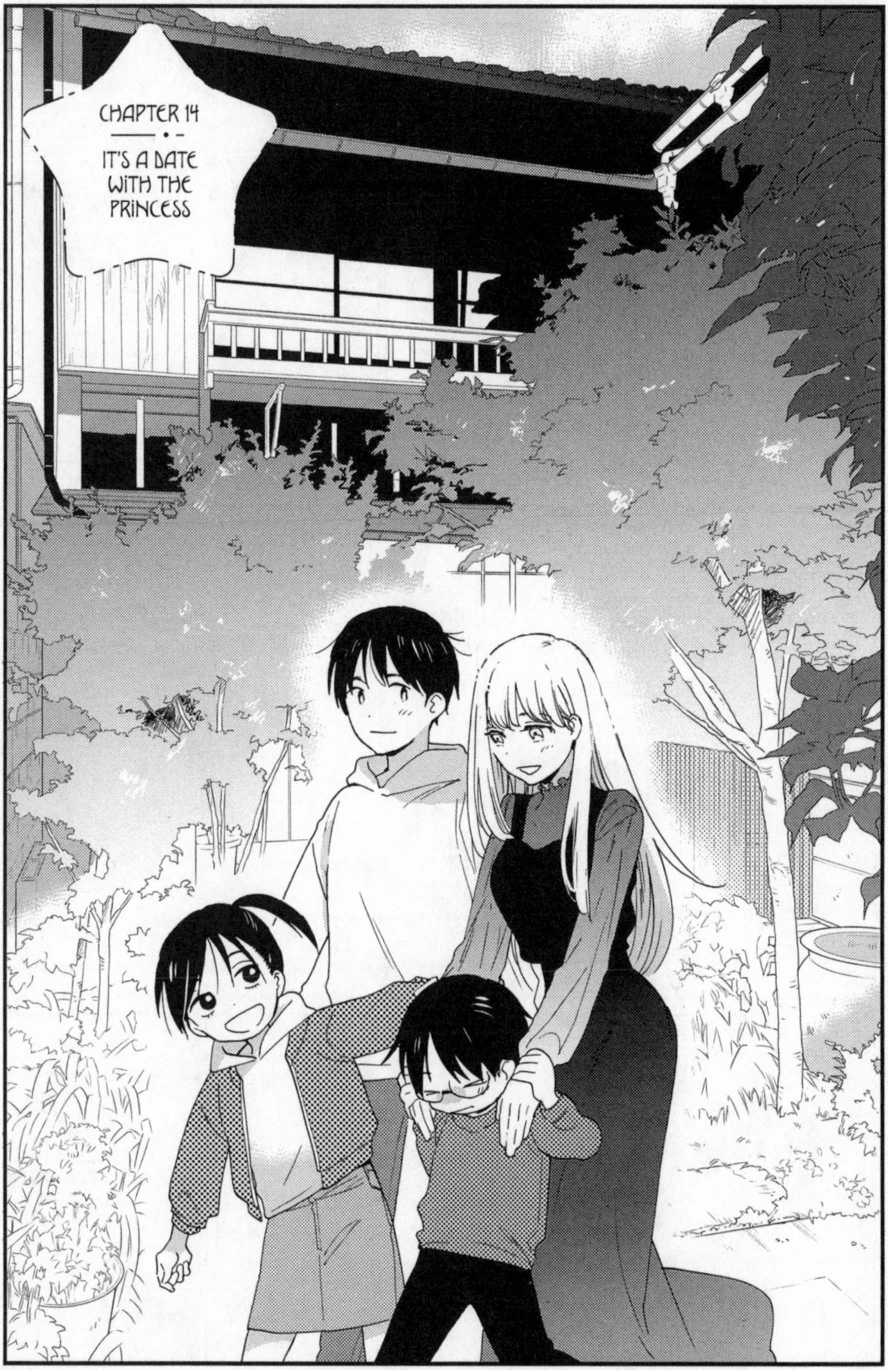
CHAPTER 14
IT'S A DATE WITH THE PRINCESS

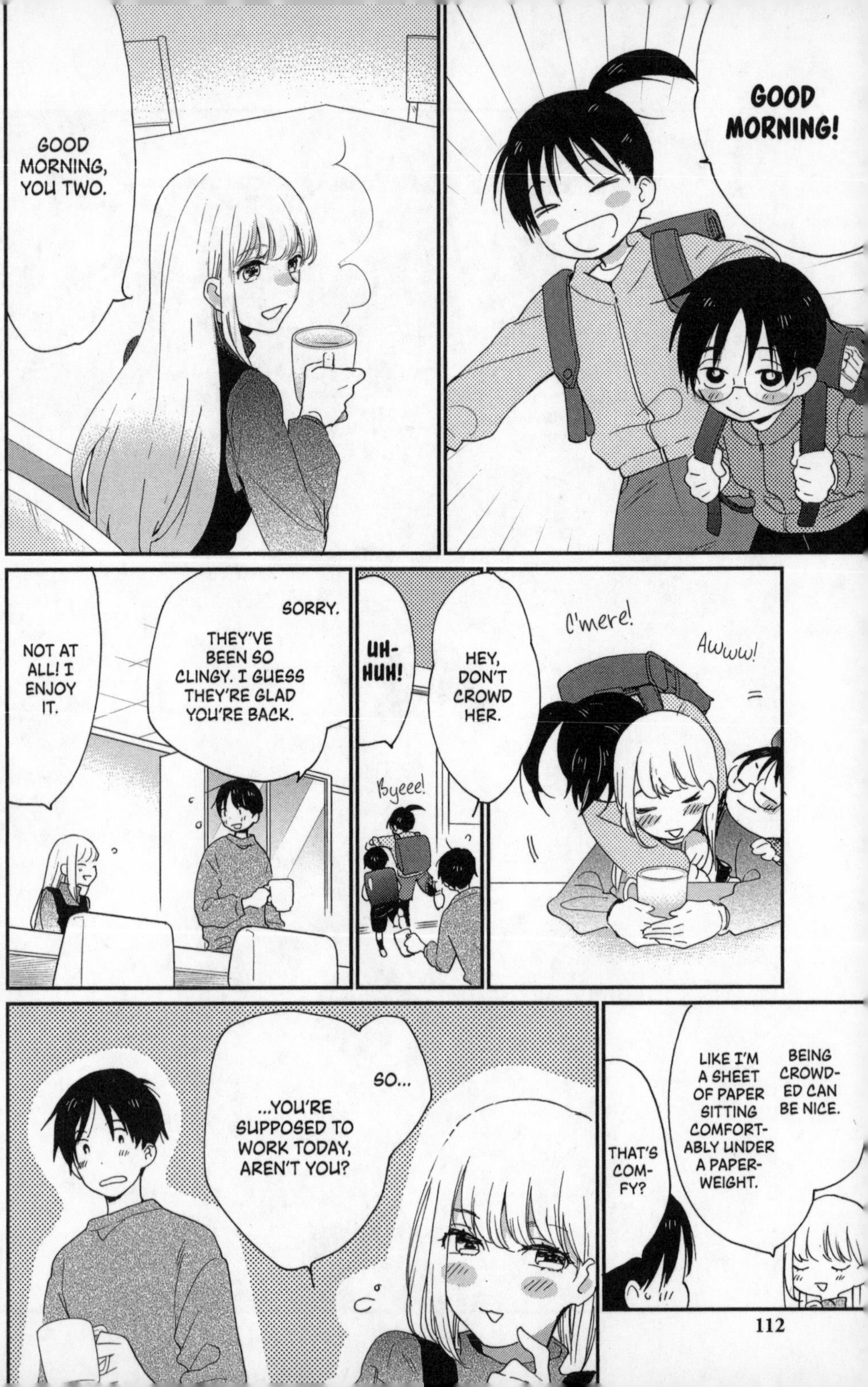
GOOD MORNING!
GOOD MORNING, YOU TWO.
C'mere!
Awww!
HEY, DON'T CROWD HER.
UH-HUH!
Byeee!
SORRY.
THEY'VE BEEN SO CLINGY. I GUESS THEY'RE GLAD YOU'RE BACK.
NOT AT ALL! I ENJOY IT.
BEING CROWDED CAN BE NICE.
LIKE I'M A SHEET OF PAPER SITTING COMFORTABLY UNDER A PAPERWEIGHT.
THAT'S COMFY?
SO...
...YOU'RE SUPPOSED TO WORK TODAY, AREN'T YOU?

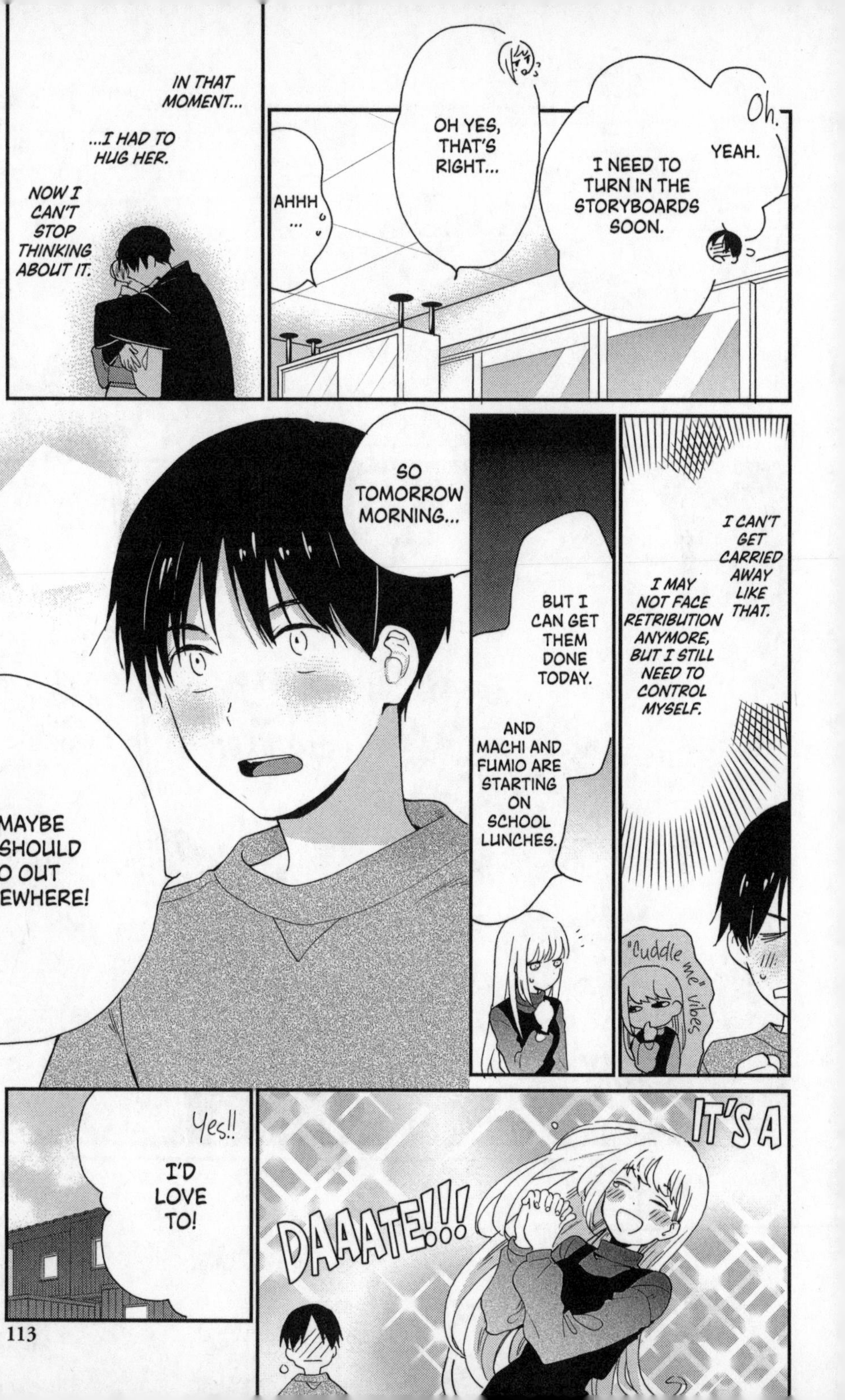
Oh.
YEAH.
I NEED TO TURN IN THE STORYBOARDS SOON.
OH YES, THAT'S RIGHT...
AHHH...
IN THAT MOMENT...
...I HAD TO HUG HER.
NOW I CAN'T STOP THINKING ABOUT IT.
I CAN'T GET CARRIED AWAY LIKE THAT.
I MAY NOT FACE RETRIBUTION ANYMORE, BUT I STILL NEED TO CONTROL MYSELF.
"Cuddle me" vibes
BUT I CAN GET THEM DONE TODAY.
AND MACHI AND FUMIO ARE STARTING ON SCHOOL LUNCHES.
SO TOMORROW MORNING...
...MAYBE WE SHOULD GO OUT SOMEWHERE!
IT'S A DAAATE!!!
Yes!!
I'D LOVE TO!

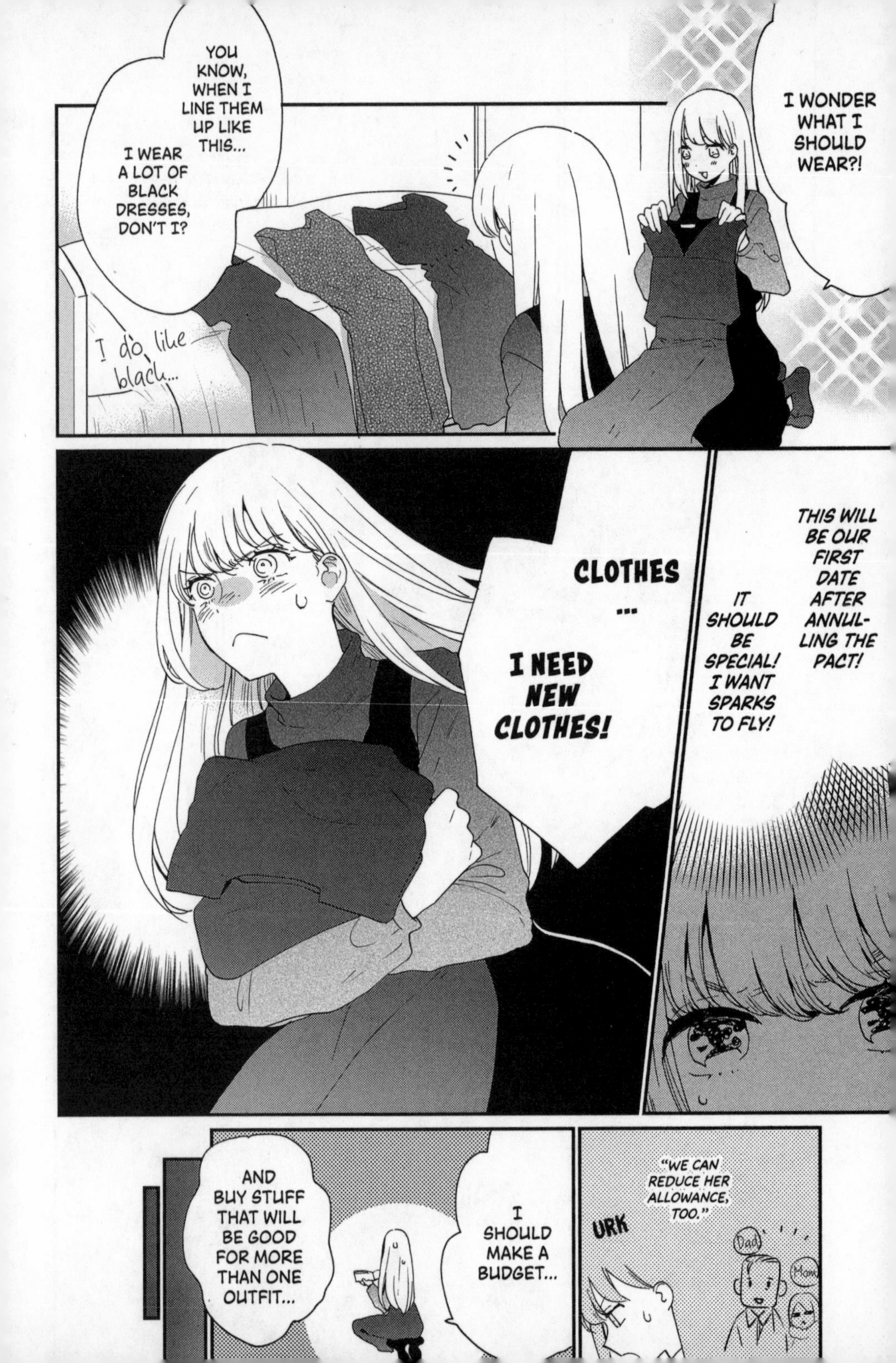
I WONDER WHAT I SHOULD WEAR?!
YOU KNOW, WHEN I LINE THEM UP LIKE THIS...
I WEAR A LOT OF BLACK DRESSES, DON'T I?
I do like black...
THIS WILL BE OUR FIRST DATE AFTER ANNUL-LING THE PACT!
IT SHOULD BE SPECIAL! I WANT SPARKS TO FLY!
CLOTHES...
I NEED NEW CLOTHES!
"WE CAN REDUCE HER ALLOWANCE, TOO."
URK
Dad
Mom
I SHOULD MAKE A BUDGET...
AND BUY STUFF THAT WILL BE GOOD FOR MORE THAN ONE OUTFIT...

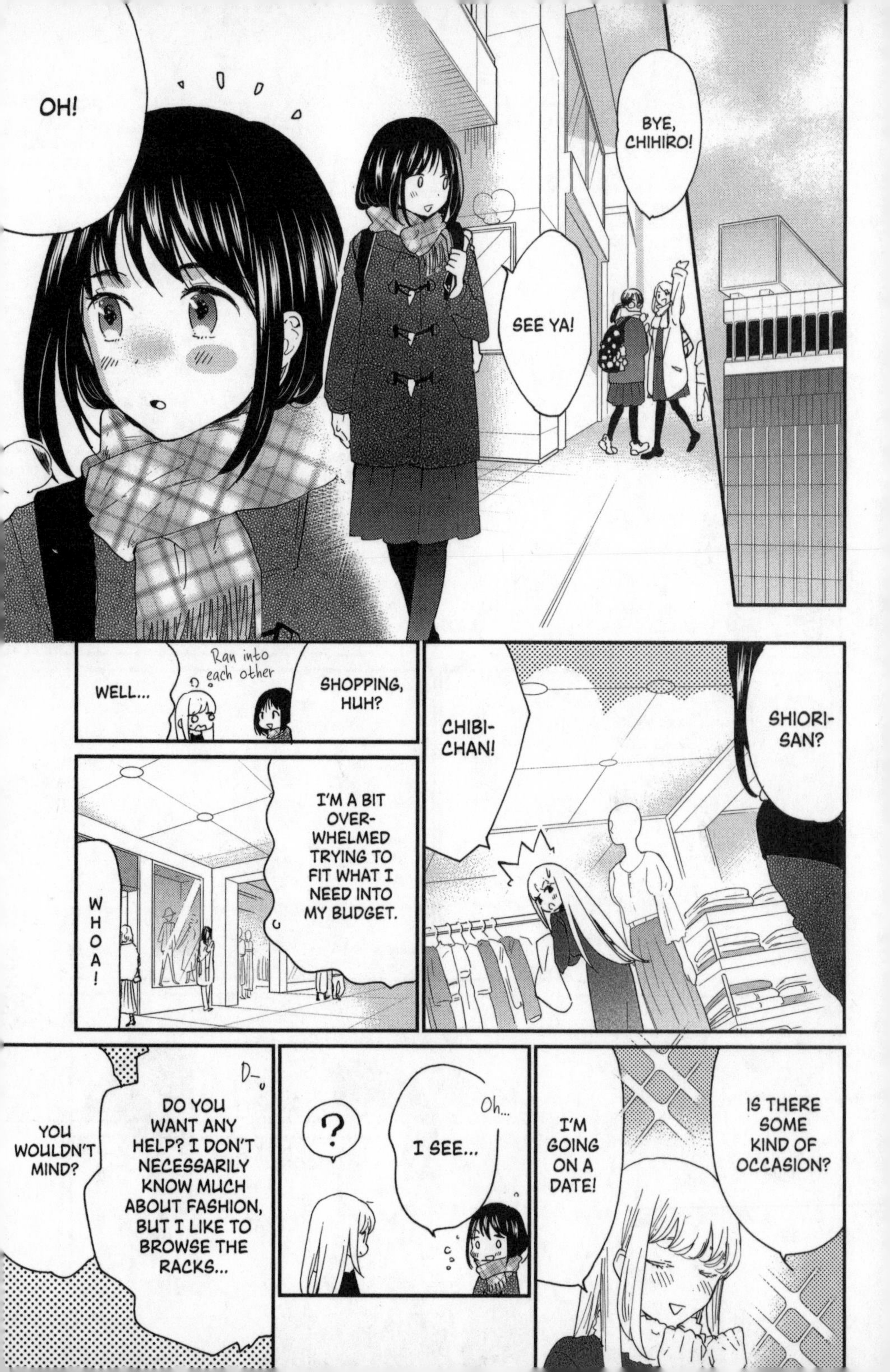
BYE, CHIHIRO!
SEE YA!
OH!
SHIORI-SAN?
CHIBI-CHAN!
SHOPPING, HUH?
Ran into each other
WELL...
I'M A BIT OVER-WHELMED TRYING TO FIT WHAT I NEED INTO MY BUDGET.
WHOA!
IS THERE SOME KIND OF OCCASION?
I'M GOING ON A DATE!
Oh...
I SEE...
?
D–
DO YOU WANT ANY HELP? I DON'T NECESSARILY KNOW MUCH ABOUT FASHION, BUT I LIKE TO BROWSE THE RACKS...
YOU WOULDN'T MIND?

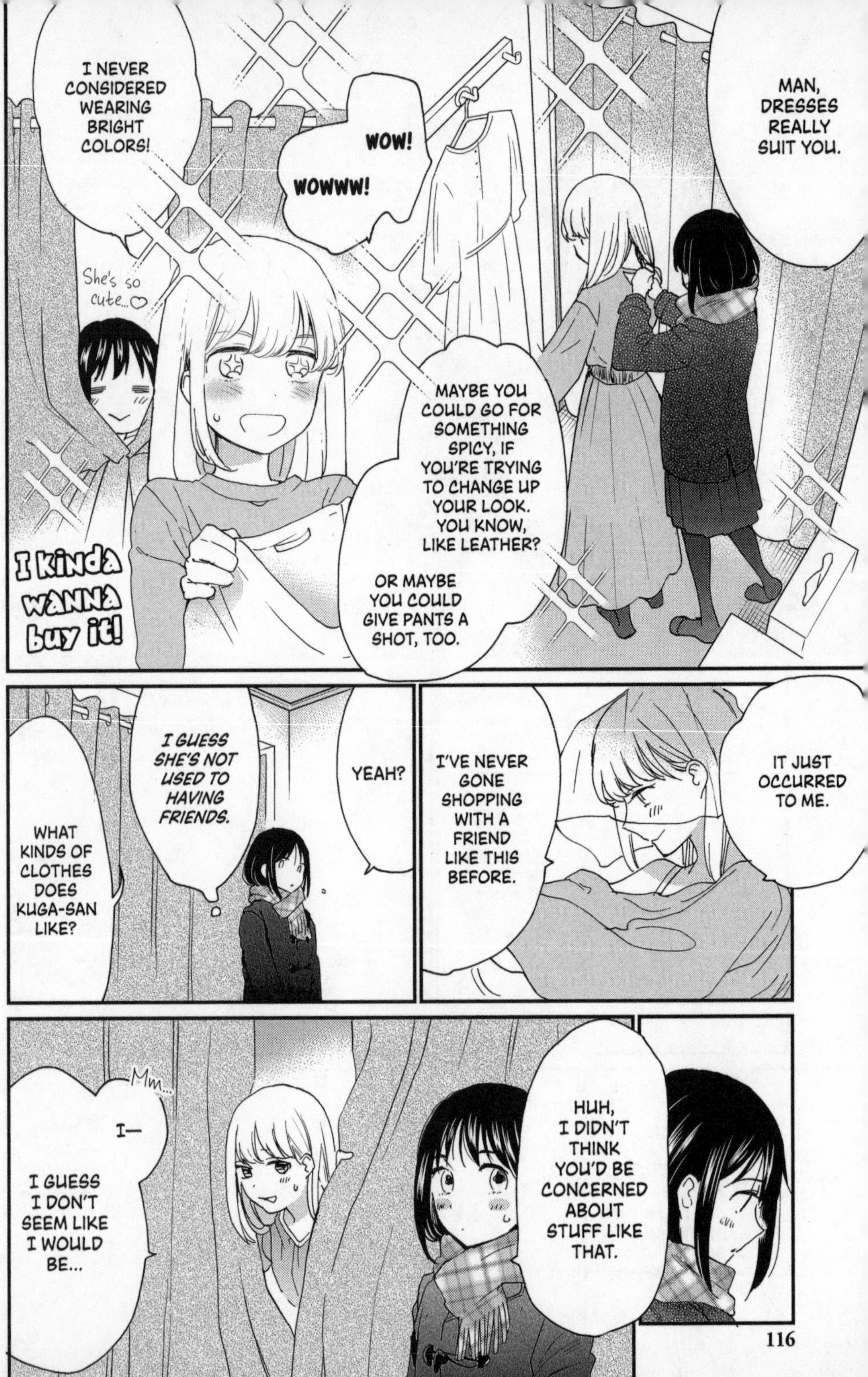
MAN, DRESSES REALLY SUIT YOU.
WOW!
WOWWW!
I NEVER CONSIDERED WEARING BRIGHT COLORS!
She's so cute...♡
MAYBE YOU COULD GO FOR SOMETHING SPICY, IF YOU'RE TRYING TO CHANGE UP YOUR LOOK. YOU KNOW, LIKE LEATHER?
OR MAYBE YOU COULD GIVE PANTS A SHOT, TOO.
I kinda wanna buy it!
IT JUST OCCURRED TO ME.
I'VE NEVER GONE SHOPPING WITH A FRIEND LIKE THIS BEFORE.
YEAH?
I GUESS SHE'S NOT USED TO HAVING FRIENDS.
WHAT KINDS OF CLOTHES DOES KUGA-SAN LIKE?
HUH, I DIDN'T THINK YOU'D BE CONCERNED ABOUT STUFF LIKE THAT.
Mm...
I—
I GUESS I DON'T SEEM LIKE I WOULD BE...

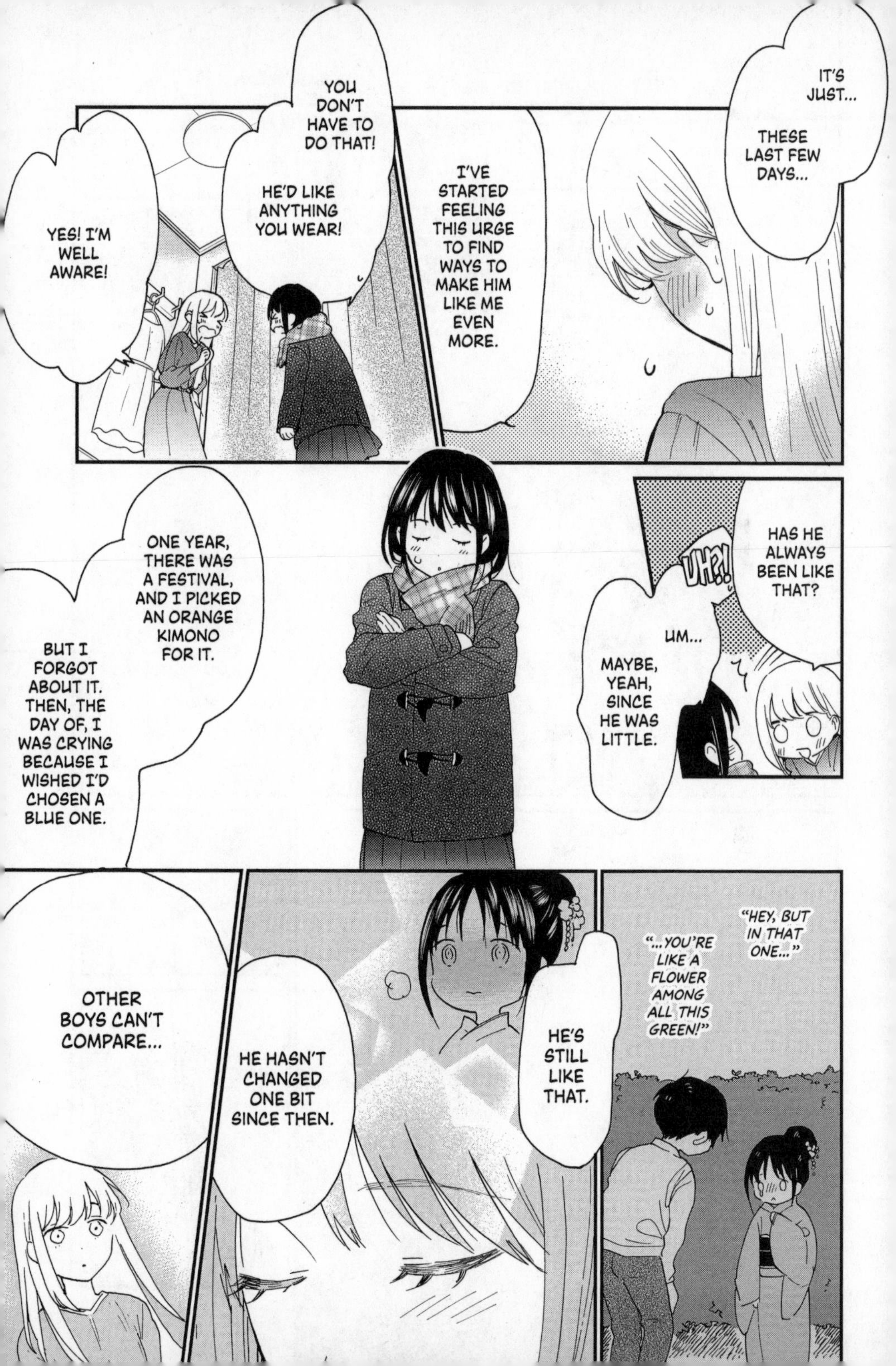
IT'S JUST...
THESE LAST FEW DAYS...
I'VE STARTED FEELING THIS URGE TO FIND WAYS TO MAKE HIM LIKE ME EVEN MORE.
YOU DON'T HAVE TO DO THAT!
HE'D LIKE ANYTHING YOU WEAR!
YES! I'M WELL AWARE!
HAS HE ALWAYS BEEN LIKE THAT?
UH?!
UM...
MAYBE, YEAH, SINCE HE WAS LITTLE.
ONE YEAR, THERE WAS A FESTIVAL, AND I PICKED AN ORANGE KIMONO FOR IT.
BUT I FORGOT ABOUT IT. THEN, THE DAY OF, I WAS CRYING BECAUSE I WISHED I'D CHOSEN A BLUE ONE.
"HEY, BUT IN THAT ONE..."
"...YOU'RE LIKE A FLOWER AMONG ALL THIS GREEN!"
HE'S STILL LIKE THAT.
HE HASN'T CHANGED ONE BIT SINCE THEN.
OTHER BOYS CAN'T COMPARE...

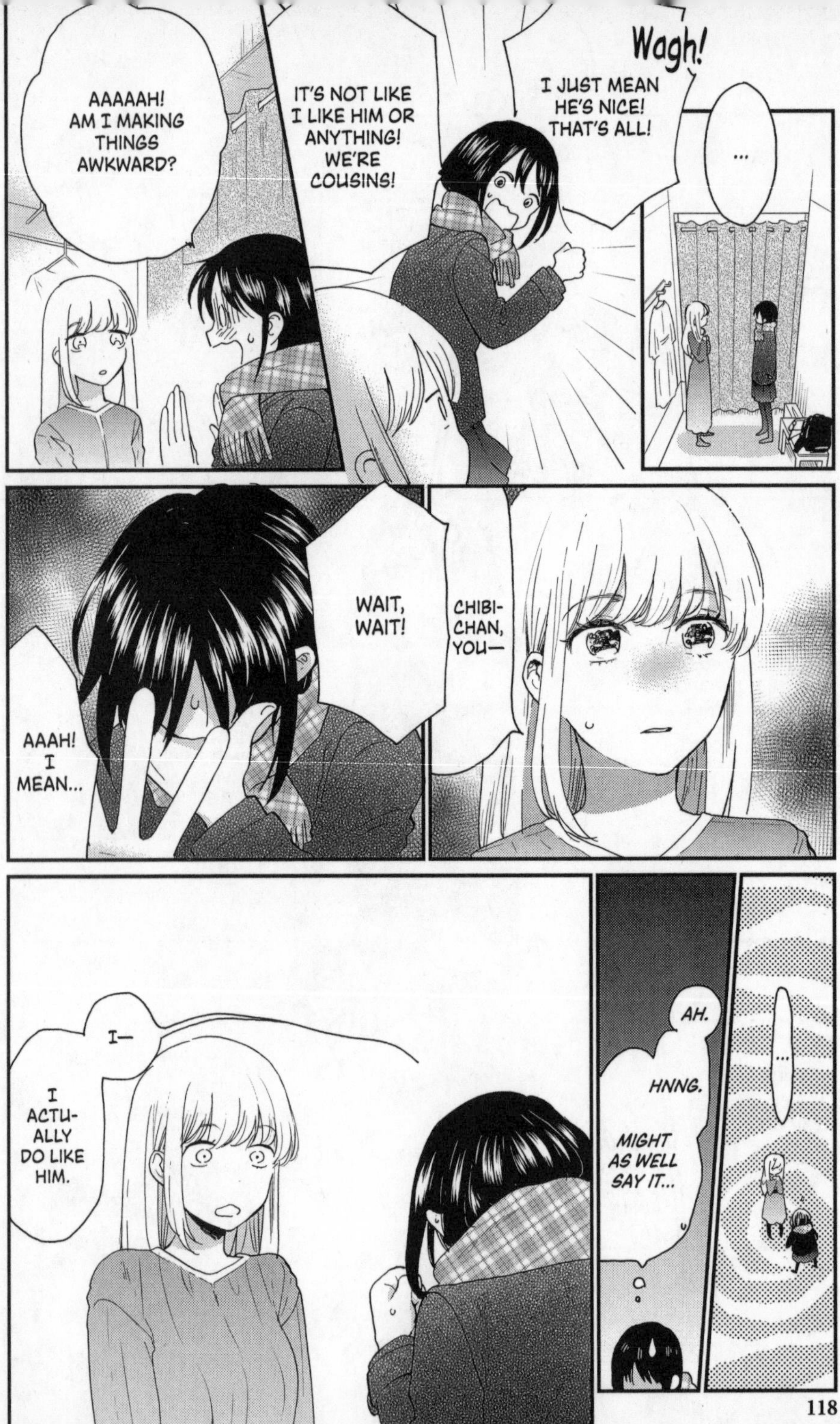
...
Wagh!
I JUST MEAN HE'S NICE! THAT'S ALL!
IT'S NOT LIKE I LIKE HIM OR ANYTHING! WE'RE COUSINS!
AAAAAH! AM I MAKING THINGS AWKWARD?
CHIBI-CHAN, YOU—
WAIT, WAIT!
AAAH! I MEAN...
...
AH.
HNNG.
MIGHT AS WELL SAY IT...
I—
I ACTU-ALLY DO LIKE HIM.

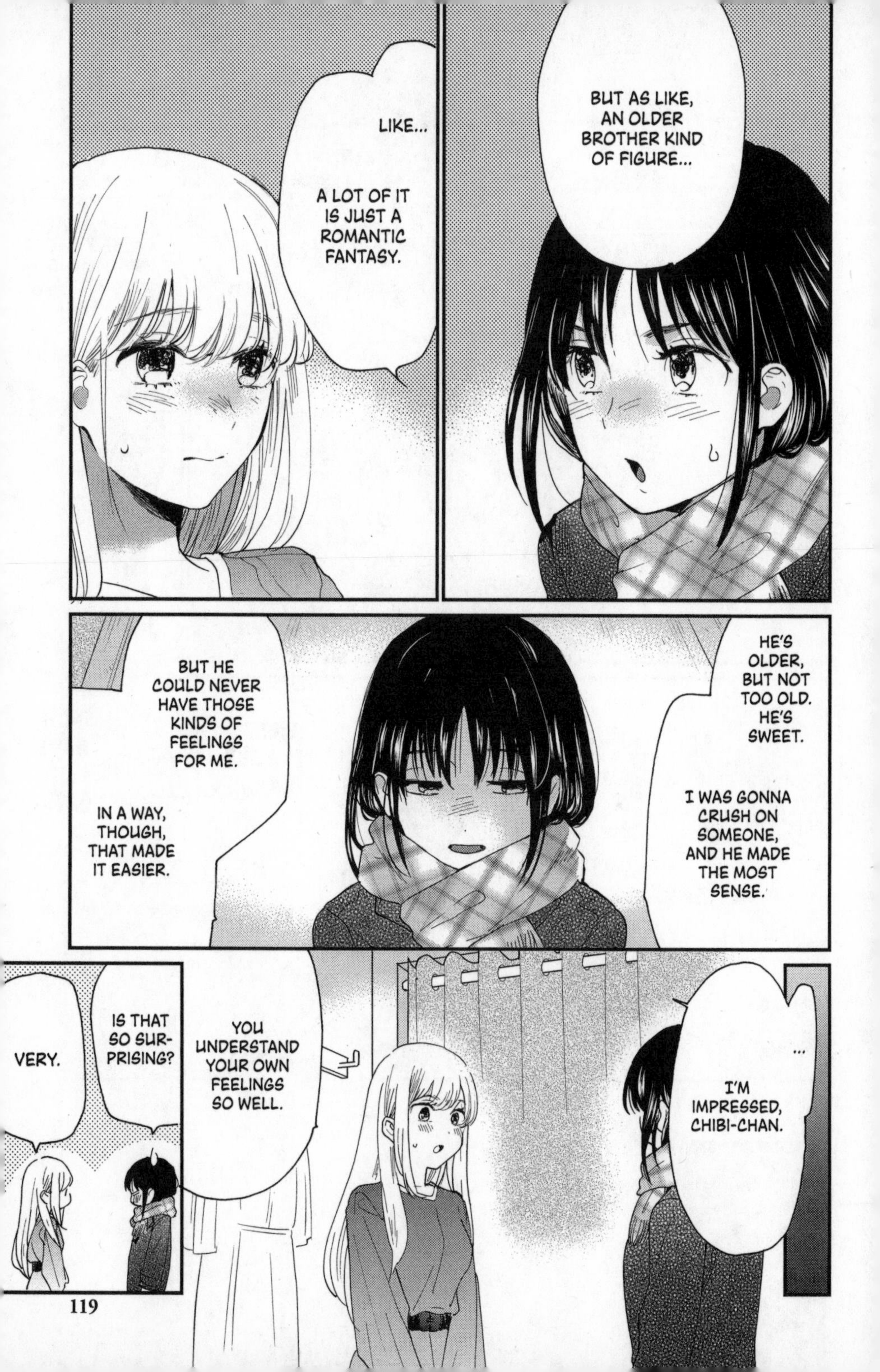
BUT AS LIKE, AN OLDER BROTHER KIND OF FIGURE...
LIKE...
A LOT OF IT IS JUST A ROMANTIC FANTASY.
HE'S OLDER, BUT NOT TOO OLD. HE'S SWEET.
I WAS GONNA CRUSH ON SOMEONE, AND HE MADE THE MOST SENSE.
BUT HE COULD NEVER HAVE THOSE KINDS OF FEELINGS FOR ME.
IN A WAY, THOUGH, THAT MADE IT EASIER.
...
I'M IMPRESSED, CHIBI-CHAN.
YOU UNDERSTAND YOUR OWN FEELINGS SO WELL.
IS THAT SO SUR-PRISING?
VERY.

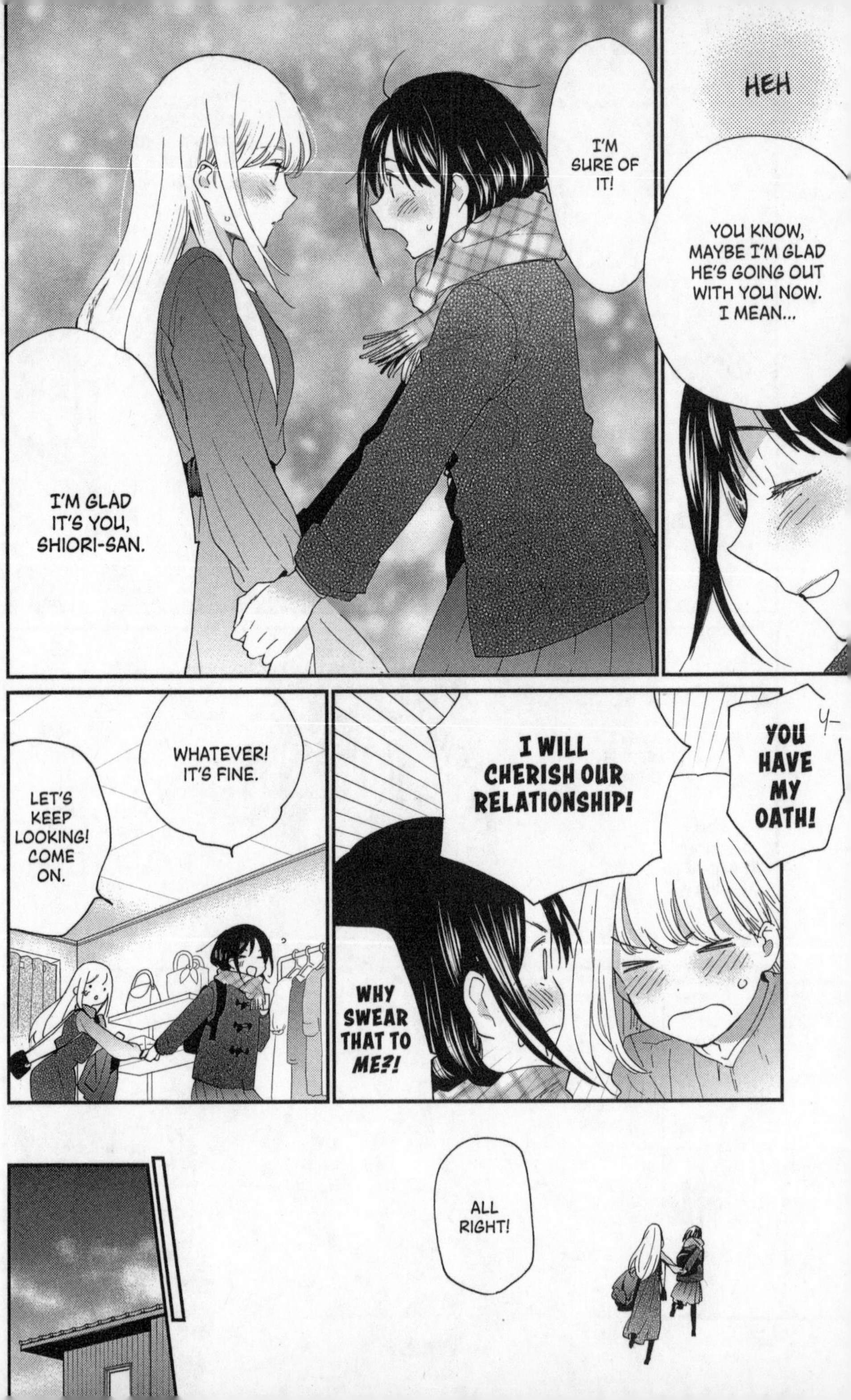
HEH
YOU KNOW, MAYBE I'M GLAD HE'S GOING OUT WITH YOU NOW. I MEAN...
I'M SURE OF IT!
I'M GLAD IT'S YOU, SHIORI-SAN.
YOU HAVE MY OATH!
I WILL CHERISH OUR RELATIONSHIP!
WHY SWEAR THAT TO ME?!
WHATEVER! IT'S FINE.
LET'S KEEP LOOKING! COME ON.
ALL RIGHT!

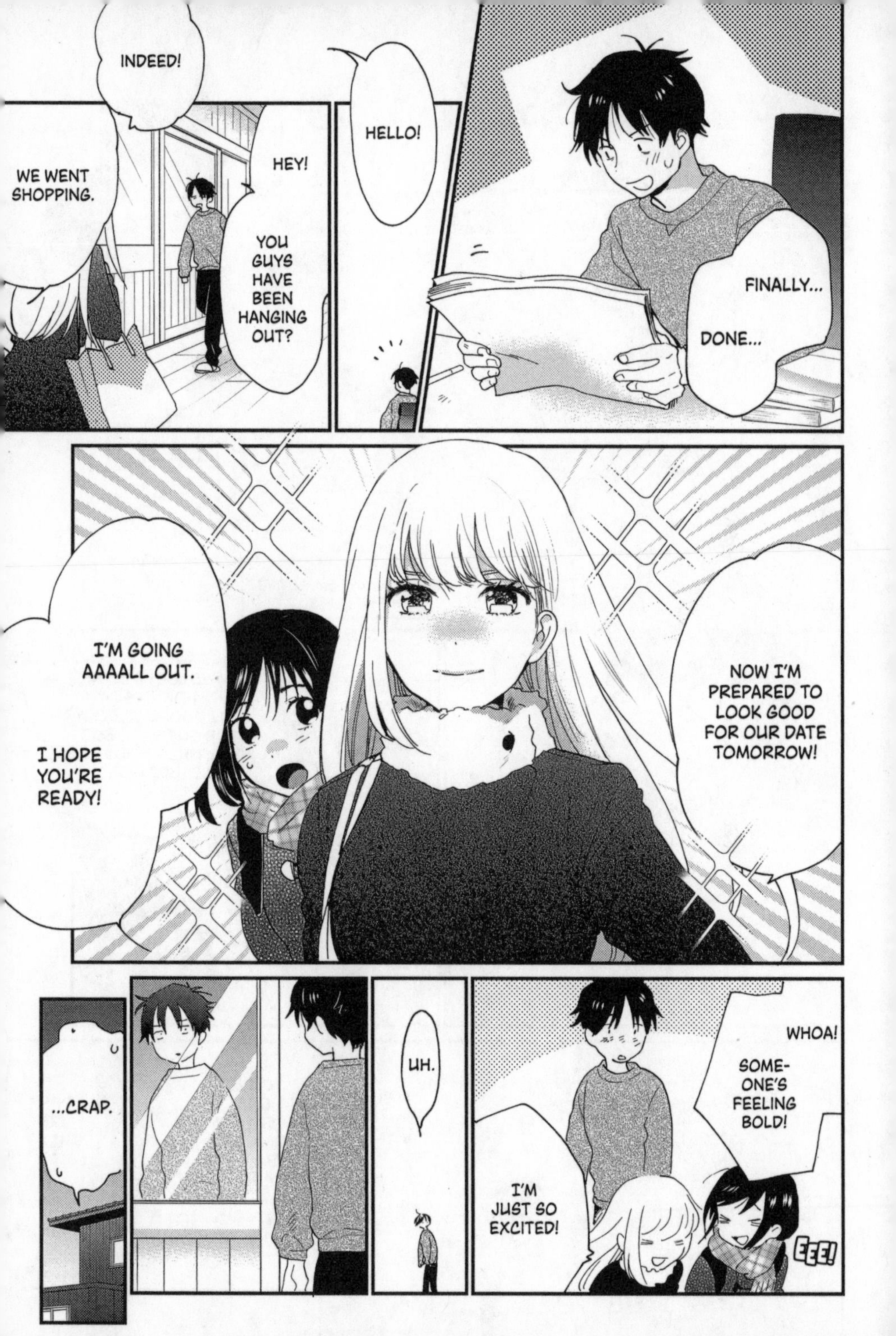
FINALLY...
DONE...
HELLO!
HEY!
YOU GUYS HAVE BEEN HANGING OUT?
INDEED!
WE WENT SHOPPING.
NOW I'M PREPARED TO LOOK GOOD FOR OUR DATE TOMORROW!
I'M GOING AAAALL OUT.
I HOPE YOU'RE READY!
WHOA!
SOME-ONE'S FEELING BOLD!
I'M JUST SO EXCITED!
EEE!
UH.
...CRAP.

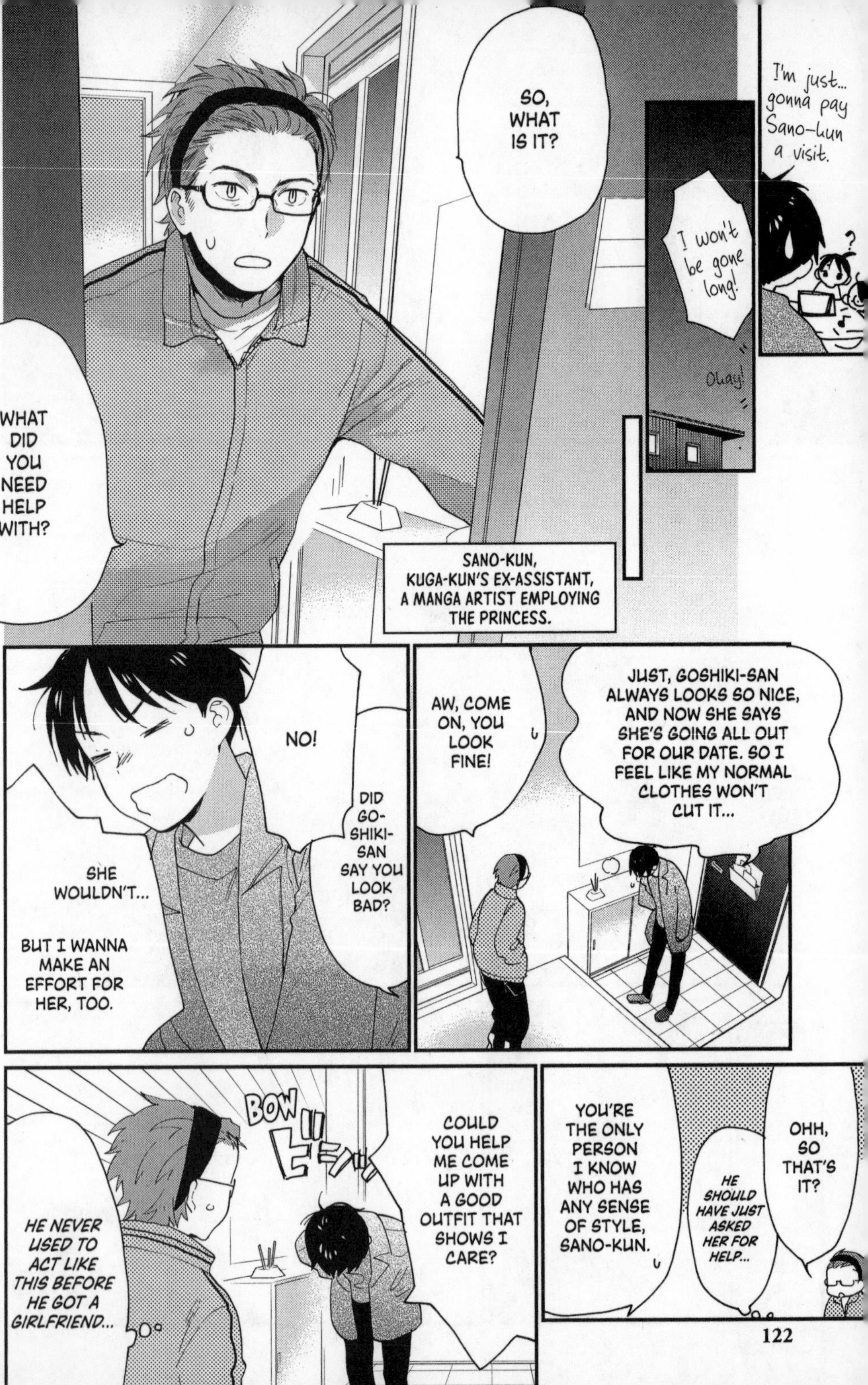
I'm just... gonna pay Sano-kun a visit.
I won't be gone long!
Okay!
SO, WHAT IS IT?
WHAT DID YOU NEED HELP WITH?
SANO-KUN, KUGA-KUN'S EX-ASSISTANT, A MANGA ARTIST EMPLOYING THE PRINCESS.
JUST, GOSHIKI-SAN ALWAYS LOOKS SO NICE, AND NOW SHE SAYS SHE'S GOING ALL OUT FOR OUR DATE. SO I FEEL LIKE MY NORMAL CLOTHES WON'T CUT IT...
AW, COME ON, YOU LOOK FINE!
DID GO-SHIKI-SAN SAY YOU LOOK BAD?
NO!
SHE WOULDN'T...
BUT I WANNA MAKE AN EFFORT FOR HER, TOO.
OHH, SO THAT'S IT?
HE SHOULD HAVE JUST ASKED HER FOR HELP...
YOU'RE THE ONLY PERSON I KNOW WHO HAS ANY SENSE OF STYLE, SANO-KUN.
COULD YOU HELP ME COME UP WITH A GOOD OUTFIT THAT SHOWS I CARE?
BOW
HE NEVER USED TO ACT LIKE THIS BEFORE HE GOT A GIRLFRIEND...

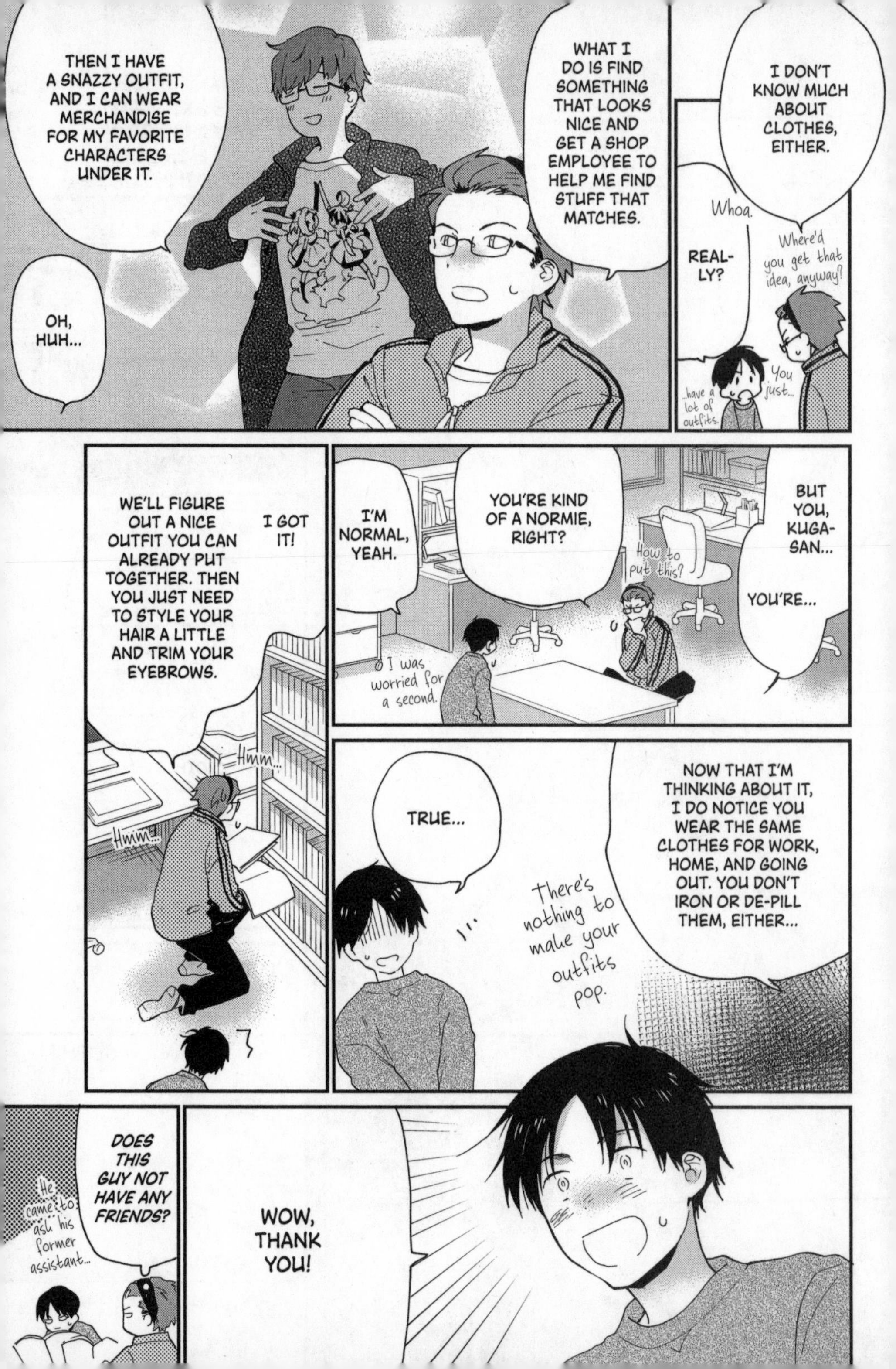
I DON'T KNOW MUCH ABOUT CLOTHES, EITHER.
Whoa.
REALLY?
Where'd you get that idea, anyway?
You just...
...have a lot of outfits.
WHAT I DO IS FIND SOMETHING THAT LOOKS NICE AND GET A SHOP EMPLOYEE TO HELP ME FIND STUFF THAT MATCHES.
THEN I HAVE A SNAZZY OUTFIT, AND I CAN WEAR MERCHANDISE FOR MY FAVORITE CHARACTERS UNDER IT.
OH, HUH...
BUT YOU, KUGA-SAN...
YOU'RE...
YOU'RE KIND OF A NORMIE, RIGHT?
How to put this?
I'M NORMAL, YEAH.
I was worried for a second.
NOW THAT I'M THINKING ABOUT IT, I DO NOTICE YOU WEAR THE SAME CLOTHES FOR WORK, HOME, AND GOING OUT. YOU DON'T IRON OR DE-PILL THEM, EITHER...
There's nothing to make your outfits pop.
TRUE...
I GOT IT!
WE'LL FIGURE OUT A NICE OUTFIT YOU CAN ALREADY PUT TOGETHER. THEN YOU JUST NEED TO STYLE YOUR HAIR A LITTLE AND TRIM YOUR EYEBROWS.
Hmm...
Hmm...
WOW, THANK YOU!
DOES THIS GUY NOT HAVE ANY FRIENDS?
He came to ask his former assistant...

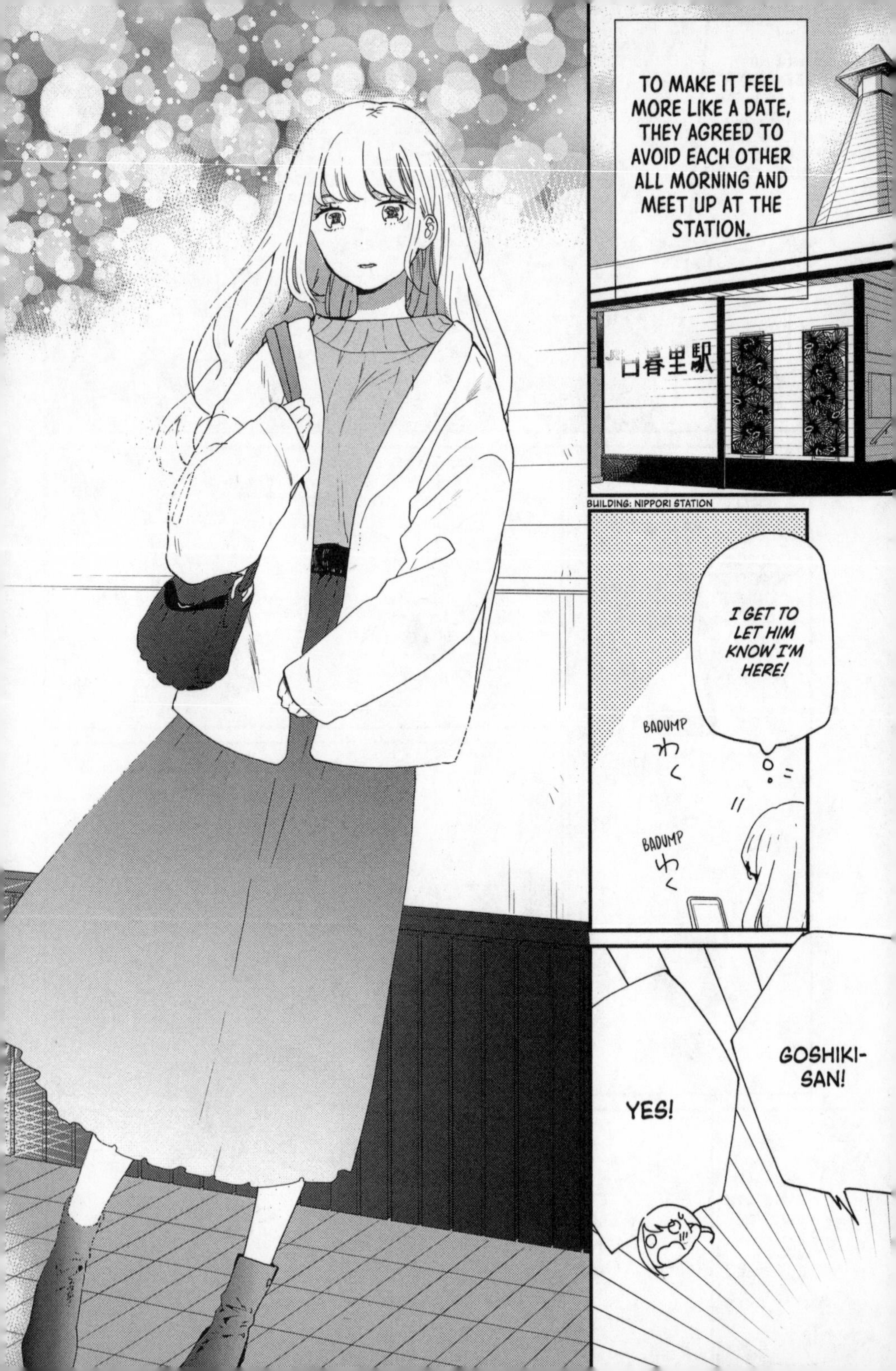

TO MAKE IT FEEL MORE LIKE A DATE, THEY AGREED TO AVOID EACH OTHER ALL MORNING AND MEET UP AT THE STATION.
JR 日暮里駅
BUILDING: NIPPORI STATION
I GET TO LET HIM KNOW I'M HERE!
BADUMP
わく
BADUMP
わく
GOSHIKI-SAN!
YES!

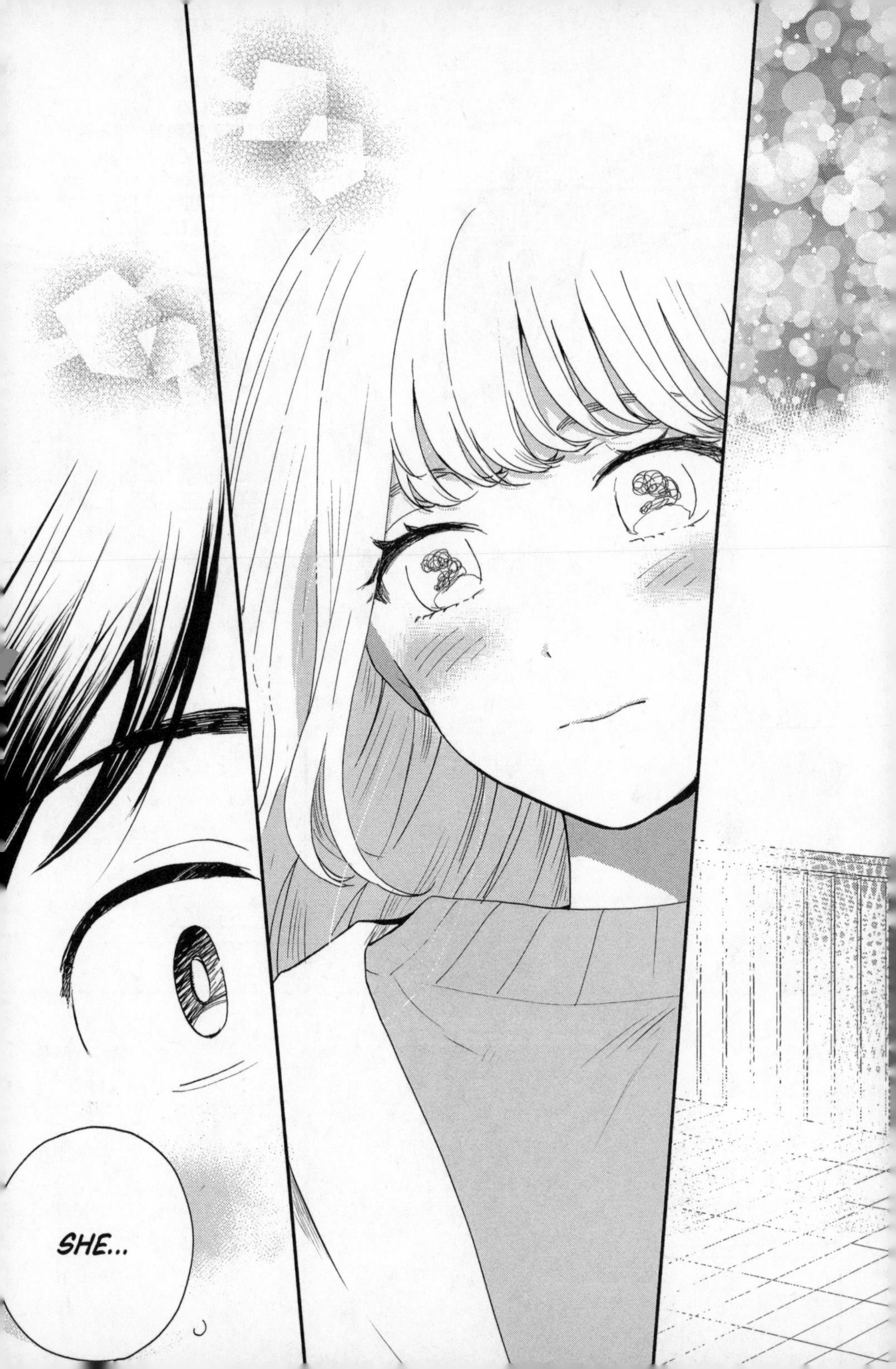
SHE...

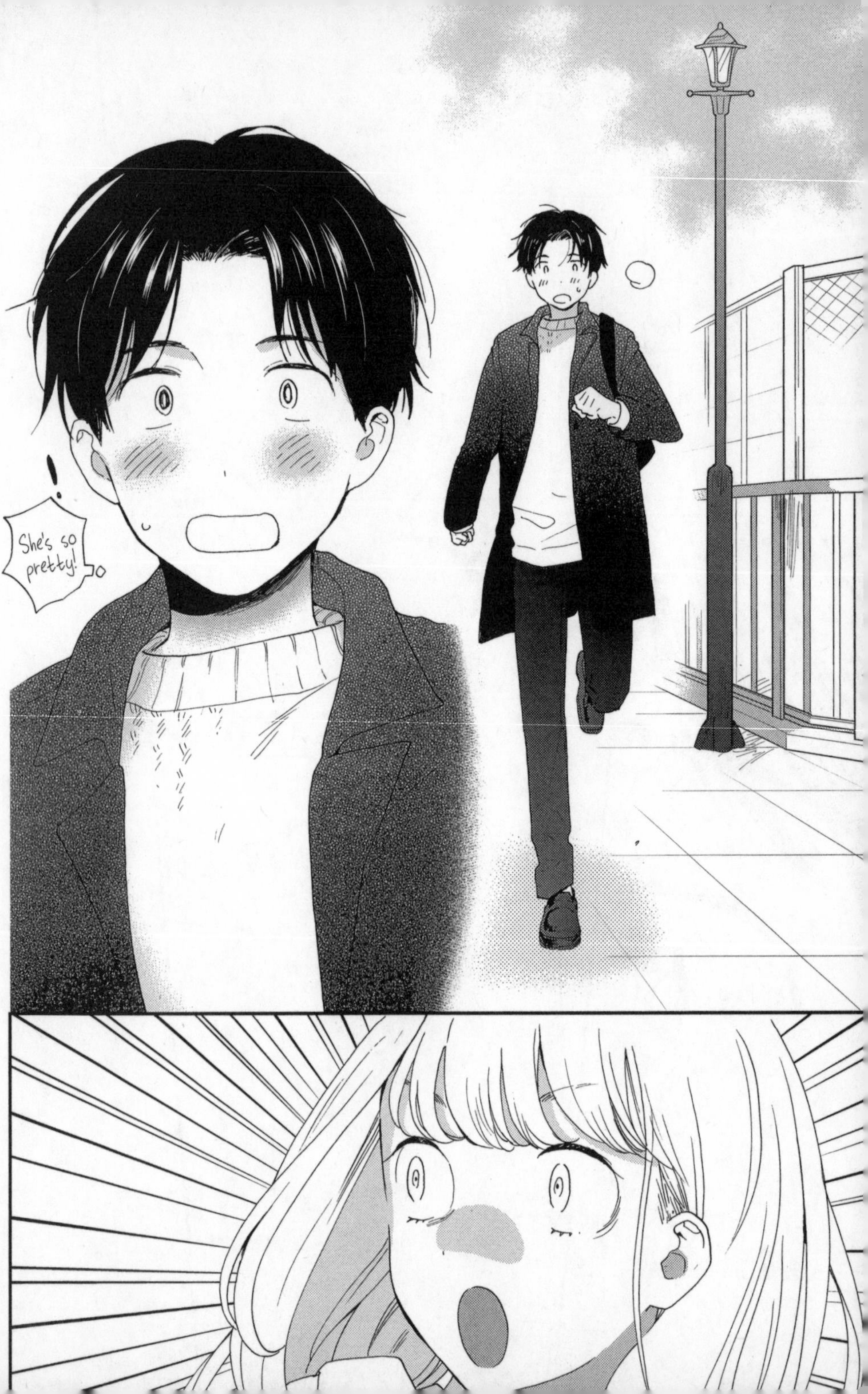
She's so pretty!

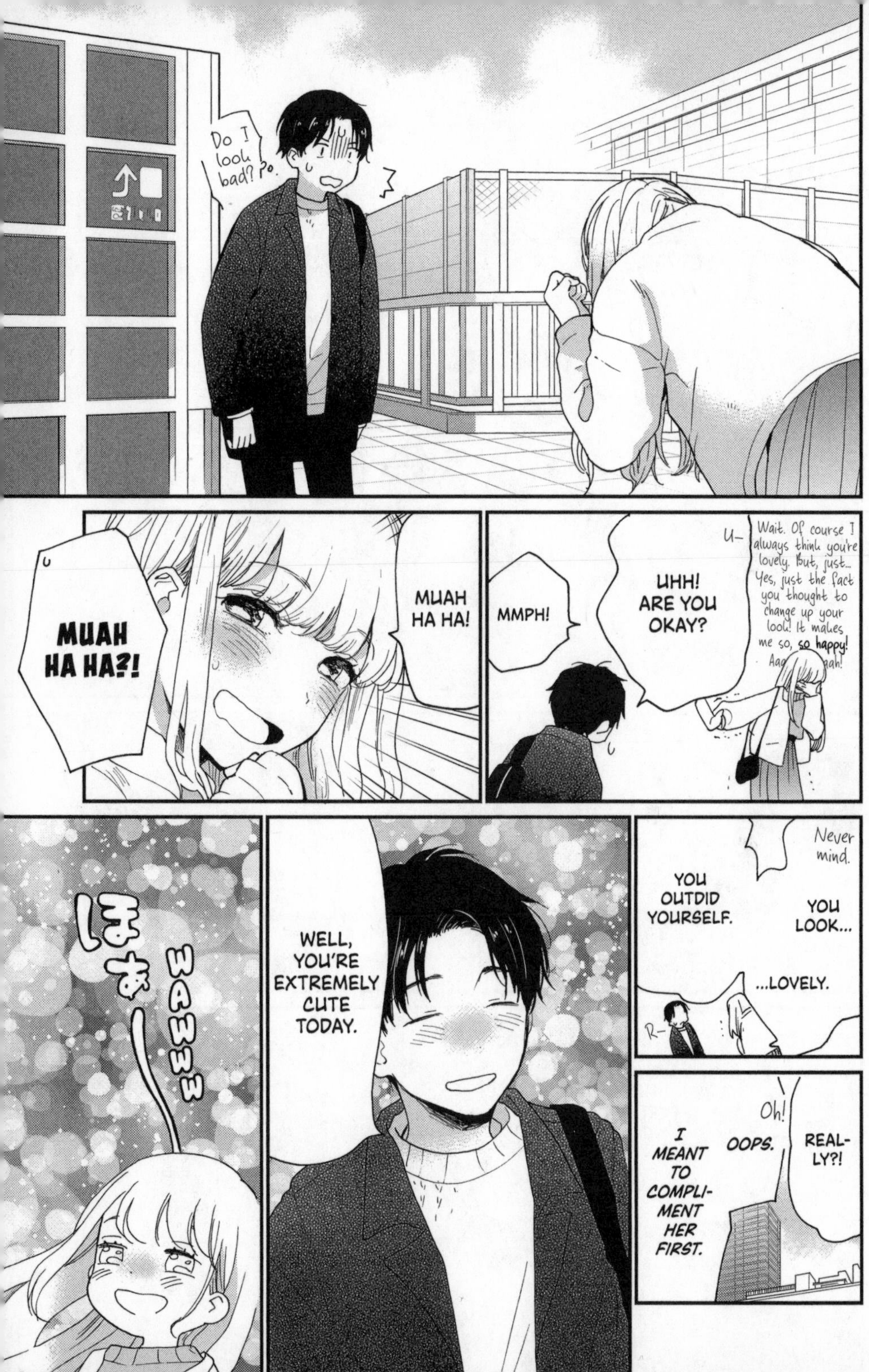
Do I look bad?
U–
Wait. Of course I always think you're lovely. But, just... Yes, just the fact you thought to change up your look! It makes me so, so happy! Aag... aah!
UHH! ARE YOU OKAY?
MMPH!
MUAH HA HA!
U
MUAH HA HA?!
Never mind.
YOU LOOK...
YOU OUTDID YOURSELF.
...LOVELY.
R–
Oh!
REAL-LY?!
OOPS.
I MEANT TO COMPLI-MENT HER FIRST.
WELL, YOU'RE EXTREMELY CUTE TODAY.
ほぁ
WAWWW

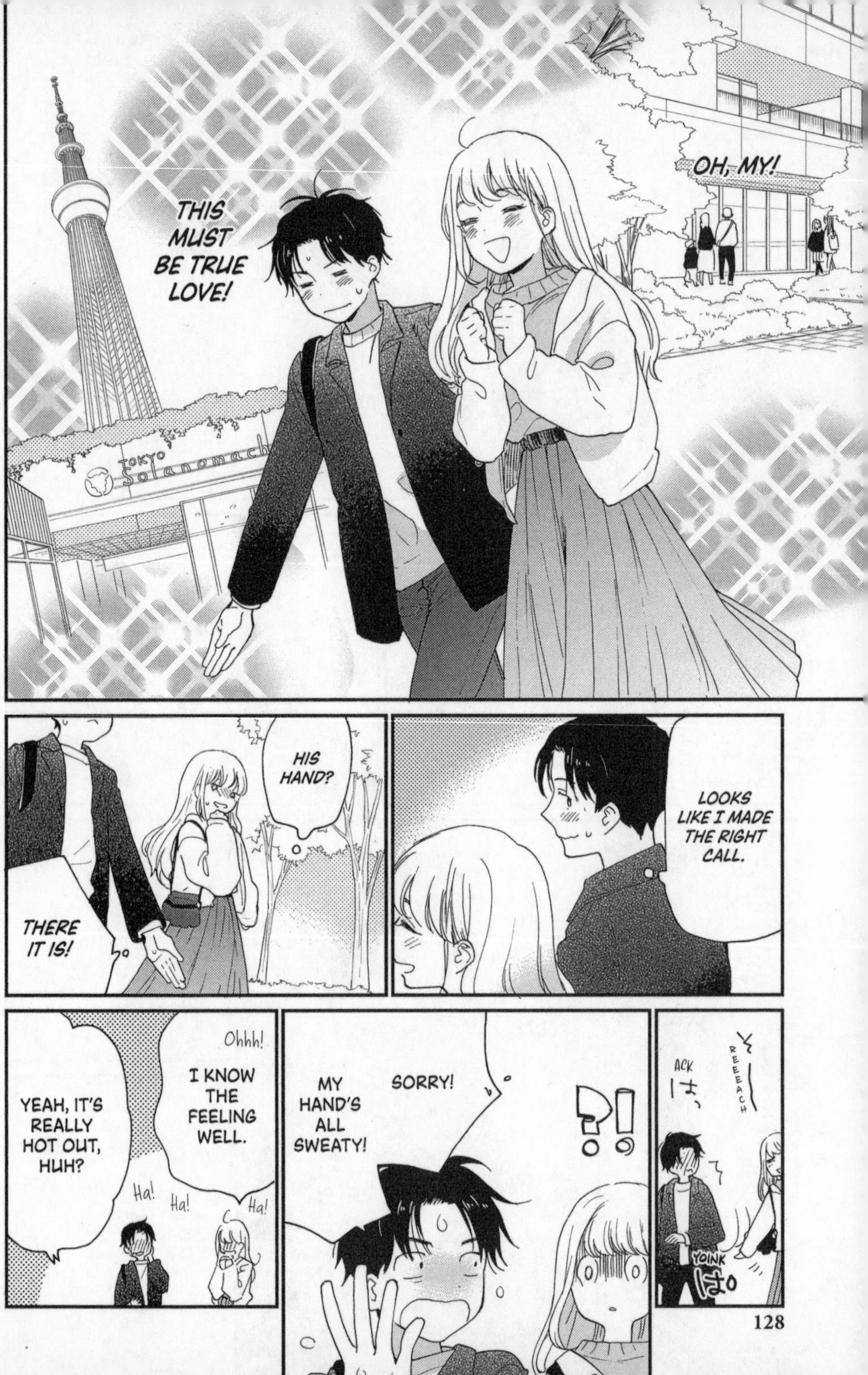
OH, MY!
THIS MUST BE TRUE LOVE!
LOOKS LIKE I MADE THE RIGHT CALL.
HIS HAND?
THERE IT IS!
そー
REEEACH
ACK
は、
YOINK
はっ
SORRY!
MY HAND'S ALL SWEATY!
Ohhh!
I KNOW THE FEELING WELL.
YEAH, IT'S REALLY HOT OUT, HUH?
Ha!
Ha!
Ha!

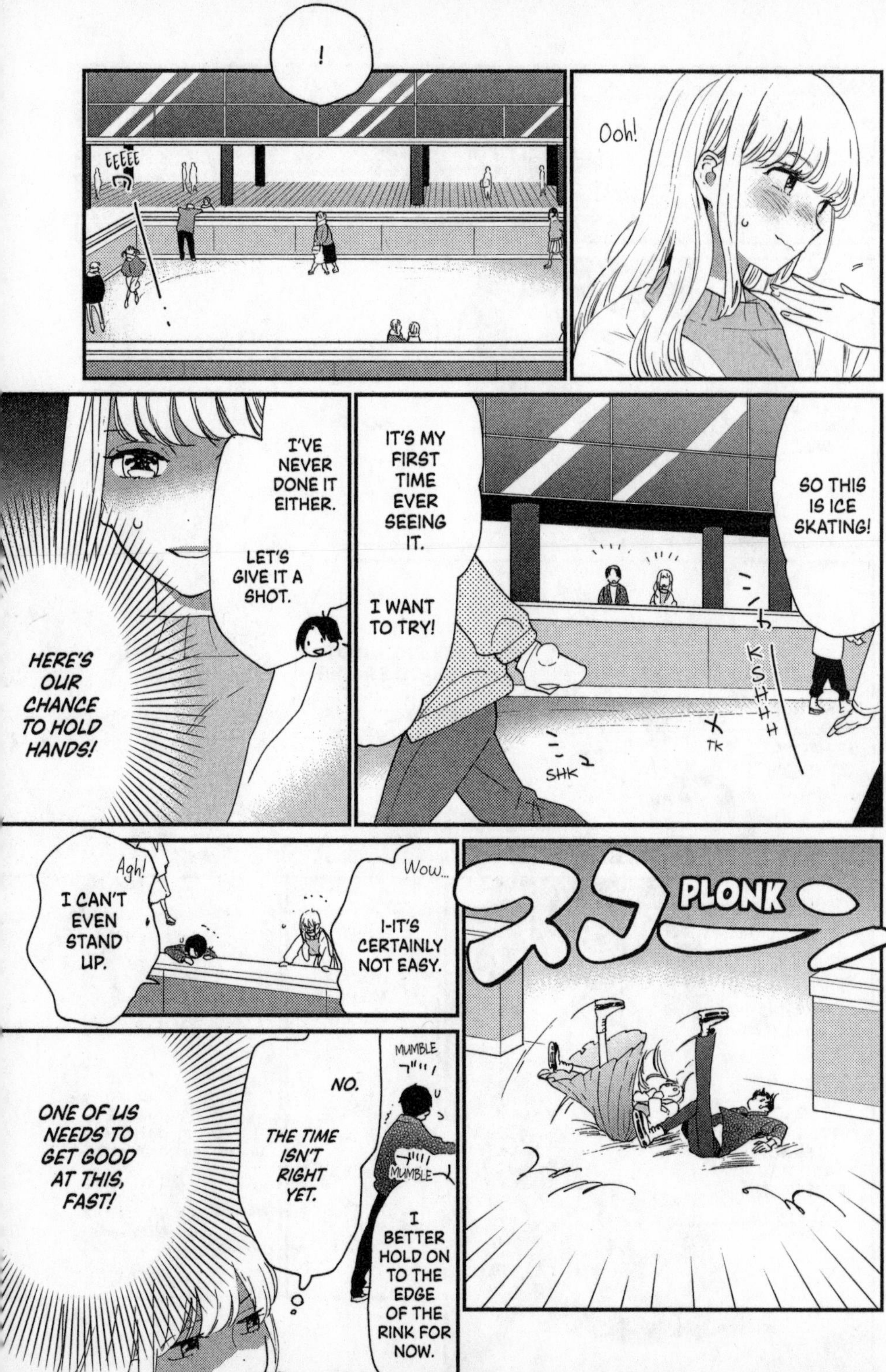
Ooh!
!
EEEEE
SO THIS IS ICE SKATING!
IT'S MY FIRST TIME EVER SEEING IT.
I WANT TO TRY!
KSHHHH
TK
SHK
I'VE NEVER DONE IT EITHER.
LET'S GIVE IT A SHOT.
HERE'S OUR CHANCE TO HOLD HANDS!
スコー
PLONK
Wow...
I-IT'S CERTAINLY NOT EASY.
Agh!
I CAN'T EVEN STAND UP.
MUMBLE
NO.
THE TIME ISN'T RIGHT YET.
MUMBLE
I BETTER HOLD ON TO THE EDGE OF THE RINK FOR NOW.
ONE OF US NEEDS TO GET GOOD AT THIS, FAST!

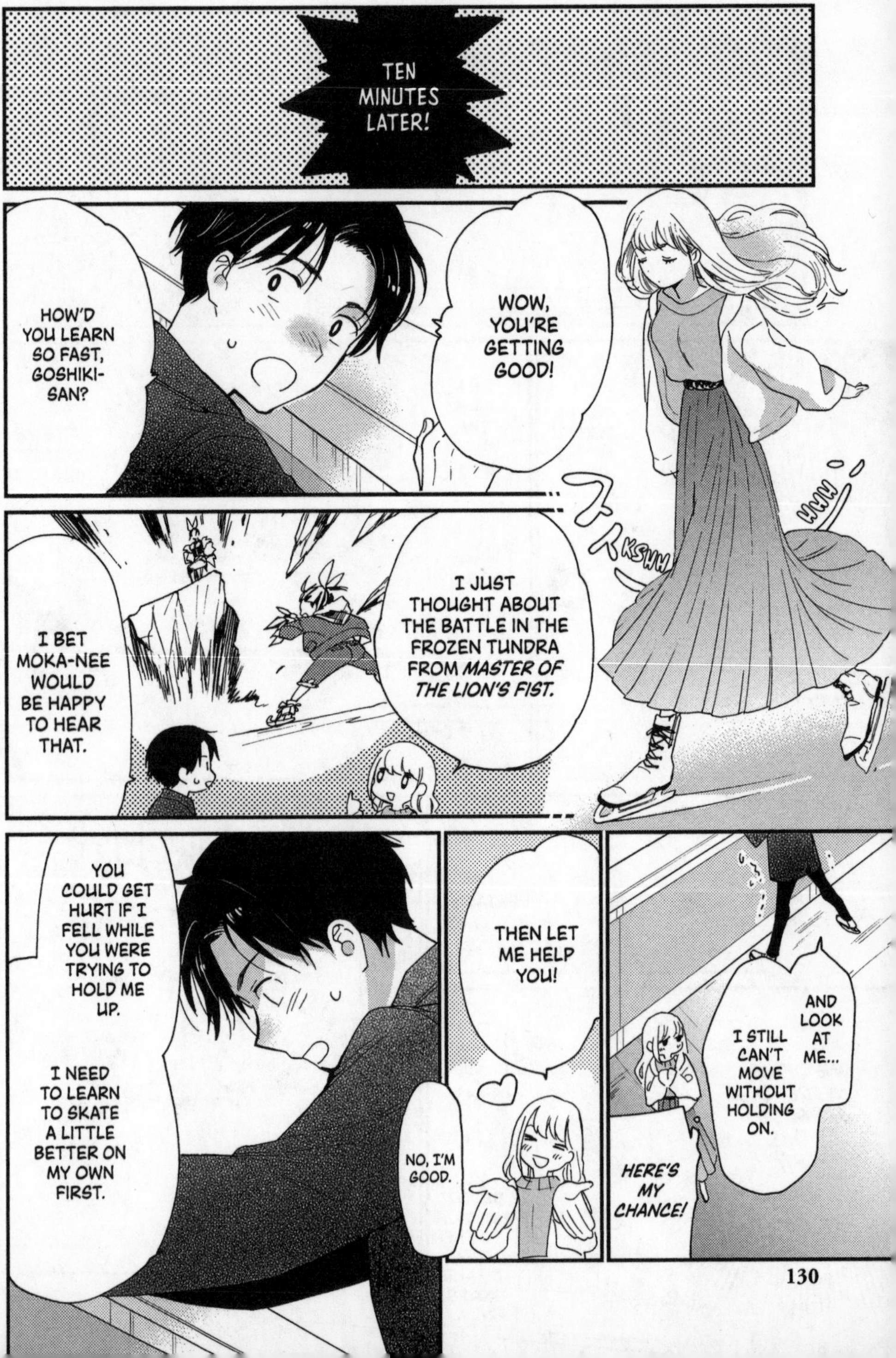
TEN MINUTES LATER!
WOW, YOU'RE GETTING GOOD!
KSHH
HMM
HOW'D YOU LEARN SO FAST, GOSHIKI-SAN?
I JUST THOUGHT ABOUT THE BATTLE IN THE FROZEN TUNDRA FROM *MASTER OF THE LION'S FIST.*
I BET MOKA-NEE WOULD BE HAPPY TO HEAR THAT.
AND LOOK AT ME...
I STILL CAN'T MOVE WITHOUT HOLDING ON.
HERE'S MY CHANCE!
THEN LET ME HELP YOU!
NO, I'M GOOD.
YOU COULD GET HURT IF I FELL WHILE YOU WERE TRYING TO HOLD ME UP.
I NEED TO LEARN TO SKATE A LITTLE BETTER ON MY OWN FIRST.

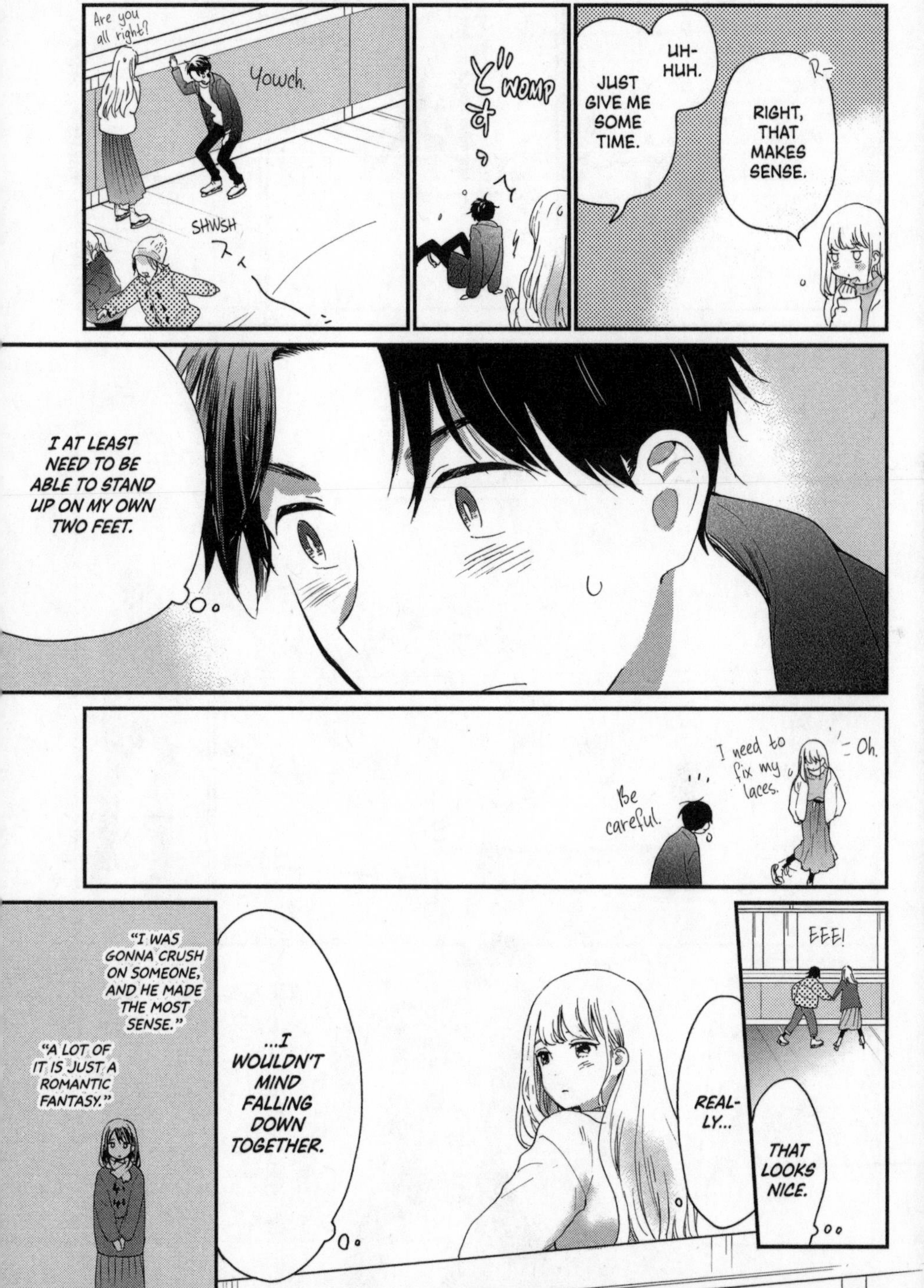
R—
RIGHT, THAT MAKES SENSE.
UH-HUH.
JUST GIVE ME SOME TIME.
どすっ
WOMP
Are you all right?
Youch.
SHWSH
スィ—
I AT LEAST NEED TO BE ABLE TO STAND UP ON MY OWN TWO FEET.
Oh.
I need to fix my laces.
Be careful.
EEE!
THAT LOOKS NICE.
REAL-LY...
...I WOULDN'T MIND FALLING DOWN TOGETHER.
"I WAS GONNA CRUSH ON SOMEONE, AND HE MADE THE MOST SENSE."
"A LOT OF IT IS JUST A ROMANTIC FANTASY."

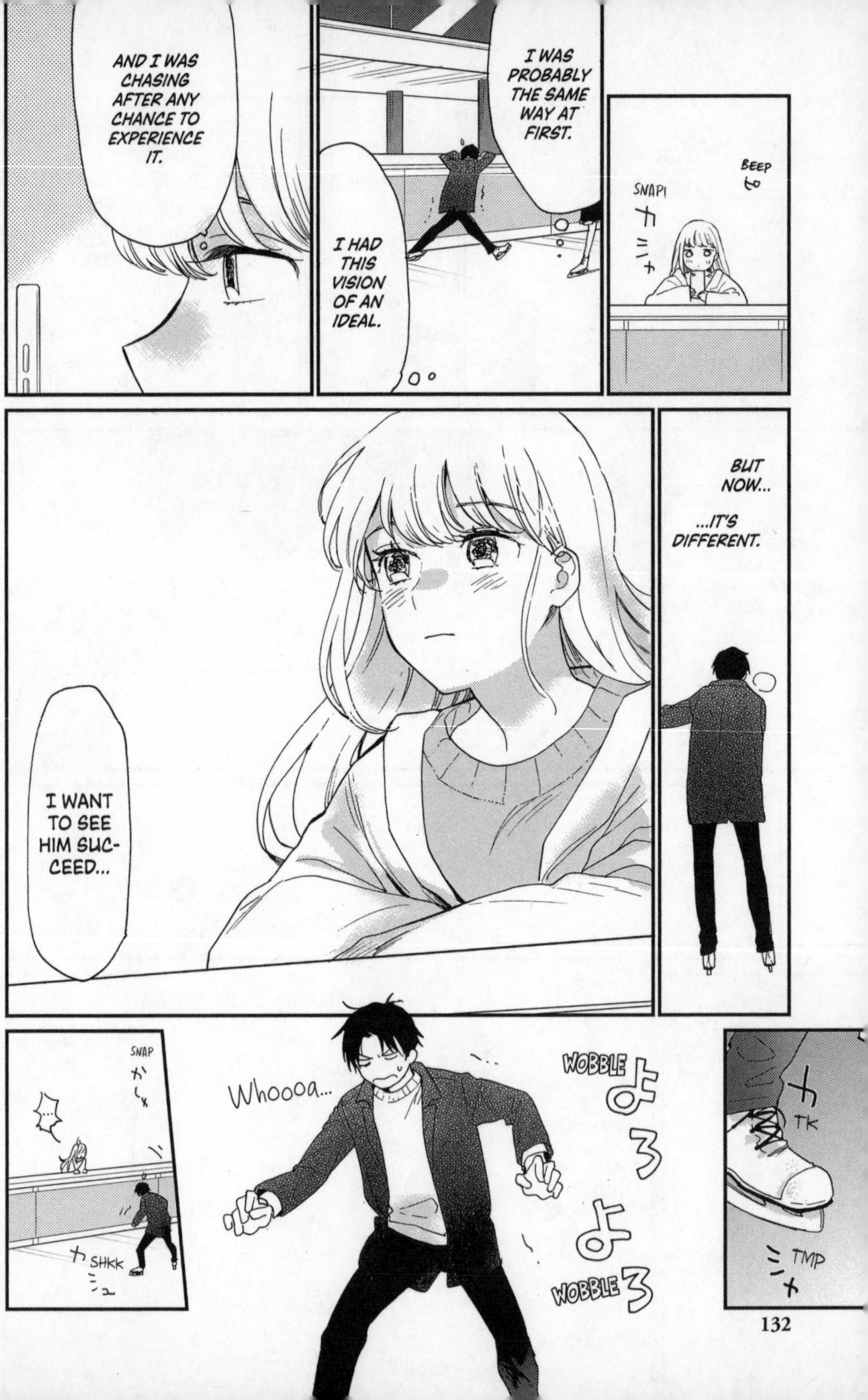
SNAP!
BEEP
I WAS PROBABLY THE SAME WAY AT FIRST.
I HAD THIS VISION OF AN IDEAL.
AND I WAS CHASING AFTER ANY CHANCE TO EXPERIENCE IT.
BUT NOW...
...IT'S DIFFERENT.
I WANT TO SEE HIM SUC-CEED...
TK
TMP
WOBBLE
Whoooa...
WOBBLE
SNAP
SHKK

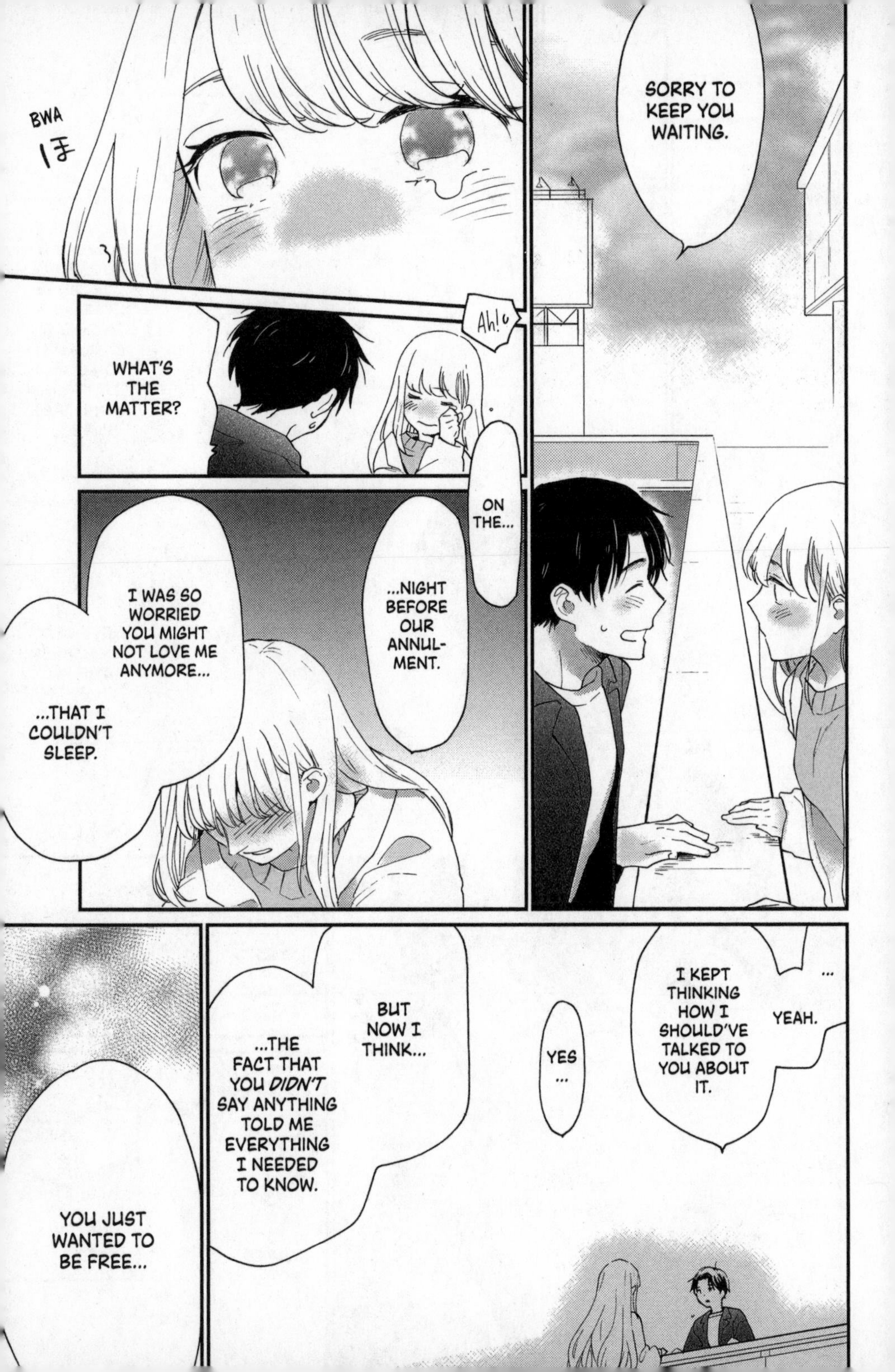
SORRY TO KEEP YOU WAITING.
BWA
ほ
Ah!
WHAT'S THE MATTER?
ON THE...
...NIGHT BEFORE OUR ANNUL-MENT.
I WAS SO WORRIED YOU MIGHT NOT LOVE ME ANYMORE...
...THAT I COULDN'T SLEEP.
...
YEAH.
I KEPT THINKING HOW I SHOULD'VE TALKED TO YOU ABOUT IT.
YES...
BUT NOW I THINK...
...THE FACT THAT YOU *DIDN'T* SAY ANYTHING TOLD ME EVERYTHING I NEEDED TO KNOW.
YOU JUST WANTED TO BE FREE...

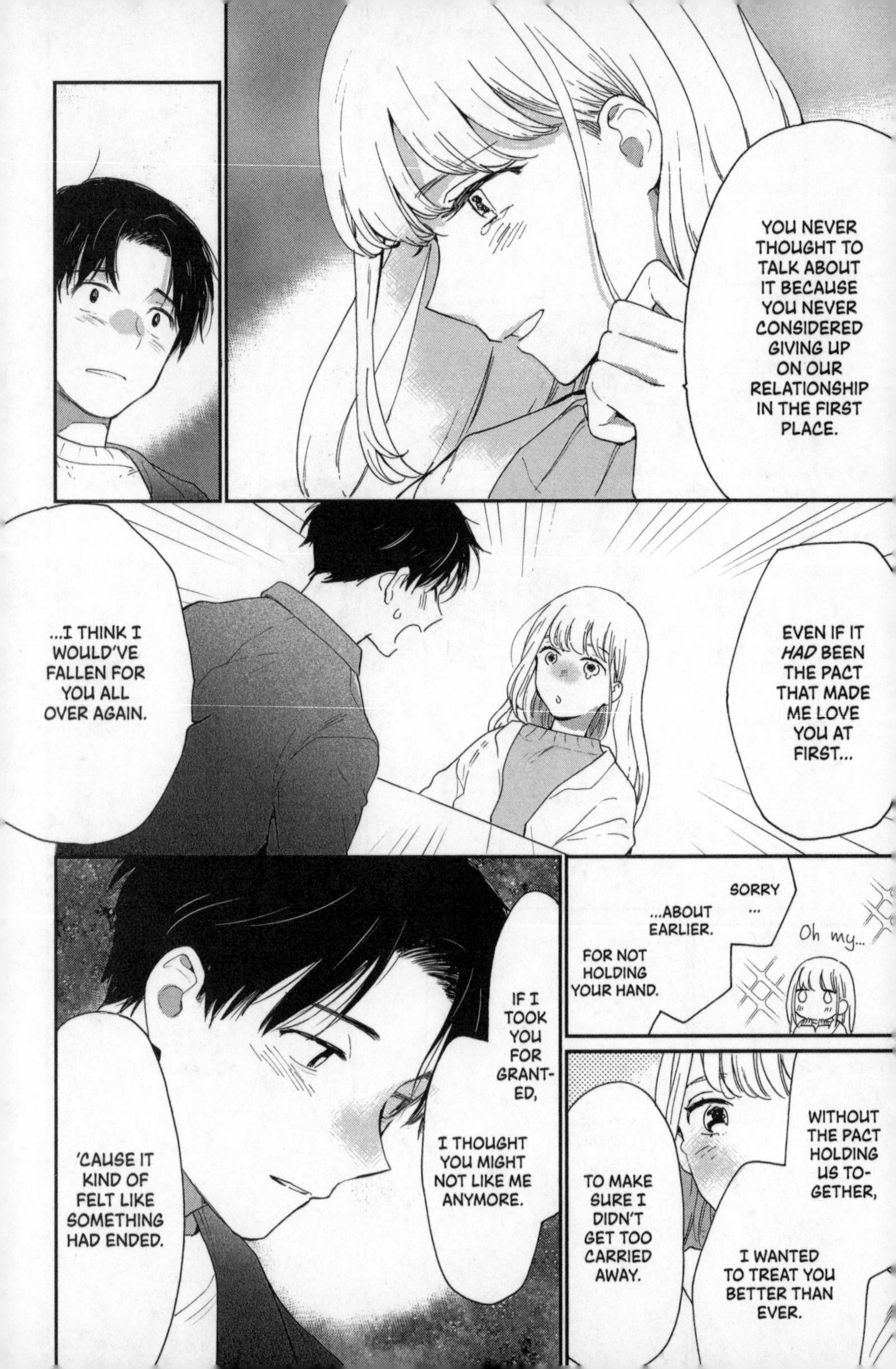
YOU NEVER THOUGHT TO TALK ABOUT IT BECAUSE YOU NEVER CONSIDERED GIVING UP ON OUR RELATIONSHIP IN THE FIRST PLACE.
EVEN IF IT *HAD* BEEN THE PACT THAT MADE ME LOVE YOU AT FIRST...
...I THINK I WOULD'VE FALLEN FOR YOU ALL OVER AGAIN.
SORRY ...
...ABOUT EARLIER.
FOR NOT HOLDING YOUR HAND.
Oh my...
WITHOUT THE PACT HOLDING US TO-GETHER,
I WANTED TO TREAT YOU BETTER THAN EVER.
TO MAKE SURE I DIDN'T GET TOO CARRIED AWAY.
IF I TOOK YOU FOR GRANT-ED,
I THOUGHT YOU MIGHT NOT LIKE ME ANYMORE.
'CAUSE IT KIND OF FELT LIKE SOMETHING HAD ENDED.

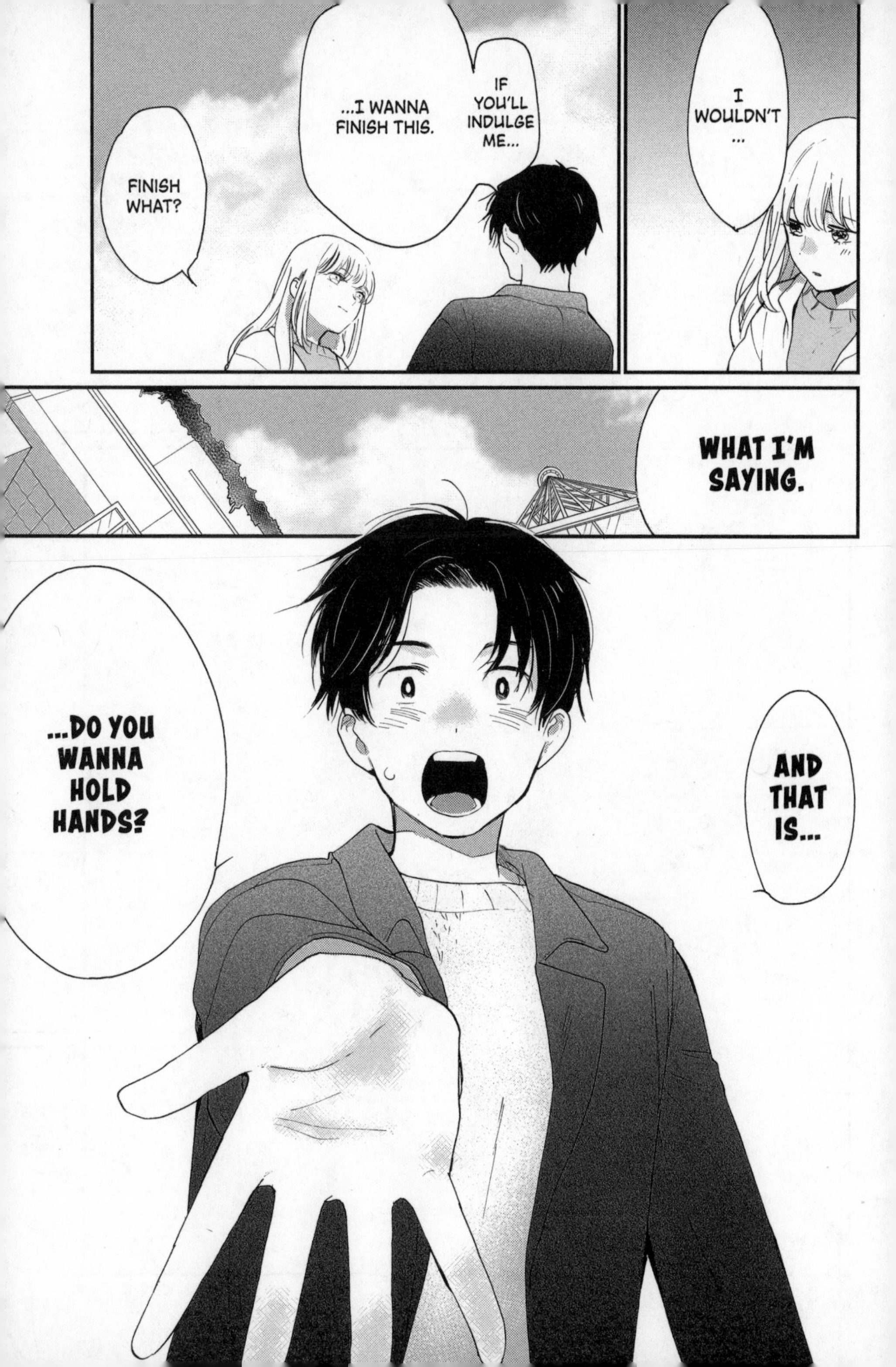
I WOULDN'T ...
IF YOU'LL INDULGE ME...
...I WANNA FINISH THIS.
FINISH WHAT?
WHAT I'M SAYING.
AND THAT IS...
...DO YOU WANNA HOLD HANDS?

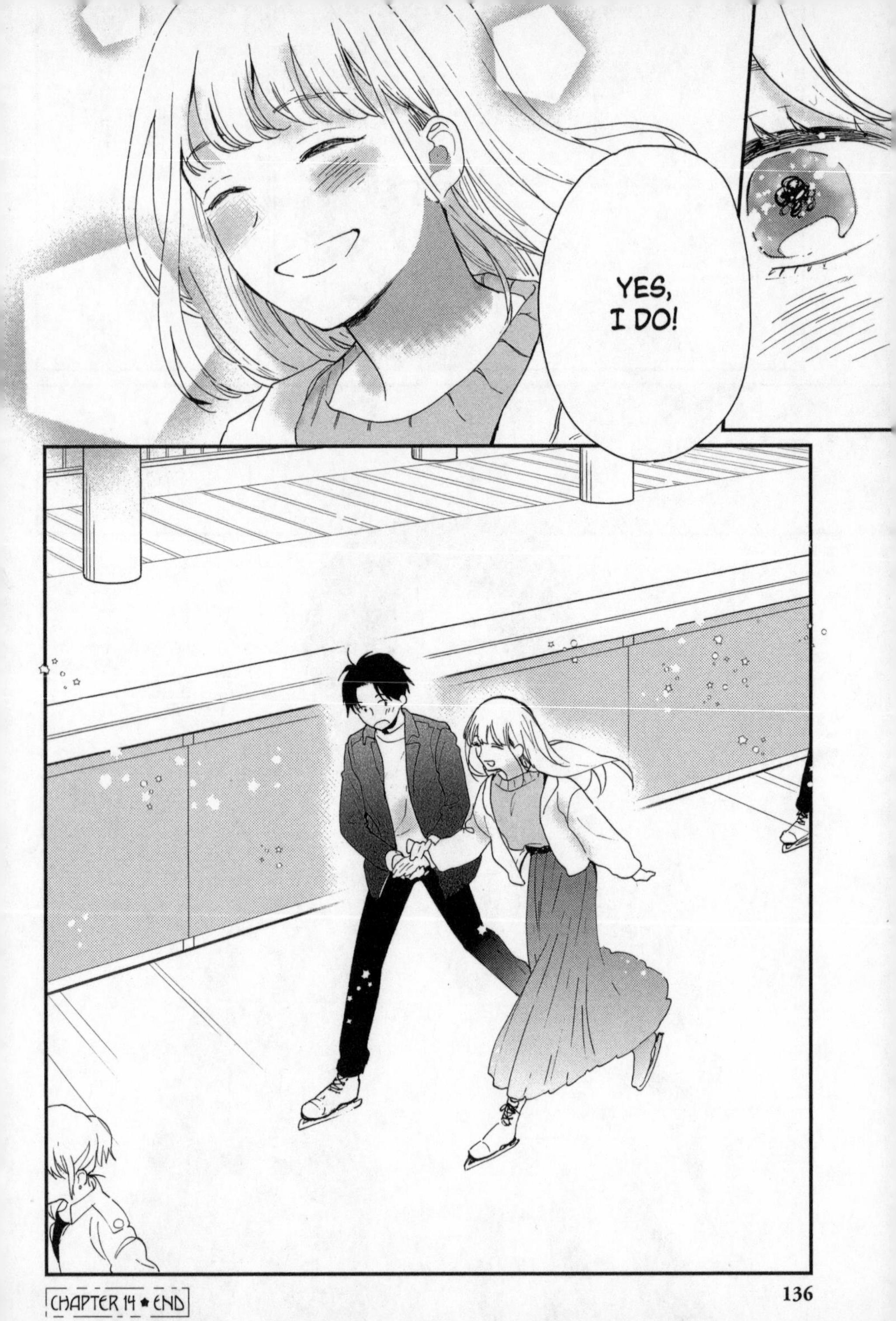
YES, I DO!

CHAPTER 14 ✦ END

A Galaxy Next Door

Gido Amagakure

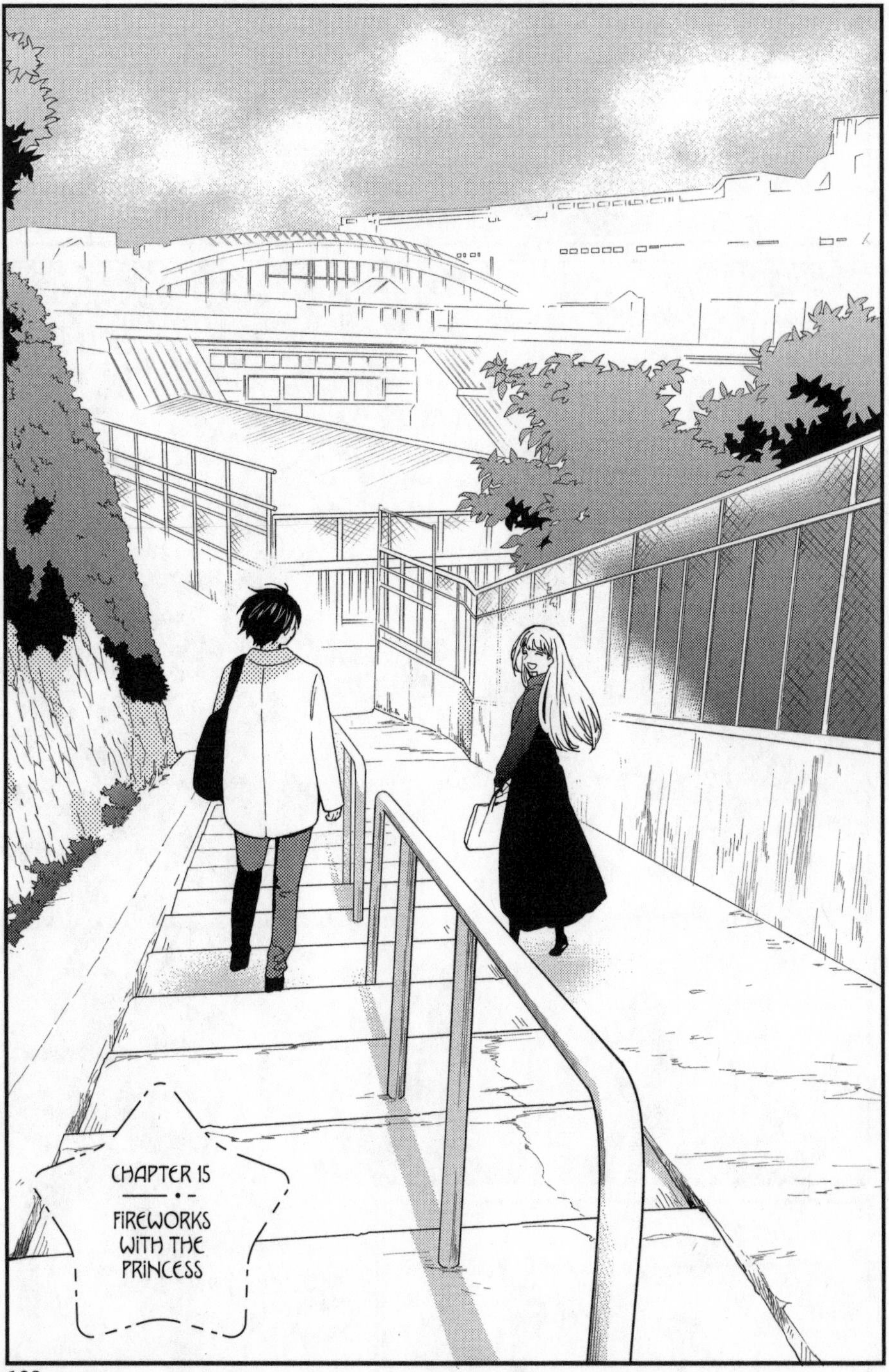
CHAPTER 15
FIREWORKS WITH THE PRINCESS

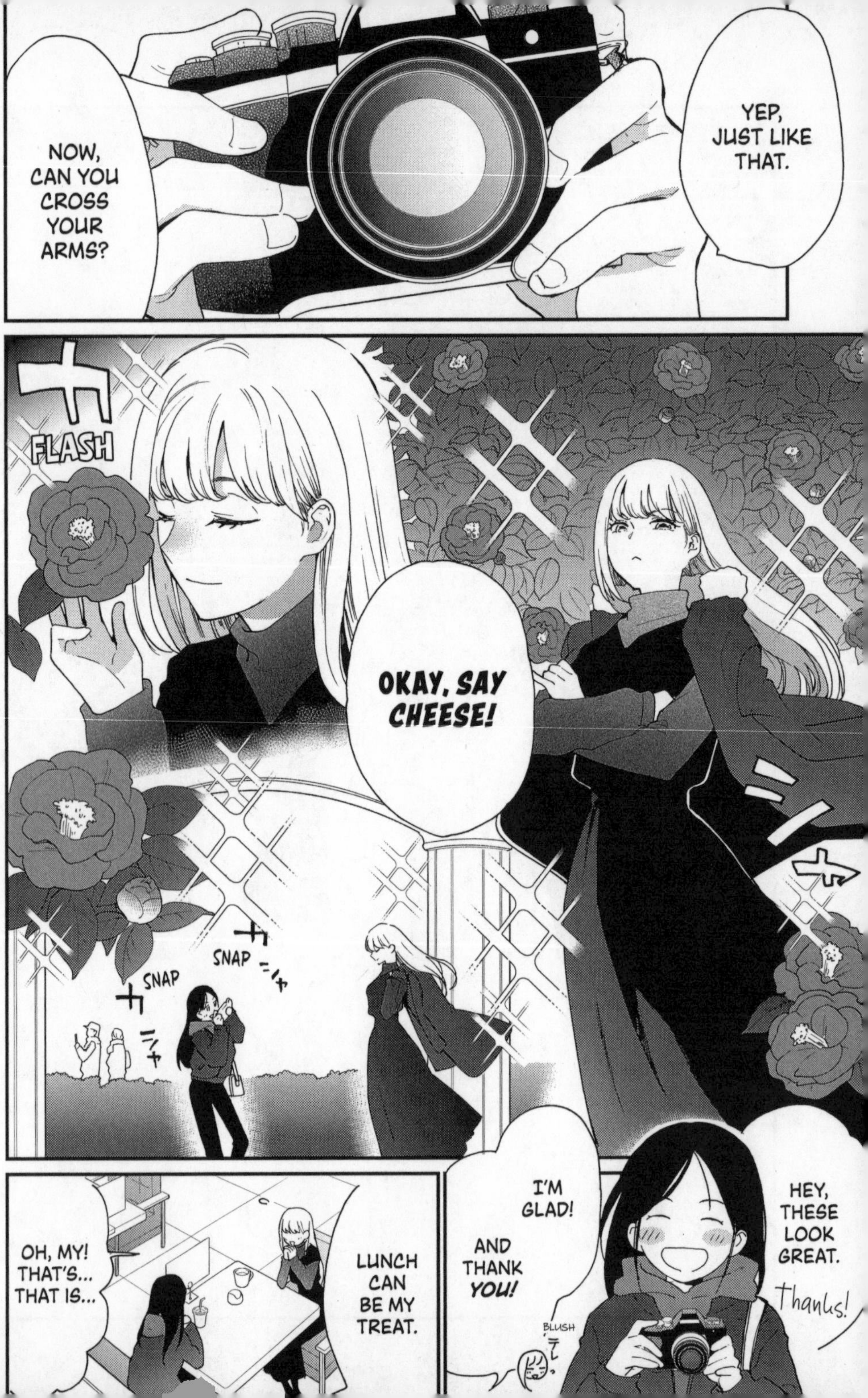
YEP, JUST LIKE THAT.
NOW, CAN YOU CROSS YOUR ARMS?
FLASH
OKAY, SAY CHEESE!
SNAP
SNAP
HEY, THESE LOOK GREAT.
Thanks!
I'M GLAD!
AND THANK YOU!
BLUSH
LUNCH CAN BE MY TREAT.
OH, MY! THAT'S... THAT IS...

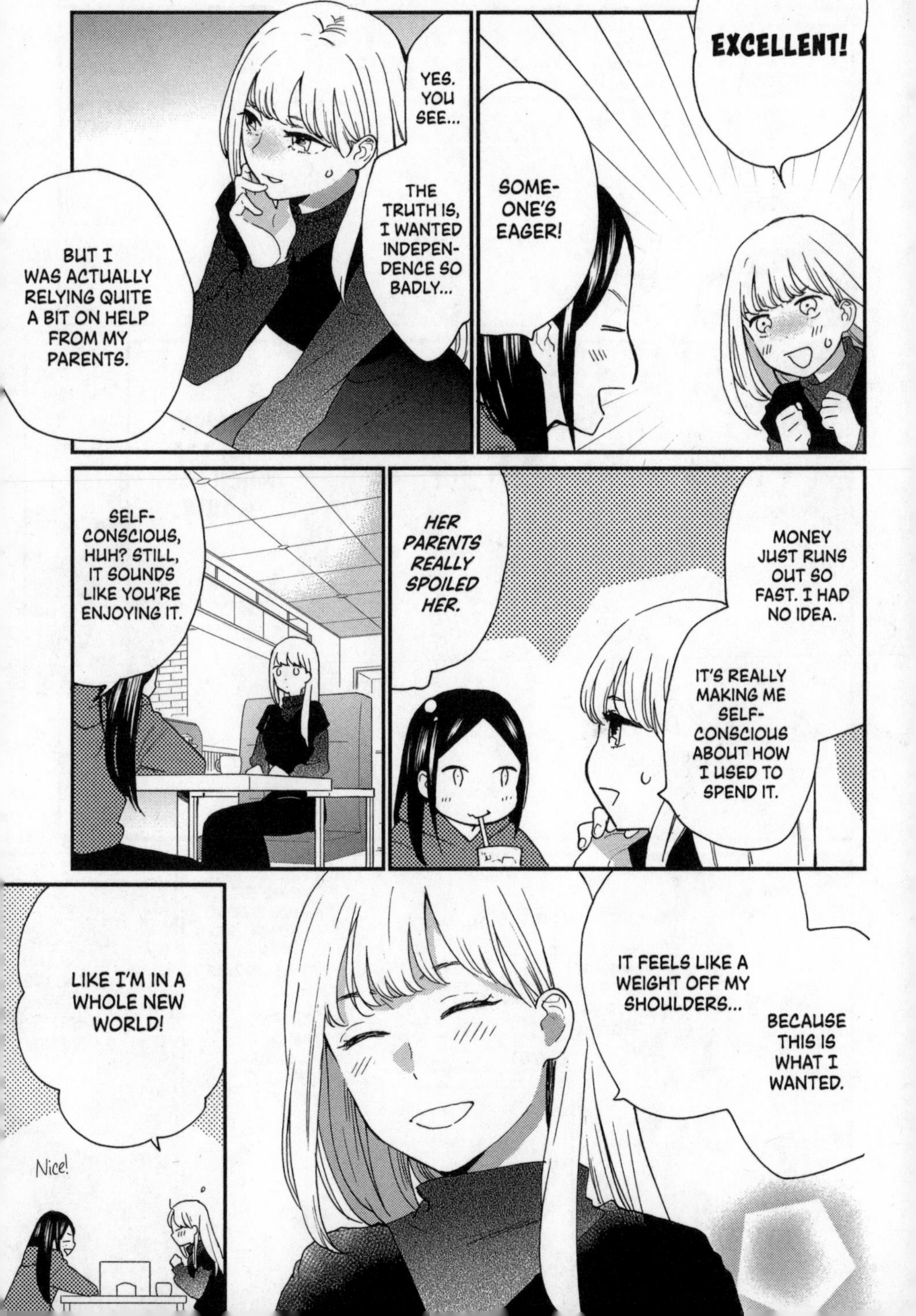
EXCELLENT!
SOME-ONE'S EAGER!
YES. YOU SEE...
THE TRUTH IS, I WANTED INDEPENDENCE SO BADLY...
BUT I WAS ACTUALLY RELYING QUITE A BIT ON HELP FROM MY PARENTS.
MONEY JUST RUNS OUT SO FAST. I HAD NO IDEA.
IT'S REALLY MAKING ME SELF-CONSCIOUS ABOUT HOW I USED TO SPEND IT.
HER PARENTS REALLY SPOILED HER.
SELF-CONSCIOUS, HUH? STILL, IT SOUNDS LIKE YOU'RE ENJOYING IT.
IT FEELS LIKE A WEIGHT OFF MY SHOULDERS...
BECAUSE THIS IS WHAT I WANTED.
LIKE I'M IN A WHOLE NEW WORLD!
Nice!

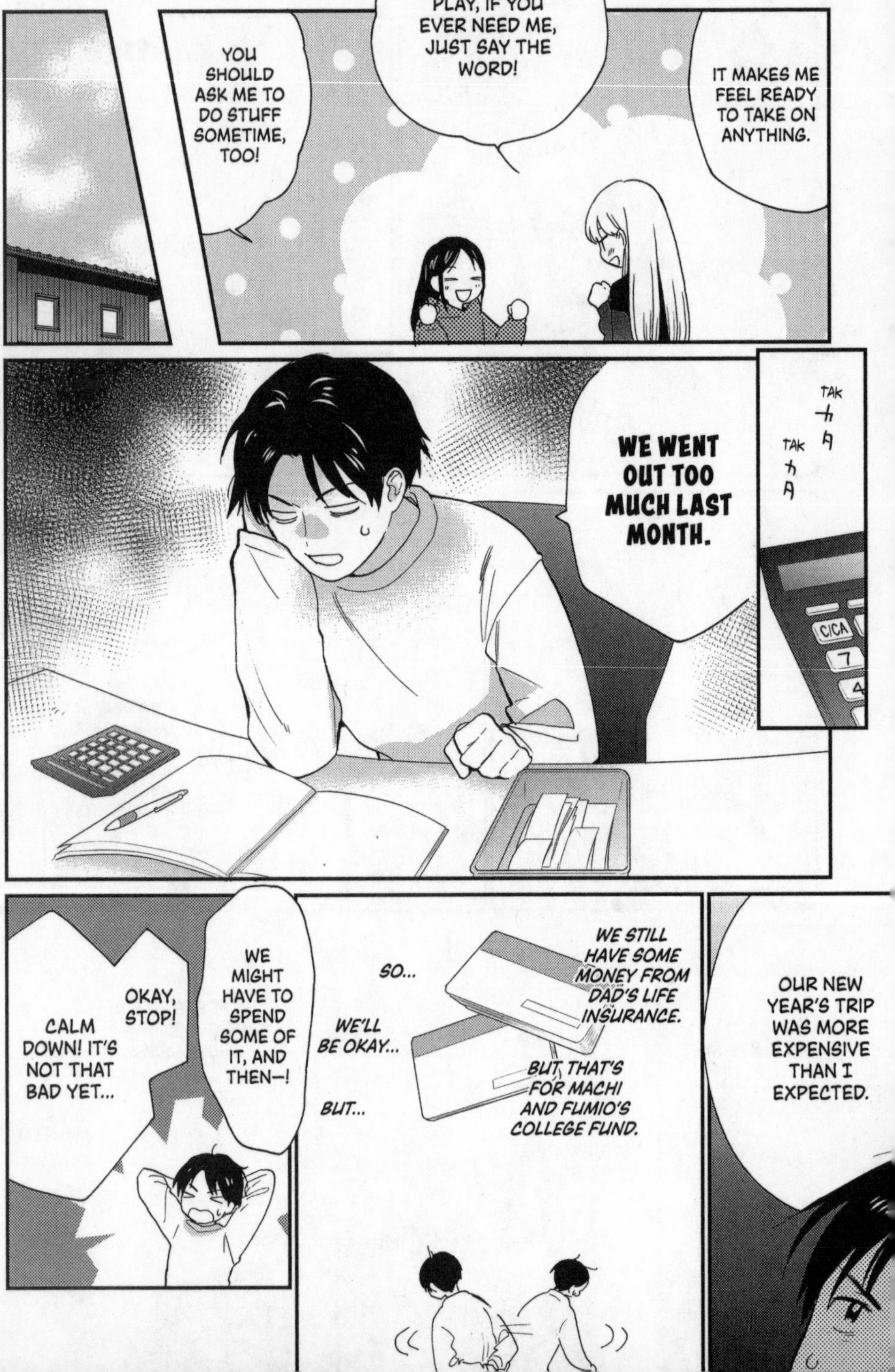
IT MAKES ME FEEL READY TO TAKE ON ANYTHING.
WORK OR PLAY, IF YOU EVER NEED ME, JUST SAY THE WORD!
YOU SHOULD ASK ME TO DO STUFF SOMETIME, TOO!
TAK カ タ
TAK カ タ
WE WENT OUT TOO MUCH LAST MONTH.
OUR NEW YEAR'S TRIP WAS MORE EXPENSIVE THAN I EXPECTED.
WE STILL HAVE SOME MONEY FROM DAD'S LIFE INSURANCE.
SO...
BUT, THAT'S FOR MACHI AND FUMIO'S COLLEGE FUND.
WE'LL BE OKAY...
BUT...
WE MIGHT HAVE TO SPEND SOME OF IT, AND THEN—!
OKAY, STOP!
CALM DOWN! IT'S NOT THAT BAD YET...

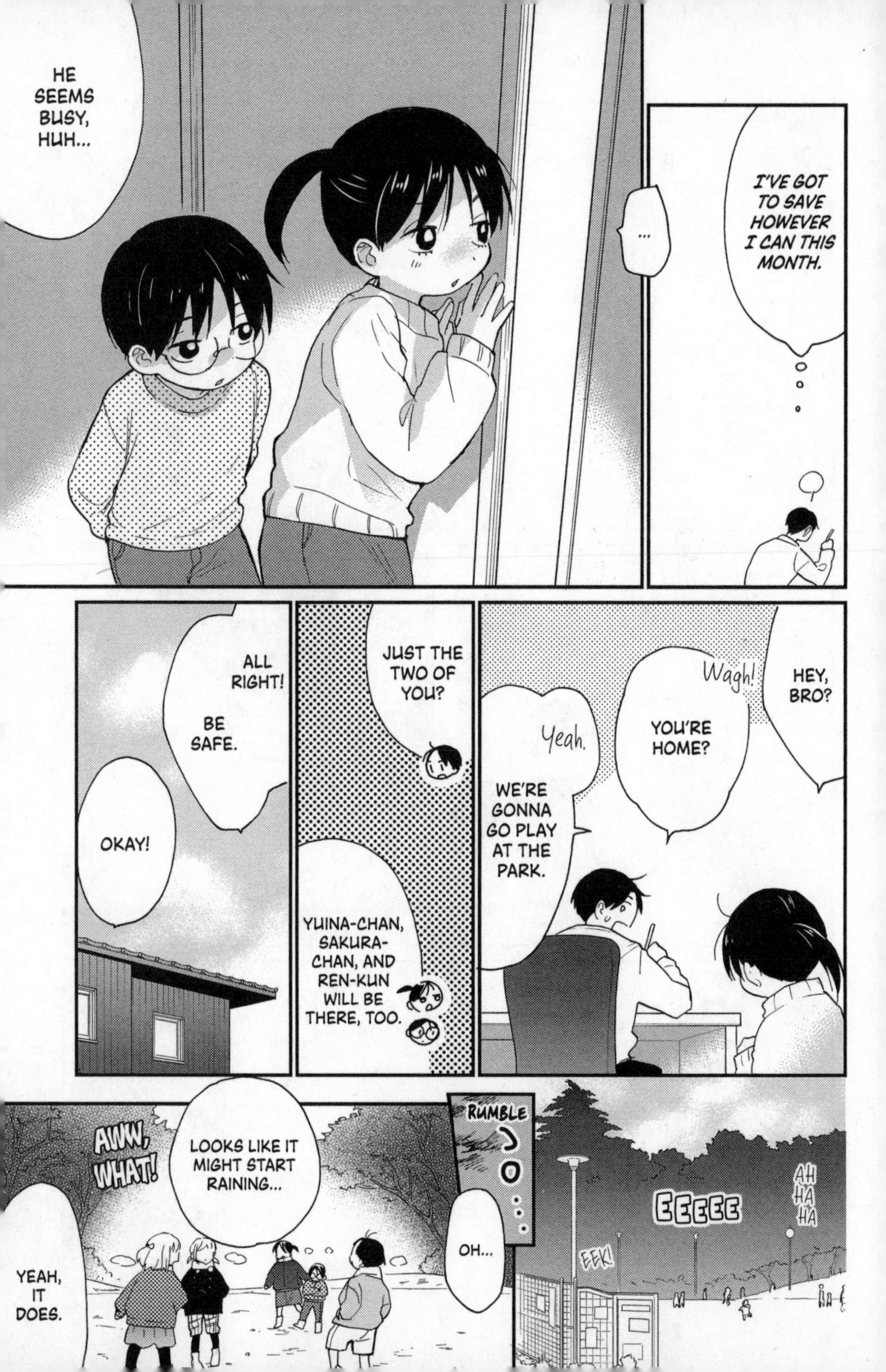
I'VE GOT TO SAVE HOWEVER I CAN THIS MONTH.
...
HE SEEMS BUSY, HUH...
HEY, BRO?
Wagh!
YOU'RE HOME?
Yeah.
WE'RE GONNA GO PLAY AT THE PARK.
JUST THE TWO OF YOU?
YUINA-CHAN, SAKURA-CHAN, AND REN-KUN WILL BE THERE, TOO.
ALL RIGHT!
BE SAFE.
OKAY!
RUMBLE
AH HA HA
EEEEE
EEK!
OH...
LOOKS LIKE IT MIGHT START RAINING...
AWW, WHAT!
YEAH, IT DOES.

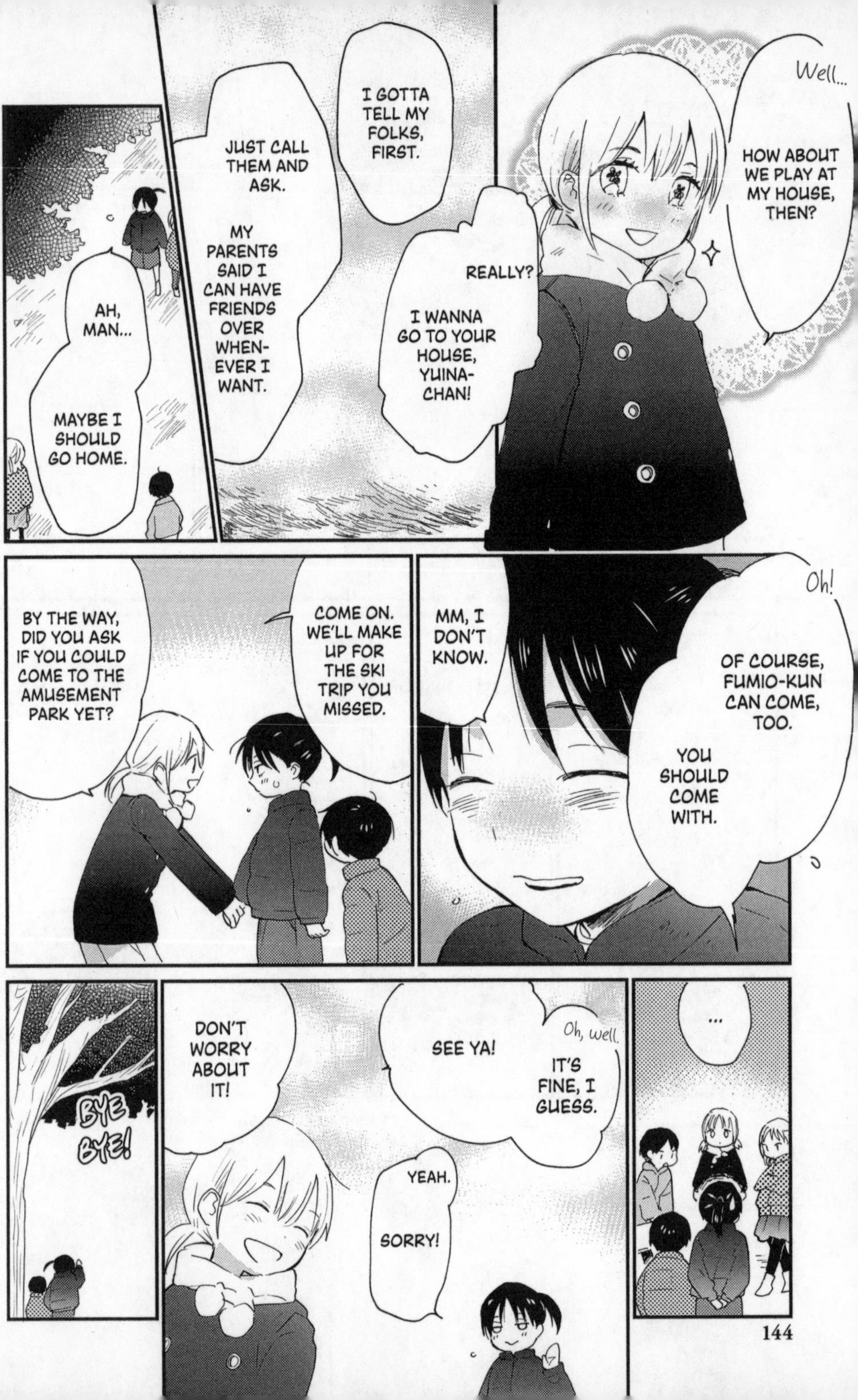

Well...
HOW ABOUT WE PLAY AT MY HOUSE, THEN?
REALLY?
I WANNA GO TO YOUR HOUSE, YUINA-CHAN!
I GOTTA TELL MY FOLKS, FIRST.
JUST CALL THEM AND ASK.
MY PARENTS SAID I CAN HAVE FRIENDS OVER WHENEVER I WANT.
AH, MAN...
MAYBE I SHOULD GO HOME.
Oh!
OF COURSE, FUMIO-KUN CAN COME, TOO.
YOU SHOULD COME WITH.
MM, I DON'T KNOW.
COME ON. WE'LL MAKE UP FOR THE SKI TRIP YOU MISSED.
BY THE WAY, DID YOU ASK IF YOU COULD COME TO THE AMUSEMENT PARK YET?
...
Oh, well.
IT'S FINE, I GUESS.
SEE YA!
DON'T WORRY ABOUT IT!
YEAH.
SORRY!
BYE BYE!

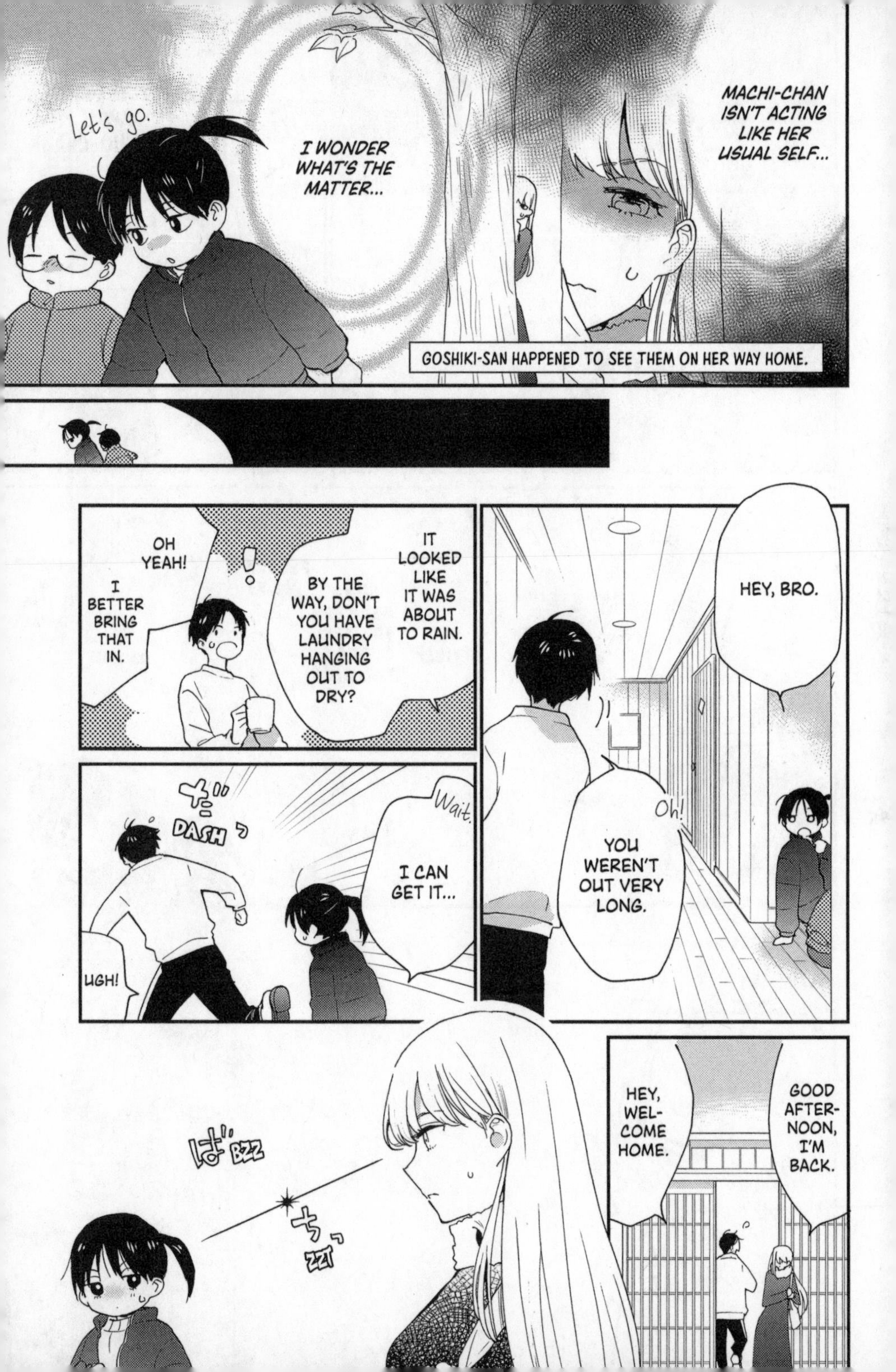
MACHI-CHAN ISN'T ACTING LIKE HER USUAL SELF...
GOSHIKI-SAN HAPPENED TO SEE THEM ON HER WAY HOME.
I WONDER WHAT'S THE MATTER...
Let's go.
HEY, BRO.
Oh!
YOU WEREN'T OUT VERY LONG.
IT LOOKED LIKE IT WAS ABOUT TO RAIN.
BY THE WAY, DON'T YOU HAVE LAUNDRY HANGING OUT TO DRY?
!
OH YEAH!
I BETTER BRING THAT IN.
Wait.
I CAN GET IT...
DASH
UGH!
GOOD AFTERNOON, I'M BACK.
HEY, WELCOME HOME.
BZZ
ZZT

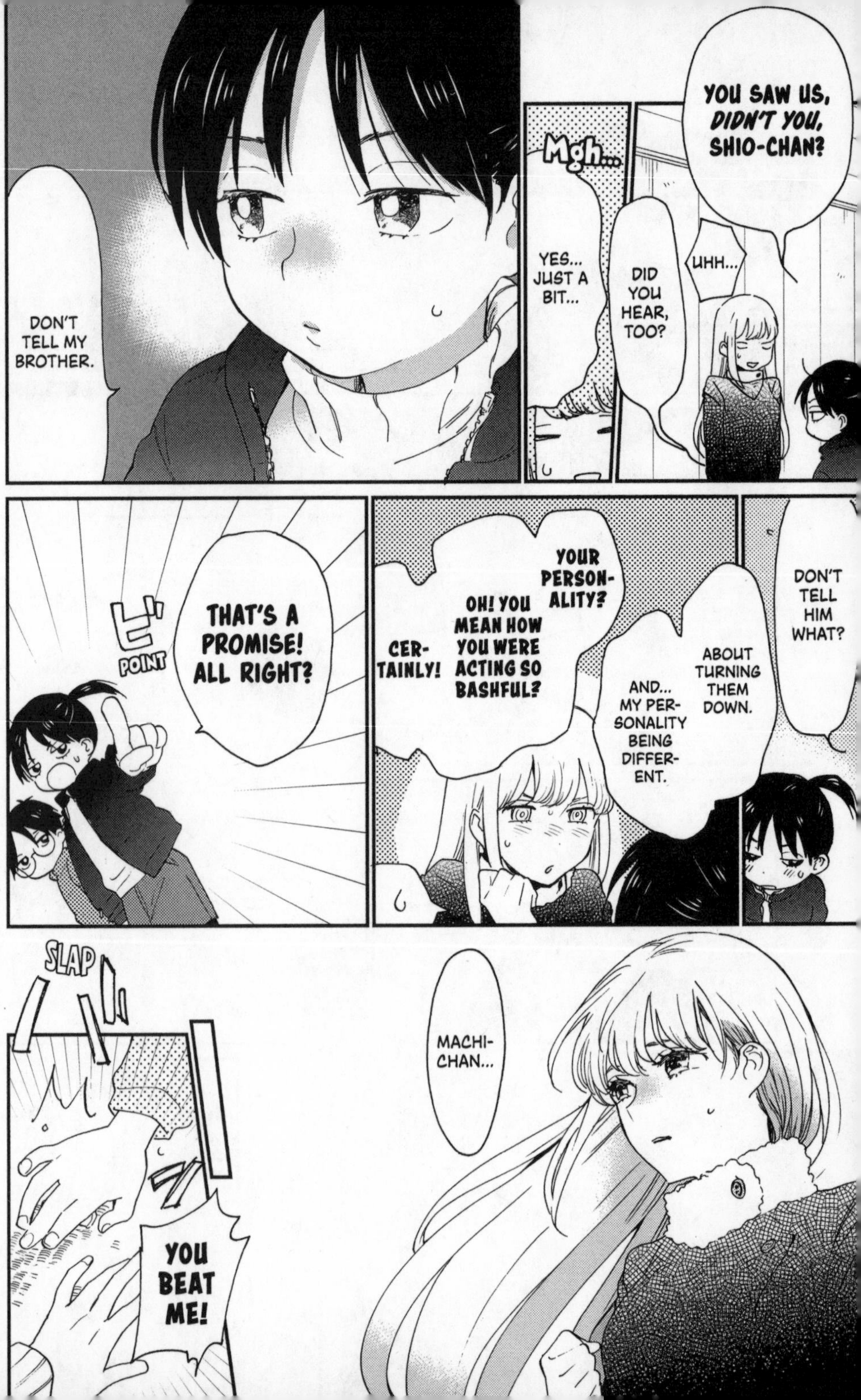
YOU SAW US, DIDN'T YOU, SHIO-CHAN?
UHH...
DID YOU HEAR, TOO?
YES... JUST A BIT...
Mgh...
DON'T TELL MY BROTHER.
DON'T TELL HIM WHAT?
ABOUT TURNING THEM DOWN.
AND... MY PERSONALITY BEING DIFFERENT.
YOUR PERSONALITY?
OH! YOU MEAN HOW YOU WERE ACTING SO BASHFUL?
CERTAINLY!
THAT'S A PROMISE! ALL RIGHT?
ビ
POINT
MACHI-CHAN...
SLAP
YOU BEAT ME!

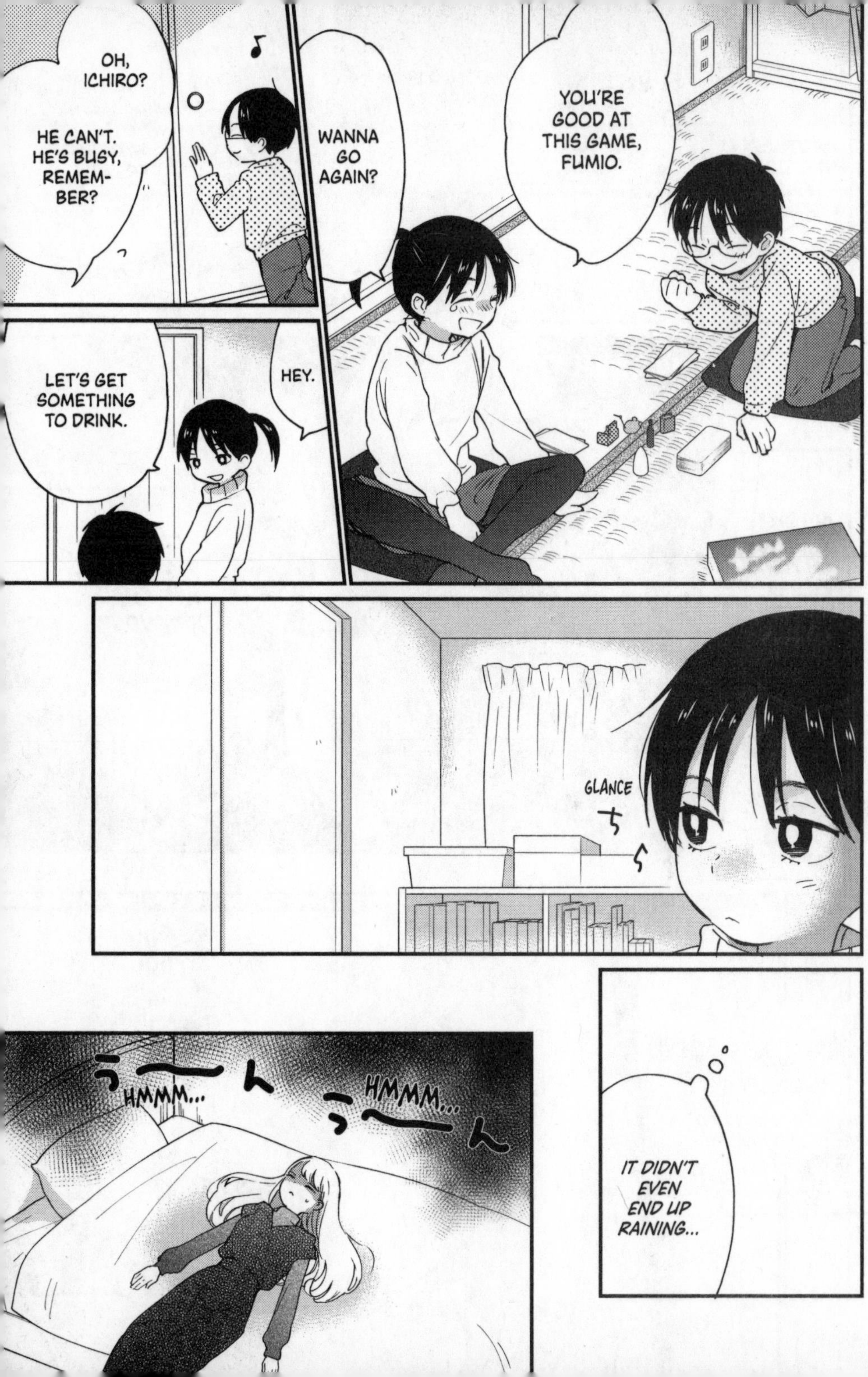
YOU'RE GOOD AT THIS GAME, FUMIO.
WANNA GO AGAIN?
OH, ICHIRO?
HE CAN'T. HE'S BUSY, REMEMBER?
HEY.
LET'S GET SOMETHING TO DRINK.
GLANCE
IT DIDN'T EVEN END UP RAINING...
うーーん HMMM...
うーーん HMMM...

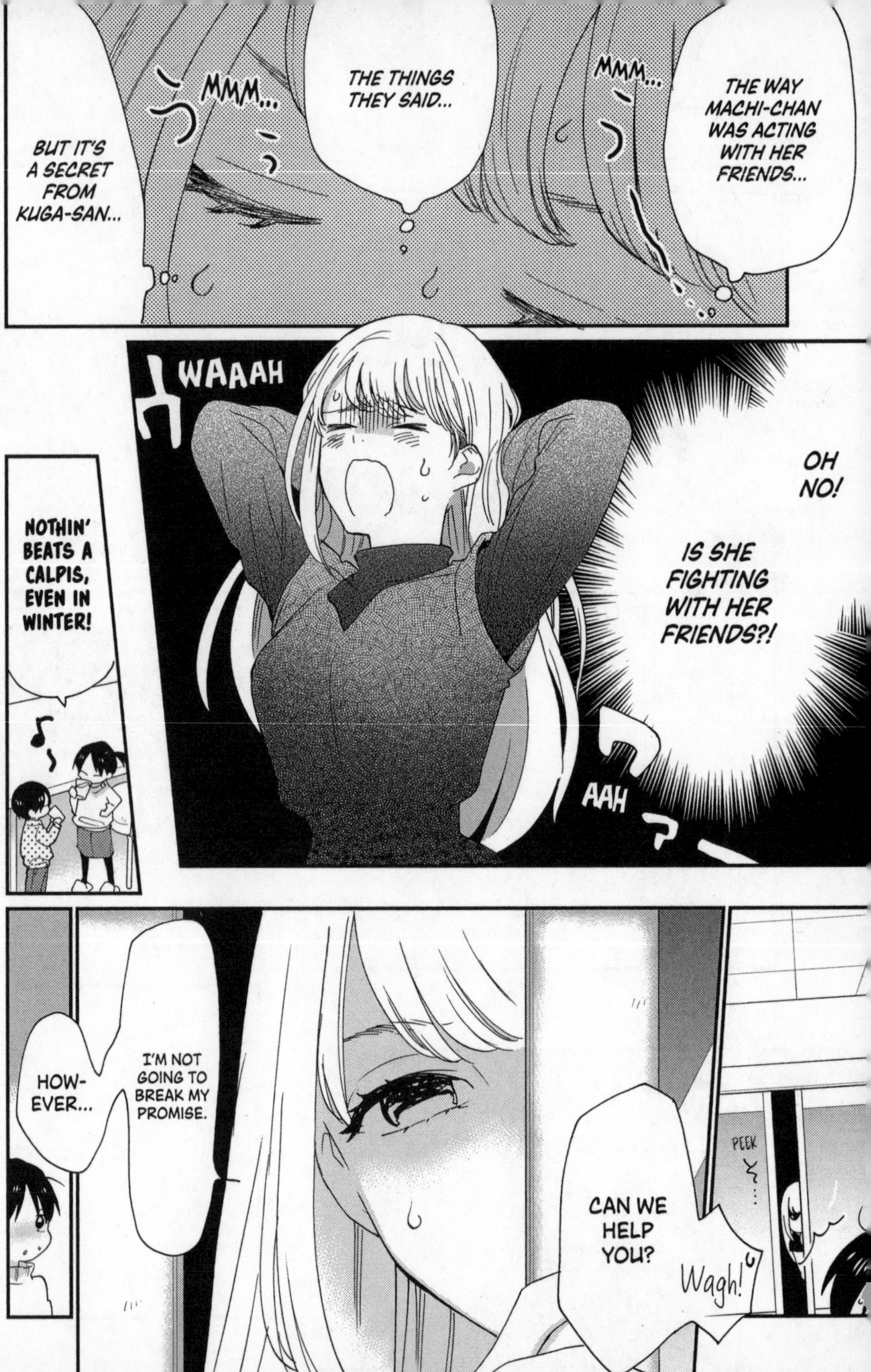

THE WAY MACHI-CHAN WAS ACTING WITH HER FRIENDS...
MMM...
THE THINGS THEY SAID...
MMM...
BUT IT'S A SECRET FROM KUGA-SAN...
OH NO!
IS SHE FIGHTING WITH HER FRIENDS?!
WAAAH
AAH
NOTHIN' BEATS A CALPIS, EVEN IN WINTER!
PEEK
CAN WE HELP YOU?
Wagh!
I'M NOT GOING TO BREAK MY PROMISE.
HOW-EVER...

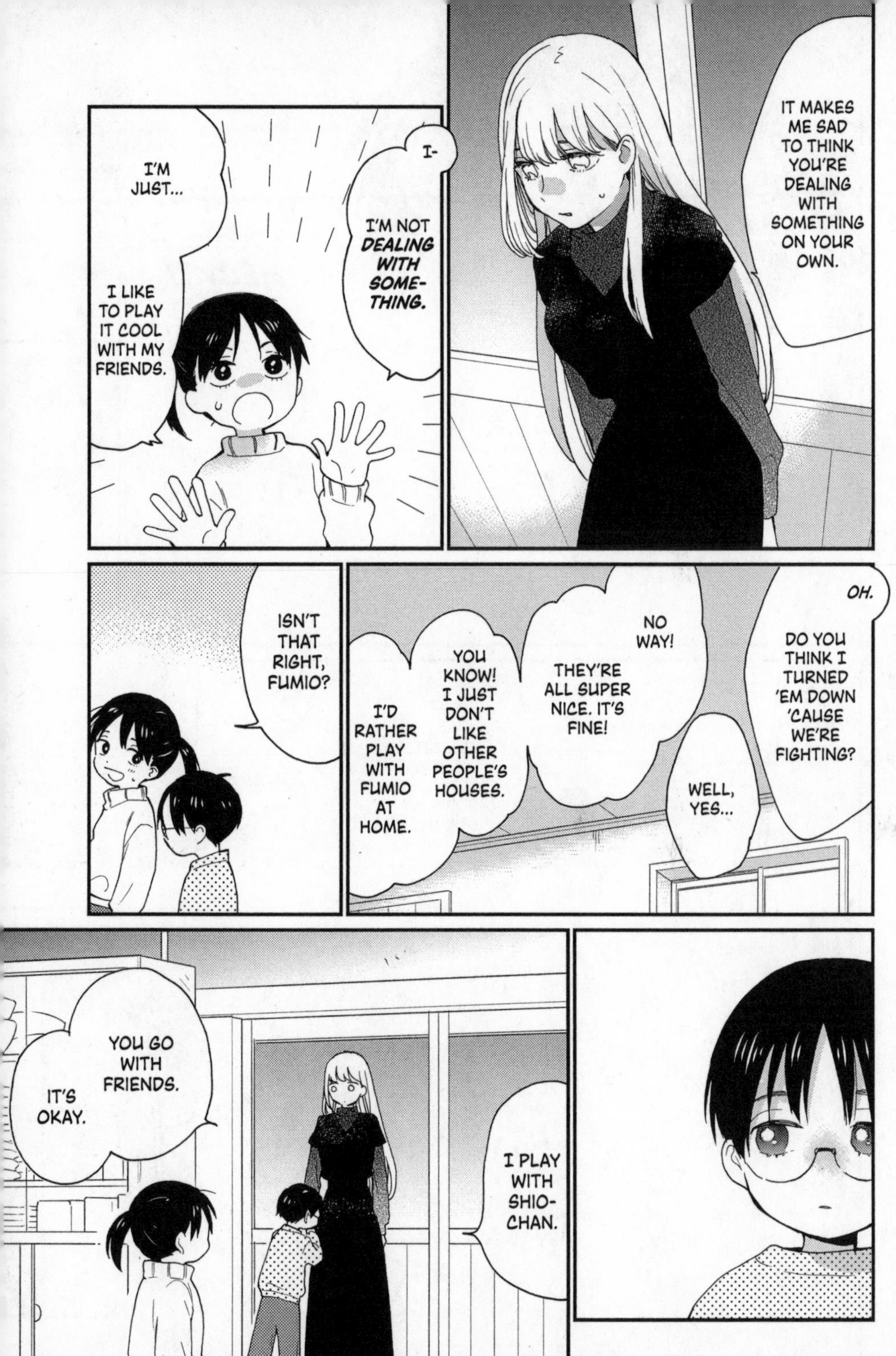
IT MAKES ME SAD TO THINK YOU'RE DEALING WITH SOMETHING ON YOUR OWN.
I-
I'M NOT *DEALING WITH SOME-THING.*
I'M JUST...
I LIKE TO PLAY IT COOL WITH MY FRIENDS.
OH.
DO YOU THINK I TURNED 'EM DOWN 'CAUSE WE'RE FIGHTING?
WELL, YES...
NO WAY!
THEY'RE ALL SUPER NICE. IT'S FINE!
YOU KNOW! I JUST DON'T LIKE OTHER PEOPLE'S HOUSES.
I'D RATHER PLAY WITH FUMIO AT HOME.
ISN'T THAT RIGHT, FUMIO?
I PLAY WITH SHIO-CHAN.
YOU GO WITH FRIENDS.
IT'S OKAY.

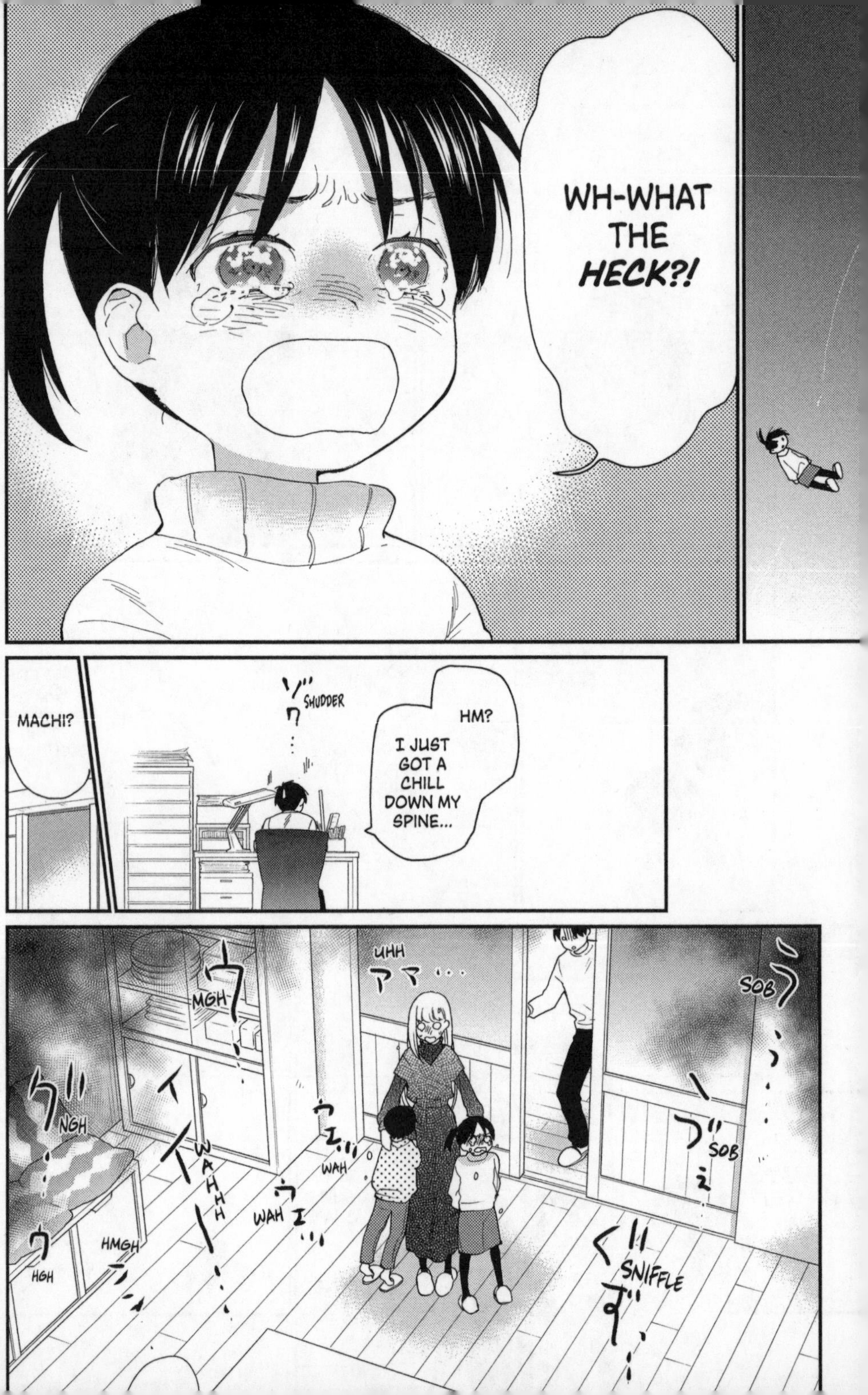
WH-WHAT THE HECK?!
SHUDDER
HM? I JUST GOT A CHILL DOWN MY SPINE...
MACHI?
SOB
SOB
SNIFFLE
UHH
WAH
WAH
MGH
WAHHH
NGH
HMGH
HGH

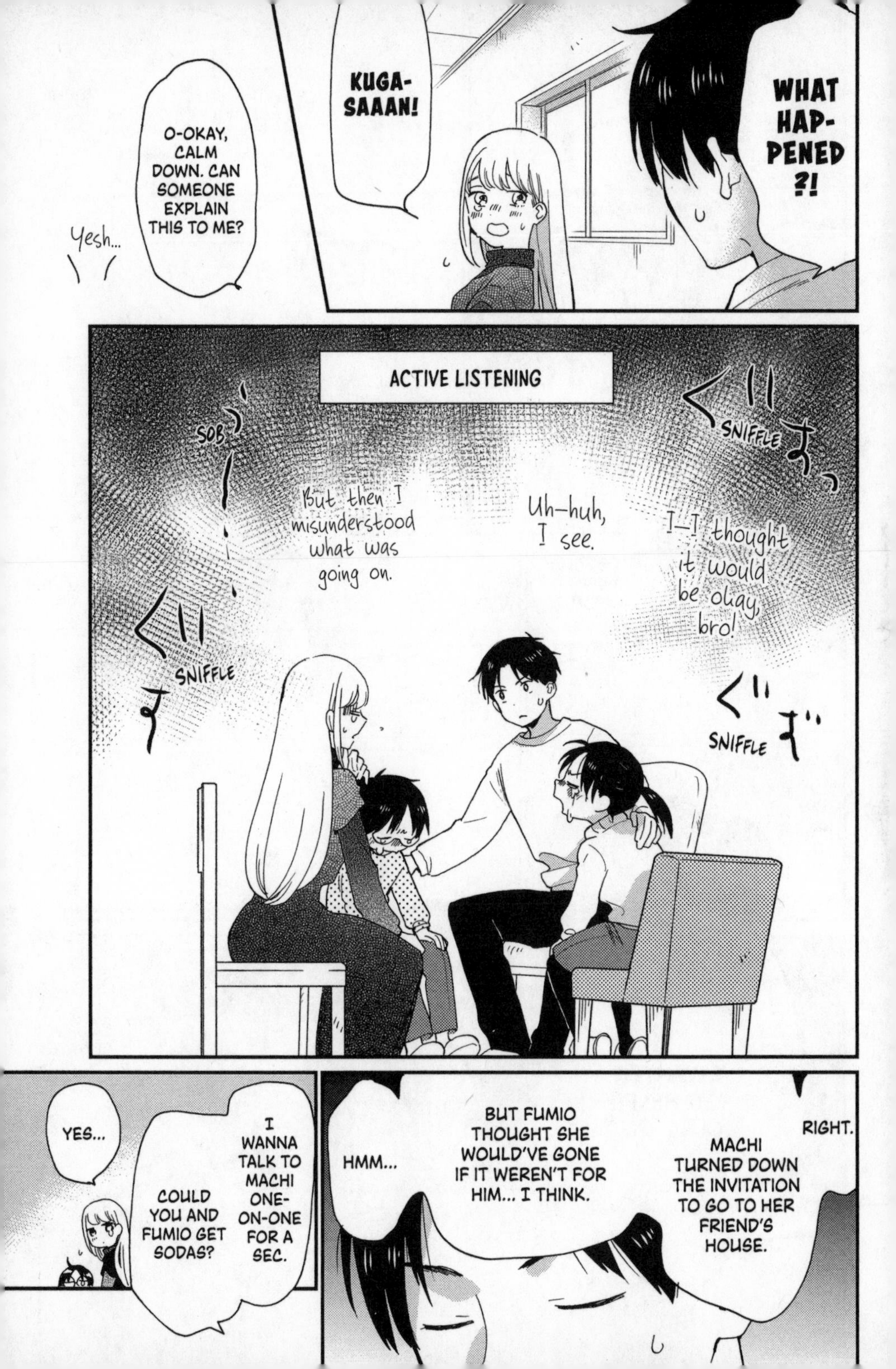
WHAT HAP-PENED ?!
KUGA-SAAAN!
O-OKAY, CALM DOWN. CAN SOMEONE EXPLAIN THIS TO ME?
Yesh...
ACTIVE LISTENING
SNIFFLE
I-I thought it would be okay, bro!
Uh-huh, I see.
But then I misunderstood what was going on.
SOB
SNIFFLE
SNIFFLE
RIGHT.
MACHI TURNED DOWN THE INVITATION TO GO TO HER FRIEND'S HOUSE.
BUT FUMIO THOUGHT SHE WOULD'VE GONE IF IT WEREN'T FOR HIM... I THINK.
HMM...
I WANNA TALK TO MACHI ONE-ON-ONE FOR A SEC.
COULD YOU AND FUMIO GET SODAS?
YES...

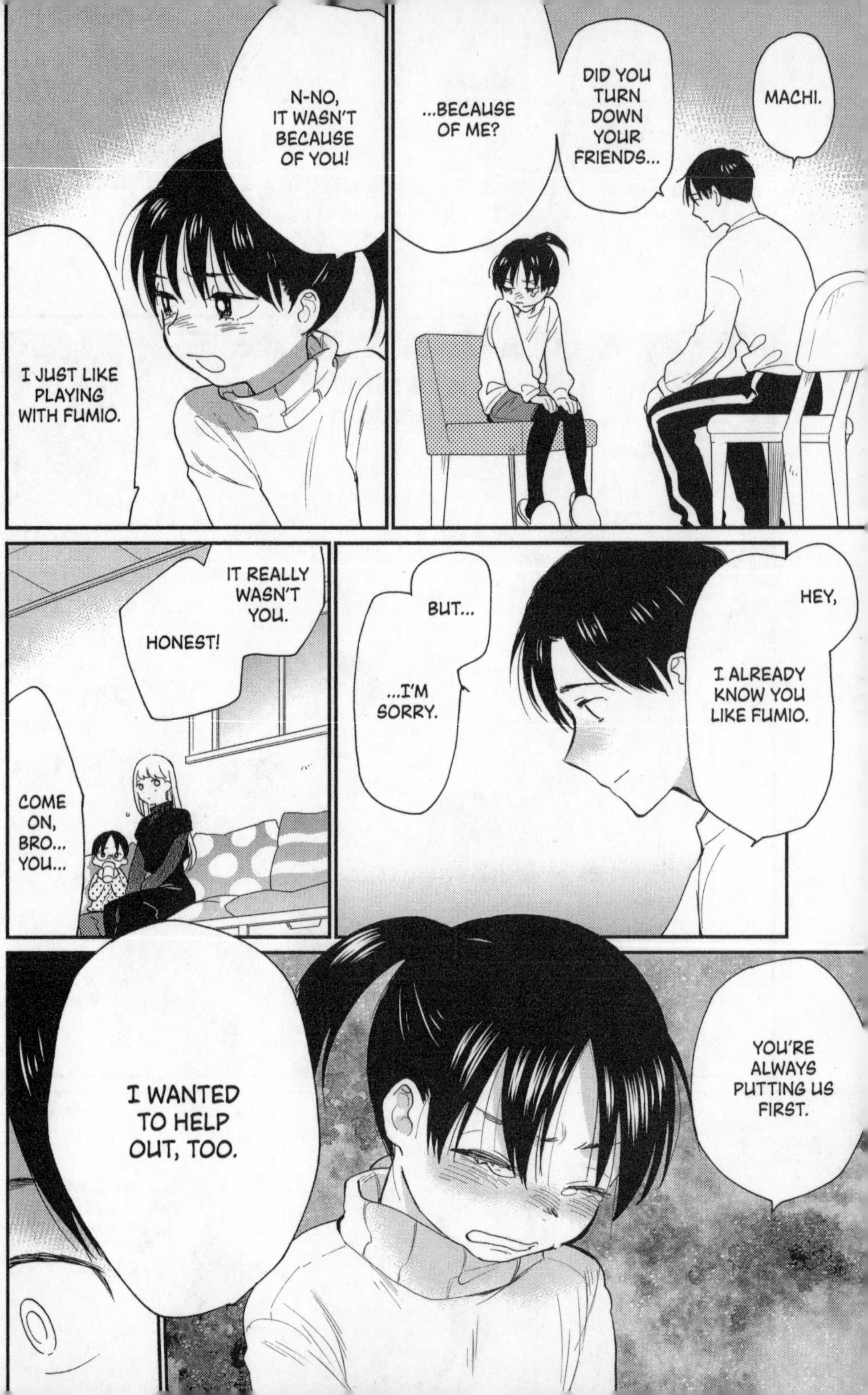
MACHI.
DID YOU TURN DOWN YOUR FRIENDS...
...BECAUSE OF ME?
N-NO, IT WASN'T BECAUSE OF YOU!
I JUST LIKE PLAYING WITH FUMIO.
HEY,
I ALREADY KNOW YOU LIKE FUMIO.
BUT...
...I'M SORRY.
IT REALLY WASN'T YOU.
HONEST!
COME ON, BRO... YOU...
YOU'RE ALWAYS PUTTING US FIRST.
I WANTED TO HELP OUT, TOO.

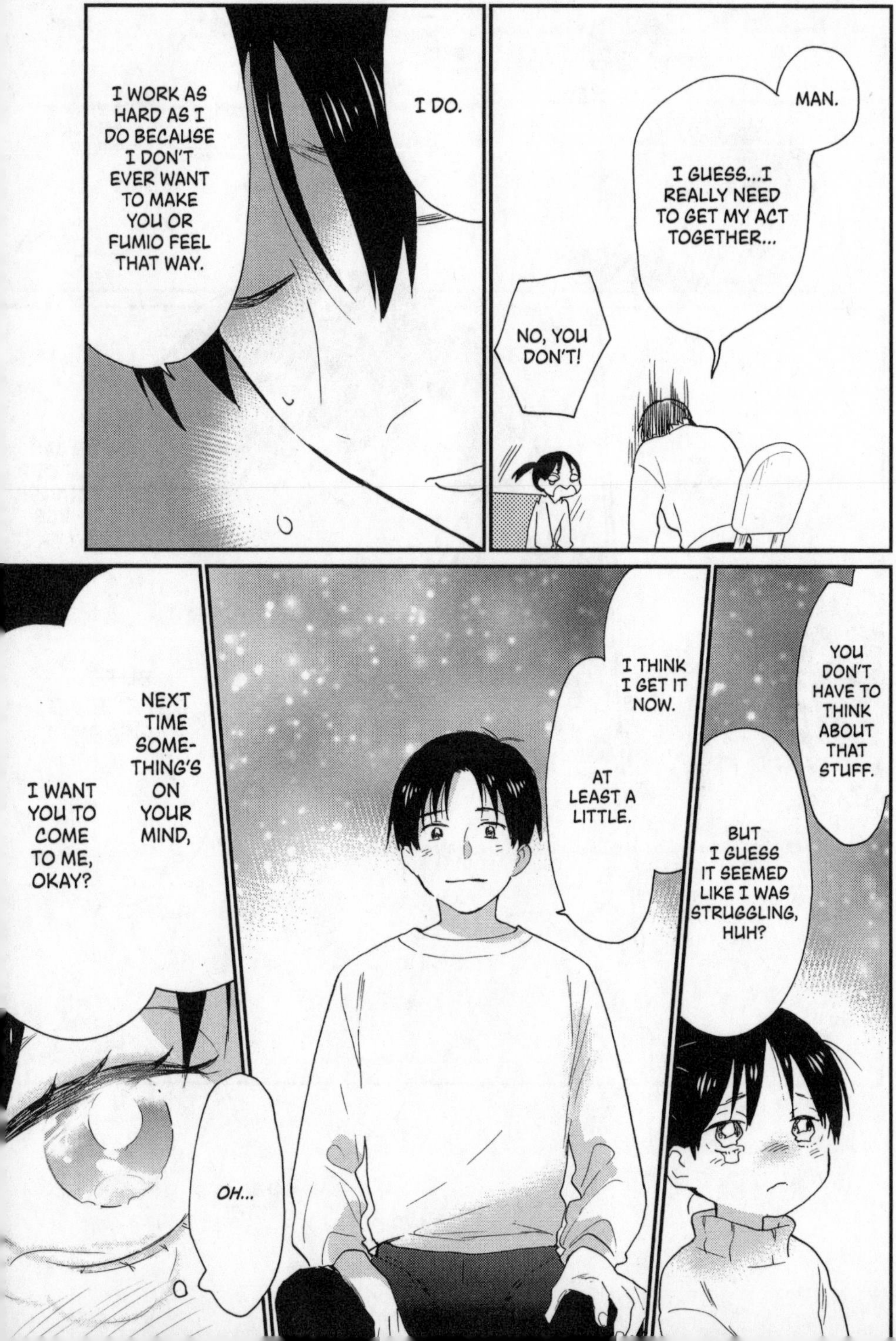
MAN.
I GUESS...I REALLY NEED TO GET MY ACT TOGETHER...
NO, YOU DON'T!
I DO.
I WORK AS HARD AS I DO BECAUSE I DON'T EVER WANT TO MAKE YOU OR FUMIO FEEL THAT WAY.
YOU DON'T HAVE TO THINK ABOUT THAT STUFF.
BUT I GUESS IT SEEMED LIKE I WAS STRUGGLING, HUH?
I THINK I GET IT NOW.
AT LEAST A LITTLE.
OH...
NEXT TIME SOMETHING'S ON YOUR MIND,
I WANT YOU TO COME TO ME, OKAY?

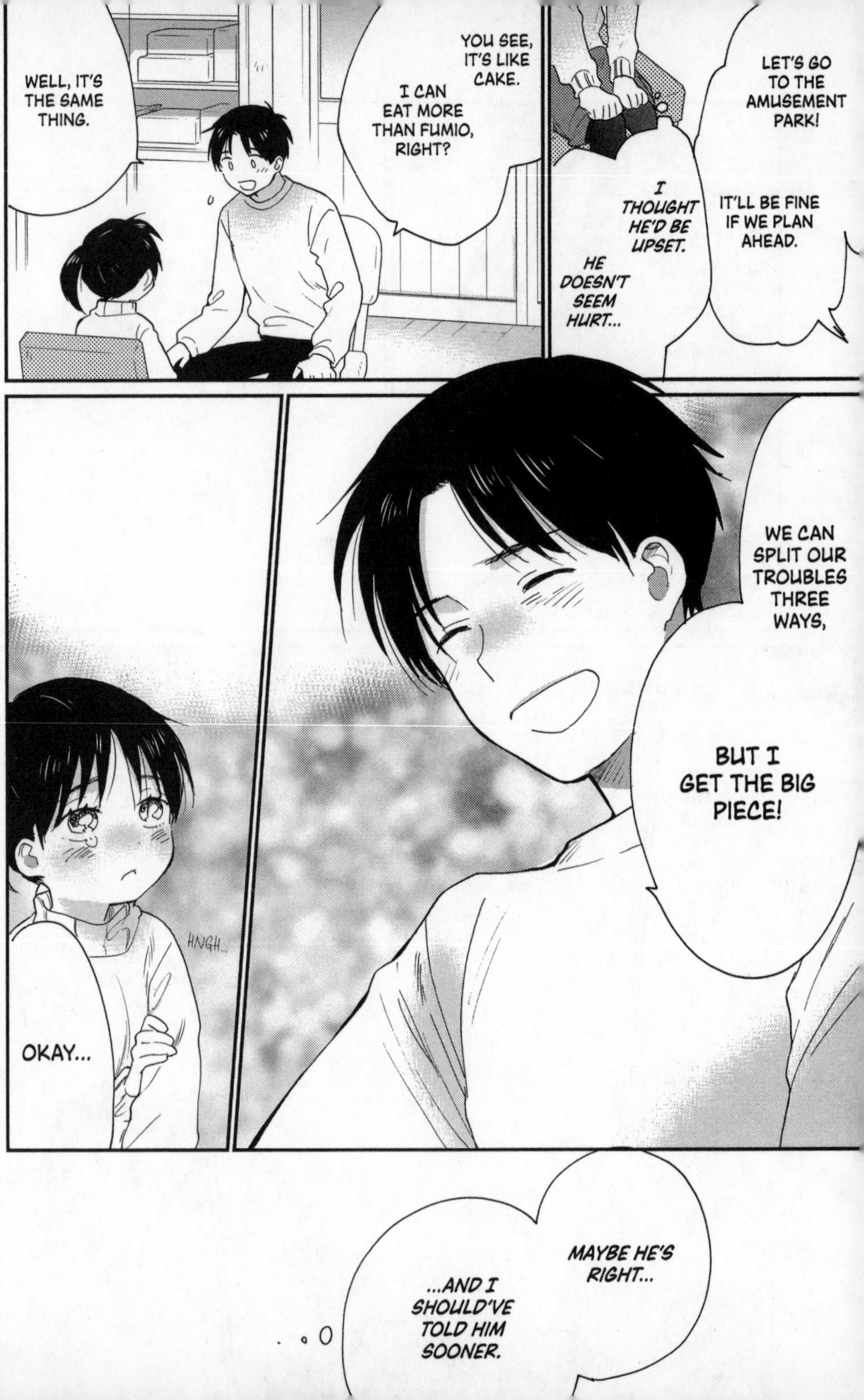
LET'S GO TO THE AMUSEMENT PARK!
IT'LL BE FINE IF WE PLAN AHEAD.
I THOUGHT HE'D BE UPSET.
HE DOESN'T SEEM HURT...
YOU SEE, IT'S LIKE CAKE.
I CAN EAT MORE THAN FUMIO, RIGHT?
WELL, IT'S THE SAME THING.
WE CAN SPLIT OUR TROUBLES THREE WAYS,
BUT I GET THE BIG PIECE!
HNGH...
OKAY...
MAYBE HE'S RIGHT...
...AND I SHOULD'VE TOLD HIM SOONER.

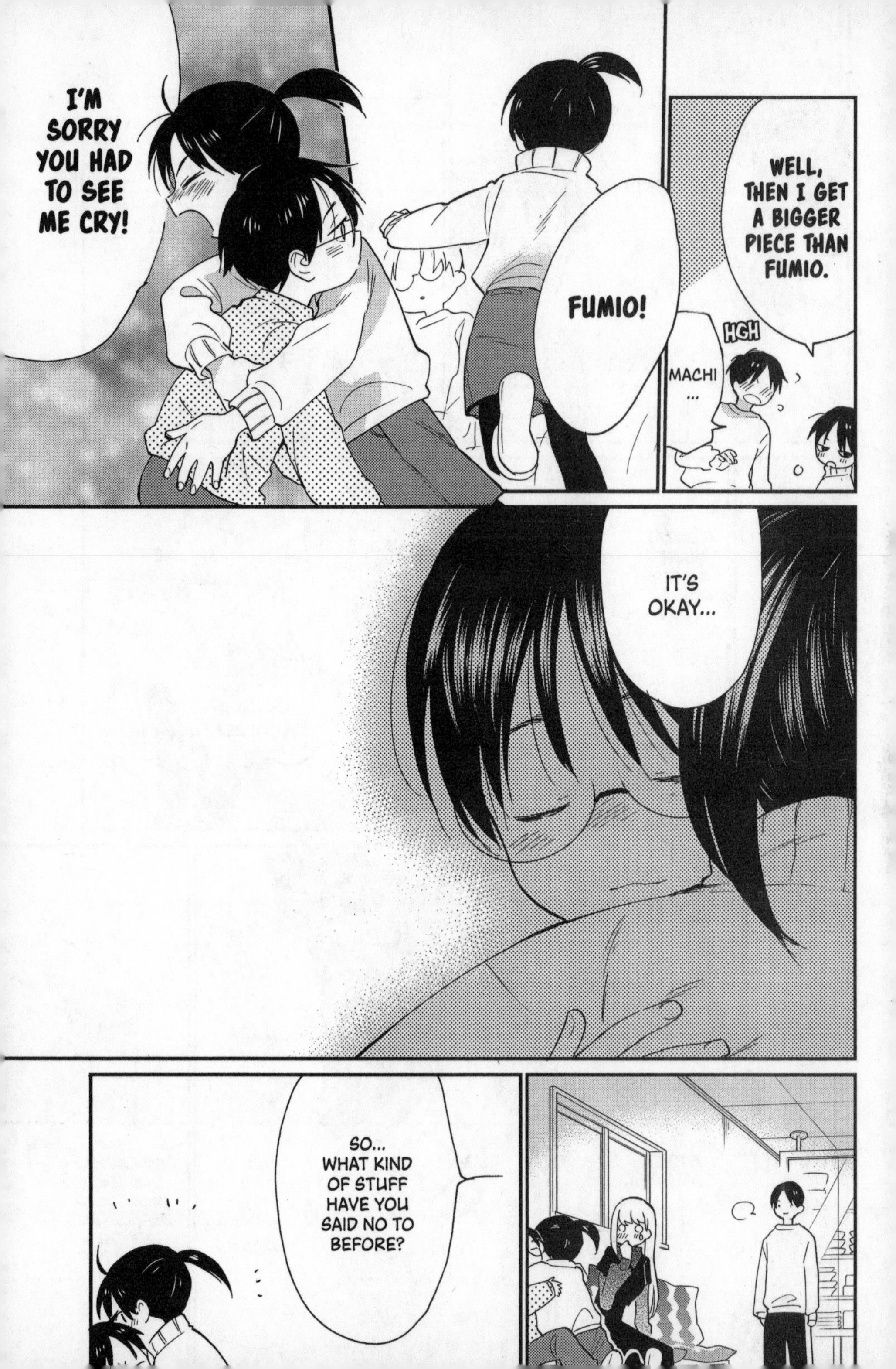
WELL, THEN I GET A BIGGER PIECE THAN FUMIO.
HGH
MACHI ...
FUMIO!
I'M SORRY YOU HAD TO SEE ME CRY!
IT'S OKAY...
SO... WHAT KIND OF STUFF HAVE YOU SAID NO TO BEFORE?

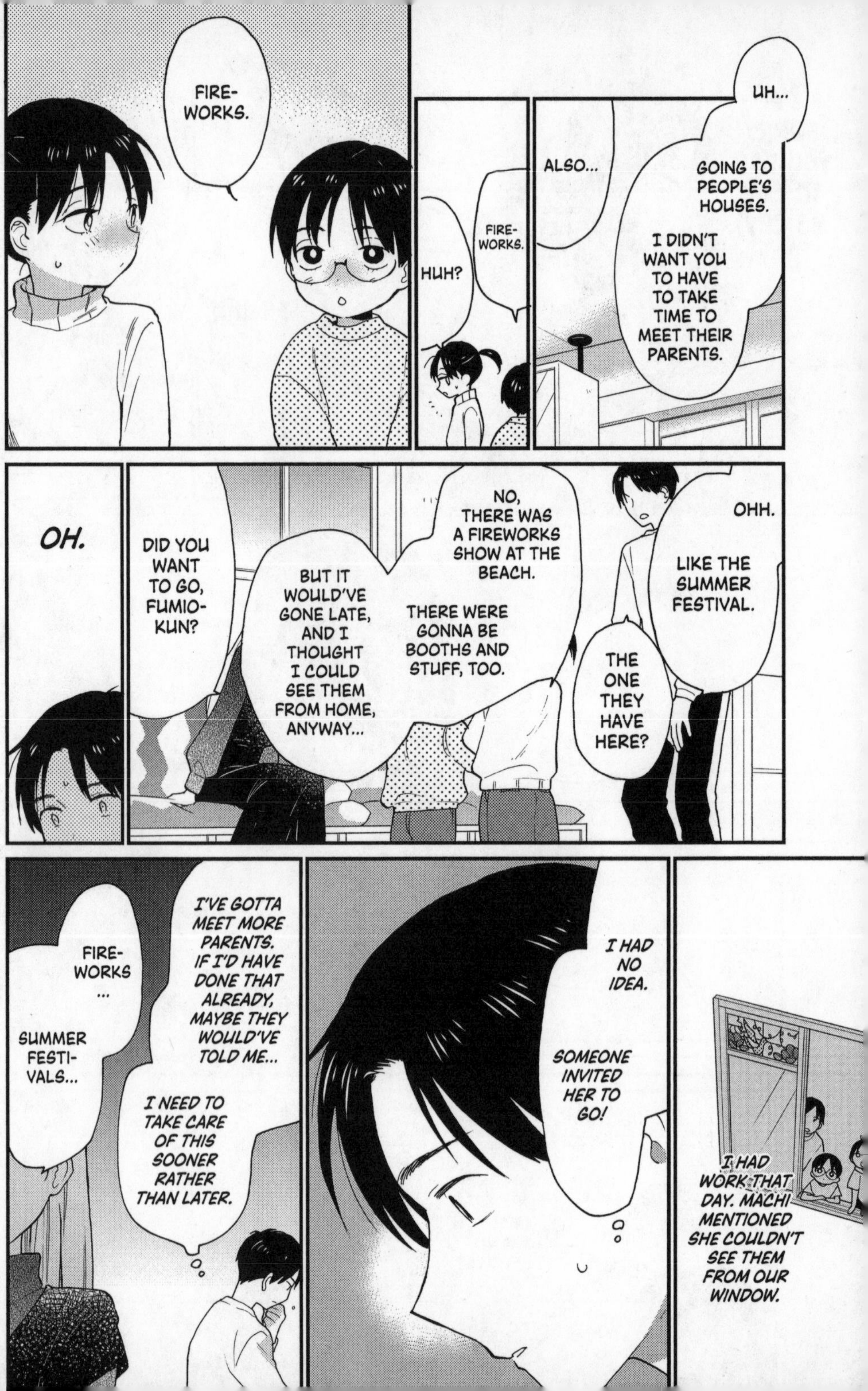
UH...
GOING TO PEOPLE'S HOUSES.
I DIDN'T WANT YOU TO HAVE TO TAKE TIME TO MEET THEIR PARENTS.
ALSO...
FIRE-WORKS.
HUH?
FIRE-WORKS.
OHH.
LIKE THE SUMMER FESTIVAL.
THE ONE THEY HAVE HERE?
NO, THERE WAS A FIREWORKS SHOW AT THE BEACH.
THERE WERE GONNA BE BOOTHS AND STUFF, TOO.
BUT IT WOULD'VE GONE LATE, AND I THOUGHT I COULD SEE THEM FROM HOME, ANYWAY...
DID YOU WANT TO GO, FUMIO-KUN?
OH.
I HAD WORK THAT DAY. MACHI MENTIONED SHE COULDN'T SEE THEM FROM OUR WINDOW.
I HAD NO IDEA.
SOMEONE INVITED HER TO GO!
I'VE GOTTA MEET MORE PARENTS. IF I'D HAVE DONE THAT ALREADY, MAYBE THEY WOULD'VE TOLD ME...
FIRE-WORKS...
SUMMER FESTI-VALS...
I NEED TO TAKE CARE OF THIS SOONER RATHER THAN LATER.

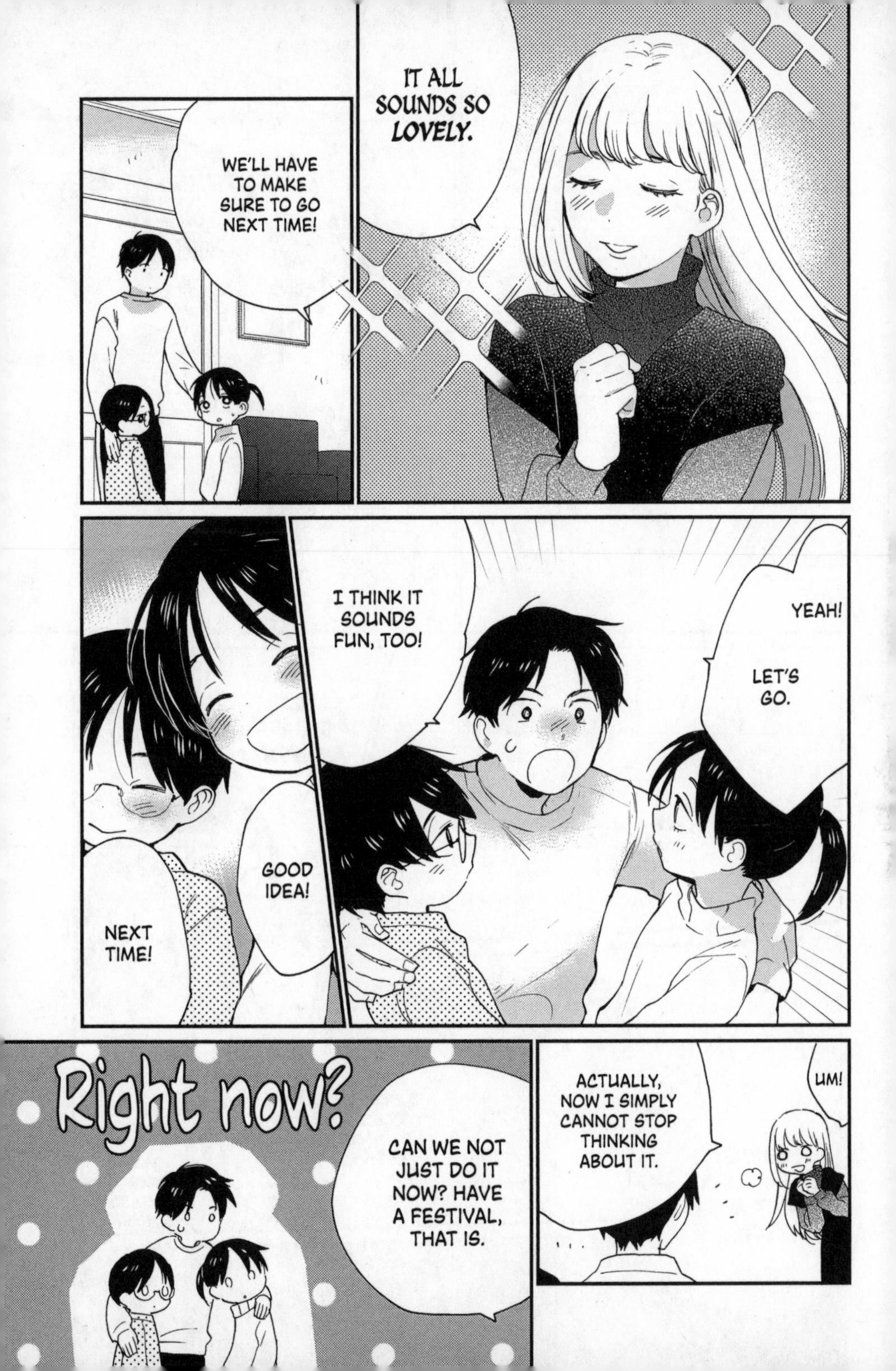
IT ALL SOUNDS SO *LOVELY.*
WE'LL HAVE TO MAKE SURE TO GO NEXT TIME!
YEAH!
LET'S GO.
I THINK IT SOUNDS FUN, TOO!
GOOD IDEA!
NEXT TIME!
UM!
ACTUALLY, NOW I SIMPLY CANNOT STOP THINKING ABOUT IT.
...
CAN WE NOT JUST DO IT NOW? HAVE A FESTIVAL, THAT IS.
Right now?

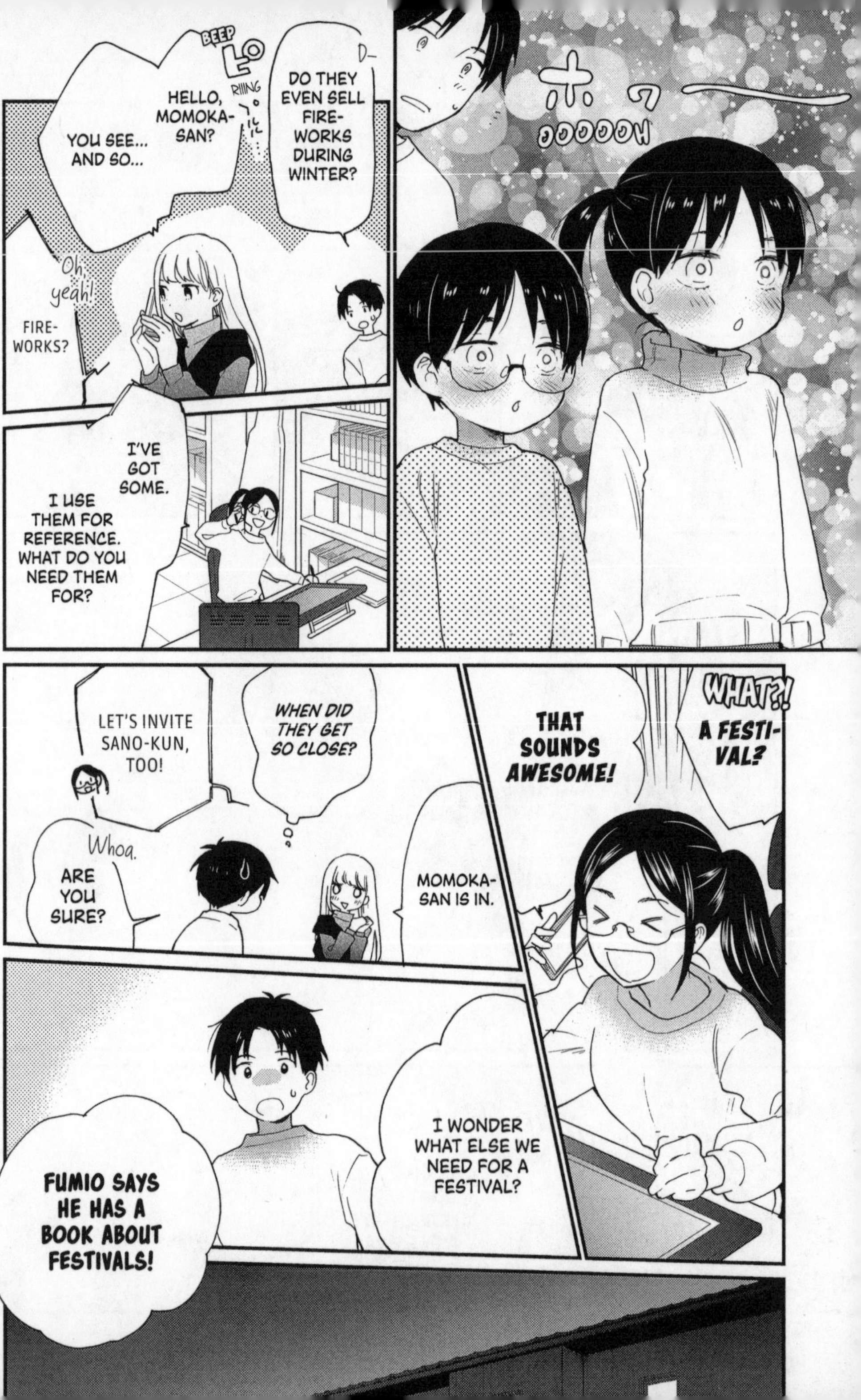
OOOOOOH
D–
DO THEY EVEN SELL FIRE-WORKS DURING WINTER?
BEEP
RIIING
HELLO, MOMOKA-SAN?
YOU SEE... AND SO...
Oh, yeah!
FIRE-WORKS?
I'VE GOT SOME.
I USE THEM FOR REFERENCE. WHAT DO YOU NEED THEM FOR?
WHAT?!
A FESTI-VAL?
THAT SOUNDS AWESOME!
MOMOKA-SAN IS IN.
WHEN DID THEY GET SO CLOSE?
LET'S INVITE SANO-KUN, TOO!
Whoa.
ARE YOU SURE?
I WONDER WHAT ELSE WE NEED FOR A FESTIVAL?
FUMIO SAYS HE HAS A BOOK ABOUT FESTIVALS!

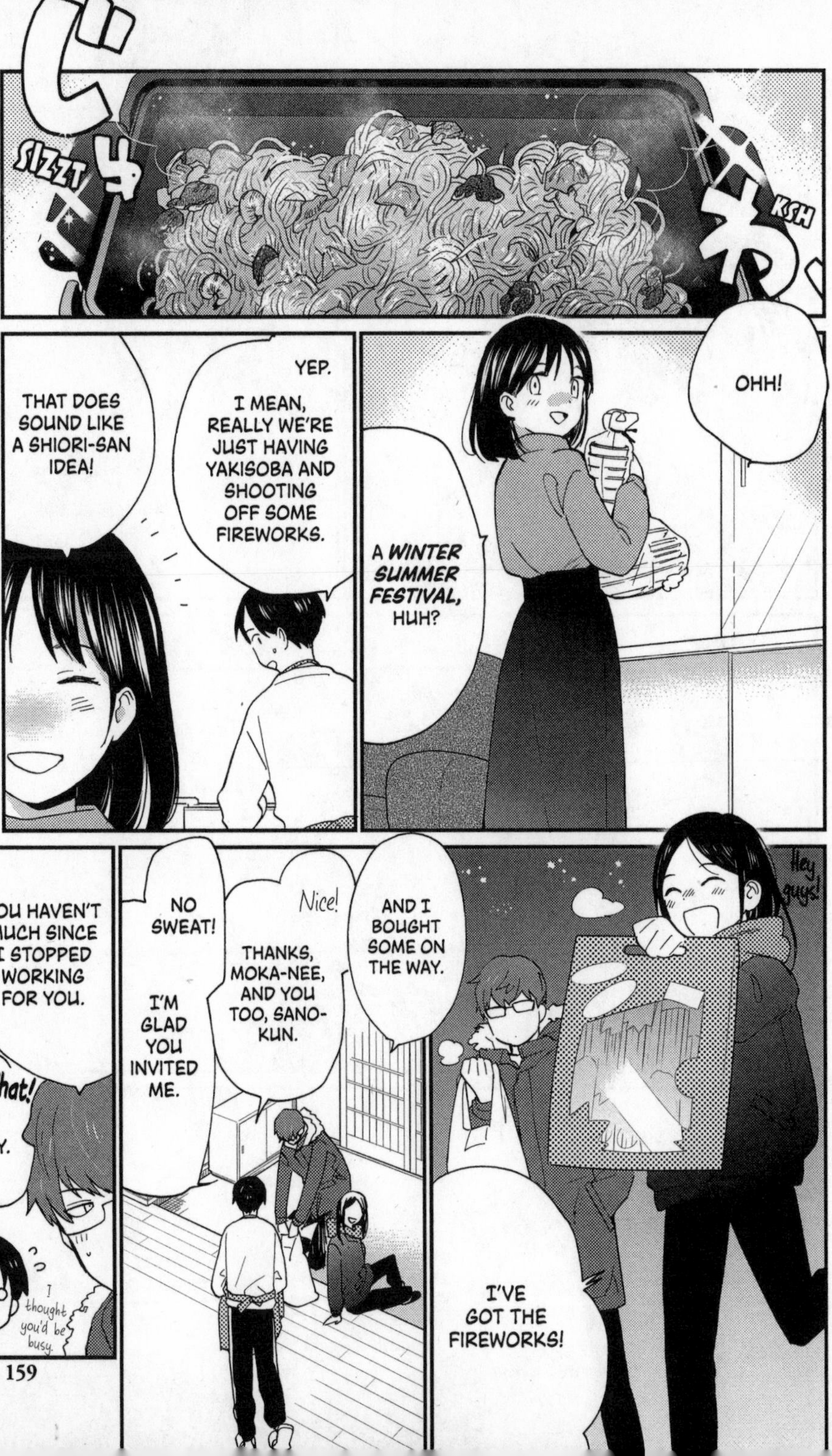
じゅ
SIZZT
わ
KSH
OHH!
A *WINTER SUMMER FESTIVAL*, HUH?
YEP.
I MEAN, REALLY WE'RE JUST HAVING YAKISOBA AND SHOOTING OFF SOME FIREWORKS.
THAT DOES SOUND LIKE A SHIORI-SAN IDEA!
Hey guys!
I'VE GOT THE FIREWORKS!
AND I BOUGHT SOME ON THE WAY.
Nice!
THANKS, MOKA-NEE, AND YOU TOO, SANO-KUN.
NO SWEAT!
I'M GLAD YOU INVITED ME.
YOU HAVEN'T MUCH SINCE I STOPPED WORKING FOR YOU.
What!
I'M SORRY.
I thought you'd be busy.

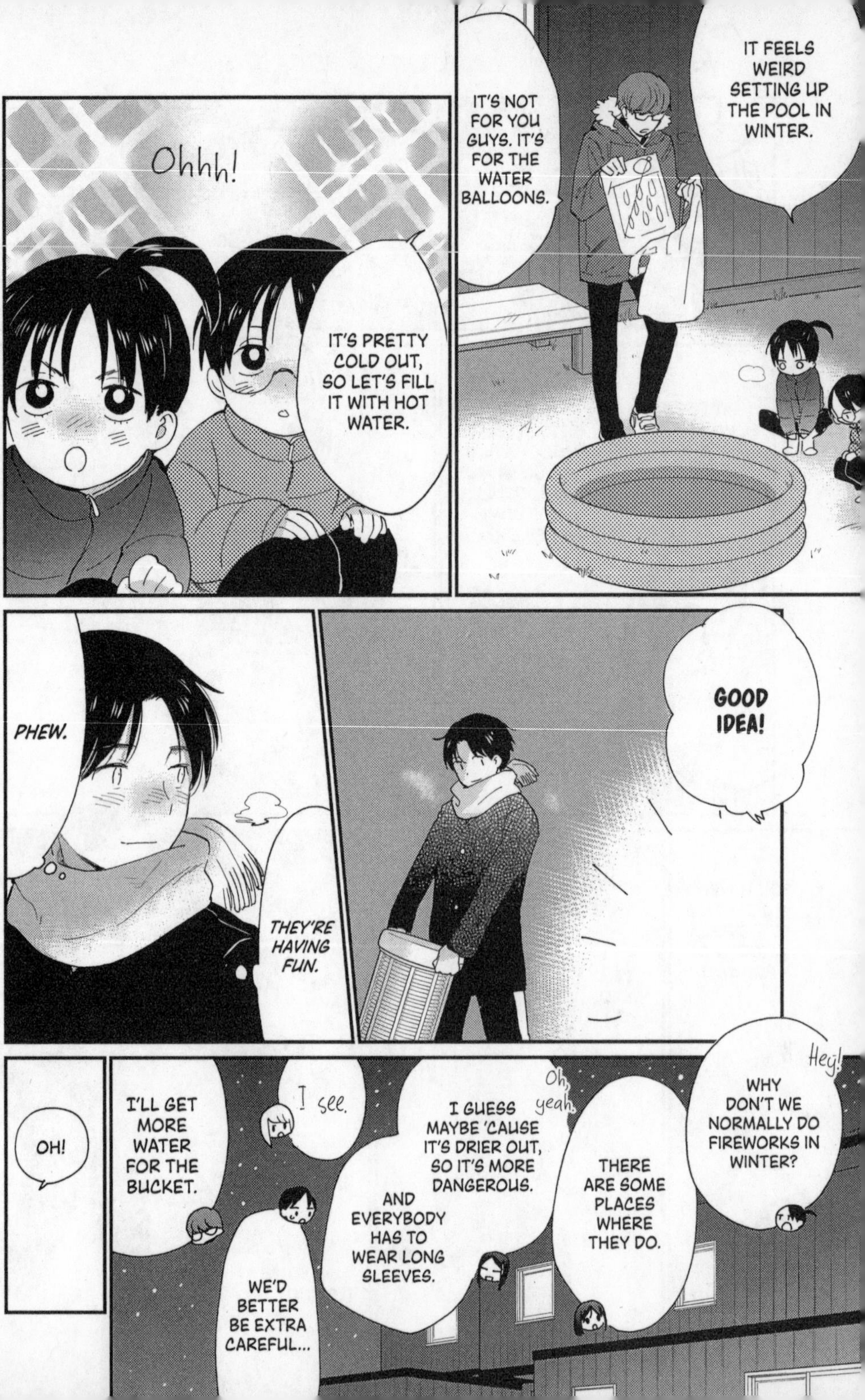

IT FEELS WEIRD SETTING UP THE POOL IN WINTER.
IT'S NOT FOR YOU GUYS. IT'S FOR THE WATER BALLOONS.
IT'S PRETTY COLD OUT, SO LET'S FILL IT WITH HOT WATER.
Ohhh!
GOOD IDEA!
PHEW.
THEY'RE HAVING FUN.
Hey!
WHY DON'T WE NORMALLY DO FIREWORKS IN WINTER?
THERE ARE SOME PLACES WHERE THEY DO.
Oh, yeah.
I GUESS MAYBE 'CAUSE IT'S DRIER OUT, SO IT'S MORE DANGEROUS.
AND EVERYBODY HAS TO WEAR LONG SLEEVES.
I see.
I'LL GET MORE WATER FOR THE BUCKET.
WE'D BETTER BE EXTRA CAREFUL...
OH!

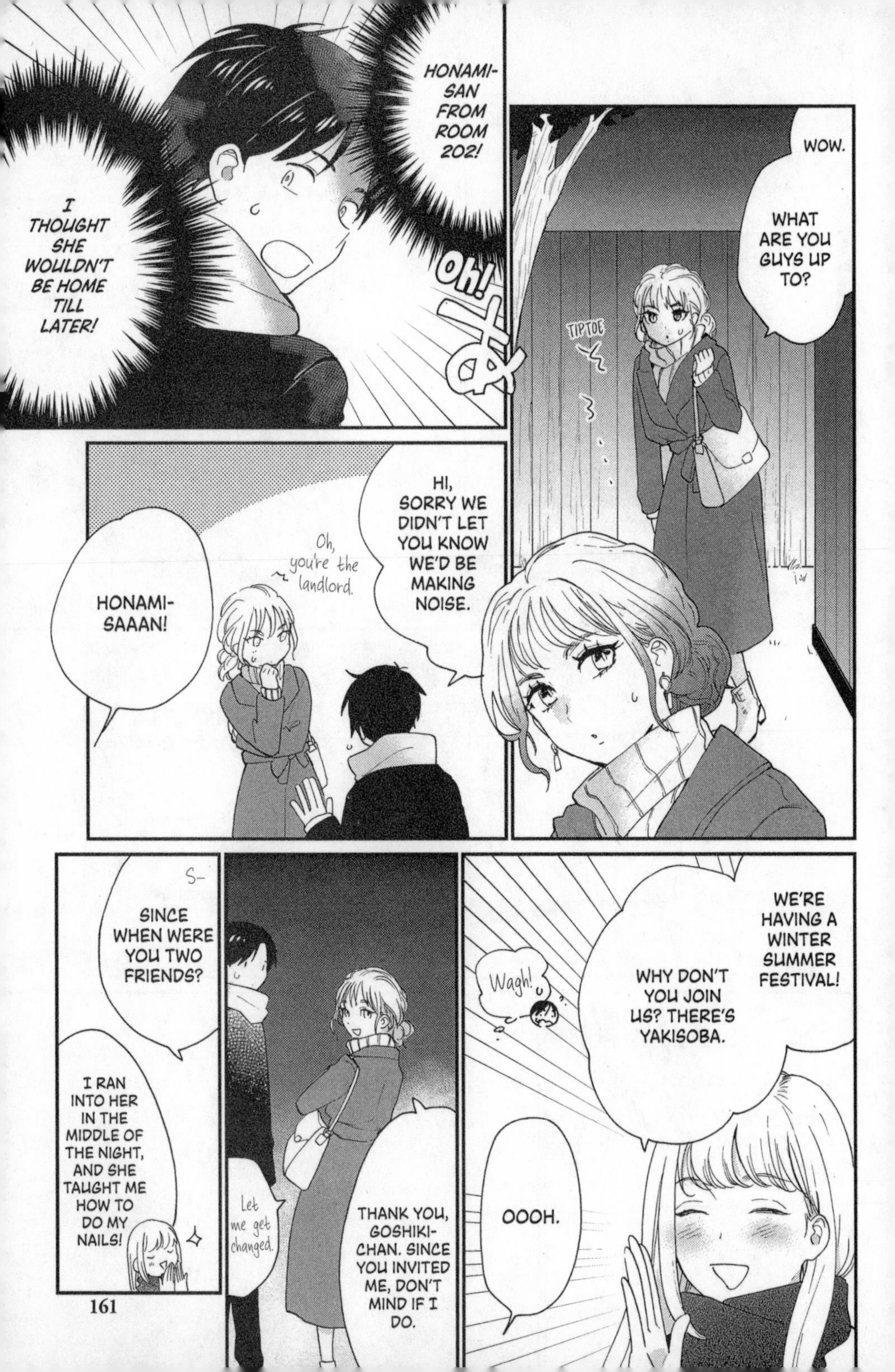
Oh!
HONAMI-SAN FROM ROOM 202!
I THOUGHT SHE WOULDN'T BE HOME TILL LATER!
WOW.
WHAT ARE YOU GUYS UP TO?
TIPTOE
HI, SORRY WE DIDN'T LET YOU KNOW WE'D BE MAKING NOISE.
Oh, you're the landlord.
HONAMI-SAAAN!
WE'RE HAVING A WINTER SUMMER FESTIVAL!
WHY DON'T YOU JOIN US? THERE'S YAKISOBA.
Wagh!
OOOH.
THANK YOU, GOSHIKI-CHAN. SINCE YOU INVITED ME, DON'T MIND IF I DO.
Let me get changed.
S-
SINCE WHEN WERE YOU TWO FRIENDS?
I RAN INTO HER IN THE MIDDLE OF THE NIGHT, AND SHE TAUGHT ME HOW TO DO MY NAILS!

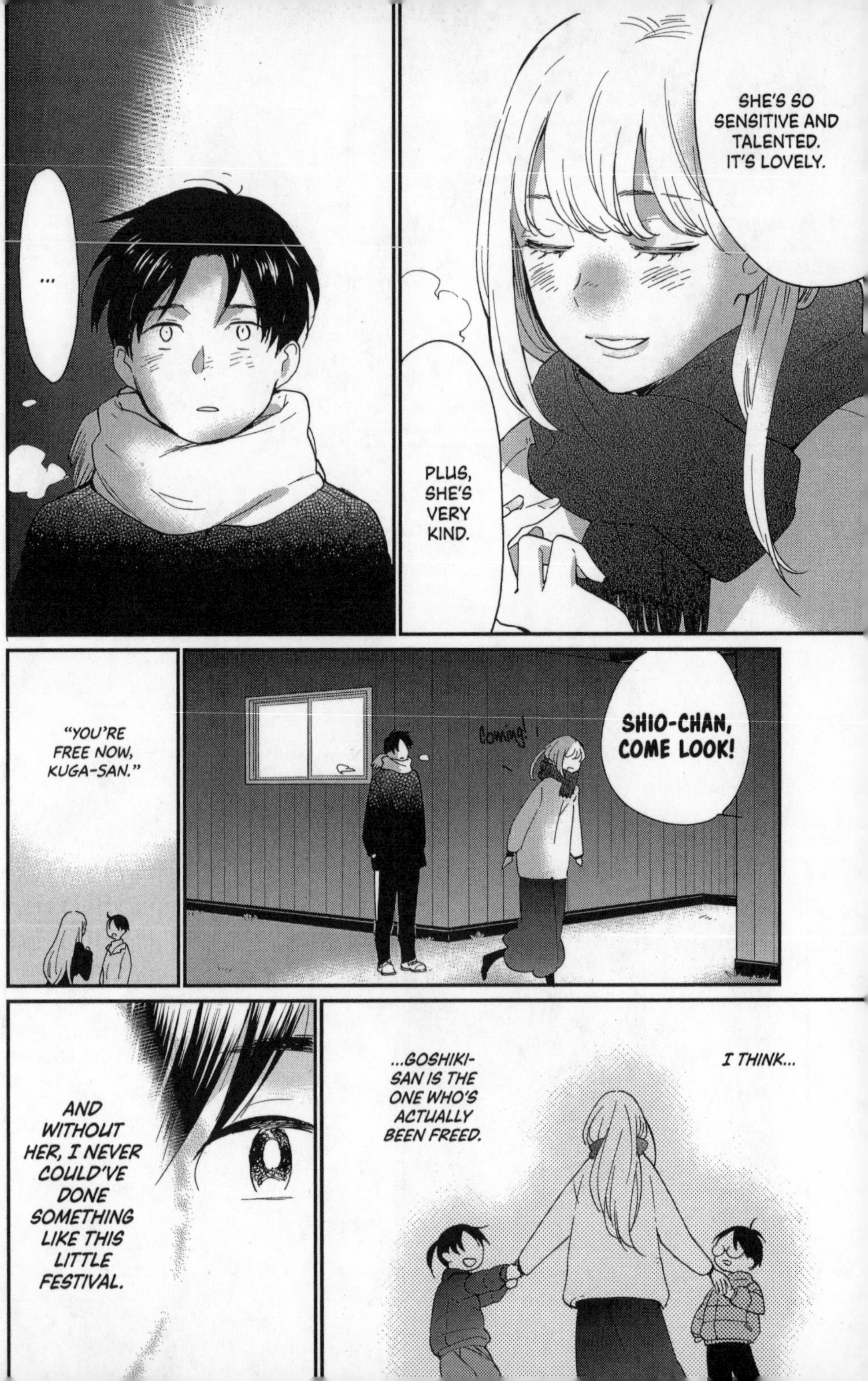
SHE'S SO SENSITIVE AND TALENTED. IT'S LOVELY.
PLUS, SHE'S VERY KIND.
...
SHIO-CHAN, COME LOOK!
Coming!
"YOU'RE FREE NOW, KUGA-SAN."
I THINK...
...GOSHIKI-SAN IS THE ONE WHO'S ACTUALLY BEEN FREED.
AND WITHOUT HER, I NEVER COULD'VE DONE SOMETHING LIKE THIS LITTLE FESTIVAL.

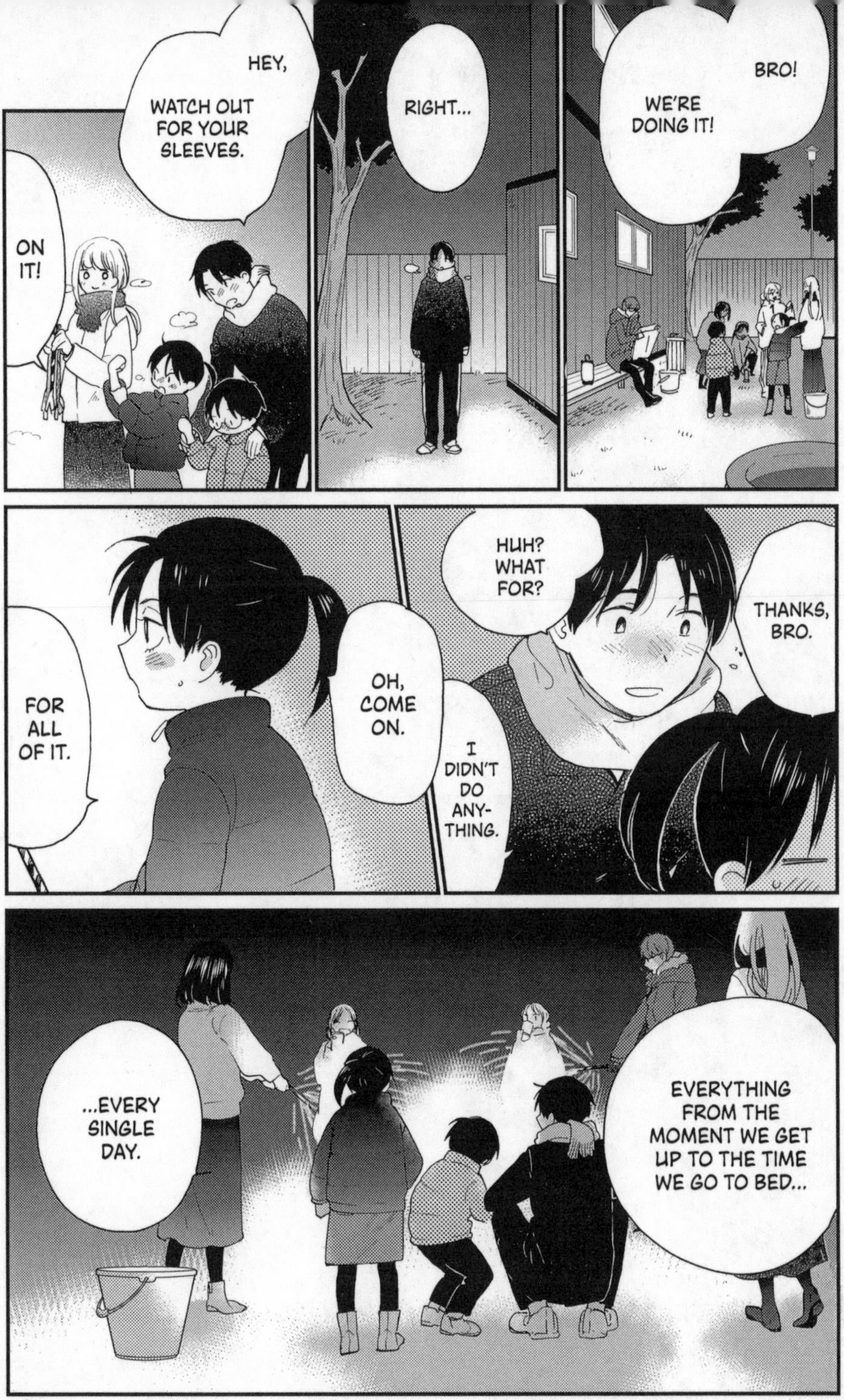
BRO!
WE'RE DOING IT!
RIGHT...
HEY,
WATCH OUT FOR YOUR SLEEVES.
ON IT!
THANKS, BRO.
HUH? WHAT FOR?
I DIDN'T DO ANY-THING.
OH, COME ON.
FOR ALL OF IT.
EVERYTHING FROM THE MOMENT WE GET UP TO THE TIME WE GO TO BED...
...EVERY SINGLE DAY.

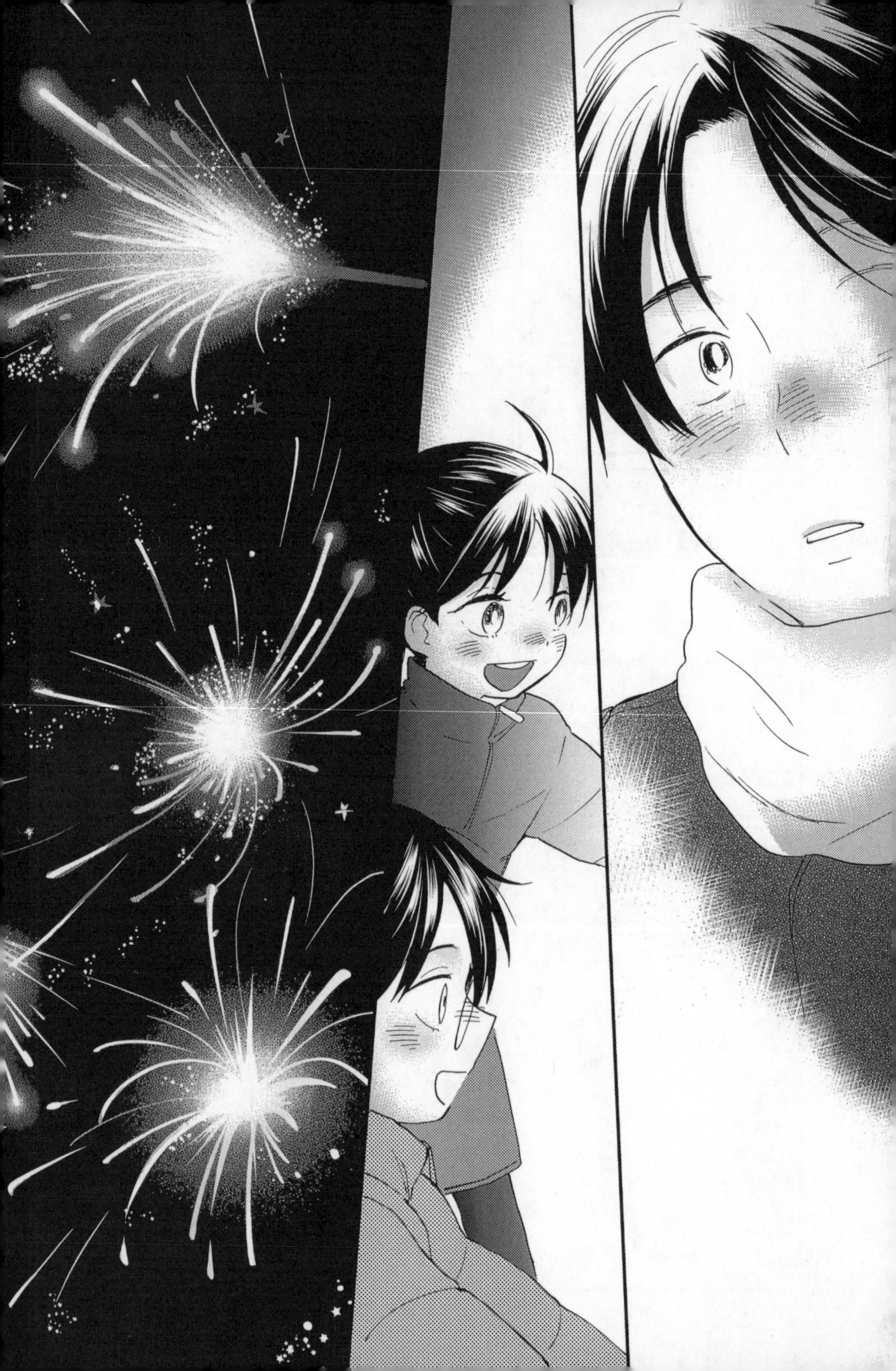

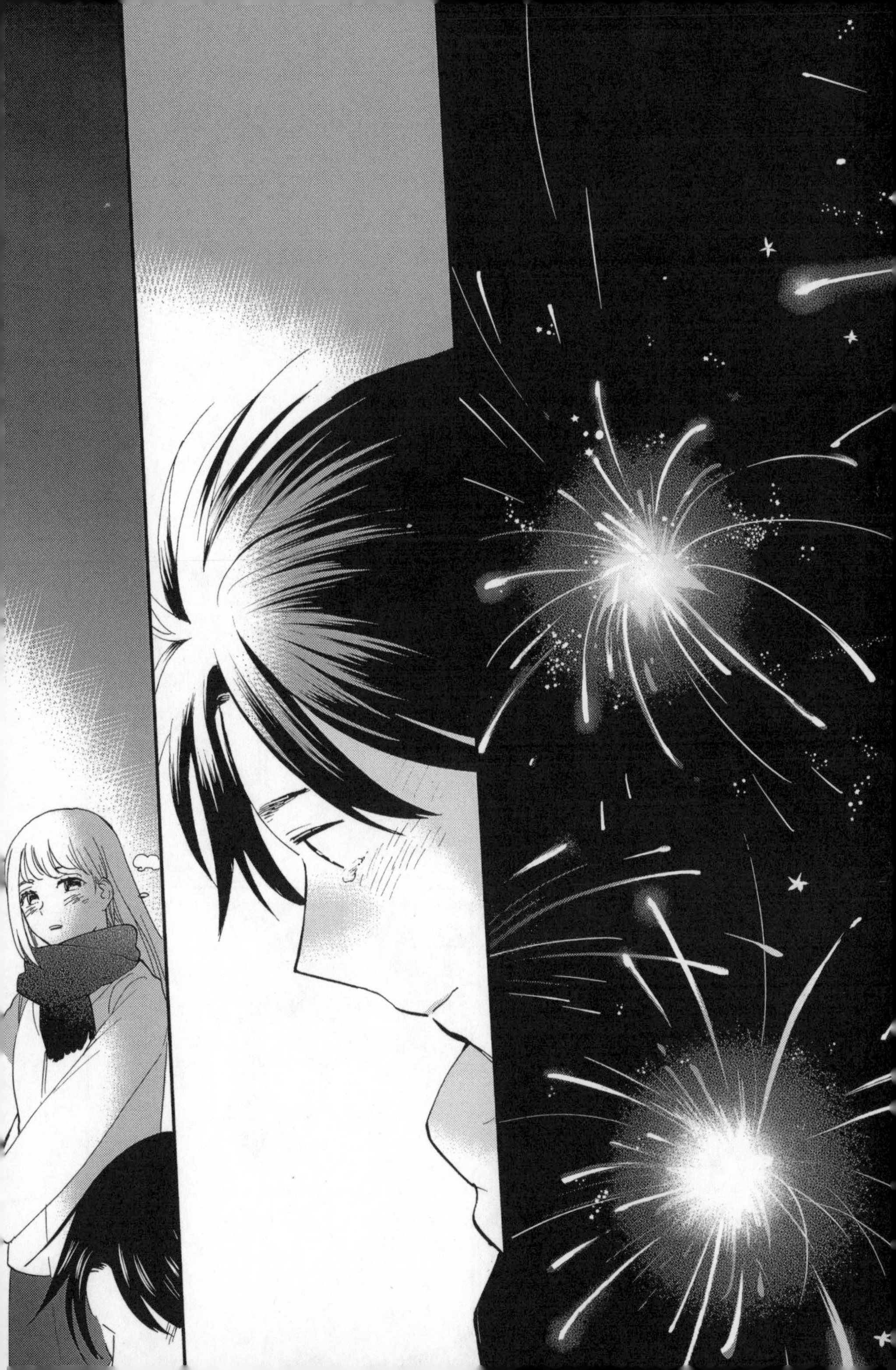

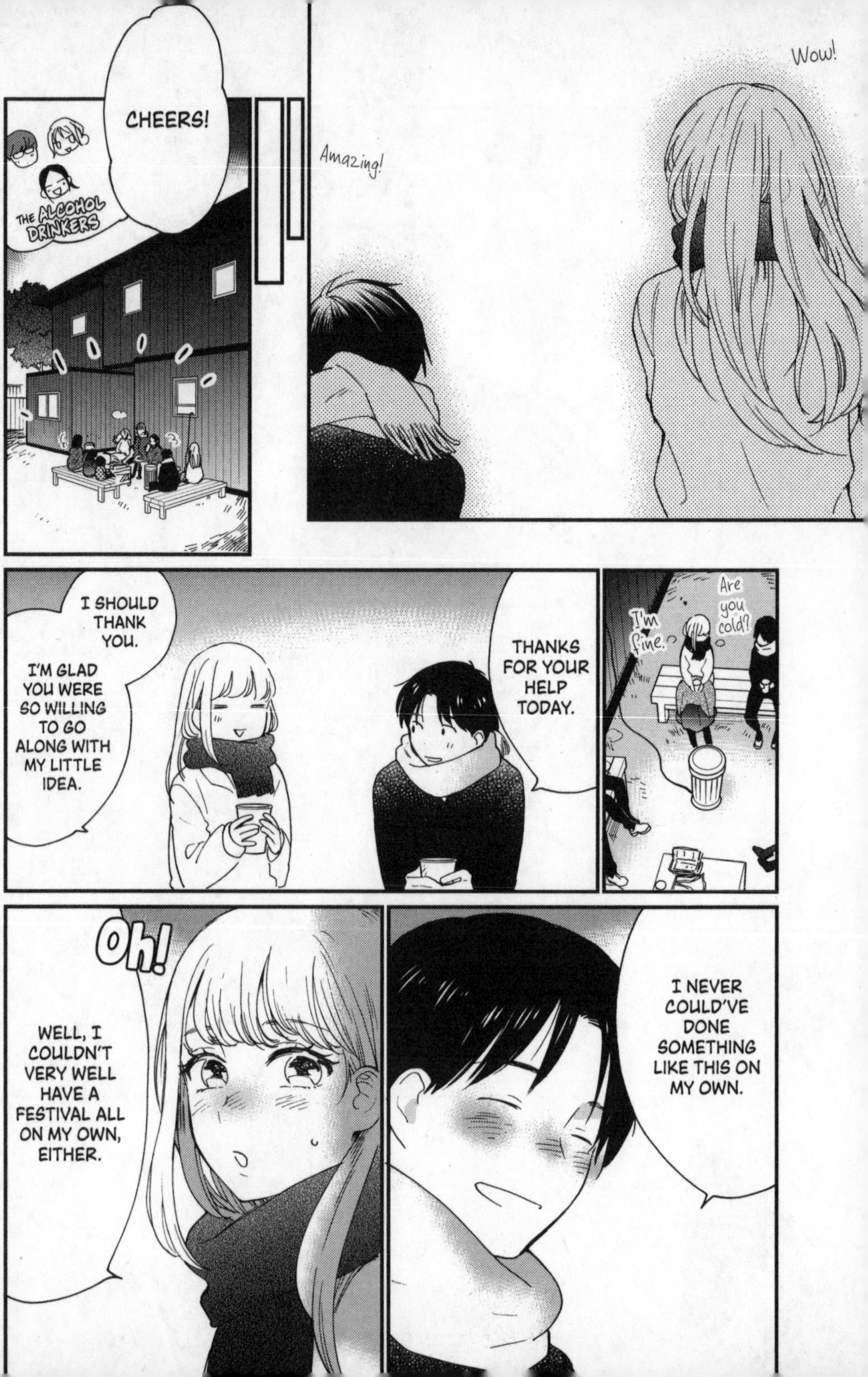

Wow!
Amazing!
CHEERS!
THE ALCOHOL DRINKERS
Are you cold?
I'm fine.
THANKS FOR YOUR HELP TODAY.
I SHOULD THANK YOU.
I'M GLAD YOU WERE SO WILLING TO GO ALONG WITH MY LITTLE IDEA.
I NEVER COULD'VE DONE SOMETHING LIKE THIS ON MY OWN.
Oh!
WELL, I COULDN'T VERY WELL HAVE A FESTIVAL ALL ON MY OWN, EITHER.

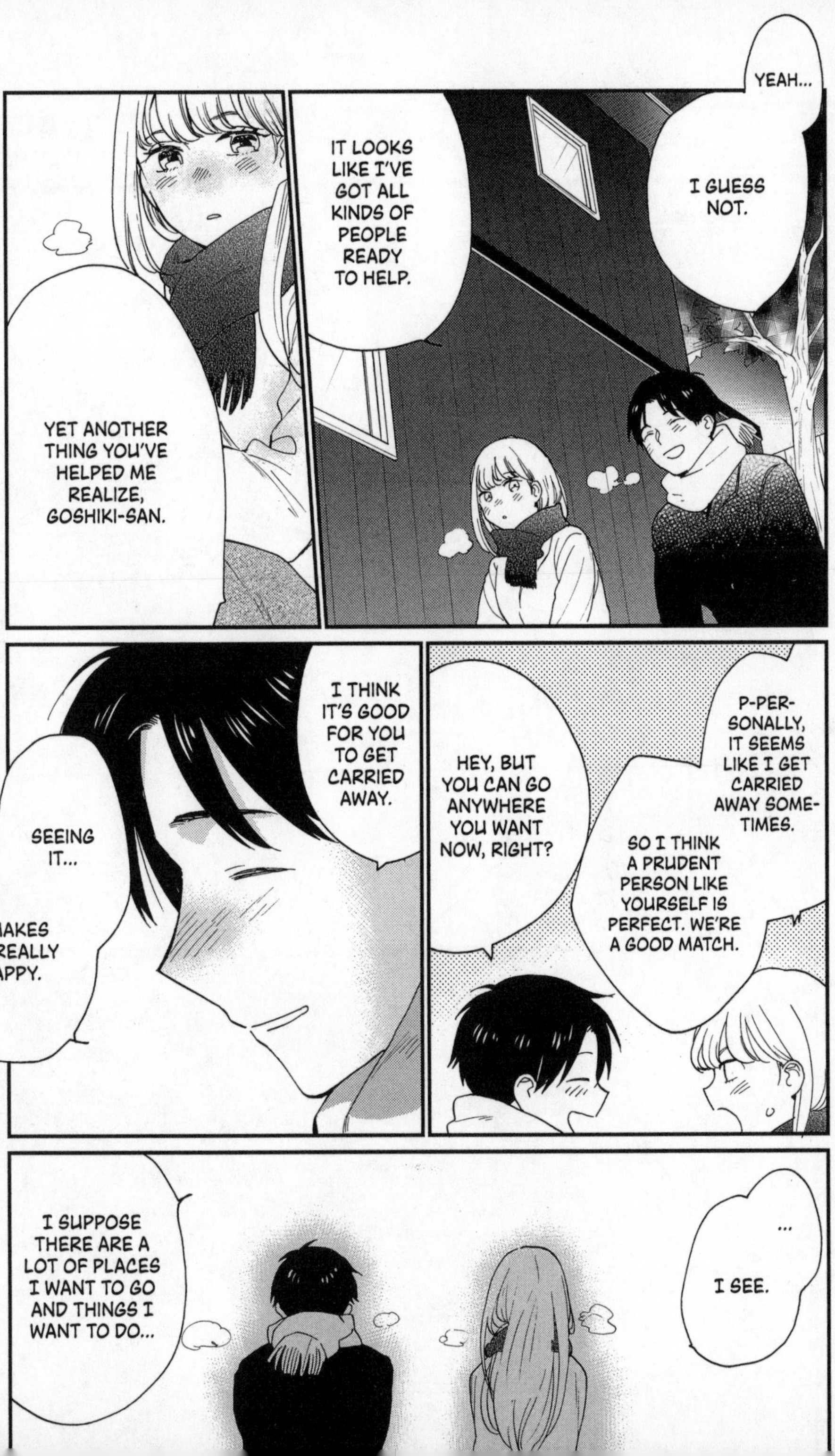
YEAH...
I GUESS NOT.
IT LOOKS LIKE I'VE GOT ALL KINDS OF PEOPLE READY TO HELP.
YET ANOTHER THING YOU'VE HELPED ME REALIZE, GOSHIKI-SAN.
P-PERSONALLY, IT SEEMS LIKE I GET CARRIED AWAY SOMETIMES.
SO I THINK A PRUDENT PERSON LIKE YOURSELF IS PERFECT. WE'RE A GOOD MATCH.
HEY, BUT YOU CAN GO ANYWHERE YOU WANT NOW, RIGHT?
I THINK IT'S GOOD FOR YOU TO GET CARRIED AWAY.
SEEING IT...
...MAKES ME REALLY HAPPY.
...
I SEE.
I SUPPOSE THERE ARE A LOT OF PLACES I WANT TO GO AND THINGS I WANT TO DO...

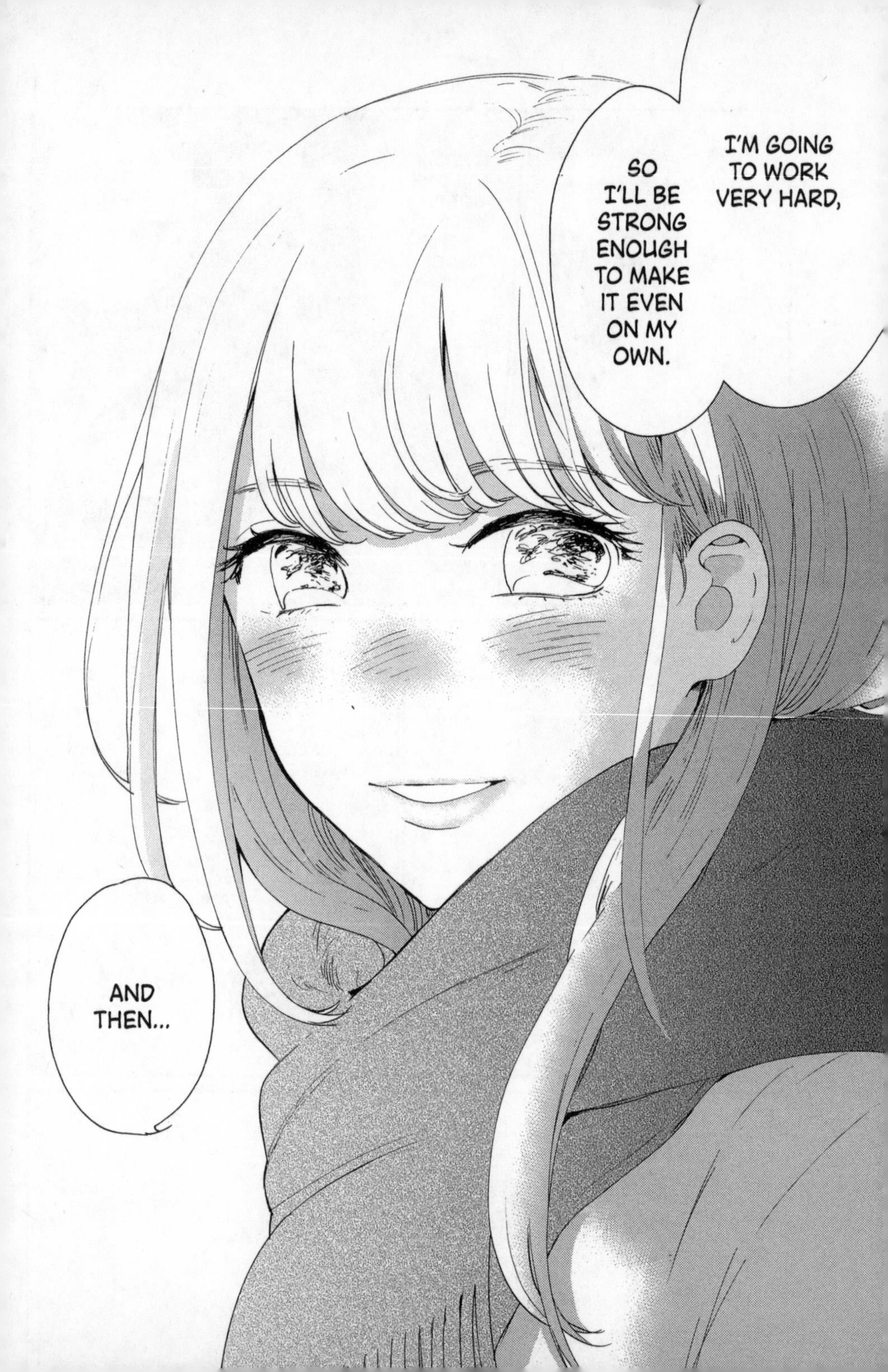
I'M GOING TO WORK VERY HARD,
SO I'LL BE STRONG ENOUGH TO MAKE IT EVEN ON MY OWN.
AND THEN...

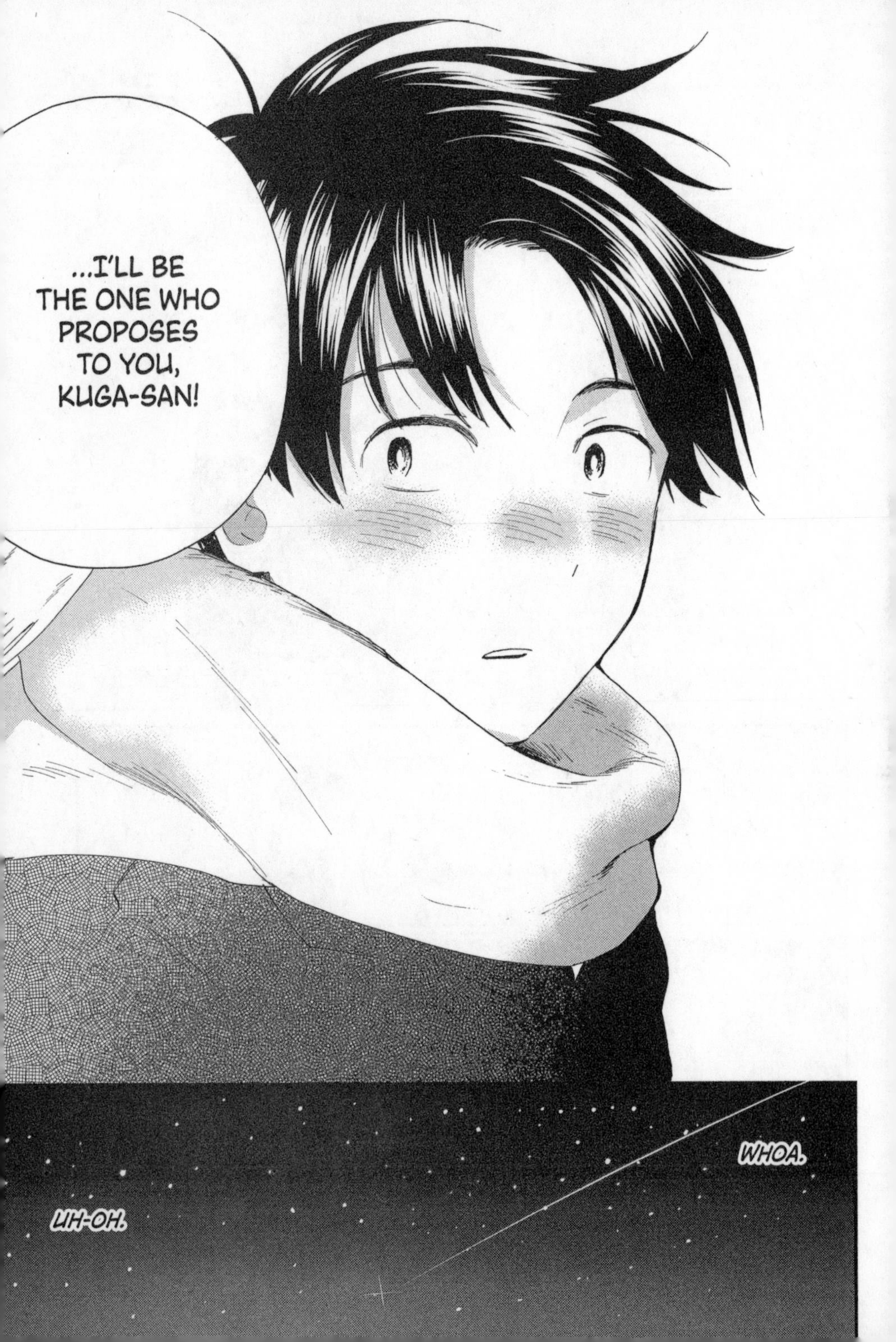
...I'LL BE THE ONE WHO PROPOSES TO YOU, KUGA-SAN!
WHOA.
UH-OH.

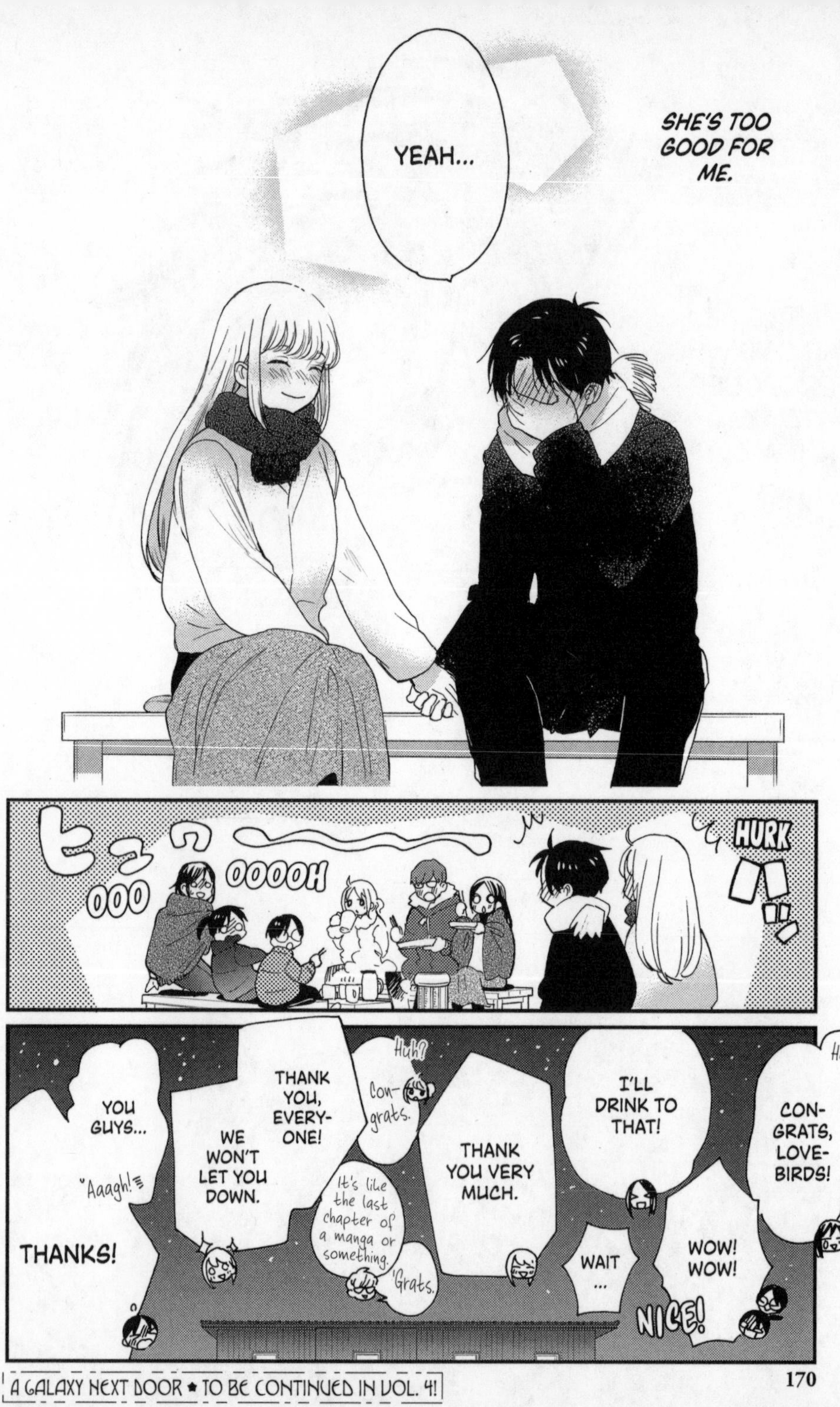
SHE'S TOO GOOD FOR ME.
YEAH...
HURK
OOOOH
OOO
ヒュウ
Hey!
CON-GRATS, LOVE-BIRDS!
WOW! WOW!
NICE!
I'LL DRINK TO THAT!
WAIT ...
THANK YOU VERY MUCH.
Huh?
Con-grats.
It's like the last chapter of a manga or something.
'Grats.
THANK YOU, EVERY-ONE!
WE WON'T LET YOU DOWN.
YOU GUYS...
Aaagh!
THANKS!

A GALAXY NEXT DOOR ★ TO BE CONTINUED IN VOL. 4!

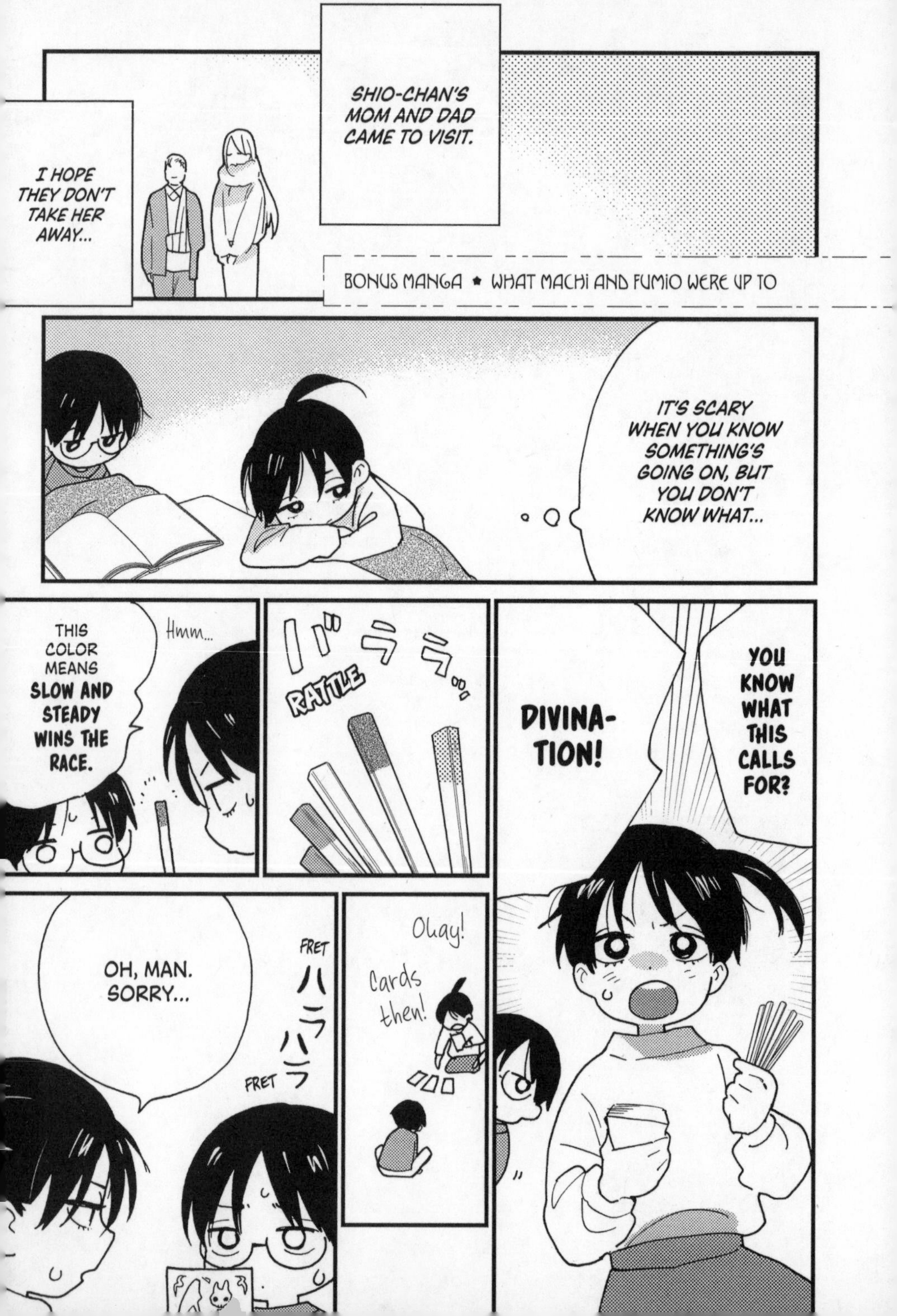
SHIO-CHAN'S MOM AND DAD CAME TO VISIT.
I HOPE THEY DON'T TAKE HER AWAY...
BONUS MANGA ★ WHAT MACHI AND FUMIO WERE UP TO
IT'S SCARY WHEN YOU KNOW SOMETHING'S GOING ON, BUT YOU DON'T KNOW WHAT...
YOU KNOW WHAT THIS CALLS FOR?
DIVINATION!
バララ
RATTLE
Hmm...
THIS COLOR MEANS SLOW AND STEADY WINS THE RACE.
Okay!
Cards then!
ハラハラ
FRET
FRET
OH, MAN. SORRY...

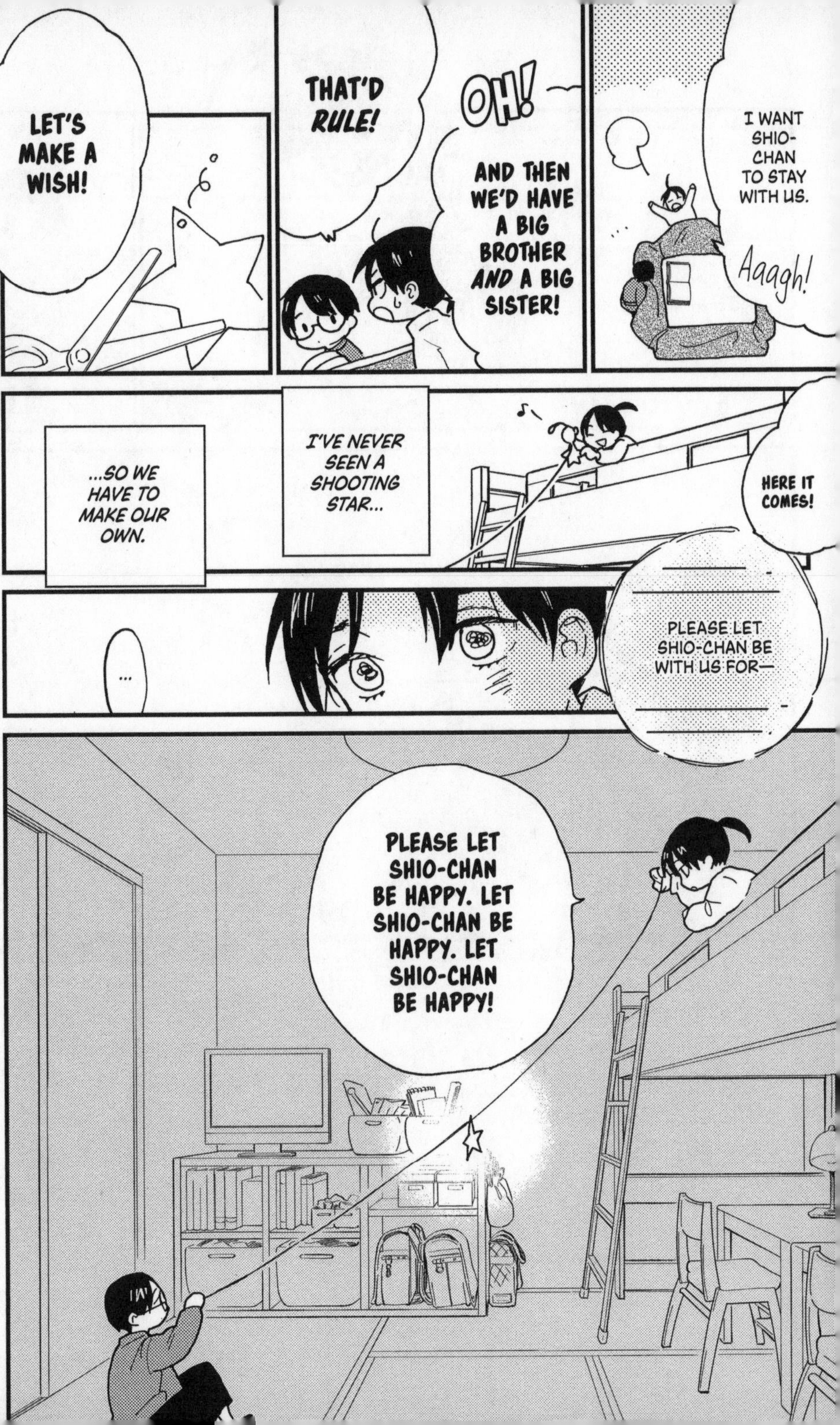
I WANT SHIO-CHAN TO STAY WITH US.
Aaagh!
OH!
AND THEN WE'D HAVE A BIG BROTHER AND A BIG SISTER!
THAT'D RULE!
LET'S MAKE A WISH!
HERE IT COMES!
I'VE NEVER SEEN A SHOOTING STAR...
...SO WE HAVE TO MAKE OUR OWN.
PLEASE LET SHIO-CHAN BE WITH US FOR—
...
PLEASE LET SHIO-CHAN BE HAPPY. LET SHIO-CHAN BE HAPPY. LET SHIO-CHAN BE HAPPY!

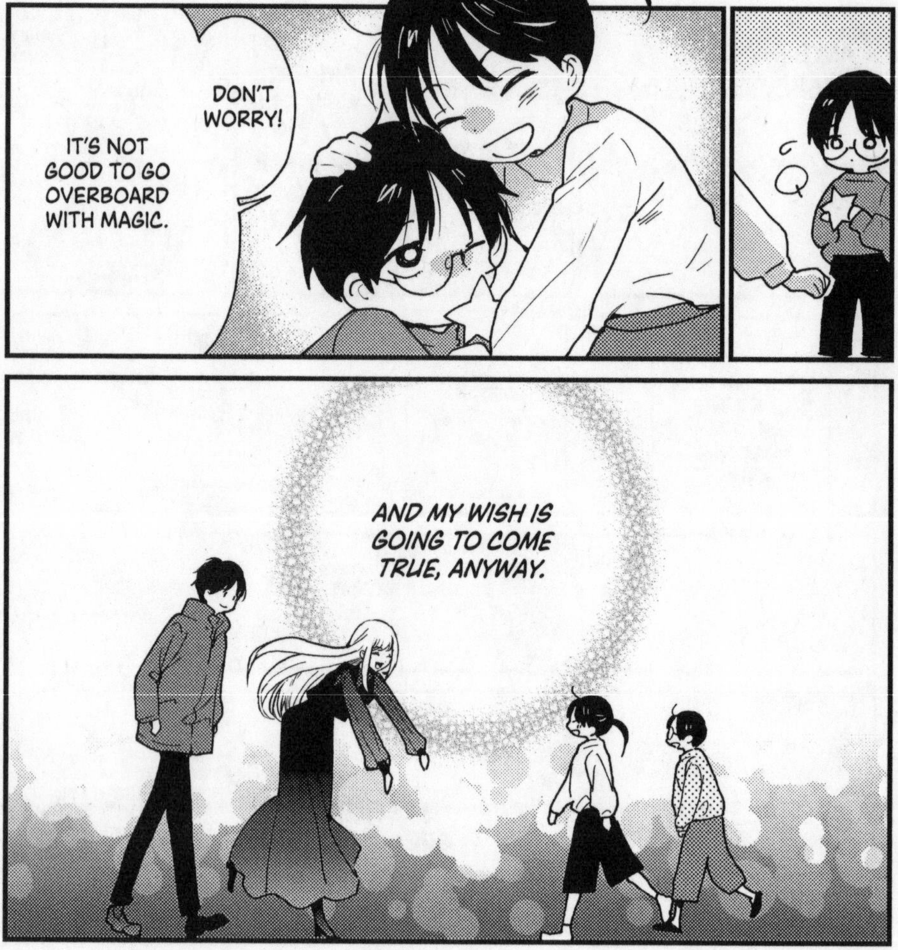
DON'T WORRY!
IT'S NOT GOOD TO GO OVERBOARD WITH MAGIC.
AND MY WISH IS GOING TO COME TRUE, ANYWAY.

Thanks to everyone who helped

Gon-chan, Chi-chan, Teba-san, M-cha,
and my editor
Graphic Design: Kohei Nawata Design Office

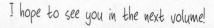

It's not over yet!

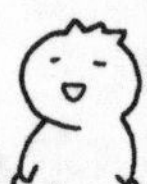

I hope to see you in the next volume!

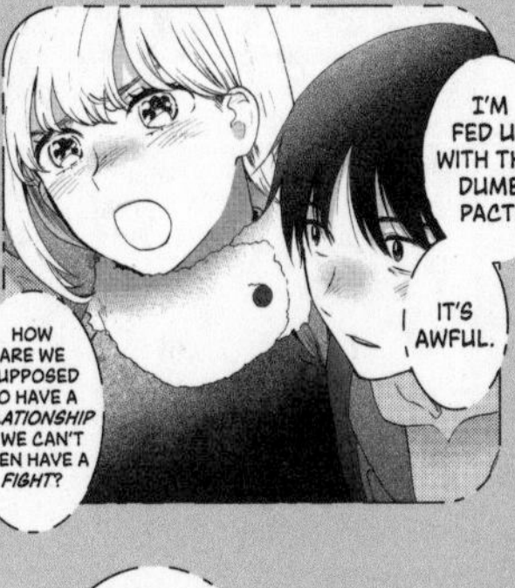
I'M FED UP WITH THIS DUMB PACT!
IT'S AWFUL.
HOW ARE WE SUPPOSED TO HAVE A *RELATIONSHIP* IF WE CAN'T EVEN HAVE A *FIGHT*?

KUGA-KUN AND GOSHIKI-SAN ARE NO LONGER BOUND BY THE TERMS OF THEIR **ENGAGEMENT PACT.**

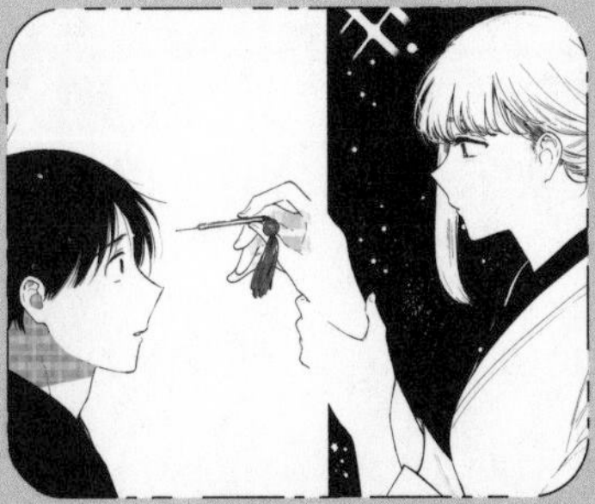

FROM NOW ON,

THEY'RE IN LOVE.

AND **THAT'S ALL.**

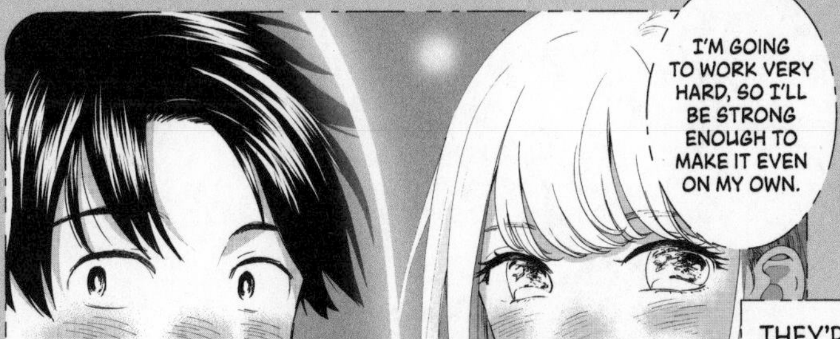
I'M GOING TO WORK VERY HARD, SO I'LL BE STRONG ENOUGH TO MAKE IT EVEN ON MY OWN.
AND THEN...
I'LL BE THE ONE WHO PROPOSES TO YOU, KUGA-SAN!

IT'S A RESTART!!

WHATEVER TROUBLES LIE AHEAD,

THEY'LL FACE THEM WITH HANDS HELD FAST!

A Galaxy Next Door 4

COMING SOON!

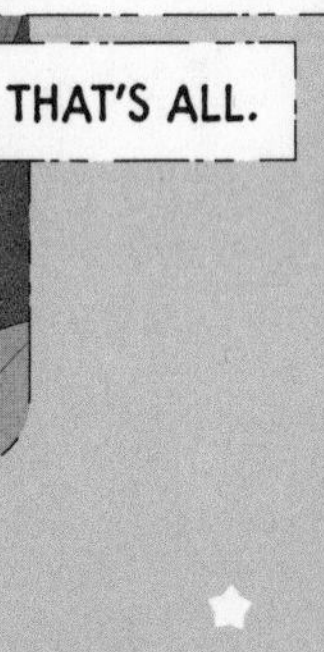
THEY'RE SO INNOCENT. DON'T SEE THAT A LOT AT THEIR AGE, BUT I'M INTO IT!

Moka-nee ten years ago

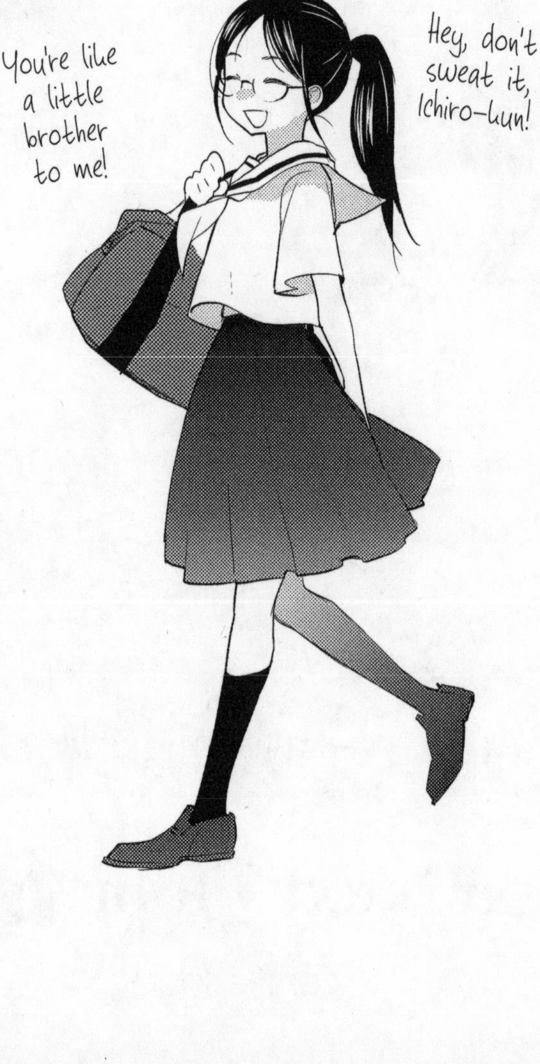
Hey, don't sweat it, Ichiro-kun!
You're like a little brother to me!

Heartbroken?

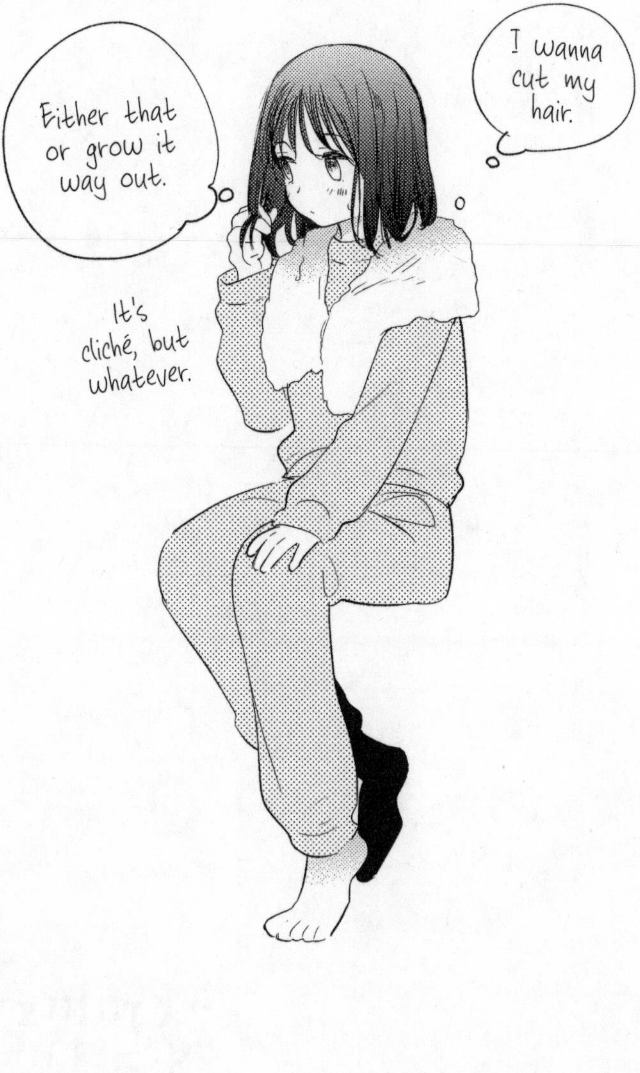
I wanna cut my hair.
Either that or grow it way out.
It's cliché, but whatever.

A Galaxy Next Door

Gido Amagakure

Translation Notes

Honorifics:
While most readers are likely familiar with many of the honorifics used in Japanese (typically attached after the addressee's name), here's a refresher:
***-kun*, pg 2:**
Typically used to address boys, or close male friends, but can also be used to refer to younger colleagues of any gender.
***-chan*, pg 3:**
Typically used by young children, female friends, family members, couples, and parents and adults to children (usually to young girls). Denotes a closeness with the addressee.
***-san*, pg 8:**
The polite default honorific, used for strangers, acquaintances, colleagues, and other non-specific relationships.
***-sama*, pg 13:**
This honorofic is one that denotes extreme respect! While less common now, it could be used when addressing anyone of a higher "rank," such as a noble or a divine entity. Today, one is more likely to hear it used when addressing customers, an honored guest, or a highly respected individual.
***-nee*, pg 74:**
A variation on older sister, denoting closeness, familiarity, and seniority. Momoka is being addressed like she is part of the family, even though they aren't blood related, as other honorifics like *-san* would be too formal and distant for their relationship.

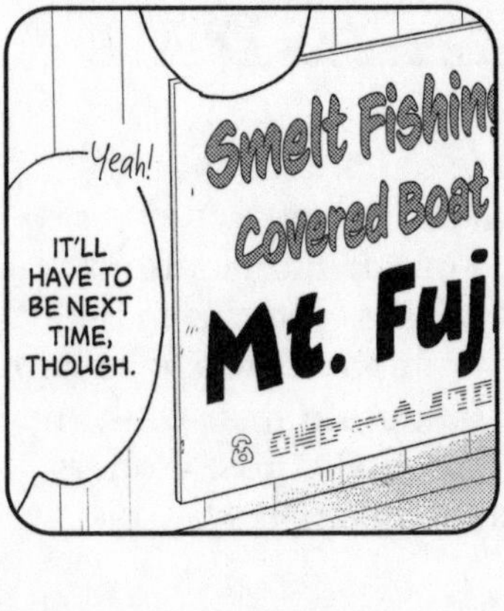
Smelt Fishin
Covered Boat
Mt. Fuj
Yeah!
IT'LL HAVE TO BE NEXT TIME, THOUGH.

Smelt fishing, pg 7:
One tourist activity on offer at the lakes near Mt. Fuji is fishing for smelt, specifically *wakasagi*, which is a fish originally native to Hokkaido. Tourists can ride on a mid-size covered boat with built-in heating. In Japanese, it's called a *dōmu-sen*, or "dome boat," in reference to its shape. Inside the boat, there might be holes in the floor for fishing out of, or fishing stations along the perimeter.

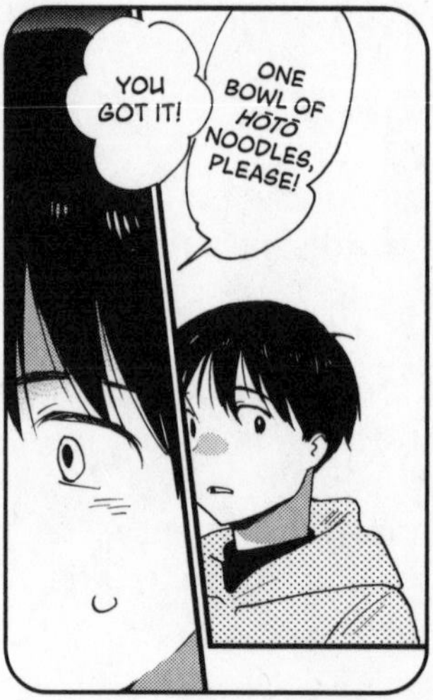
ONE BOWL OF HŌTŌ NOODLES, PLEASE!
YOU GOT IT!

Hōtō noodles, pg 8:
Hōtō noodle soup is a popular, local cuisine from Yamanashi Prefecture, home to Mt. Fuji. The dish is vegetarian and has a miso base. Though it is commonly considered a type of udon, the noodles are actually larger and flatter. In fact, some people do not consider *hōtō* a type of udon at all!

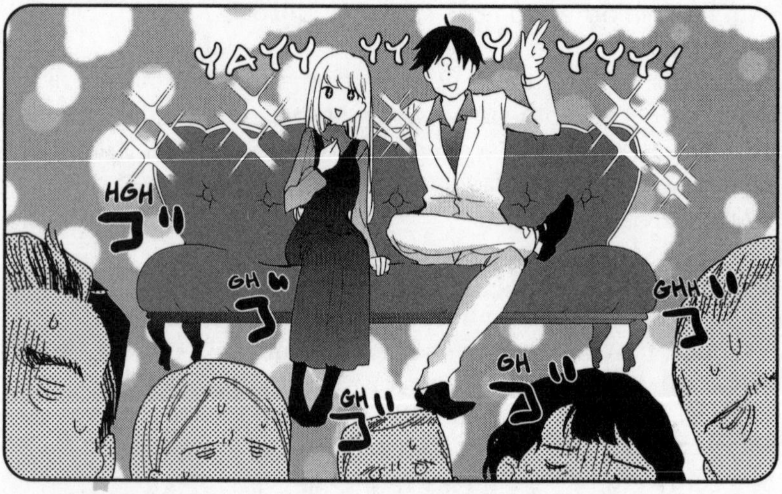
YAYY YY Y YYY!
GHH
GH
GH
GH
HGH

Night club host, pg 11:
A host (or hostess) club is a type of night life bar or club where customers pay to be waited on and entertained by young men or women. Hosts are generally expected to be lavish in their attentions, and are often portrayed in media as sweet talkers who charm their guests into spending excessively due to their infatuation. Those with more traditional sensibilities, such as the islanders in this scene, may therefore have the impression that hosts are cunning gold diggers looking to take advantage of young, wealthy women like Goshiki.

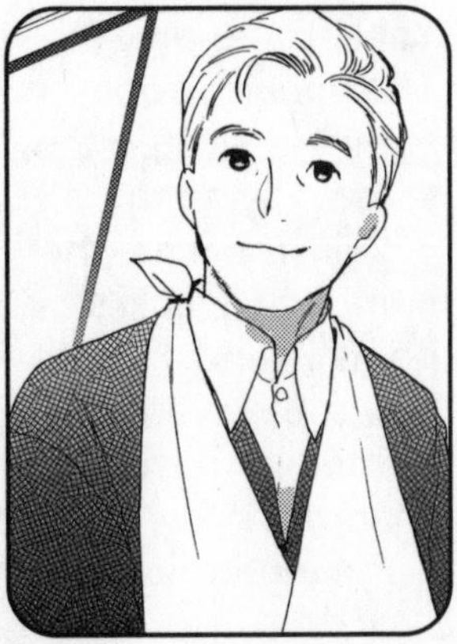

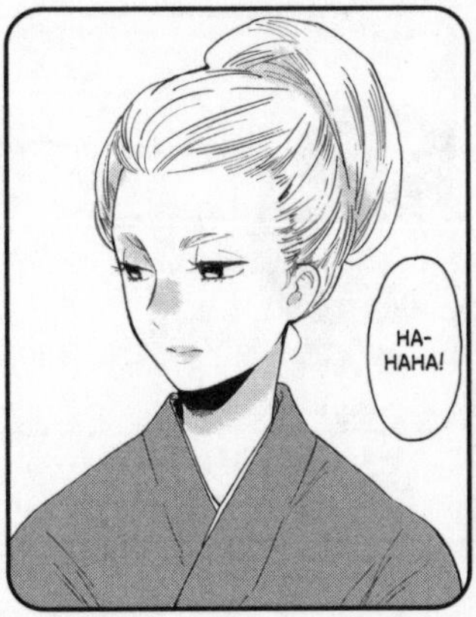
HA-
HAHA!

Miyako and Takeru's names, pgs 13 & 14: Goshiki's family members have meaningful names, so it's worth noting some of the details. Miyako's name is written with the character for "capital." The word *miyako* in Japanese has a strong association with the old, traditional capital of Kyoto. One of the original names for Kyoto, which actually means "captial city," was *kyo no miyako* (or just *miyako*). Takeru's name is written with the character for "healthy," and could convey a sense that he is hearty and strong. It is also worth noting that an alternative way to pronounce his name is "Ken"!

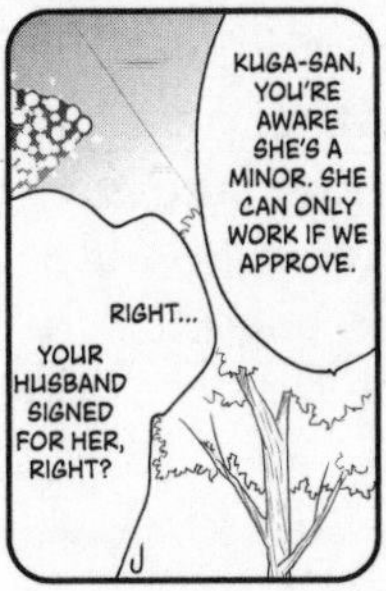
KUGA-SAN, YOU'RE AWARE SHE'S A MINOR. SHE CAN ONLY WORK IF WE APPROVE.
RIGHT...
YOUR HUSBAND SIGNED FOR HER, RIGHT?

Goshiki is a minor, pg 57: Some readers who remember that Goshiki is currently 19 may be wondering why she is being described as a minor, but the age of majority in Japan is actually 20!

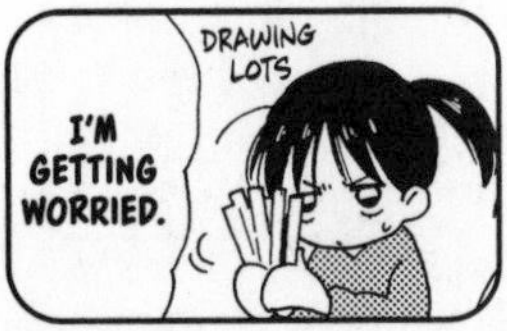
DRAWING LOTS
I'M GETTING WORRIED.

Drawing lots, pgs 70 & 74: Machi is drawing lots to tell the future again, and just a few pages later, Kuga finds himself thinking back to the winning lot he drew from a popsicle stick. Some popsicle companies in Japan have been known to print numbers on their popsicle sticks as a marketing gimmick—either as collectibles or as the means to win a prize. In this case, it seems like Kuga has found one that is considered a winning stick, though it is unclear what—if anything—he may have won!

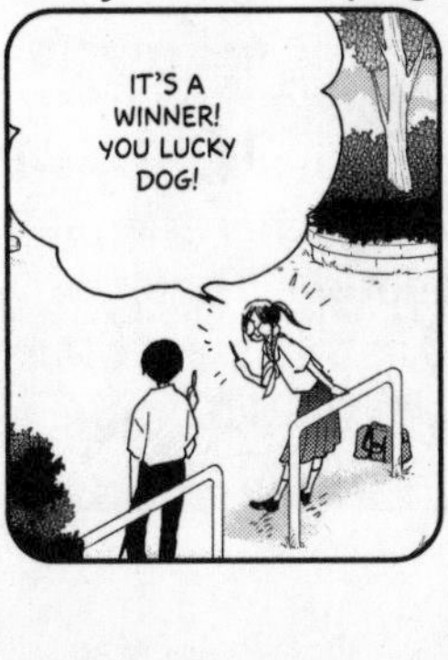
IT'S A WINNER! YOU LUCKY DOG!

Yobi stone, pg 77:
The *yobi* in "Yobi stone" is written the same way as the *yobi* in Yobijima, the name of Goshiki's home island. In both cases, the word is written with the two characters for "summon" and "princess." Presumably, the Yobi stone is the meteorite that gave birth to their way of life.

IT'S REALLY THEM...
YES.
THOSE ARE THE TWEEZERS MADE FROM THE YOBI STONE.

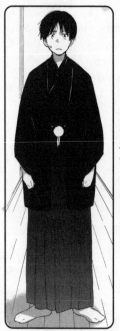

***Haori* and *hakama*, pg 79:**
Haori and *hakama* are two items of traditional Japanese clothing that often go together as a very formal outfit. A *haori* is a lengthy, short-sleeved overcoat, and *hakama* are a kind of long, pleated pants. In contrast, the *yukata* Kuga is used to aren't as fancy, and are instead worn for occasions such as summer festivals.

Aya's name, pg 80:
Goshiki's grandmother's name is written with the character for "writing" or "literacy." This seems significant, considering her role in Goshiki's life!

OUR FORE-MOTHER, AYA-SAMA, CHANCED UPON A FALLEN STAR.
THAT STAR GRANTED HER WISH.
IT BROUGHT PEACE AND JOY TO THE PEOPLE OF THE ISLAND.

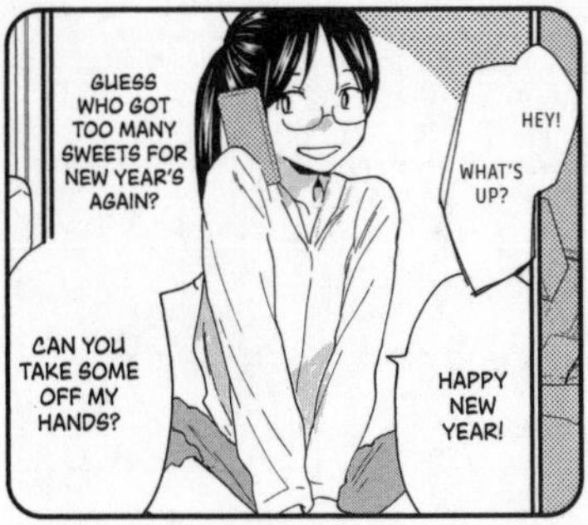
HEY!
WHAT'S UP?
GUESS WHO GOT TOO MANY SWEETS FOR NEW YEAR'S AGAIN?
HAPPY NEW YEAR!
CAN YOU TAKE SOME OFF MY HANDS?

Sweets for New Year's, pg 90:
Actually, Moka didn't necessarily receive only sweets. Specifically, she says that she got a lot of *o-nenga* and would like to share some with Ichiro. *O-nenga* can refer to any kind of small New Year's gift, though sweets are common.

Calpis soda, pg 148:
Calpis is a popular brand of Japanese soft drink. It has a milky, vanilla-like flavor, and is available in both carbonated and non-carbonated varieties.

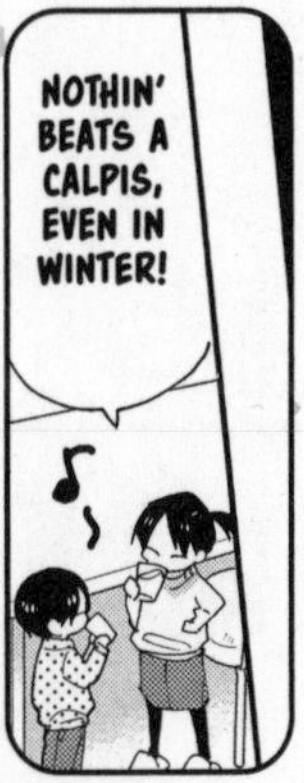
NOTHIN' BEATS A CALPIS, EVEN IN WINTER!

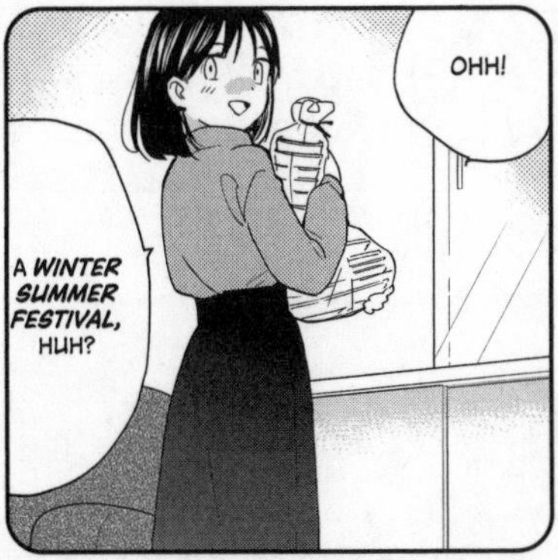
OHH!
A *WINTER SUMMER FESTIVAL*, HUH?

Winter summer festival, pg 159:
A very popular summer activity is the summer festival. These events are usually organized by a local shrine. Local vendors set up booths on the grounds offering food, such as *yakisoba*, merchandise, and games. Traditional fireworks and hand-held sparklers are often included as part of the festivities. The "fireworks" that are used in this scene are actually sparklers, hence all the caution against catching anything on fire!

Having lost his wife, high school teacher Kōhei Inuzuka is doing his best to raise his young daughter Tsumugi as a single father. He's pretty bad at cooking and doesn't have a huge appetite to begin with, but chance brings his little family together with one of his students, the lonely Kotori. The three of them are anything but comfortable in the kitchen, but the healing power of home cooking might just work on their grieving hearts.

"This season's number-one feel-good anime!" —Anime News Network

"A beautifully-drawn story about comfort food and family and grief. Recommended." —Otaku USA Magazine

sweetness & lightning

By Gido Amagakure

PERFECT WORLD

Rie Aruga

A TOUCHING NEW SERIES ABOUT LOVE AND COPING WITH DISABILITY

An office party reunites Tsugumi with her high school crush Itsuki. He's realized his dream of becoming an architect, but along the way, he experienced a spinal injury that put him in a wheelchair. Now Tsugumi's rekindled feelings will butt up against prejudices she never considered — and Itsuki will have to decide if he's ready to let someone into his heart...

"Depicts with great delicacy and courage the difficulties some with disabilities experience getting involved in romantic relationships... Rie Aruga refuses to romanticize, pushing her heroine to face the reality of disability. She invites her readers to the same tasks of empathy, knowledge and recognition."
—Slate.fr

"An important entry [in manga romance]... The emotional core of both plot and characters indicates thoughtfulness... [Aruga's] research is readily apparent in the text and artwork, making this feel like a real story."
—Anime News Network

A SMART, NEW ROMANTIC COMEDY FOR FANS OF *SHORTCAKE CAKE* AND *TERRACE HOUSE!*

Living-Room Matsunaga-san © Keiko Iwashita / Kodansha Ltd.

A romance manga starring high school girl Meeko, who learns to live on her own in a boarding house whose living room is home to the odd (but handsome) Matsunaga-san. She begins to adjust to her new life away from her parents, but Meeko soon learns that no matter how far away from home she is, she's still a young girl at heart — especially when she finds herself falling for Matsunaga-san.

In love, there are
no save points.

ヲ
タ
ク
に
恋
は
難
し
い

NOW AN
ANIME!

WOTAKOI:
LOVE IS HARD FOR OTAKU
by FUJITA

Narumi has had it rough: Every boyfriend she's had dumped her once they found out she was an otaku, so she's gone to great lengths to hide it. At her new job, she bumps into Hirotaka, her childhood friend and fellow otaku. When Hirotaka almost gets her secret outed at work, she comes up with a plan to keep him quiet. But he comes up with a counter-proposal: Why doesn't she just date him instead?

THE SWEET SCENT OF LOVE IS IN THE AIR! FOR FANS OF OFFBEAT ROMANCES LIKE *WOTAKOI*

Sweat and Soap © Kintetsu Yamada / Kodansha Ltd.

In an office romance, there's a fine line between sexy and awkward... and that line is where Asako — a woman who sweats copiously — meets Koutarou — a perfume developer who can't get enough of Asako's, er, scent. Don't miss a romcom manga like no other!

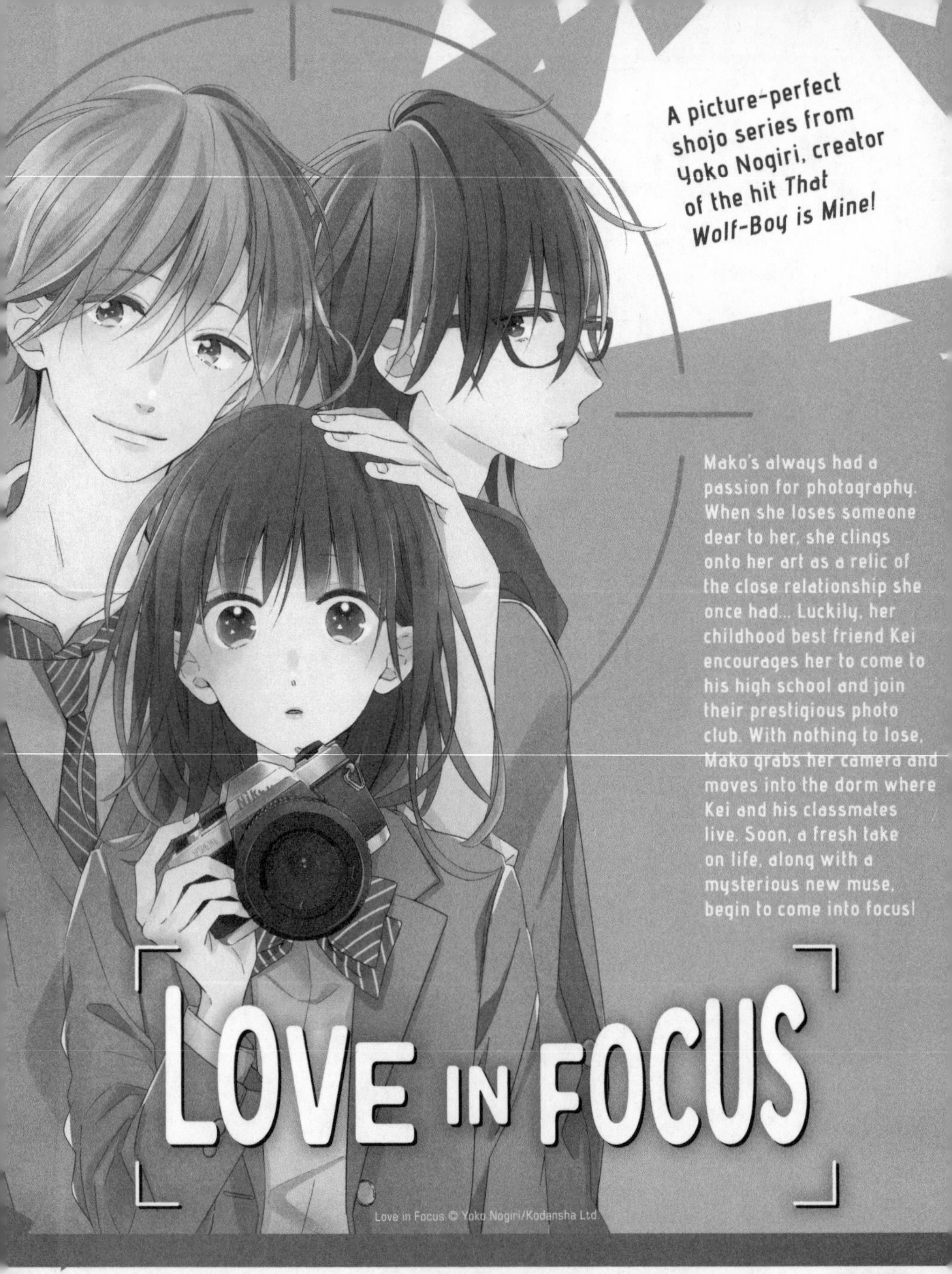

A picture-perfect shojo series from Yoko Nogiri, creator of the hit *That Wolf-Boy is Mine!*
Mako's always had a passion for photography. When she loses someone dear to her, she clings onto her art as a relic of the close relationship she once had... Luckily, her childhood best friend Kei encourages her to come to his high school and join their prestigious photo club. With nothing to lose, Mako grabs her camera and moves into the dorm where Kei and his classmates live. Soon, a fresh take on life, along with a mysterious new muse, begin to come into focus!
LOVE IN FOCUS

Praise for Yoko Nogiri's *That Wolf-Boy is Mine!*

KC KODANSHA COMICS

"Emotional squees...will-they-won't-they plot...[and a] pleasantly quick pace."
–Otaku USA Magazine

"A series that is pure shojo sugar—a cute love story about two nice people looking for their places in the world, and finding them with each other." –Anime News Network

Young characters and steampunk setting, like *Howl's Moving Castle* and *Battle Angel Alita*

Beyond the Clouds © 2018 Nicke / Ki-oon

A boy with a talent for machines and a mysterious girl whose wings he's fixed will take you beyond the clouds! In the tradition of the high-flying, resonant adventure stories of Studio Ghibli comes a gorgeous tale about the longing of young hearts for adventure and friendship!

A Kodansha Trade Paperback Original

Published in the United States by
Kodansha USA Publishing, LLC, New York.

Publication rights for this English edition arranged through
Kodansha Ltd., Tokyo.

First published in Japan in 2021 by Kodansha Ltd., Tokyo
as *Otonari ni ginga*, volume 3.

ISBN 978-1-64651-563-9

Printed in the United States of America.

9 8 7 6 5 4 3 2 1

Translation: Rose Padgett
Lettering: Lys Blakeslee
Editing: Cayley Last
Kodansha USA Publishing edition cover design by Matthew Akuginow

This English edition is dedicated to the beloved memory of Fall Rose Padgett.

Publisher: Kiichiro Sugawara

Director of Publishing Services: Ben Applegate
Director of Publishing Operations: Dave Barrett
Associate Director of Publishing Operations: Stephen Pakula
Publishing Services Managing Editors: Alanna Ruse, Madison Salters,
with Grace Chen
Senior Production Manager: Angela Zurlo

KODANSHA.US

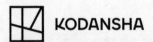

KODANSHA